Praise for *Generative Deep Learning*

Generative Deep Learning is an accessible introduction to the deep learning toolkit for generative modeling. If you are a creative practitioner who loves to tinker with code and want to apply deep learning to your work, then this is the book for you.

—*David Ha, Head of Strategy, Stability AI*

An excellent book that dives right into all of the major techniques behind state-of-the-art generative deep learning. You'll find intuitive explanations and clever analogies—backed by didactic, highly readable code examples. An exciting exploration of one of the most fascinating domains in AI!

—*François Chollet, Creator of Keras*

David Foster's explanations of complex concepts are clear and concise, enriched with intuitive visuals, code examples, and exercises. An excellent resource for students and practitioners!

—*Suzana Ilić, Principal Program Manager Responsible AI, Microsoft Azure OpenAI*

Generative AI is the next revolutionary step in AI technology that will have a massive impact on the world. This book provides a great introduction to this field and its incredible potential and potential risks.

—*Connor Leahy, CEO at Conjecture and Cofounder of EleutherAI*

Predicting the world means understanding the world—in all modalities. In that sense, generative AI is solving the very core of intelligence.

—*Jonas Andrulis, Founder & CEO Aleph Alpha*

Generative AI is reshaping countless industries and powering a new generation of creative tools. This book is the perfect way to get going with generative modeling and start building with this revolutionary technology yourself.

—*Ed Newton-Rex, VP Audio at Stability AI and composer*

David taught me everything I know about machine learning and has a knack for explaining the underlying concepts. *Generative Deep Learning* is my go-to resource for generative AI and lives on a shelf next to my work desk amongst my small collection of favorite technical books.

—*Zack Thoutt, CPO at AutoSalesVelocity*

Generative AI is likely to have a profound impact on society. This book gives an introduction to the field that is accessible without skimping on technical detail.

—*Raza Habib, Cofounder of Humanloop*

When people ask me how to get started with generative AI, I always recommend David's book. The second edition is awesome because it covers the strongest models, such as diffusion models and Transformers. Definitely a must-have for anyone interested in computational creativity!

—*Dr. Tristan Behrens, AI Expert and AI Music Artist in Residence at KI Salon Heilbronn*

Dense in tech knowledge, this is my number one go-to literature when I have ideas around generative AI. It should be on every data scientist's bookshelf.

—*Martin Musiol, Founder of generativeAI.net*

The book covers the full taxonomy of generative models in excellent detail. One of the best things I found about the book is that it covers the important theory behind the models as well as solidifying the reader's understanding with practical examples. I must point out that the chapter on GANs is one of the best explanations I have read and provides intuitive means to fine-tune your models. The book covers a wide range of generative AI modalities including text, image, and music. A great resource for anyone getting started with GenAI.

—*Aishwarya Srinivasan, Data Scientist, Google Cloud*

SECOND EDITION

Generative Deep Learning

Teaching Machines to Paint, Write, Compose, and Play

David Foster
Foreword by Karl Friston

Beijing · Boston · Farnham · Sebastopol · Tokyo

Generative Deep Learning
by David Foster

Copyright © 2023 Applied Data Science Partners Ltd. All rights reserved.

Published by O'Reilly Media, Inc., 1005 Gravenstein Highway North, Sebastopol, CA 95472.

O'Reilly books may be purchased for educational, business, or sales promotional use. Online editions are also available for most titles (*http://oreilly.com*). For more information, contact our corporate/institutional sales department: 800-998-9938 or *corporate@oreilly.com*.

Acquisitions Editor: Nicole Butterfield	**Indexer:** Judith McConville
Development Editor: Michele Cronin	**Interior Designer:** David Futato
Production Editor: Christopher Faucher	**Cover Designer:** Karen Montgomery
Copyeditor: Charles Roumeliotis	**Illustrator:** Kate Dullea
Proofreader: Rachel Head	

July 2019:	First Edition
May 2023:	Second Edition

Revision History for the Second Edition

2023-04-28:	First Release
2024-03-01:	Second Release

See *http://oreilly.com/catalog/errata.csp?isbn=0636920733492* for release details.

978-1-098-13418-1

[LSI]

For Alina, the loveliest noise vector of them all.

Table of Contents

Part II.   Methods

Part III.   Applications

Foreword

This book is becoming part of my life. On finding a copy in my living room I asked my son, "When did you get this?" He replied, "When you gave it to me," bemused by my senior moment. Going through various sections together, I came to regard *Generative Deep Learning* as the *Gray's Anatomy* of Generative AI.

The author dissects the anatomy of generative AI with an incredible clarity and reassuring authority. He offers a truly remarkable account of a fast-moving field, underwritten with pragmatic examples, engaging narratives, and references that are so current, it reads like a living history.

Throughout his deconstructions, the author maintains a sense of wonder and excitement about the potential of generative AI—especially evident in the book's compelling dénouement. Having laid bare the technology, he reminds us that we are at the dawn of a new age of intelligence, an age in which generative AI holds a mirror up to our language, our art, our creativity; reflecting not just what we have created, but what we could create—what we can create—limited only by "your own imagination."

The central theme of generative models in artificial intelligence resonates deeply with me, because I see exactly the same themes emerging in the natural sciences; namely, a view of ourselves as generative models of our lived world. I suspect in the next edition of this book we will read about the confluence of artificial and natural intelligence. Until that time, I will keep this edition next to my copy of *Gray's Anatomy*, and other treasures on my bookshelf.

— Karl Friston, FRS
Professor of Neuroscience
University College London

Preface

What I cannot create, I do not understand.

    —Richard Feynman

Generative AI is one of the most revolutionary technologies of our time, transforming the way we interact with machines. Its potential to revolutionize the way we live, work, and play has been the subject of countless conversations, debates, and predictions. But what if there was an even greater potential to this powerful technology? What if the possibilities of generative AI extend beyond our current imagination? The future of generative AI may be more exciting than we ever thought possible...

Since our earliest days, we have sought opportunities to generate original and beautiful creations. For early humans, this took the form of cave paintings depicting wild animals and abstract patterns, created with pigments placed carefully and methodically onto rock. The Romantic Era gave us the mastery of Tchaikovsky symphonies, with their ability to inspire feelings of triumph and tragedy through sound waves, woven together to form beautiful melodies and harmonies. And in recent times, we have found ourselves rushing to bookshops at midnight to buy stories about a fictional wizard, because the combination of letters creates a narrative that wills us to turn the page and find out what happens to our hero.

It is therefore not surprising that humanity has started to ask the ultimate question of creativity: can we create something that is in itself creative?

This is the question that generative AI aims to answer. With recent advances in methodology and technology, we are now able to build machines that can paint original artwork in a given style, write coherent blocks of text with long-term structure, compose music that is pleasant to listen to, and develop winning strategies for complex games by generating imaginary future scenarios. This is just the start of a generative revolution that will leave us with no choice but to find answers to some of the biggest questions about the mechanics of creativity, and ultimately, what it means to be human.

In short, there has never been a better time to learn about generative AI—so let's get started!

Objective and Approach

This book assumes no prior knowledge of generative AI. We will build up all of the key concepts from scratch in a way that is intuitive and easy to follow, so don't worry if you have no experience with generative AI. You have come to the right place!

Rather than only covering the techniques that are currently in vogue, this book serves as a complete guide to generative modeling that covers a broad range of model families. There is no one technique that is objectively *better* or *worse* than any other—in fact, many state-of-the-art models now mix together ideas from across the broad spectrum of approaches to generative modeling. For this reason, it is important to keep abreast of developments across all areas of generative AI, rather than focusing on one particular kind of technique. One thing is certain: the field of generative AI is moving fast, and you never know where the next groundbreaking idea will come from!

With this in mind, the approach I will take is to show you how to train your own generative models on your own data, rather than relying on pre-trained off-the-shelf models. While there are now many impressive open source generative models that can be downloaded and run in a few lines of code, the aim of this book is to dig deeper into their architecture and design from first principles, so that you gain a complete understanding of how they work and can code up examples of each technique from scratch using Python and Keras.

In summary, this book can be thought of as a map of the current generative AI landscape that covers both theory and practical applications, including full working examples of key models from the literature. We will walk through the code for each step by step, with clear signposts that show how the code implements the theory underpinning each technique. This book can be read cover to cover or used as a reference book that you can dip into. Above all, I hope you find it a useful and enjoyable read!

 Throughout the book, you will find short, allegorical stories that help explain the mechanics of some of the models we will be building. I believe that one of the best ways to teach a new abstract theory is to first convert it into something that isn't quite so abstract, such as a story, before diving into the technical explanation. The story and the model explanation are just the same mechanics explained in two different domains—you might therefore find it useful to refer back to the relevant story while learning about the technical details of each model!

Prerequisites

This book assumes that you have experience coding in Python. If you are not familiar with Python, the best place to start is through LearnPython.org. There are many free resources online that will allow you to develop enough Python knowledge to work with the examples in this book.

Also, since some of the models are described using mathematical notation, it will be useful to have a solid understanding of linear algebra (for example, matrix multiplication) and general probability theory. A useful resource is Deisenroth et al.'s book *Mathematics for Machine Learning* (*https://mml-book.com*) (Cambridge University Press), which is freely available.

The book assumes no prior knowledge of generative modeling (we will examine the key concepts in Chapter 1) or TensorFlow and Keras (these libraries will be introduced in Chapter 2).

Roadmap

This book is divided into three parts.

Part I is a general introduction to generative modeling and deep learning, where we explore the core concepts that underpin all of the techniques in later parts of the book:

- In Chapter 1, "Generative Modeling", we define generative modeling and consider a toy example that we can use to understand some of the key concepts that are important to all generative models. We also lay out the taxonomy of generative model families that we will explore in Part II of this book.

- In Chapter 2, "Deep Learning", we begin our exploration of deep learning and neural networks by building our first example of a multilayer perceptron (MLP) using Keras. We then adapt this to include convolutional layers and other improvements, to observe the difference in performance.

Part II walks through the six key techniques that we will be using to build generative models, with practical examples for each:

- In Chapter 3, "Variational Autoencoders", we consider the variational autoencoder (VAE) and see how it can be used to generate images of faces and morph between faces in the model's latent space.

- In Chapter 4, "Generative Adversarial Networks", we explore generative adversarial networks (GANs) for image generation, including deep convolutional GANs, conditional GANs, and improvements such as the Wasserstein GAN that make the training process more stable.

- In Chapter 5, "Autoregressive Models", we turn our attention to autoregressive models, starting with an introduction to recurrent neural networks such as long short-term memory networks (LSTMs) for text generation and PixelCNN for image generation.

- In Chapter 6, "Normalizing Flow Models", we focus on normalizing flows, including an intuitive theoretical exploration of the technique and a practical example of how to build a RealNVP model to generate images.

- In Chapter 7, "Energy-Based Models", we cover energy-based models, including important methods such as how to train using contrastive divergence and sample using Langevin dynamics.

- In Chapter 8, "Diffusion Models", we dive into a practical guide to building diffusion models, which drive many state-of-the-art image generation models such as DALL.E 2 and Stable Diffusion.

Finally, in Part III we build on these foundations to explore the inner workings of state-of-the-art models for image generation, writing, composing music, and model-based reinforcement learning:

- In Chapter 9, "Transformers", we explore the lineage and technical details of the StyleGAN models, as well as other state-of-the-art GANs for image generation such as VQ-GAN.

- In Chapter 10, "Advanced GANs", we consider the Transformer architecture, including a practical walkthrough for building your own version of GPT for text generation.

- In Chapter 11, "Music Generation", we turn our attention to music generation, including a guide to working with music data and application of techniques such as Transformers and MuseGAN.

- In Chapter 12, "World Models", we see how generative models can be used in the context of reinforcement learning, with the application of world models and Transformer-based methods.

- In Chapter 13, "Multimodal Models", we explain the inner workings of four state-of-the-art multimodal models that incorporate more than one type of data, including DALL.E 2, Imagen, and Stable Diffusion for text-to-image generation and Flamingo, a visual language model.

- In Chapter 14, "Conclusion", we recap the key milestones of generative AI to date and discuss the ways in which generative AI will revolutionize our daily lives in years to come.

Changes in the Second Edition

Thank you to everyone who read the first edition of this book—I am really pleased that so many of you have found it a useful resource and provided feedback on things that you would like to see in the second edition. The field of generative deep learning has progressed significantly since the first edition was published in 2019, so as well as refreshing the existing content I have added several new chapters to bring the material in line with the current state of the art.

The following is a summary of the main updates, in terms of the individual chapters and general book improvements:

- Chapter 1 now includes a section on the different families of generative models and a taxonomy of how they are related.

- Chapter 2 contains improved diagrams and more detailed explanations of key concepts.

- Chapter 3 is refreshed with a new worked example and accompanying explanations.

- Chapter 4 now includes an explanation of conditional GAN architectures.

- Chapter 5 now includes a section on autoregressive models for images (e.g., PixelCNN).

- Chapter 6 is an entirely new chapter, describing the RealNVP model.

- Chapter 7 is also a new chapter, focusing on techniques such as Langevin dynamics and contrastive divergence.

- Chapter 8 is a newly written chapter on denoising the diffusion models that power many of today's state-of-the-art applications.

- Chapter 9 is an expansion of the material provided in the conclusion of the first edition, with deeper focus on architectures of the various StyleGAN models and new material on VQ-GAN.

- Chapter 10 is a new chapter that explores the Transformer architecture in detail.

- Chapter 11 includes modern Transformer architectures, replacing the LSTM models from the first edition.

- Chapter 12 includes updated diagrams and descriptions, with a section on how this approach is informing state-of-the-art reinforcement learning today.

- Chapter 13 is a new chapter that explains in detail how impressive models like DALL.E 2, Imagen, Stable Diffusion, and Flamingo work.

- Chapter 14 is updated to reflect the outstanding progress in the field since the first edition and give a more complete and detailed view of where generative AI is heading in the future.

- All comments given as feedback to the first edition and typos identified have been addressed (to the best of my knowledge!).
- Chapter goals have been added at the start of each chapter, so that you can see the key topics covered in the chapter before you start reading.
- Some of the allegorical stories have been rewritten to be more concise and clear—I am pleased that so many readers have said that the stories have helped them to better understand the key concepts!
- The headings and subheadings of each chapter have been aligned so that is it clear which parts of the chapter are focused on explanation and which are focused on building your own models.

Other Resources

I highly recommend the following books as general introductions to machine learning and deep learning:

- *Hands-On Machine Learning with Scikit-Learn, Keras, and TensorFlow: Concepts, Tools, and Techniques to Build Intelligent Systems* by Aurélien Géron (O'Reilly)
- *Deep Learning with Python* by Francois Chollet (Manning)

Most of the papers in this book are sourced through arXiv (*https://arxiv.org*), a free repository of scientific research papers. It is now common for authors to post papers to arXiv before they are fully peer-reviewed. Reviewing the recent submissions is a great way to keep on top of the most cutting-edge developments in the field.

I also highly recommend the website Papers with Code (*https://paperswithcode.com*), where you can find the latest state-of-the-art results in a variety of machine learning tasks, alongside links to the papers and official GitHub repositories. It is an excellent resource for anyone wanting to quickly understand which techniques are currently achieving the highest scores in a range of tasks and has certainly helped me to decide which techniques to include in this book.

Conventions Used in This Book

The following typographical conventions are used in this book:

Italic
  Indicates new terms, URLs, email addresses, filenames, and file extensions.

`Constant width`
  Used for commands and program listings, as well as within paragraphs to refer to program elements such as variable or function names.

Constant width italic

Shows text that should be replaced with user-supplied values or by values determined by context.

This element signifies a tip or suggestion.

This element signifies a general note.

This element signifies a warning or caution.

Codebase

The code examples in this book can be found in a GitHub repository (*https://github.com/davidADSP/Generative_Deep_Learning_2nd_Edition*). I have deliberately ensured that none of the models require prohibitively large amounts of computational resources to train, so that you can start training your own models without having to spend lots of time or money on expensive hardware. There is a comprehensive guide in the repository on how to get started with Docker and set up cloud resources with GPUs on Google Cloud if required.

The following changes have been made to the codebase since the first edition:

- All examples are now runnable from within a single notebook, instead of some code being imported from modules across the codebase. This is so that you can run each example cell by cell and delve into exactly how each model is built, piece by piece.

- The sections of each notebook are now broadly aligned between examples.

- Many of the examples in this book now utilize code snippets from the amazing open source Keras repository (*https://oreil.ly/1UTwa*)—this is to avoid creating a completely detached open source repository of Keras generative AI examples, when there already exist excellent implementations available through the Keras website. I have added references and links to the original authors of code that I have utilized from the Keras website throughout this book and in the repository.

- I have added new data sources and improved the data collection process from the first edition—now, there is a script that can be easily run to collect data from the required sources in order to train the examples in the book, using tools such as the Kaggle API (*https://oreil.ly/8ibPw*).

Using Code Examples

Supplemental material (code examples, exercises, etc.) is available for download at *https://github.com/davidADSP/Generative_Deep_Learning_2nd_Edition*.

If you have a technical question or a problem using the code examples, please send email to *bookquestions@oreilly.com*.

This book is here to help you get your job done. In general, if example code is offered with this book, you may use it in your programs and documentation. You do not need to contact us for permission unless you're reproducing a significant portion of the code. For example, writing a program that uses several chunks of code from this book does not require permission. Selling or distributing examples from O'Reilly books does require permission. Answering a question by citing this book and quoting example code does not require permission. Incorporating a significant amount of example code from this book into your product's documentation does require permission.

We appreciate, but do not require, attribution. An attribution usually includes the title, author, publisher, and ISBN. For example: "*Generative Deep Learning*, 2nd edition, by David Foster (O'Reilly). Copyright 2023 Applied Data Science Partners Ltd., 978-1-098-13418-1."

If you feel your use of code examples falls outside fair use or the permission given above, feel free to contact us at *permissions@oreilly.com*.

O'Reilly Online Learning

For more than 40 years, *O'Reilly Media* has provided technology and business training, knowledge, and insight to help companies succeed.

Our unique network of experts and innovators share their knowledge and expertise through books, articles, and our online learning platform. O'Reilly's online learning platform gives you on-demand access to live training courses, in-depth learning paths, interactive coding environments, and a vast collection of text and video from O'Reilly and 200+ other publishers. For more information, visit *https://oreilly.com*.

How to Contact Us

Please address comments and questions concerning this book to the publisher:

O'Reilly Media, Inc.
1005 Gravenstein Highway North
Sebastopol, CA 95472
800-889-8969 (in the United States or Canada)
707-827-7019 (international or local)
707-829-0104 (fax)
support@oreilly.com
https://www.oreilly.com/about/contact.html

We have a web page for this book, where we list errata, examples, and any additional information. You can access this page at *https://oreil.ly/generative-dl-2e*.

For news and information about our books and courses, visit *https://oreilly.com*.

Find us on LinkedIn: *https://linkedin.com/company/oreilly-media*

Watch us on YouTube: *https://youtube.com/oreillymedia*

Acknowledgments

There are so many people I would like to thank for helping me write this book.

First, I would like to thank everyone who has taken time to technically review the book—in particular Vishwesh Ravi Shrimali, Lipi Deepaakshi Patnaik, Luba Elliot, and Lorna Barclay. Thanks also to Samir Bico for helping to review and test the codebase that accompanies this book. Your input has been invaluable.

Also, a huge thanks to my colleagues at Applied Data Science Partners (*https://adsp.ai*), Ross Witeszczak, Amy Bull, Ali Parandeh, Zine Eddine, Joe Rowe, Gerta Salillari, Aleshia Parkes, Evelina Kireilyte, Riccardo Tolli, Mai Do, Khaleel Syed, and Will Holmes. Your patience with me while I have taken time to finish the book is hugely appreciated, and I am greatly looking forward to all the machine learning projects we will complete together in the future! Particular thanks to Ross—had we not decided to start a business together, this book might never have taken shape, so thank you for believing in me as your business partner!

I also want to thank anyone who has ever taught me anything mathematical—I was extremely fortunate to have fantastic math teachers at school, who developed my interest in the subject and encouraged me to pursue it further at university. I would like to thank you for your commitment and for going out of your way to share your knowledge of the subject with me.

A huge thank you goes to the staff at O'Reilly for guiding me through the process of writing this book. A special thanks goes to Michele Cronin, who has been there at each step, providing useful feedback and sending me friendly reminders to keep completing chapters! Also to Nicole Butterfield, Christopher Faucher, Charles Roumeliotis, and Suzanne Huston for getting the book into production, and Mike Loukides for first reaching out to ask if I'd be interested in writing a book. You have all been so supportive of this project from the start, and I want to thank you for providing me with a platform on which to write about something that I love.

Throughout the writing process, my family has been a constant source of encouragement and support. A huge thank you goes to my mum, Gillian Foster, for checking every single line of text for typos and for teaching me how to add up in the first place! Your attention to detail has been extremely helpful while proofreading this book, and I'm really grateful for all the opportunities that both you and dad have given me. My dad, Clive Foster, originally taught me how to program a computer—this book is full of practical examples, and that's thanks to his early patience while I fumbled around in BASIC trying to make football games as a teenager. My brother, Rob Foster, is the most modest genius you will ever find, particularly within linguistics—chatting with him about AI and the future of text-based machine learning has been amazingly helpful. Last, I would like to thank my Nana, who was always a constant source of inspiration and fun for all of us. Her love of literature was one of the reasons I first decided that writing a book would be an exciting thing to do.

I would also like to thank my wife, Lorna Barclay. As well as providing me with endless support and cups of tea throughout the writing process, you have rigorously checked every word of this book in meticulous detail. I couldn't have done it without you. Thank you for always being there for me, and for making this journey so much more enjoyable. I promise I won't talk about generative AI at the dinner table for at least a few days after the book is published.

Lastly, I would like to thank our beautiful baby daughter Alina for providing endless entertainment during the long nights of book-writing. Your adorable giggles have been the perfect background music to my typing. Thanks for being my inspiration and for always keeping me on my toes. You're the real brains behind this operation.

Introduction to Generative Deep Learning

Part I is a general introduction to generative modeling and deep learning—the two fields that we need to understand in order to get started with generative deep learning!

In Chapter 1 we will define generative modeling and consider a toy example that we can use to understand some of the key concepts that are important to all generative models. We will also lay out the taxonomy of generative model families that we will explore in Part II of this book.

Chapter 2 provides a guide to the deep learning tools and techniques that we will need to start building more complex generative models. In particular, we will build our first example of a deep neural network—a multilayer perceptron (MLP)—using Keras. We will then adapt this to include convolutional layers and other improvements, to observe the difference in performance.

By the end of Part I you will have a good understanding of the core concepts that underpin all of the techniques in later parts of the book.

CHAPTER 1

Generative Modeling

Chapter Goals

In this chapter you will:

- Learn the key differences between generative and discriminative models.
- Understand the desirable properties of a generative model through a simple example.
- Learn about the core probabilistic concepts that underpin generative models.
- Explore the different families of generative models.
- Clone the codebase that accompanies this book, so that you can get started building generative models!

This chapter is a general introduction to the field of generative modeling.

We will start with a gentle theoretical introduction to generative modeling and see how it is the natural counterpart to the more widely studied discriminative modeling. We will then establish a framework that describes the desirable properties that a good generative model should have. We will also lay out the core probabilistic concepts that are important to know, in order to fully appreciate how different approaches tackle the challenge of generative modeling.

This will lead us naturally to the penultimate section, which lays out the six broad families of generative models that dominate the field today. The final section explains how to get started with the codebase that accompanies this book.

What Is Generative Modeling?

Generative modeling can be broadly defined as follows:

> Generative modeling is a branch of machine learning that involves training a model to produce new data that is similar to a given dataset.

What does this mean in practice? Suppose we have a dataset containing photos of horses. We can *train* a generative model on this dataset to capture the rules that govern the complex relationships between pixels in images of horses. Then we can *sample* from this model to create novel, realistic images of horses that did not exist in the original dataset. This process is illustrated in Figure 1-1.

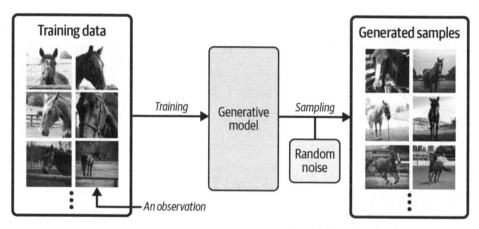

Figure 1-1. A generative model trained to generate realistic photos of horses

In order to build a generative model, we require a dataset consisting of many examples of the entity we are trying to generate. This is known as the *training data*, and one such data point is called an *observation*.

Each observation consists of many *features*. For an image generation problem, the features are usually the individual pixel values; for a text generation problem, the features could be individual words or groups of letters. It is our goal to build a model that can generate new sets of features that look as if they have been created using the same rules as the original data. Conceptually, for image generation this is an incredibly difficult task, considering the vast number of ways that individual pixel values can be assigned and the relatively tiny number of such arrangements that constitute an image of the entity we are trying to generate.

A generative model must also be *probabilistic* rather than *deterministic*, because we want to be able to sample many different variations of the output, rather than get the same output every time. If our model is merely a fixed calculation, such as taking the average value of each pixel in the training dataset, it is not generative. A generative model must include a random component that influences the individual samples generated by the model.

In other words, we can imagine that there is some unknown probabilistic distribution that explains why some images are likely to be found in the training dataset and other images are not. It is our job to build a model that mimics this distribution as closely as possible and then sample from it to generate new, distinct observations that look as if they could have been included in the original training set.

Generative Versus Discriminative Modeling

In order to truly understand what generative modeling aims to achieve and why this is important, it is useful to compare it to its counterpart, *discriminative modeling*. If you have studied machine learning, most problems you will have faced will have most likely been discriminative in nature. To understand the difference, let's look at an example.

Suppose we have a dataset of paintings, some painted by Van Gogh and some by other artists. With enough data, we could train a discriminative model to predict if a given painting was painted by Van Gogh. Our model would learn that certain colors, shapes, and textures are more likely to indicate that a painting is by the Dutch master, and for paintings with these features, the model would upweight its prediction accordingly. Figure 1-2 shows the discriminative modeling process—note how it differs from the generative modeling process shown in Figure 1-1.

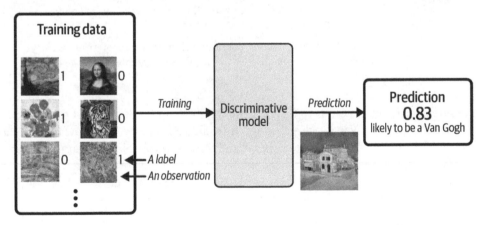

Figure 1-2. A discriminative model trained to predict if a given image is painted by Van Gogh

When performing discriminative modeling, each observation in the training data has a *label*. For a binary classification problem such as our artist discriminator, Van Gogh paintings would be labeled 1 and non–Van Gogh paintings labeled 0. Our model then learns how to discriminate between these two groups and outputs the probability that a new observation has label 1—i.e., that it was painted by Van Gogh.

In contrast, generative modeling doesn't require the dataset to be labeled because it concerns itself with generating entirely new images, rather than trying to predict a label of a given image.

Let's define these types of modeling formally, using mathematical notation:

> *Discriminative modeling* estimates $p(y|\mathbf{x})$.
>
> That is, discriminative modeling aims to model the probability of a label y given some observation $\mathbf{x}$.

> *Generative modeling* estimates $p(\mathbf{x})$.
>
> That is, generative modeling aims to model the probability of observing an observation $\mathbf{x}$. Sampling from this distribution allows us to generate new observations.

Conditional Generative Models

Note that we can also build a generative model to model the conditional probability $p(\mathbf{x}|y)$—the probability of seeing an observation $\mathbf{x}$ with a specific label y.

For example, if our dataset contains different types of fruit, we could tell our generative model to specifically generate an image of an apple.

An important point to note is that even if we were able to build a perfect discriminative model to identify Van Gogh paintings, it would still have no idea how to create a painting that looks like a Van Gogh. It can only output probabilities against existing images, as this is what it has been trained to do. We would instead need to train a generative model and sample from this model to generate images that have a high chance of belonging to the original training dataset.

The Rise of Generative Modeling

Until recently, discriminative modeling has been the driving force behind most progress in machine learning. This is because for any discriminative problem, the corresponding generative modeling problem is typically much more difficult to tackle. For example, it is much easier to train a model to predict if a painting is by Van Gogh than it is to train a model to generate a Van Gogh–style painting from scratch.

Similarly, it is much easier to train a model to predict if a page of text was written by Charles Dickens than it is to build a model to generate a set of paragraphs in the style of Dickens. Until recently, most generative challenges were simply out of reach and many doubted that they could ever be solved. Creativity was considered a purely human capability that couldn't be rivaled by AI.

However, as machine learning technologies have matured, this assumption has gradually weakened. In the last 10 years many of the most interesting advancements in the field have come through novel applications of machine learning to generative modeling tasks. For example, Figure 1-3 shows the striking progress that has already been made in facial image generation since 2014.

Figure 1-3. Face generation using generative modeling has improved significantly over the last decade (adapted from Brundage et al., 2018)[1]

As well as being easier to tackle, discriminative modeling has historically been more readily applicable to practical problems across industry than generative modeling. For example, a doctor may benefit from a model that predicts if a given retinal image shows signs of glaucoma, but wouldn't necessarily benefit from a model that can generate novel pictures of the back of an eye.

However, this is also starting to change, with the proliferation of companies offering generative services that target specific business problems. For example, it is now possible to access APIs that generate original blog posts given a particular subject matter, produce a variety of images of your product in any setting you desire, or write social media content and ad copy to match your brand and target message. There are also clear positive applications of generative AI for industries such as game design and cinematography, where models trained to output video and music are beginning to add value.

Generative Modeling and AI

As well as the practical uses of generative modeling (many of which are yet to be discovered), there are three deeper reasons why generative modeling can be considered the key to unlocking a far more sophisticated form of artificial intelligence that goes beyond what discriminative modeling alone can achieve.

Firstly, purely from a theoretical point of view, we shouldn't limit our machine training to simply categorizing data. For completeness, we should also be concerned with training models that capture a more complete understanding of the data distribution, beyond any particular label. This is undoubtedly a more difficult problem to solve, due to the high dimensionality of the space of feasible outputs and the relatively small number of creations that we would class as belonging to the dataset. However, as we shall see, many of the same techniques that have driven development in discriminative modeling, such as deep learning, can be utilized by generative models too.

Secondly, as we shall see in Chapter 12, generative modeling is now being used to drive progress in other fields of AI, such as reinforcement learning (the study of teaching agents to optimize a goal in an environment through trial and error). Suppose we want to train a robot to walk across a given terrain. A traditional approach would be to run many experiments where the agent tries out different strategies in the terrain, or a computer simulation of the terrain. Over time the agent would learn which strategies are more successful than others and therefore gradually improve. A challenge with this approach is that it is fairly inflexible because it is trained to optimize the policy for one particular task. An alternative approach that has recently gained traction is to instead train the agent to learn a *world model* of the environment using a generative model, independent of any particular task. The agent can quickly adapt to new tasks by testing strategies in its own world model, rather than in the real environment, which is often computationally more efficient and does not require retraining from scratch for each new task.

Finally, if we are to truly say that we have built a machine that has acquired a form of intelligence that is comparable to a human's, generative modeling must surely be part of the solution. One of the finest examples of a generative model in the natural world is the person reading this book. Take a moment to consider what an incredible generative model you are. You can close your eyes and imagine what an elephant would look like from any possible angle. You can imagine a number of plausible different endings to your favorite TV show, and you can plan your week ahead by working through various futures in your mind's eye and taking action accordingly. Current neuroscientific theory suggests that our perception of reality is not a highly complex discriminative model operating on our sensory input to produce predictions of what we are experiencing, but is instead a generative model that is trained from birth to produce simulations of our surroundings that accurately match the future. Some theories even suggest that the output from this generative model is what we directly perceive as reality. Clearly, a deep understanding of how we can build machines to acquire this ability will be central to our continued understanding of the workings of the brain and general artificial intelligence.

Our First Generative Model

With this in mind, let's begin our journey into the exciting world of generative modeling. To begin with, we'll look at a toy example of a generative model and introduce some of the ideas that will help us to work through the more complex architectures that we will encounter later in the book.

Hello World!

Let's start by playing a generative modeling game in just two dimensions. I have chosen a rule that has been used to generate the set of points $\mathbf{X}$ in Figure 1-4. Let's call this rule p_{data}. Your challenge is to choose a different point $\mathbf{x} = (x_1, x_2)$ in the space that looks like it has been generated by the same rule.

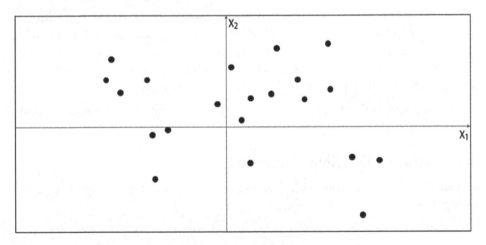

Figure 1-4. A set of points in two dimensions, generated by an unknown rule p_{data}

Where did you choose? You probably used your knowledge of the existing data points to construct a mental model, p_{model}, of whereabouts in the space the point is more likely to be found. In this respect, p_{model} is an *estimate* of p_{data}. Perhaps you decided that p_{model} should look like Figure 1-5—a rectangular box where points may be found, and an area outside of the box where there is no chance of finding any points.

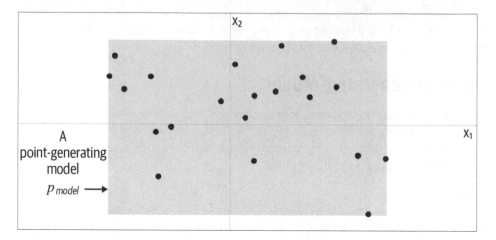

Figure 1-5. The orange box, p_{model}, is an estimate of the true data-generating distribution, p_{data}

To generate a new observation, you can simply choose a point at random within the box, or more formally, *sample* from the distribution p_{model}. Congratulations, you have just built your first generative model! You have used the training data (the black points) to construct a model (the orange region) that you can easily sample from to generate other points that appear to belong to the training set.

Let's now formalize this thinking into a framework that can help us understand what generative modeling is trying to achieve.

The Generative Modeling Framework

We can capture our motivations and goals for building a generative model in the following framework.

The Generative Modeling Framework

- We have a dataset of observations **X**.
- We assume that the observations have been generated according to some unknown distribution, p_{data}.
- We want to build a generative model p_{model} that mimics p_{data}. If we achieve this goal, we can sample from p_{model} to generate observations that appear to have been drawn from p_{data}.
- Therefore, the desirable properties of p_{model} are:

Let's now reveal the true data-generating distribution, p_{data}, and see how the framework applies to this example. As we can see from Figure 1-6, the data-generating rule is simply a uniform distribution over the land mass of the world, with no chance of finding a point in the sea.

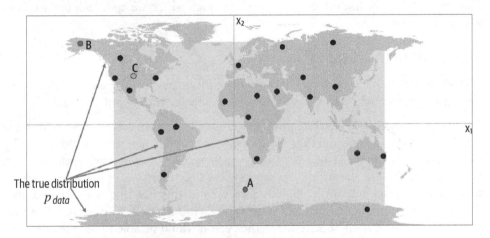

Figure 1-6. The orange box, p_{model}, is an estimate of the true data-generating distribution, p_{data} (the gray area)

Clearly, our model, p_{model}, is an oversimplification of p_{data}. We can inspect points A, B, and C to understand the successes and failures of our model in terms of how accurately it mimics p_{data}:

- Point A is an observation that is generated by our model but does not appear to have been generated by p_{data} as it's in the middle of the sea.

- Point B could never have been generated by p_{model} as it sits outside the orange box. Therefore, our model has some gaps in its ability to produce observations across the entire range of potential possibilities.

- Point C is an observation that could be generated by p_{model} and also by p_{data}.

Despite its shortcomings, the model is easy to sample from, because it is simply a uniform distribution over the orange box. We can easily choose a point at random from inside this box, in order to sample from it.

Also, we can certainly say that our model is a simple representation of the underlying complex distribution that captures some of the underlying high-level features. The true distribution is separated into areas with lots of land mass (continents) and those with no land mass (the sea). This is a high-level feature that is also true of our model, except we have one large continent, rather than many.

This example has demonstrated the fundamental concepts behind generative modeling. The problems we will be tackling in this book will be far more complex and high-dimensional, but the underlying framework through which we approach the problem will be the same.

Representation Learning

It is worth delving a little deeper into what we mean by learning a *representation* of the high-dimensional data, as it is a topic that will recur throughout this book.

Suppose you wanted to describe your appearance to someone who was looking for you in a crowd of people and didn't know what you looked like. You wouldn't start by stating the color of pixel 1 of a photo of you, then pixel 2, then pixel 3, etc. Instead, you would make the reasonable assumption that the other person has a general idea of what an average human looks like, then amend this baseline with features that describe groups of pixels, such as *I have very blond hair* or *I wear glasses*. With no more than 10 or so of these statements, the person would be able to map the description back into pixels to generate an image of you in their head. The image wouldn't be perfect, but it would be a close enough likeness to your actual appearance for them to find you among possibly hundreds of other people, even if they've never seen you before.

This is the core idea behind *representation learning*. Instead of trying to model the high-dimensional sample space directly, we describe each observation in the training set using some lower-dimensional *latent space* and then learn a mapping function that can take a point in the latent space and map it to a point in the original domain. In other words, each point in the latent space is a *representation* of some high-dimensional observation.

What does this mean in practice? Let's suppose we have a training set consisting of grayscale images of biscuit tins (Figure 1-7).

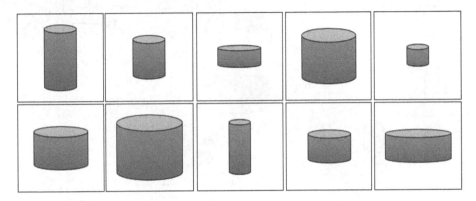

Figure 1-7. The biscuit tin dataset

To us, it is obvious that there are two features that can uniquely represent each of these tins: the height and width of the tin. That is, we can convert each image of a tin to a point in a latent space of just two dimensions, even though the training set of images is provided in high-dimensional pixel space. Notably, this means that we can also produce images of tins that do not exist in the training set, by applying a suitable mapping function f to a new point in the latent space, as shown in Figure 1-8.

Realizing that the original dataset can be described by the simpler latent space is not so easy for a machine—it would first need to establish that height and width are the two latent space dimensions that best describe this dataset, then learn the mapping function f that can take a point in this space and map it to a grayscale biscuit tin image. Machine learning (and specifically, deep learning) gives us the ability to train machines that can find these complex relationships without human guidance.

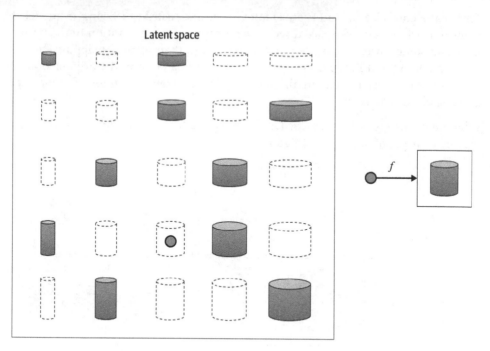

Figure 1-8. The 2D latent space of biscuit tins and the function f that maps a point in the latent space back to the original image domain

One of the benefits of training models that utilize a latent space is that we can perform operations that affect high-level properties of the image by manipulating its representation vector within the more manageable latent space. For example, it is not obvious how to adjust the shading of every single pixel to make an image of a biscuit tin *taller*. However, in the latent space, it's simply a case of increasing the *height* latent dimension, then applying the mapping function to return to the image domain. We shall see an explicit example of this in the next chapter, applied not to biscuit tins but to faces.

The concept of encoding the training dataset into a latent space so that we can sample from it and decode the point back to the original domain is common to many generative modeling techniques, as we shall see in later chapters of this book. Mathematically speaking, *encoder-decoder* techniques try to transform the highly nonlinear *manifold* on which the data lies (e.g., in pixel space) into a simpler latent space that can be sampled from, so that it is likely that any point in the latent space is the representation of a well-formed image, as shown in Figure 1-9.

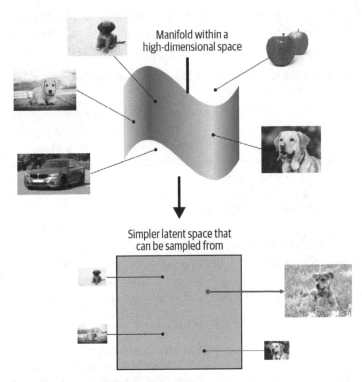

Figure 1-9. The dog manifold in high-dimensional pixel space is mapped to a simpler latent space that can be sampled from

Core Probability Theory

We have already seen that generative modeling is closely connected to statistical modeling of probability distributions. Therefore, it now makes sense to introduce some core probabilistic and statistical concepts that will be used throughout this book to explain the theoretical background of each model.

If you have never studied probability or statistics, don't worry. To build many of the deep learning models that we shall see later in this book, it is not essential to have a deep understanding of statistical theory. However, to gain a full appreciation of the task that we are trying to tackle, it's worth trying to build up a solid understanding of basic probabilistic theory. This way, you will have the foundations in place to understand the different families of generative models that will be introduced later in this chapter.

As a first step, we shall define five key terms, linking each one back to our earlier example of a generative model that models the world map in two dimensions:

Sample space

The *sample space* is the complete set of all values an observation **x** can take.

In our previous example, the sample space consists of all points of latitude and longitude **x** = (x_1, x_2) on the world map. For example, **x** = (40.7306, −73.9352) is a point in the sample space (New York City) that belongs to the true data-generating distribution. **x** = (11.3493, 142.1996) is a point in the sample space that does not belong to the true data-generating distribution (it's in the sea).

Probability density function

A *probability density function* (or simply *density function*) is a function $p(\mathbf{x})$ that represents the relative likelihood of a continuous random variable falling within different intervals, with the integral of $p(\mathbf{x})$ over the entire range of possible values being equal to 1.

In the world map example, the density function of our generative model is 0 outside of the orange box and constant inside of the box, so that the integral of the density function over the entire sample space equals 1.

While there is only one true density function $p_{data}(\mathbf{x})$ that is assumed to have generated the observable dataset, there are infinitely many density functions $p_{model}(\mathbf{x})$ that we can use to estimate $p_{data}(\mathbf{x})$.

Parametric modeling

Parametric modeling is a technique that we can use to structure our approach to finding a suitable $p_{model}(\mathbf{x})$. A *parametric model* is a family of density functions $p_\theta(\mathbf{x})$ that can be described using a finite number of parameters, θ.

If we assume a uniform distribution as our model family, then the set all possible boxes we could draw on Figure 1-5 is an example of a parametric model. In this case, there are four parameters: the coordinates of the bottom-left (θ_1, θ_2) and top-right (θ_3, θ_4) corners of the box.

Thus, each density function $p_\theta(\mathbf{x})$ in this parametric model (i.e., each box) can be uniquely represented by four numbers, $\theta = (\theta_1, \theta_2, \theta_3, \theta_4)$.

Likelihood

The *likelihood* $\mathscr{L}(\theta|\mathbf{x})$ of a parameter set θ is a function that measures the plausibility of θ, given some observed point $\mathbf{x}$. It is defined as follows:

$$\mathscr{L}(\theta|\mathbf{x}) = p_\theta(\mathbf{x})$$

That is, the likelihood of θ given some observed point $\mathbf{x}$ is defined to be the value of the density function parameterized by θ, at the point $\mathbf{x}$. If we have a whole dataset $\mathbf{X}$ of independent observations, then we can write:

$$\mathscr{L}(\theta|\mathbf{X}) = \prod_{\mathbf{x} \in \mathbf{X}} p_\theta(\mathbf{x})$$

In the world map example, an orange box that only covered the left half of the map would have a likelihood of 0—it couldn't possibly have generated the dataset, as we have observed points in the right half of the map. The orange box in Figure 1-5 has a positive likelihood, as the density function is positive for all data points under this model.

Since the product of a large number of terms between 0 and 1 can be quite computationally difficult to work with, we often use the *log-likelihood* ℓ instead:

$$\ell(\theta|\mathbf{X}) = \sum_{\mathbf{x} \in \mathbf{X}} \log p_\theta(\mathbf{x})$$

There are statistical reasons why the likelihood is defined in this way, but we can also see that this definition intuitively makes sense. The likelihood of a set of parameters θ is defined to be the probability of seeing the data if the true data-generating distribution was the model parameterized by θ.

Note that the likelihood is a function of the *parameters*, not the data. It should *not* be interpreted as the probability that a given parameter set is correct—in other words, it is not a probability distribution over the parameter space (i.e., it doesn't sum/integrate to 1, with respect to the parameters).

It makes intuitive sense that the focus of parametric modeling should be to find the optimal value $\hat{\theta}$ of the parameter set that maximizes the likelihood of observing the dataset $\mathbf{X}$.

Maximum likelihood estimation

Maximum likelihood estimation is the technique that allows us to estimate $\hat{\theta}$—the set of parameters θ of a density function $p_\theta(\mathbf{x})$ that is most likely to explain some observed data $\mathbf{X}$. More formally:

$$\hat{\theta} = \arg_\theta \max\ell(\theta|\mathbf{X})$$

$\hat{\theta}$ is also called the *maximum likelihood estimate* (MLE).

In the world map example, the MLE is the smallest rectangle that still contains all of the points in the training set.

Neural networks typically *minimize* a loss function, so we can equivalently talk about finding the set of parameters that *minimize the negative log-likelihood*:

$$\hat{\theta} = \arg_\theta \min(-\ell(\theta|\mathbf{X})) = \arg_\theta \min(-\log p_\theta(\mathbf{X}))$$

Generative modeling can be thought of as a form of maximum likelihood estimation, where the parameters θ are the weights of the neural networks contained in the model. We are trying to find the values of these parameters that maximize the likelihood of observing the given data (or equivalently, minimize the negative log-likelihood).

However, for high-dimensional problems, it is generally not possible to directly calculate $p_\theta(\mathbf{x})$—it is *intractable*. As we shall see in the next section, different families of generative models take different approaches to tackling this problem.

Generative Model Taxonomy

While all types of generative models ultimately aim to solve the same task, they all take slightly different approaches to modeling the density function $p_\theta(\mathbf{x})$. Broadly speaking, there are three possible approaches:

1. Explicitly model the density function, but constrain the model in some way, so that the density function is tractable (i.e., it can be calculated).

2. Explicitly model a tractable approximation of the density function.

3. Implicitly model the density function, through a stochastic process that directly generates data.

These are shown in Figure 1-10 as a taxonomy, alongside the six families of generative models that we will explore in Part II of this book. Note that these families are not mutually exclusive—there are many examples of models that are hybrids between two different kinds of approaches. You should think of the families as different general approaches to generative modeling, rather than explicit model architectures.

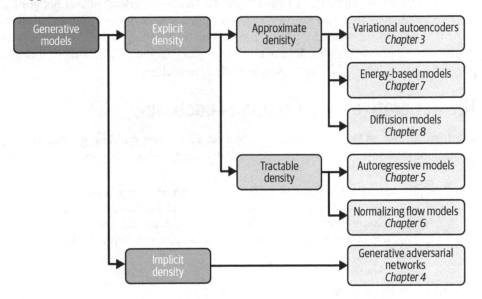

Figure 1-10. A taxonomy of generative modeling approaches

The first split that we can make is between models where the probability density function $p(\mathbf{x})$ is modeled *explicitly* and those where it is modeled *implicitly*.

Implicit density models do not aim to estimate the probability density at all, but instead focus solely on producing a stochastic process that directly generates data. The best-known example of an implicit generative model is a *generative adversarial network*. We can further split *explicit density models* into those that directly optimize the density function (tractable models) and those that only optimize an approximation of it.

Tractable models place constraints on the model architecture, so that the density function has a form that makes it easy to calculate. For example, *autoregressive models* impose an ordering on the input features, so that the output can be generated sequentially—e.g., word by word, or pixel by pixel. *Normalizing flow models* apply a series of tractable, invertible functions to a simple distribution, in order to generate more complex distributions.

Approximate density models include *variational autoencoders*, which introduce a latent variable and optimize an approximation of the joint density function. *Energy-based models* also utilize approximate methods, but do so via Markov chain sampling, rather than variational methods. *Diffusion models* approximate the density function by training a model to gradually denoise a given image that has been previously corrupted.

A common thread that runs through all of the generative model family types is *deep learning*. Almost all sophisticated generative models have a deep neural network at their core, because they can be trained from scratch to learn the complex relationships that govern the structure of the data, rather than having to be hardcoded with information a priori. We'll explore deep learning in Chapter 2, with practical examples of how to get started building your own deep neural networks.

The Generative Deep Learning Codebase

The final section of this chapter will get you set up to start building generative deep learning models by introducing the codebase that accompanies this book.

Many of the examples in this book are adapted from the excellent open source implementations that are available through the Keras website (*https://oreil.ly/1UTwa*). I highly recommend you check out this resource, as new models and examples are constantly being added.

Cloning the Repository

To get started, you'll first need to clone the Git repository. *Git* is an open source version control system and will allow you to copy the code locally so that you can run the notebooks on your own machine, or in a cloud-based environment. You may already have this installed, but if not, follow the instructions relevant to your operating system (*https://oreil.ly/tFOdN*).

To clone the repository for this book, navigate to the folder where you would like to store the files and type the following into your terminal:

```
git clone https://github.com/davidADSP/Generative_Deep_Learning_2nd_Edition.git
```

You should now be able to see the files in a folder on your machine.

Using Docker

The codebase for this book is intended to be used with *Docker*, a free containerization technology that makes getting started with a new codebase extremely easy, regardless of your architecture or operating system. If you have never used Docker, don't worry—there is a description of how to get started in the *README* file in the book repository.

Running on a GPU

If you don't have access to your own GPU, that's also no problem! All of the examples in this book will train on a CPU, though this will take longer than if you use a GPU-enabled machine. There is also a section in the *README* about setting up a Google Cloud environment that gives you access to a GPU on a pay-as-you-go basis.

Summary

This chapter introduced the field of generative modeling, an important branch of machine learning that complements the more widely studied discriminative modeling. We discussed how generative modeling is currently one of the most active and exciting areas of AI research, with many recent advances in both theory and applications.

We started with a simple toy example and saw how generative modeling ultimately focuses on modeling the underlying distribution of the data. This presents many complex and interesting challenges, which we summarized into a framework for understanding the desirable properties of any generative model.

We then walked through the key probabilistic concepts that will help to fully understand the theoretical foundations of each approach to generative modeling and laid out the six different families of generative models that we will explore in Part II of this book. We also saw how to get started with the *Generative Deep Learning* codebase, by cloning the repository.

In Chapter 2, we will begin our exploration of deep learning and see how to use Keras to build models that can perform discriminative modeling tasks. This will give us the necessary foundation to tackle generative deep learning problems in later chapters.

References

1. Miles Brundage et al., "The Malicious Use of Artificial Intelligence: Forecasting, Prevention, and Mitigation," February 20, 2018, *https://www.eff.org/files/2018/02/20/malicious_ai_report_final.pdf*.

CHAPTER 2

Deep Learning

Chapter Goals

In this chapter you will:

- Learn about the different types of unstructured data that can be modeled using deep learning.
- Define a deep neural network and understand how it can be used to model complex datasets.
- Build a multilayer perceptron to predict the content of an image.
- Improve the performance of the model by using convolutional layers, dropout, and batch normalization layers.

Let's start with a basic definition of deep learning:

> Deep learning is a class of machine learning algorithms that uses *multiple stacked layers of processing units* to learn high-level representations from *unstructured* data.

To understand deep learning fully, we need to delve into this definition a bit further. First, we'll take a look at the different types of unstructured data that deep learning can be used to model, then we'll dive into the mechanics of building multiple stacked layers of processing units to solve classification tasks. This will provide the foundation for future chapters where we focus on deep learning for generative tasks.

Data for Deep Learning

Many types of machine learning algorithms require *structured*, tabular data as input, arranged into columns of features that describe each observation. For example, a person's age, income, and number of website visits in the last month are all features that could help to predict if the person will subscribe to a particular online service in the coming month. We could use a structured table of these features to train a logistic regression, random forest, or XGBoost model to predict the binary response variable—did the person subscribe (1) or not (0)? Here, each individual feature contains a nugget of information about the observation, and the model would learn how these features interact to influence the response.

Unstructured data refers to any data that is not naturally arranged into columns of features, such as images, audio, and text. There is of course spatial structure to an image, temporal structure to a recording or passage of text, and both spatial and temporal structure to video data, but since the data does not arrive in columns of features, it is considered unstructured, as shown in Figure 2-1.

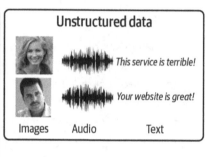

Figure 2-1. The difference between structured and unstructured data

When our data is unstructured, individual pixels, frequencies, or characters are almost entirely uninformative. For example, knowing that pixel 234 of an image is a muddy shade of brown doesn't really help identify if the image is of a house or a dog, and knowing that character 24 of a sentence is an *e* doesn't help predict if the text is about football or politics.

Pixels or characters are really just the dimples of the canvas into which higher-level informative features, such as an image of a chimney or the word *striker*, are embedded. If the chimney in the image were placed on the other side of the house, the image would still contain a chimney, but this information would now be carried by completely different pixels. If the word *striker* appeared slightly earlier or later in the text, the text would still be about football, but different character positions would provide this information. The granularity of the data combined with the high degree of spatial dependence destroys the concept of the pixel or character as an informative feature in its own right.

For this reason, if we train logistic regression, random forest, or XGBoost models on raw pixel values, the trained model will often perform poorly for all but the simplest of classification tasks. These models rely on the input features to be informative and not spatially dependent. A deep learning model, on the other hand, can learn how to build high-level informative features by itself, directly from the unstructured data.

Deep learning can be applied to structured data, but its real power, especially with regard to generative modeling, comes from its ability to work with unstructured data. Most often, we want to generate unstructured data such as new images or original strings of text, which is why deep learning has had such a profound impact on the field of generative modeling.

Deep Neural Networks

The majority of deep learning systems are *artificial neural networks* (ANNs, or just *neural networks* for short) with multiple stacked hidden layers. For this reason, *deep learning* has now almost become synonymous with *deep neural networks*. However, any system that employs many layers to learn high-level representations of the input data is also a form of deep learning (e.g., deep belief networks).

Let's start by breaking down exactly what we mean by a neural network and then see how they can be used to learn high-level features from unstructured data.

What Is a Neural Network?

A neural network consists of a series of stacked *layers*. Each layer contains *units* that are connected to the previous layer's units through a set of *weights*. As we shall see, there are many different types of layers, but one of the most common is the *fully connected* (or *dense*) layer that connects all units in the layer directly to every unit in the previous layer.

Neural networks where all adjacent layers are fully connected are called *multilayer perceptrons* (MLPs). This is the first type of neural network that we will study. An example of an MLP is shown in Figure 2-2.

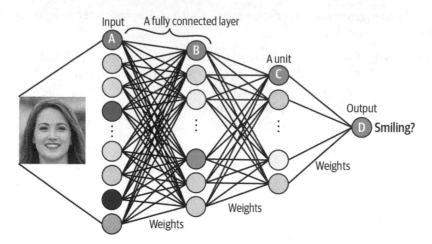

Figure 2-2. An example of a multilayer perceptron that predicts if a face is smiling

The input (e.g., an image) is transformed by each layer in turn, in what is known as a *forward pass* through the network, until it reaches the output layer. Specifically, each unit applies a nonlinear transformation to a weighted sum of its inputs and passes the output through to the subsequent layer. The final output layer is the culmination of this process, where the single unit outputs a probability that the original input belongs to a particular category (e.g., *smiling*).

The magic of deep neural networks lies in finding the set of weights for each layer that results in the most accurate predictions. The process of finding these weights is what we mean by *training* the network.

During the training process, batches of images are passed through the network and the predicted outputs are compared to the ground truth. For example, the network might output a probability of 80% for an image of someone who really is smiling and a probability of 23% for an image of someone who really isn't smiling. A perfect prediction would output 100% and 0% for these examples, so there is a small amount of error. The error in the prediction is then propagated backward through the network, adjusting each set of weights a small amount in the direction that improves the prediction most significantly. This process is appropriately called *backpropagation*. Gradually, each unit becomes skilled at identifying a particular feature that ultimately helps the network to make better predictions.

Learning High-Level Features

The critical property that makes neural networks so powerful is their ability to learn features from the input data, without human guidance. In other words, we do not need to do any feature engineering, which is why neural networks are so useful! We can let the model decide how it wants to arrange its weights, guided only by its desire to minimize the error in its predictions.

For example, let's walk through the network shown in Figure 2-2, assuming it has already been trained to accurately predict if a given input face is smiling:

1. Unit A receives the value for an individual channel of an input pixel.

2. Unit B combines its input values so that it fires strongest when a particular low-level feature such as an edge is present.

3. Unit C combines the low-level features so that it fires strongest when a higher-level feature such as *teeth* are seen in the image.

4. Unit D combines the high-level features so that it fires strongest when the person in the original image is smiling.

Units in each subsequent layer are able to represent increasingly sophisticated aspects of the original input, by combining lower-level features from the previous layer. Amazingly, this arises naturally out of the training process—we do not need to *tell* each unit what to look for, or whether it should look for high-level features or low-level features.

The layers between the input and output layers are called *hidden* layers. While our example only has two hidden layers, deep neural networks can have many more. Stacking large numbers of layers allows the neural network to learn progressively higher-level features by gradually building up information from the lower-level features in previous layers. For example, ResNet,[1] designed for image recognition, contains 152 layers.

Next, we'll dive straight into the practical side of deep learning and get set up with TensorFlow and Keras so that you can start building your own deep neural networks.

TensorFlow and Keras

TensorFlow (*https://www.tensorflow.org*) is an open source Python library for machine learning, developed by Google. TensorFlow is one of the most utilized frameworks for building machine learning solutions, with particular emphasis on the manipulation of tensors (hence the name). It provides the low-level functionality required to train neural networks, such as computing the gradient of arbitrary differentiable expressions and efficiently executing tensor operations.

Keras (*https://keras.io*) is a high-level API for building neural networks, built on top of TensorFlow (Figure 2-3). It is extremely flexible and very user-friendly, making it an ideal choice for getting started with deep learning. Moreover, Keras provides numerous useful building blocks that can be plugged together to create highly complex deep learning architectures through its functional API.

Figure 2-3. TensorFlow and Keras are excellent tools for building deep learning solutions

If you are just getting started with deep learning, I can highly recommend using TensorFlow and Keras. This setup will allow you to build any network that you can think of in a production environment, while also giving you an easy-to-learn API that enables rapid development of new ideas and concepts. Let's start by seeing how easy it is to build a multilayer perceptron using Keras.

Multilayer Perceptron (MLP)

In this section, we will train an MLP to classify a given image using *supervised learning*. Supervised learning is a type of machine learning algorithm in which the computer is trained on a labeled dataset. In other words, the dataset used for training includes input data with corresponding output labels. The goal of the algorithm is to learn a mapping between the input data and the output labels, so that it can make predictions on new, unseen data.

The MLP is a discriminative (rather than generative) model, but supervised learning will still play a role in many types of generative models that we will explore in later chapters of this book, so it is a good place to start our journey.

Running the Code for This Example

The code for this example can be found in the Jupyter notebook located at *notebooks/02_deeplearning/01_mlp/mlp.ipynb* in the book repository.

Preparing the Data

For this example we will be using the CIFAR-10 (*https://oreil.ly/cNbFG*) dataset, a collection of 60,000 32 × 32–pixel color images that comes bundled with Keras out of the box. Each image is classified into exactly one of 10 classes, as shown in Figure 2-4.

Airplane
Automobile
Bird
Cat
Deer
Dog
Frog
Horse
Ship
Truck

Figure 2-4. Example images from the CIFAR-10 dataset (source: Krizhevsky, 2009)[2]

By default, the image data consists of integers between 0 and 255 for each pixel channel. We first need to preprocess the images by scaling these values to lie between 0 and 1, as neural networks work best when the absolute value of each input is less than 1.

We also need to change the integer labeling of the images to one-hot encoded vectors, because the neural network output will be a probability that the image belongs to each class. If the class integer label of an image is *i*, then its one-hot encoding is a vector of length 10 (the number of classes) that has 0s in all but the *i*th element, which is 1. These steps are shown in Example 2-1.

Example 2-1. Preprocessing the CIFAR-10 dataset

```
import numpy as np
from tensorflow.keras import datasets, utils

(x_train, y_train), (x_test, y_test) = datasets.cifar10.load_data() ❶
```

```
NUM_CLASSES = 10

x_train = x_train.astype('float32') / 255.0  ❷
x_test = x_test.astype('float32') / 255.0

y_train = utils.to_categorical(y_train, NUM_CLASSES)  ❸
y_test = utils.to_categorical(y_test, NUM_CLASSES)
```

❶ Load the CIFAR-10 dataset. x_train and x_test are numpy arrays of shape [50000, 32, 32, 3] and [10000, 32, 32, 3], respectively. y_train and y_test are numpy arrays of shape [50000, 1] and [10000, 1], respectively, containing the integer labels in the range 0 to 9 for the class of each image.

❷ Scale each image so that the pixel channel values lie between 0 and 1.

❸ One-hot encode the labels—the new shapes of y_train and y_test are [50000, 10] and [10000, 10], respectively.

We can see that the training image data (x_train) is stored in a *tensor* of shape [50000, 32, 32, 3]. There are no *columns* or *rows* in this dataset; instead, this is a tensor with four dimensions. A tensor is just a multidimensional array—it is the natural extension of a matrix to more than two dimensions. The first dimension of this tensor references the index of the image in the dataset, the second and third relate to the size of the image, and the last is the channel (i.e., red, green, or blue, since these are RGB images).

For example, Example 2-2 shows how we can find the channel value of a specific pixel in an image.

Example 2-2. The green channel (1) value of the pixel in the (12,13) position of image 54

```
x_train[54, 12, 13, 1]
# 0.36862746
```

Building the Model

In Keras you can either define the structure of a neural network as a Sequential model or using the functional API.

A Sequential model is useful for quickly defining a linear stack of layers (i.e., where one layer follows on directly from the previous layer without any branching). We can define our MLP model using the Sequential class as shown in Example 2-3.

Example 2-3. Building our MLP using a Sequential model

```python
from tensorflow.keras import layers, models

model = models.Sequential([
    layers.Flatten(input_shape=(32, 32, 3)),
    layers.Dense(200, activation = 'relu'),
    layers.Dense(150, activation = 'relu'),
    layers.Dense(10, activation = 'softmax'),
])
```

Many of the models in this book require that the output from a layer is passed to multiple subsequent layers, or conversely, that a layer receives input from multiple preceding layers. For these models, the `Sequential` class is not suitable and we would need to use the functional API instead, which is a lot more flexible.

 I recommend that even if you are just starting out building linear models with Keras, you still use the functional API rather than `Sequential` models, since it will serve you better in the long run as your neural networks become more architecturally complex. The functional API will give you complete freedom over the design of your deep neural network.

Example 2-4 shows the same MLP coded using the functional API. When using the functional API, we use the `Model` class to define the overall input and output layers of the model.

Example 2-4. Building our MLP using the functional API

```python
from tensorflow.keras import layers, models

input_layer = layers.Input(shape=(32, 32, 3))
x = layers.Flatten()(input_layer)
x = layers.Dense(units=200, activation = 'relu')(x)
x = layers.Dense(units=150, activation = 'relu')(x)
output_layer = layers.Dense(units=10, activation = 'softmax')(x)
model = models.Model(input_layer, output_layer)
```

Both methods give identical models—a diagram of the architecture is shown in Figure 2-5.

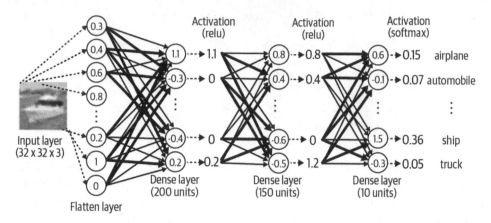

Figure 2-5. A diagram of the MLP architecture

Let's now look in more detail at the different layers and activation functions used within the MLP.

Layers

To build our MLP, we used three different types of layers: Input, Flatten, and Dense.

The Input layer is an entry point into the network. We tell the network the shape of each data element to expect as a tuple. Notice that we do not specify the batch size; this isn't necessary as we can pass any number of images into the Input layer simultaneously. We do not need to explicitly state the batch size in the Input layer definition.

Next we flatten this input into a vector, using a Flatten layer. This results in a vector of length 3,072 (= 32 × 32 × 3). The reason we do this is because the subsequent Dense layer requires that its input is flat, rather than a multidimensional array. As we shall see later, other layer types require multidimensional arrays as input, so you need to be aware of the required input and output shape of each layer type to understand when it is necessary to use Flatten.

The Dense layer is one of the most fundamental building blocks of a neural network. It contains a given number of units that are densely connected to the previous layer—that is, every unit in the layer is connected to every unit in the previous layer, through a single connection that carries a weight (which can be positive or negative). The output from a given unit is the weighted sum of the inputs it receives from the previous layer, which is then passed through a nonlinear *activation function* before being sent to the following layer. The activation function is critical to ensure the neural network is able to learn complex functions and doesn't just output a linear combination of its inputs.

Activation functions

There are many kinds of activation function, but three of the most important are ReLU, sigmoid, and softmax.

The *ReLU* (rectified linear unit) activation function is defined to be 0 if the input is negative and is otherwise equal to the input. The *LeakyReLU* activation function is very similar to ReLU, with one key difference: whereas the ReLU activation function returns 0 for input values less than 0, the LeakyReLU function returns a small negative number proportional to the input. ReLU units can sometimes die if they always output 0, because of a large bias toward negative values pre-activation. In this case, the gradient is 0 and therefore no error is propagated back through this unit. LeakyReLU activations fix this issue by always ensuring the gradient is nonzero. ReLU-based functions are among the most reliable activations to use between the layers of a deep network to encourage stable training.

The *sigmoid* activation is useful if you wish the output from the layer to be scaled between 0 and 1—for example, for binary classification problems with one output unit or multilabel classification problems, where each observation can belong to more than one class. Figure 2-6 shows ReLU, LeakyReLU, and sigmoid activation functions side by side for comparison.

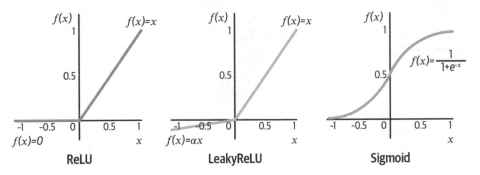

Figure 2-6. The ReLU, LeakyReLU, and sigmoid activation functions

The *softmax* activation function is useful if you want the total sum of the output from the layer to equal 1; for example, for multiclass classification problems where each observation only belongs to exactly one class. It is defined as:

$$y_i = \frac{e^{x_i}}{\sum_{j=1}^{J} e^{x_j}}$$

Here, J is the total number of units in the layer. In our neural network, we use a softmax activation in the final layer to ensure that the output is a set of 10 probabilities that sum to 1, which can be interpreted as the likelihood that the image belongs to each class.

In Keras, activation functions can be defined within a layer (Example 2-5) or as a separate layer (Example 2-6).

Example 2-5. A ReLU activation function defined as part of a Dense layer

```
x = layers.Dense(units=200, activation = 'relu')(x)
```

Example 2-6. A ReLU activation function defined as its own layer

```
x = layers.Dense(units=200)(x)
x = layers.Activation('relu')(x)
```

In our example, we pass the input through two Dense layers, the first with 200 units and the second with 150, both with ReLU activation functions.

Inspecting the model

We can use the model.summary() method to inspect the shape of the network at each layer, as shown in Table 2-1.

Table 2-1. Output from the model.summary() method

Layer (type)	Output shape	Param #
InputLayer	(None, 32, 32, 3)	0
Flatten	(None, 3072)	0
Dense	(None, 200)	614,600
Dense	(None, 150)	30,150
Dense	(None, 10)	1,510

Total params	646,260
Trainable params	646,260
Non-trainable params	0

Notice how the shape of our Input layer matches the shape of x_train and the shape of our Dense output layer matches the shape of y_train. Keras uses None as a marker for the first dimension to show that it doesn't yet know the number of observations that will be passed into the network. In fact, it doesn't need to; we could just as easily pass 1 observation through the network at a time as 1,000. That's because tensor operations are conducted across all observations simultaneously using linear algebra—this is the part handled by TensorFlow. It is also the reason why you get a performance increase when training deep neural networks on GPUs instead of CPUs: GPUs are optimized for large tensor operations since these calculations are also necessary for complex graphics manipulation.

The `summary` method also gives the number of parameters (weights) that will be trained at each layer. If ever you find that your model is training too slowly, check the summary to see if there are any layers that contain a huge number of weights. If so, you should consider whether the number of units in the layer could be reduced to speed up training.

 Make sure you understand how the number of parameters is calculated in each layer! It's important to remember that by default, each unit within a given layer is also connected to one additional *bias* unit that always outputs 1. This ensures that the output from the unit can still be nonzero even when all inputs from the previous layer are 0.

Therefore, the number of parameters in the 200-unit `Dense` layer is 200 * (3,072 + 1) = 614,600.

Compiling the Model

In this step, we compile the model with an optimizer and a loss function, as shown in Example 2-7.

Example 2-7. Defining the optimizer and the loss function

```
from tensorflow.keras import optimizers

opt = optimizers.Adam(learning_rate=0.0005)
model.compile(loss='categorical_crossentropy', optimizer=opt,
              metrics=['accuracy'])
```

Let's now look in more detail at what we mean by loss functions and optimizers.

Loss functions

The *loss function* is used by the neural network to compare its predicted output to the ground truth. It returns a single number for each observation; the greater this number, the worse the network has performed for this observation.

Keras provides many built-in loss functions to choose from, or you can create your own. Three of the most commonly used are mean squared error, categorical cross-entropy, and binary cross-entropy. It is important to understand when it is appropriate to use each.

If your neural network is designed to solve a regression problem (i.e., the output is continuous), then you might use the *mean squared error* loss. This is the mean of the squared difference between the ground truth y_i and predicted value p_i of each output unit, where the mean is taken over all n output units:

$$\text{MSE} = \frac{1}{n} \sum_{i=1}^{n} (y_i - p_i)^2$$

If you are working on a classification problem where each observation only belongs to one class, then *categorical cross-entropy* is the correct loss function. This is defined as follows:

$$-\sum_{i=1}^{n} y_i \log (p_i)$$

Finally, if you are working on a binary classification problem with one output unit, or a multilabel problem where each observation can belong to multiple classes simultaneously, you should use *binary cross-entropy*:

$$-\frac{1}{n} \sum_{i=1}^{n} (y_i \log (p_i) + (1 - y_i) \log (1 - p_i))$$

Optimizers

The *optimizer* is the algorithm that will be used to update the weights in the neural network based on the gradient of the loss function. One of the most commonly used and stable optimizers is *Adam* (Adaptive Moment Estimation).[3] In most cases, you shouldn't need to tweak the default parameters of the Adam optimizer, except the *learning rate*. The greater the learning rate, the larger the change in weights at each training step. While training is initially faster with a large learning rate, the downside is that it may result in less stable training and may not find the global minimum of the loss function. This is a parameter that you may want to tune or adjust during training.

Another common optimizer that you may come across is *RMSProp* (Root Mean Squared Propagation). Again, you shouldn't need to adjust the parameters of this optimizer too much, but it is worth reading the Keras documentation (*https://keras.io/optimizers*) to understand the role of each parameter.

We pass both the loss function and the optimizer into the `compile` method of the model, as well as a `metrics` parameter where we can specify any additional metrics that we would like to report on during training, such as accuracy.

Training the Model

Thus far, we haven't shown the model any data. We have just set up the architecture and compiled the model with a loss function and optimizer.

To train the model against the data, we simply call the `fit` method, as shown in Example 2-8.

Example 2-8. Calling the `fit` method to train the model

```
model.fit(x_train ❶
        , y_train ❷
        , batch_size = 32 ❸
        , epochs = 10 ❹
        , shuffle = True ❺
        )
```

❶ The raw image data.

❷ The one-hot encoded class labels.

❸ The `batch_size` determines how many observations will be passed to the network at each training step.

❹ The `epochs` determine how many times the network will be shown the full training data.

❺ If `shuffle = True`, the batches will be drawn randomly without replacement from the training data at each training step.

This will start training a deep neural network to predict the category of an image from the CIFAR-10 dataset. The training process works as follows.

First, the weights of the network are initialized to small random values. Then the network performs a series of training steps. At each training step, one *batch* of images is passed through the network and the errors are backpropagated to update the weights. The `batch_size` determines how many images are in each training step batch. The larger the batch size, the more stable the gradient calculation, but the slower each training step.

It would be far too time-consuming and computationally intensive to use the entire dataset to calculate the gradient at each training step, so generally a batch size between 32 and 256 is used. It is also now recommended practice to increase the batch size as training progresses.[4]

This continues until all observations in the dataset have been seen once. This completes the first *epoch*. The data is then passed through the network again in batches as part of the second epoch. This process repeats until the specified number of epochs have elapsed.

During training, Keras outputs the progress of the procedure, as shown in Figure 2-7. We can see that the training dataset has been split into 1,563 batches (each containing 32 images) and it has been shown to the network 10 times (i.e., over 10 epochs), at a rate of approximately 2 milliseconds per batch. The categorical cross-entropy loss has fallen from 1.8377 to 1.3696, resulting in an accuracy increase from 33.69% after the first epoch to 51.67% after the tenth epoch.

```
model.fit(x_train, y_train, batch_size=32, epochs=10, shuffle=True)    🗐 ↑ ↓ ± ꝗ 🗑
Epoch 1/10
1563/1563 [==============================] - 3s 2ms/step - loss: 1.8377 - accuracy: 0.3369
Epoch 2/10
1563/1563 [==============================] - 3s 2ms/step - loss: 1.6552 - accuracy: 0.4076
Epoch 3/10
1563/1563 [==============================] - 3s 2ms/step - loss: 1.5743 - accuracy: 0.4396
Epoch 4/10
1563/1563 [==============================] - 3s 2ms/step - loss: 1.5288 - accuracy: 0.4549
Epoch 5/10
1563/1563 [==============================] - 3s 2ms/step - loss: 1.4888 - accuracy: 0.4706
Epoch 6/10
1563/1563 [==============================] - 2s 2ms/step - loss: 1.4542 - accuracy: 0.4851
Epoch 7/10
1563/1563 [==============================] - 3s 2ms/step - loss: 1.4332 - accuracy: 0.4908
Epoch 8/10
1563/1563 [==============================] - 2s 2ms/step - loss: 1.4094 - accuracy: 0.4992
Epoch 9/10
1563/1563 [==============================] - 2s 2ms/step - loss: 1.3896 - accuracy: 0.5045
Epoch 10/10
1563/1563 [==============================] - 3s 2ms/step - loss: 1.3696 - accuracy: 0.5167
```

Figure 2-7. The output from the `fit` *method*

Evaluating the Model

We know the model achieves an accuracy of 51.9% on the training set, but how does it perform on data it has never seen?

To answer this question we can use the `evaluate` method provided by Keras, as shown in Example 2-9.

Example 2-9. Evaluating the model performance on the test set

```
model.evaluate(x_test, y_test)
```

Figure 2-8 shows the output from this method.

```
10000/10000 [==============================] - 1s 55us/step
[1.4358007415771485, 0.4896]
```

Figure 2-8. The output from the evaluate method

The output is a list of the metrics we are monitoring: categorical cross-entropy and accuracy. We can see that model accuracy is still 49.0% even on images that it has never seen before. Note that if the model were guessing randomly, it would achieve approximately 10% accuracy (because there are 10 classes), so 49.0% is a good result, given that we have used a very basic neural network.

We can view some of the predictions on the test set using the predict method, as shown in Example 2-10.

Example 2-10. Viewing predictions on the test set using the predict method

```
CLASSES = np.array(['airplane', 'automobile', 'bird', 'cat', 'deer', 'dog'
                , 'frog', 'horse', 'ship', 'truck'])

preds = model.predict(x_test) ❶
preds_single = CLASSES[np.argmax(preds, axis = -1)] ❷
actual_single = CLASSES[np.argmax(y_test, axis = -1)]
```

❶   preds is an array of shape [10000, 10]—i.e., a vector of 10 class probabilities for each observation.

❷   We convert this array of probabilities back into a single prediction using numpy's argmax function. Here, axis = -1 tells the function to collapse the array over the last dimension (the classes dimension), so that the shape of preds_single is then [10000, 1].

We can view some of the images alongside their labels and predictions with the code in Example 2-11. As expected, around half are correct.

Example 2-11. Displaying predictions of the MLP against the actual labels

```
import matplotlib.pyplot as plt

n_to_show = 10
indices = np.random.choice(range(len(x_test)), n_to_show)

fig = plt.figure(figsize=(15, 3))
fig.subplots_adjust(hspace=0.4, wspace=0.4)
```

```
for i, idx in enumerate(indices):
    img = x_test[idx]
    ax = fig.add_subplot(1, n_to_show, i+1)
    ax.axis('off')
    ax.text(0.5, -0.35, 'pred = ' + str(preds_single[idx]), fontsize=10
        , ha='center', transform=ax.transAxes)
    ax.text(0.5, -0.7, 'act = ' + str(actual_single[idx]), fontsize=10
        , ha='center', transform=ax.transAxes)
    ax.imshow(img)
```

Figure 2-9 shows a randomly chosen selection of predictions made by the model, alongside the true labels.

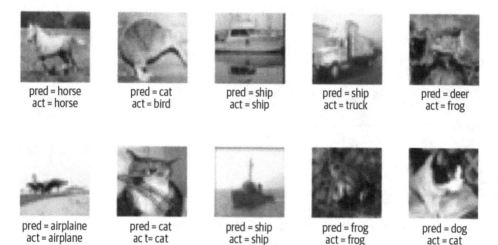

Figure 2-9. Some predictions made by the model, alongside the actual labels

Congratulations! You've just built a multilayer perceptron using Keras and used it to make predictions on new data. Even though this is a supervised learning problem, when we come to building generative models in future chapters many of the core ideas from this chapter (such as loss functions, activation functions, and understanding layer shapes) will still be extremely important. Next we'll look at ways of improving this model, by introducing a few new layer types.

Convolutional Neural Network (CNN)

One of the reasons our network isn't yet performing as well as it might is because there isn't anything in the network that takes into account the spatial structure of the input images. In fact, our first step is to flatten the image into a single vector, so that we can pass it to the first Dense layer!

To achieve this we need to use a *convolutional layer*.

Convolutional Layers

First, we need to understand what is meant by a *convolution* in the context of deep learning.

Figure 2-10 shows two different $3 \times 3 \times 1$ portions of a grayscale image being convoluted with a $3 \times 3 \times 1$ *filter* (or *kernel*). The convolution is performed by multiplying the filter pixelwise with the portion of the image, and summing the results. The output is more positive when the portion of the image closely matches the filter and more negative when the portion of the image is the inverse of the filter. The top example resonates strongly with the filter, so it produces a large positive value. The bottom example does not resonate much with the filter, so it produces a value near zero.

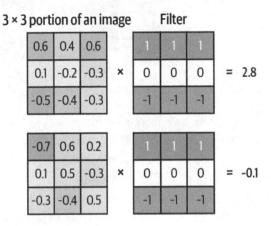

Figure 2-10. A 3×3 convolutional filter applied to two portions of a grayscale image

If we move the filter across the entire image from left to right and top to bottom, recording the convolutional output as we go, we obtain a new array that picks out a particular feature of the input, depending on the values in the filter. For example, Figure 2-11 shows two different filters that highlight horizontal and vertical edges.

Running the Code for This Example

You can see this convolutional process worked through manually in the Jupyter notebook located at *notebooks/02_deeplearning/ 02_cnn/convolutions.ipynb* in the book repository.

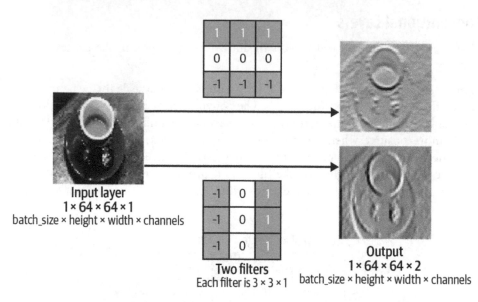

Input layer
1 × 64 × 64 × 1
batch_size × height × width × channels

Two filters
Each filter is 3 × 3 × 1

Output
1 × 64 × 64 × 2
batch_size × height × width × channels

Figure 2-11. Two convolutional filters applied to a grayscale image

A convolutional layer is simply a collection of filters, where the values stored in the filters are the weights that are learned by the neural network through training. Initially these are random, but gradually the filters adapt their weights to start picking out interesting features such as edges or particular color combinations.

In Keras, the Conv2D layer applies convolutions to an input tensor with two spatial dimensions (such as an image). For example, the code shown in Example 2-12 builds a convolutional layer with two filters, to match the example in Figure 2-11.

Example 2-12. A Conv2D layer applied to grayscale input images

```
from tensorflow.keras import layers

input_layer = layers.Input(shape=(64,64,1))
conv_layer_1 = layers.Conv2D(
    filters = 2
    , kernel_size = (3,3)
    , strides = 1
    , padding = "same"
    )(input_layer)
```

Next, let's look at two of the arguments to the Conv2D layer in more detail—strides and padding.

Stride

The `strides` parameter is the step size used by the layer to move the filters across the input. Increasing the stride therefore reduces the size of the output tensor. For example, when `strides = 2`, the height and width of the output tensor will be half the size of the input tensor. This is useful for reducing the spatial size of the tensor as it passes through the network, while increasing the number of channels.

Padding

The `padding = "same"` input parameter pads the input data with zeros so that the output size from the layer is exactly the same as the input size when `strides = 1`.

Figure 2-12 shows a 3 × 3 kernel being passed over a 5 × 5 input image, with `padding = "same"` and `strides = 1`. The output size from this convolutional layer would also be 5 × 5, as the padding allows the kernel to extend over the edge of the image, so that it fits five times in both directions. Without padding, the kernel could only fit three times along each direction, giving an output size of 3 × 3.

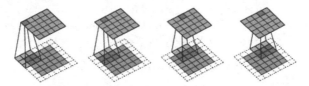

Figure 2-12. A 3 × 3 × 1 kernel (gray) being passed over a 5 × 5 × 1 input image (blue), with `padding = "same"` and `strides = 1`, to generate the 5 × 5 × 1 output (green) (source: Dumoulin and Visin, 2018)[5]

Setting `padding = "same"` is a good way to ensure that you are able to easily keep track of the size of the tensor as it passes through many convolutional layers. The shape of the output from a convolutional layer with `padding = "same"` is:

$$\left(\frac{input\ height}{stride}, \frac{input\ width}{stride}, filters \right)$$

Stacking convolutional layers

The output of a `Conv2D` layer is another four-dimensional tensor, now of shape (`batch_size, height, width, filters`), so we can stack `Conv2D` layers on top of each other to grow the depth of our neural network and make it more powerful. To demonstrate this, let's imagine we are applying `Conv2D` layers to the CIFAR-10 dataset and wish to predict the label of a given image. Note that this time, instead of one input channel (grayscale) we have three (red, green, and blue).

Example 2-13 shows how to build a simple convolutional neural network that we could train to succeed at this task.

Example 2-13. Code to build a convolutional neural network model using Keras

```
from tensorflow.keras import layers, models

input_layer = layers.Input(shape=(32,32,3))
conv_layer_1 = layers.Conv2D(
    filters = 10
    , kernel_size = (4,4)
    , strides = 2
    , padding = 'same'
    )(input_layer)
conv_layer_2 = layers.Conv2D(
    filters = 20
    , kernel_size = (3,3)
    , strides = 2
    , padding = 'same'
    )(conv_layer_1)
flatten_layer = layers.Flatten()(conv_layer_2)
output_layer = layers.Dense(units=10, activation = 'softmax')(flatten_layer)
model = models.Model(input_layer, output_layer)
```

This code corresponds to the diagram shown in Figure 2-13.

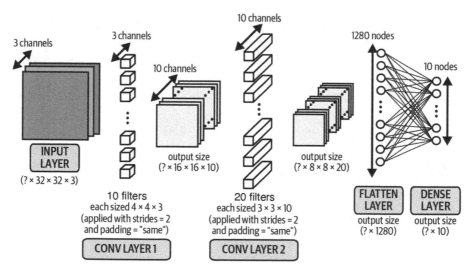

Figure 2-13. A diagram of a convolutional neural network

Note that now that we are working with color images, each filter in the first convolutional layer has a depth of 3 rather than 1 (i.e., each filter has shape 4 × 4 × 3, rather than 4 × 4 × 1). This is to match the three channels (red, green, blue) of the input image. The same idea applies to the filters in the second convolutional layer that have a depth of 10, to match the 10 channels output by the first convolutional layer.

 In general, the depth of the filters in a layer is always equal to the number of channels output by the preceding layer.

Inspecting the model

It's really informative to look at how the shape of the tensor changes as data flows through from one convolutional layer to the next. We can use the `model.summary()` method to inspect the shape of the tensor as it passes through the network (Table 2-2).

Table 2-2. CNN model summary

Layer (type)	Output shape	Param #
InputLayer	(None, 32, 32, 3)	0
Conv2D	(None, 16, 16, 10)	490
Conv2D	(None, 8, 8, 20)	1,820
Flatten	(None, 1280)	0
Dense	(None, 10)	12,810

Total params	15,120
Trainable params	15,120
Non-trainable params	0

Let's walk through our network layer by layer, noting the shape of the tensor as we go:

1. The input shape is (`None, 32, 32, 3`)—Keras uses `None` to represent the fact that we can pass any number of images through the network simultaneously. Since the network is just performing tensor algebra, we don't need to pass images through the network individually, but instead can pass them through together as a batch.

2. The shape of each of the 10 filters in the first convolutional layer is $4 \times 4 \times 3$. This is because we have chosen each filter to have a height and width of 4 (`ker nel_size = (4,4)`) and there are three channels in the preceding layer (red, green, and blue). Therefore, the number of parameters (or weights) in the layer is $(4 \times 4 \times 3 + 1) \times 10 = 490$, where the + 1 is due to the inclusion of a bias term attached to each of the filters. The output from each filter will be the pixelwise multiplication of the filter weights and the $4 \times 4 \times 3$ section of the image it is

covering. As `strides = 2` and `padding = "same"`, the width and height of the output are both halved to 16, and since there are 10 filters the output of the first layer is a batch of tensors each having shape [`16, 16, 10`].

3. In the second convolutional layer, we choose the filters to be 3 × 3 and they now have depth 10, to match the number of channels in the previous layer. Since there are 20 filters in this layer, this gives a total number of parameters (weights) of (3 × 3 × 10 + 1) × 20 = 1,820. Again, we use `strides = 2 and padding = "same"`, so the width and height both halve. This gives us an overall output shape of (`None, 8, 8, 20`).

4. We now flatten the tensor using the Keras `Flatten` layer. This results in a set of 8 × 8 × 20 = 1,280 units. Note that there are no parameters to learn in a `Flatten` layer as the operation is just a restructuring of the tensor.

5. We finally connect these units to a 10-unit `Dense` layer with softmax activation, which represents the probability of each category in a 10-category classification task. This creates an extra 1,280 × 10 = 12,810 parameters (weights) to learn.

This example demonstrates how we can chain convolutional layers together to create a convolutional neural network. Before we see how this compares in accuracy to our densely connected neural network, we'll examine two more techniques that can also improve performance: batch normalization and dropout.

Batch Normalization

One common problem when training a deep neural network is ensuring that the weights of the network remain within a reasonable range of values—if they start to become too large, this is a sign that your network is suffering from what is known as the *exploding gradient* problem. As errors are propagated backward through the network, the calculation of the gradient in the earlier layers can sometimes grow exponentially large, causing wild fluctuations in the weight values.

 If your loss function starts to return `NaN`, chances are that your weights have grown large enough to cause an overflow error.

This doesn't necessarily happen immediately as you start training the network. Sometimes it can be happily training for hours when suddenly the loss function returns `NaN` and your network has exploded. This can be incredibly annoying. To prevent it from happening, you need to understand the root cause of the exploding gradient problem.

Covariate shift

One of the reasons for scaling input data to a neural network is to ensure a stable start to training over the first few iterations. Since the weights of the network are initially randomized, unscaled input could potentially create huge activation values that immediately lead to exploding gradients. For example, instead of passing pixel values from 0–255 into the input layer, we usually scale these values to between −1 and 1.

Because the input is scaled, it's natural to expect the activations from all future layers to be relatively well scaled as well. Initially this may be true, but as the network trains and the weights move further away from their random initial values, this assumption can start to break down. This phenomenon is known as *covariate shift*.

Covariate Shift Analogy

Imagine you're carrying a tall pile of books, and you get hit by a gust of wind. You move the books in a direction opposite to the wind to compensate, but as you do so, some of the books shift, so that the tower is slightly more unstable than before. Initially, this is OK, but with every gust the pile becomes more and more unstable, until eventually the books have shifted so much that the pile collapses. This is covariate shift.

Relating this to neural networks, each layer is like a book in the pile. To remain stable, when the network updates the weights, each layer implicitly assumes that the distribution of its input from the layer beneath is approximately consistent across iterations. However, since there is nothing to stop any of the activation distributions shifting significantly in a certain direction, this can sometimes lead to runaway weight values and an overall collapse of the network.

Training using batch normalization

Batch normalization is a technique that was originally proposed as a solution to this problem and has since been shown to bring other benefits such as a smoother parameter space and smoother gradients. The solution is surprisingly simple. During training, a batch normalization layer calculates the mean and standard deviation of each of its input channels across the batch and normalizes by subtracting the mean and dividing by the standard deviation. There are then two learned parameters for each channel, the scale (gamma) and shift (beta). The output is simply the normalized input, scaled by gamma and shifted by beta. Figure 2-14 shows the whole process.

Input: Values of x over a mini-batch: $\mathcal{B} = \{x_{1...m}\}$;
Parameters to be learned: γ, β
Output: $\{y_i = \mathrm{BN}_{\gamma,\beta}(x_i)\}$

$$\mu_{\mathcal{B}} \leftarrow \frac{1}{m}\sum_{i=1}^{m} x_i \qquad\qquad \text{// mini-batch mean}$$

$$\sigma_{\mathcal{B}}^2 \leftarrow \frac{1}{m}\sum_{i=1}^{m}(x_i - \mu_{\mathcal{B}})^2 \qquad\qquad \text{// mini-batch variance}$$

$$\widehat{x}_i \leftarrow \frac{x_i - \mu_{\mathcal{B}}}{\sqrt{\sigma_{\mathcal{B}}^2 + \epsilon}} \qquad\qquad \text{// normalize}$$

$$y_i \leftarrow \gamma\widehat{x}_i + \beta \equiv \mathrm{BN}_{\gamma,\beta}(x_i) \qquad\qquad \text{// scale and shift}$$

Algorithm 1: Batch Normalizing Transform, applied to activation x over a mini-batch.

Figure 2-14. The batch normalization process (source: Ioffe and Szegedy, 2015)[6]

We can place batch normalization layers after dense or convolutional layers to normalize the output.

> Referring to our previous example, it's a bit like connecting the layers of books with small sets of adjustable springs that ensure there aren't any overall huge shifts in their positions over time.

Prediction using batch normalization

You might be wondering how this layer works at prediction time. When it comes to prediction, we may only want to predict a single observation, so there is no *batch* over which to calculate the mean and standard deviation. To get around this problem, during training a batch normalization layer also calculates the moving average of the mean and standard deviation of each channel and stores this value as part of the layer to use at test time.

How many parameters are contained within a batch normalization layer? For every channel in the preceding layer, two weights need to be learned: the scale (gamma) and shift (beta). These are the *trainable* parameters. The moving average and standard deviation also need to be calculated for each channel, but since they are derived from the data passing through the layer rather than trained through backpropagation, they are called *nontrainable* parameters. In total, this gives four parameters for each channel in the preceding layer, where two are trainable and two are nontrainable.

In Keras, the `BatchNormalization` layer implements the batch normalization functionality, as shown in Example 2-14.

Example 2-14. A `BatchNormalization` layer in Keras

```
from tensorflow.keras import layers
layers.BatchNormalization(momentum = 0.9)
```

The `momentum` parameter is the weight given to the previous value when calculating the moving average and moving standard deviation.

Dropout

When studying for an exam, it is common practice for students to use past papers and sample questions to improve their knowledge of the subject material. Some students try to memorize the answers to these questions, but then come unstuck in the exam because they haven't truly understood the subject matter. The best students use the practice material to further their general understanding, so that they are still able to answer correctly when faced with new questions that they haven't seen before.

The same principle holds for machine learning. Any successful machine learning algorithm must ensure that it generalizes to unseen data, rather than simply *remembering* the training dataset. If an algorithm performs well on the training dataset, but not the test dataset, we say that it is suffering from *overfitting*. To counteract this problem, we use *regularization* techniques, which ensure that the model is penalized if it starts to overfit.

There are many ways to regularize a machine learning algorithm, but for deep learning, one of the most common is by using *dropout* layers. This idea was introduced by Hinton et al. in 2012[7] and presented in a 2014 paper by Srivastava et al.[8]

Dropout layers are very simple. During training, each dropout layer chooses a random set of units from the preceding layer and sets their output to 0, as shown in Figure 2-15.

Incredibly, this simple addition drastically reduces overfitting by ensuring that the network doesn't become overdependent on certain units or groups of units that, in effect, just remember observations from the training set. If we use dropout layers, the network cannot rely too much on any one unit and therefore knowledge is more evenly spread across the whole network.

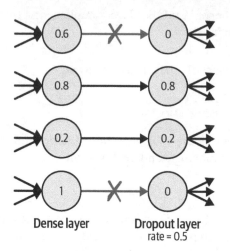

Figure 2-15. A dropout layer

This makes the model much better at generalizing to unseen data, because the network has been trained to produce accurate predictions even under unfamiliar conditions, such as those caused by dropping random units. There are no weights to learn within a dropout layer, as the units to drop are decided stochastically. At prediction time, the dropout layer doesn't drop any units, so that the full network is used to make predictions.

Dropout Analogy

Returning to our analogy, it's a bit like a math student practicing past papers with a random selection of key formulae missing from their formula book. This way, they learn how to answer questions through an understanding of the core principles, rather than always looking up the formulae in the same places in the book. When it comes to test time, they will find it much easier to answer questions that they have never seen before, due to their ability to generalize beyond the training material.

The `Dropout` layer in Keras implements this functionality, with the `rate` parameter specifying the proportion of units to drop from the preceding layer, as shown in Example 2-15.

Example 2-15. A `Dropout` layer in Keras

```
from tensorflow.keras import layers
layers.Dropout(rate = 0.25)
```

Dropout layers are used most commonly after dense layers since these are the most prone to overfitting due to the higher number of weights, though you can also use them after convolutional layers.

Batch normalization also has been shown to reduce overfitting, and therefore many modern deep learning architectures don't use dropout at all, relying solely on batch normalization for regularization. As with most deep learning principles, there is no golden rule that applies in every situation—the only way to know for sure what's best is to test different architectures and see which performs best on a holdout set of data.

Building the CNN

You've now seen three new Keras layer types: `Conv2D`, `BatchNormalization`, and `Dropout`. Let's put these pieces together into a CNN model and see how it performs on the CIFAR-10 dataset.

Running the Code for This Example

You can run the following example in the Jupyter notebook in the book repository called *notebooks/02_deeplearning/02_cnn/ cnn.ipynb*.

The model architecture we shall test is shown in Example 2-16.

Example 2-16. Code to build a CNN model using Keras

```
from tensorflow.keras import layers, models

input_layer = layers.Input((32,32,3))

x = layers.Conv2D(filters = 32, kernel_size = 3
        , strides = 1, padding = 'same')(input_layer)
x = layers.BatchNormalization()(x)
x = layers.LeakyReLU()(x)

x = layers.Conv2D(filters = 32, kernel_size = 3, strides = 2, padding = 'same')(x)
x = layers.BatchNormalization()(x)
x = layers.LeakyReLU()(x)

x = layers.Conv2D(filters = 64, kernel_size = 3, strides = 1, padding = 'same')(x)
x = layers.BatchNormalization()(x)
x = layers.LeakyReLU()(x)

x = layers.Conv2D(filters = 64, kernel_size = 3, strides = 2, padding = 'same')(x)
x = layers.BatchNormalization()(x)
```

```
x = layers.LeakyReLU()(x)

x = layers.Flatten()(x)

x = layers.Dense(128)(x)
x = layers.BatchNormalization()(x)
x = layers.LeakyReLU()(x)
x = layers.Dropout(rate = 0.5)(x)

output_layer = layers.Dense(10, activation = 'softmax')(x)

model = models.Model(input_layer, output_layer)
```

We use four stacked `Conv2D` layers, each followed by a `BatchNormalization` and a `LeakyReLU` layer. After flattening the resulting tensor, we pass the data through a `Dense` layer of size 128, again followed by a `BatchNormalization` and a `LeakyReLU` layer. This is immediately followed by a `Dropout` layer for regularization, and the network is concluded with an output `Dense` layer of size 10.

 The order in which to use the batch normalization and activation layers is a matter of preference. Usually batch normalization layers are placed before the activation, but some successful architectures use these layers the other way around. If you do choose to use batch normalization before activation, you can remember the order using the acronym *BAD* (batch normalization, activation, then dropout)!

The model summary is shown in Table 2-3.

Table 2-3. Model summary of the CNN for CIFAR-10

Layer (type)	Output shape	Param #
InputLayer	(None, 32, 32, 3)	0
Conv2D	(None, 32, 32, 32)	896
BatchNormalization	(None, 32, 32, 32)	128
LeakyReLU	(None, 32, 32, 32)	0
Conv2D	(None, 16, 16, 32)	9,248
BatchNormalization	(None, 16, 16, 32)	128
LeakyReLU	(None, 16, 16, 32)	0
Conv2D	(None, 16, 16, 64)	18,496
BatchNormalization	(None, 16, 16, 64)	256
LeakyReLU	(None, 16, 16, 64)	0
Conv2D	(None, 8, 8, 64)	36,928
BatchNormalization	(None, 8, 8, 64)	256

Layer (type)	Output shape	Param #
LeakyReLU	(None, 8, 8, 64)	0
Flatten	(None, 4096)	0
Dense	(None, 128)	524,416
BatchNormalization	(None, 128)	512
LeakyReLU	(None, 128)	0
Dropout	(None, 128)	0
Dense	(None, 10)	1290

Total params	592,554
Trainable params	591,914
Non-trainable params	640

 Before moving on, make sure you are able to calculate the output shape and number of parameters for each layer by hand. It's a good exercise to prove to yourself that you have fully understood how each layer is constructed and how it is connected to the preceding layer! Don't forget to include the bias weights that are included as part of the Conv2D and Dense layers.

Training and Evaluating the CNN

We compile and train the model in exactly the same way as before and call the evaluate method to determine its accuracy on the holdout set (Figure 2-16).

```
model.evaluate(x_test, y_test, batch_size=1000)

10000/10000 [==============================] - 15s 1ms/step

[0.8423407137393951, 0.7155999958515167]
```

Figure 2-16. CNN performance

As you can see, this model is now achieving 71.5% accuracy, up from 49.0% previously. Much better! Figure 2-17 shows some predictions from our new convolutional model.

This improvement has been achieved simply by changing the architecture of the model to include convolutional, batch normalization, and dropout layers. Notice that the number of parameters is actually fewer in our new model than the previous model, even though the number of layers is far greater. This demonstrates the importance of being experimental with your model design and being comfortable with how the different layer types can be used to your advantage. When building generative models, it becomes even more important to understand the inner workings of your model since it is the middle layers of your network that capture the high-level features that you are most interested in.

| pred = dog | pred = frog | pred = truck | pred = ship | pred = ship |
| act = dog | act = frog | act = truck | act = ship | act = ship |

| pred = dog | pred = cat | pred = horse | pred = airplaine | pred = ship |
| act = dog | act = cat | act = deer | act = airplane | act = airplane |

Figure 2-17. CNN predictions

Summary

This chapter introduced the core deep learning concepts that you will need to start building deep generative models. We started by building a multilayer perceptron (MLP) using Keras and trained the model to predict the category of a given image from the CIFAR-10 dataset. Then, we improved upon this architecture by introducing convolutional, batch normalization, and dropout layers to create a convolutional neural network (CNN).

A really important point to take away from this chapter is that deep neural networks are completely flexible by design, and there really are no fixed rules when it comes to model architecture. There are guidelines and best practices, but you should feel free to experiment with layers and the order in which they appear. Don't feel constrained to only use the architectures that you have read about in this book or elsewhere! Like a child with a set of building blocks, the design of your neural network is only limited by your own imagination.

In the next chapter, we shall see how we can use these building blocks to design a network that can generate images.

References

1. Kaiming He et al., "Deep Residual Learning for Image Recognition," December 10, 2015, *https://arxiv.org/abs/1512.03385*.

2. Alex Krizhevsky, "Learning Multiple Layers of Features from Tiny Images," April 8, 2009, *https://www.cs.toronto.edu/~kriz/learning-features-2009-TR.pdf*.

3. Diederik Kingma and Jimmy Ba, "Adam: A Method for Stochastic Optimization," December 22, 2014, *https://arxiv.org/abs/1412.6980v8*.

4. Samuel L. Smith et al., "Don't Decay the Learning Rate, Increase the Batch Size," November 1, 2017, *https://arxiv.org/abs/1711.00489*.

5. Vincent Dumoulin and Francesco Visin, "A Guide to Convolution Arithmetic for Deep Learning," January 12, 2018, *https://arxiv.org/abs/1603.07285*.

6. Sergey Ioffe and Christian Szegedy, "Batch Normalization: Accelerating Deep Network Training by Reducing Internal Covariate Shift," February 11, 2015, *https://arxiv.org/abs/1502.03167*.

7. Hinton et al., "Improving Neural Networks by Preventing Co-Adaptation of Feature Detectors," July 3, 2012, *https://arxiv.org/abs/1207.0580*.

8. Nitish Srivastava et al., "Dropout: A Simple Way to Prevent Neural Networks from Overfitting," *Journal of Machine Learning Research* 15 (2014): 1929–1958, *http://jmlr.org/papers/volume15/srivastava14a/srivastava14a.pdf*.

PART II

Methods

In Part II we will dive into the six families of generative models, including the theory behind how they work and practical examples of how to build each type of model.

In Chapter 3 we shall take a look at our first generative deep learning model, the *variational autoencoder*. This technique will allow us to not only generate realistic faces, but also alter existing images—for example, by adding a smile or changing the color of someone's hair.

Chapter 4 explores one of the most successful generative modeling techniques of recent years, the *generative adversarial network*. We shall see the ways that GAN training has been fine-tuned and adapted to continually push the boundaries of what generative modeling is able to achieve.

In Chapter 5 we will delve into several examples of *autoregressive models*, including LSTMs and PixelCNN. This family of models treats the generation process as a sequence prediction problem—it underpins today's state-of-the-art text generation models and can also be used for image generation.

In Chapter 6 we will cover the family of *normalizing flow models*, including RealNVP. This model is based on a change of variables formula, which allows the transformation of a simple distribution, such as a Gaussian distribution, into a more complex distribution in way that preserves tractability.

Chapter 7 introduces the family of *energy-based models*. These models train a scalar energy function to score the validity of a given input. We will explore a technique for training energy-based models called contrastive divergence and a technique for sampling new observations called Langevin dynamics.

Finally, in Chapter 8 we shall explore the family of *diffusion models*. This technique is based on the idea of iteratively adding noise to an image and then training a model to remove the noise, giving us the ability to transform pure noise into realistic samples.

By the end of Part II you will have built practical examples of generative models from each of the six generative modeling families and be able to explain how each works from a theoretical perspective.

CHAPTER 3

Variational Autoencoders

Chapter Goals

In this chapter you will:

- Learn how the architectural design of autoencoders makes them perfectly suited to generative modeling.
- Build and train an autoencoder from scratch using Keras.
- Use autoencoders to generate new images, but understand the limitations of this approach.
- Learn about the architecture of the variational autoencoder and how it solves many of the problems associated with standard autoencoders.
- Build a variational autoencoder from scratch using Keras.
- Use variational autoencoders to generate new images.
- Use variational autoencoders to manipulate generated images using latent space arithmetic.

In 2013, Diederik P. Kingma and Max Welling published a paper that laid the foundations for a type of neural network known as a *variational autoencoder* (VAE).[1] This is now one of the most fundamental and well-known deep learning architectures for generative modeling and an excellent place to start our journey into generative deep learning.

In this chapter, we shall start by building a standard autoencoder and then see how we can extend this framework to develop a variational autoencoder. Along the way, we will pick apart both types of models, to understand how they work at a granular level. By the end of the chapter you should have a complete understanding of how to build and manipulate autoencoder-based models and, in particular, how to build a variational autoencoder from scratch to generate images based on your own dataset.

Introduction

Let's start with a simple story that will help to explain the fundamental problem that an autoencoder is trying to solve.

Brian, the Stitch, and the Wardrobe

Imagine that on the floor in front of you is a pile of all the clothing you own—trousers, tops, shoes, and coats, all of different styles. Your stylist, Brian, is becoming increasingly frustrated with how long it takes him to find the items you require, so he devises a clever plan.

He tells you to organize your clothes into a wardrobe that is infinitely high and wide (Figure 3-1). When you want to request a particular item, you simply need to tell Brian its location and he will sew the item from scratch using his trusty sewing machine. It soon becomes obvious that you will need to place similar items near to each other, so that Brian can accurately re-create each item given only its location.

Figure 3-1. A man standing in front of an infinite 2D wardrobe (created with Midjourney)

After several weeks of practice, you and Brian have adjusted to each other's understandings of the wardrobe layout. It is now possible for you to tell Brian the location of any item of clothing that you desire, and he can accurately sew it from scratch!

This gives you an idea—what would happen if you gave Brian a wardrobe location that was empty? To your amazement, you find that Brian is able to generate entirely new items of clothing that haven't existed before! The process isn't perfect, but you now have limitless options for generating new clothing, just by picking an empty location in the infinite wardrobe and letting Brian work his magic with the sewing machine.

Let's now explore how this story relates to building autoencoders.

Autoencoders

A diagram of the process described by the story is shown in Figure 3-2. You play the part of the *encoder*, moving each item of clothing to a location in the wardrobe. This process is called *encoding*. Brian plays the part of the *decoder*, taking a location in the wardrobe and attempting to re-create the item. This process is called *decoding*.

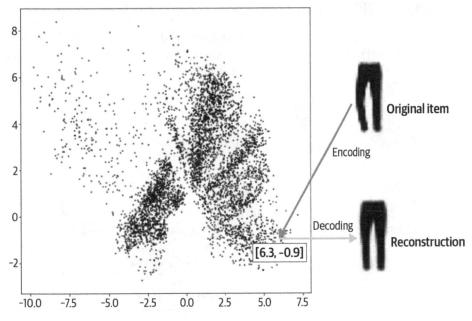

Figure 3-2. Items of clothing in the infinite wardrobe—each black dot represents an item of clothing

Each location in the wardrobe is represented by two numbers (i.e., a 2D vector). For example, the trousers in Figure 3-2 are encoded to the point [6.3, –0.9]. This vector is also known as an *embedding* because the encoder attempts to embed as much information into it as possible, so that the decoder can produce an accurate reconstruction.

An *autoencoder* is simply a neural network that is trained to perform the task of encoding and decoding an item, such that the output from this process is as close to the original item as possible. Crucially, it can be used as a generative model, because we can decode any point in the 2D space that we want (in particular, those that are not embeddings of original items) to produce a novel item of clothing.

Let's now see how we can build an autoencoder using Keras and apply it to a real dataset!

Running the Code for This Example

The code for this example can be found in the Jupyter notebook located at *notebooks/03_vae/01_autoencoder/autoencoder.ipynb* in the book repository.

The Fashion-MNIST Dataset

For this example, we'll be using the Fashion-MNIST dataset (*https://oreil.ly/DS4-4*)—a collection of grayscale images of clothing items, each of size 28 × 28 pixels. Some example images from the dataset are shown in Figure 3-3.

Figure 3-3. Examples of images from the Fashion-MNIST dataset

The dataset comes prepackaged with TensorFlow, so it can be downloaded as shown in Example 3-1.

Example 3-1. Loading the Fashion-MNIST dataset

```
from tensorflow.keras import datasets
(x_train,y_train), (x_test,y_test) = datasets.fashion_mnist.load_data()
```

These are 28 × 28 grayscale images (pixel values between 0 and 255) out of the box, which we need to preprocess to ensure that the pixel values are scaled between 0 and 1. We will also pad each image to 32 × 32 for easier manipulation of the tensor shape as it passes through the network, as shown in Example 3-2.

Example 3-2. Preprocessing the data

```python
def preprocess(imgs):
    imgs = imgs.astype("float32") / 255.0
    imgs = np.pad(imgs, ((0, 0), (2, 2), (2, 2)), constant_values=0.0)
    imgs = np.expand_dims(imgs, -1)
    return imgs

x_train = preprocess(x_train)
x_test = preprocess(x_test)
```

Next, we need to understand the overall structure of an autoencoder, so that we can code it up using TensorFlow and Keras.

The Autoencoder Architecture

An *autoencoder* is a neural network made up of two parts:

- An *encoder* network that compresses high-dimensional input data such as an image into a lower-dimensional embedding vector
- A *decoder* network that decompresses a given embedding vector back to the original domain (e.g., back to an image)

A diagram of the network architecture is shown in Figure 3-4. An input image is encoded to a latent embedding vector z, which is then decoded back to the original pixel space.

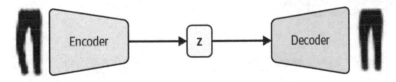

Figure 3-4. Autoencoder architecture diagram

The autoencoder is trained to reconstruct an image, after it has passed through the encoder and back out through the decoder. This may seem strange at first—why would you want to reconstruct a set of images that you already have available to you? However, as we shall see, it is the embedding space (also called the *latent space*) that is the interesting part of the autoencoder, as sampling from this space will allow us to generate new images.

Let's first define what we mean by an embedding. The embedding (z) is a compression of the original image into a lower-dimensional latent space. The idea is that by choosing any point in the latent space, we can generate novel images by passing this point through the decoder, since the decoder has learned how to convert points in the latent space into viable images.

In our example, we will embed images into a two-dimensional latent space. This will help us to visualize the latent space, since we can easily plot points in 2D. In practice, the latent space of an autoencoder will usually have more than two dimensions in order to have more freedom to capture greater nuance in the images.

Autoencoders as Denoising Models

Autoencoders can be used to clean noisy images, since the encoder learns that it is not useful to capture the position of the random noise inside the latent space in order to reconstruct the original. For tasks such as this, a 2D latent space is probably too small to encode sufficient relevant information from the input. However, as we shall see, increasing the dimensionality of the latent space quickly leads to problems if we want to use the autoencoder as a generative model.

Let's now see how to build the encoder and decoder.

The Encoder

In an autoencoder, the encoder's job is to take the input image and map it to an embedding vector in the latent space. The architecture of the encoder we will be building is shown in Table 3-1.

Table 3-1. Model summary of the encoder

Layer (type)	Output shape	Param #
InputLayer	(None, 32, 32, 1)	0
Conv2D	(None, 16, 16, 32)	320
Conv2D	(None, 8, 8, 64)	18,496
Conv2D	(None, 4, 4, 128)	73,856
Flatten	(None, 2048)	0
Dense	(None, 2)	4,098

Total params	96,770
Trainable params	96,770
Non-trainable params	0

To achieve this, we first create an `Input` layer for the image and pass this through three `Conv2D` layers in sequence, each capturing increasingly high-level features. We use a stride of 2 to halve the size of the output of each layer, while increasing the number of channels. The last convolutional layer is flattened and connected to a `Dense` layer of size 2, which represents our two-dimensional latent space.

Example 3-3 shows how to build this in Keras.

Example 3-3. The encoder

```
encoder_input = layers.Input(
    shape=(32, 32, 1), name = "encoder_input"
) ❶
x = layers.Conv2D(32, (3, 3), strides = 2, activation = 'relu', padding="same")(
    encoder_input
) ❷
x = layers.Conv2D(64, (3, 3), strides = 2, activation = 'relu', padding="same")(x)
x = layers.Conv2D(128, (3, 3), strides = 2, activation = 'relu', padding="same")(x)
shape_before_flattening = K.int_shape(x)[1:]

x = layers.Flatten()(x) ❸
encoder_output = layers.Dense(2, name="encoder_output")(x) ❹

encoder = models.Model(encoder_input, encoder_output) ❺
```

❶ Define the `Input` layer of the encoder (the image).

❷ Stack `Conv2D` layers sequentially on top of each other.

❸ Flatten the last convolutional layer to a vector.

❹ Connect this vector to the 2D embeddings with a `Dense` layer.

❺ The Keras `Model` that defines the encoder—a model that takes an input image and encodes it into a 2D embedding.

> I strongly encourage you to experiment with the number of convolutional layers and filters to understand how the architecture affects the overall number of model parameters, model performance, and model runtime.

The Decoder

The decoder is a mirror image of the encoder—instead of convolutional layers, we use *convolutional transpose* layers, as shown in Table 3-2.

Table 3-2. Model summary of the decoder

Layer (type)	Output shape	Param #
InputLayer	(None, 2)	0
Dense	(None, 2048)	6,144

Layer (type)	Output shape	Param #
Reshape	(None, 4, 4, 128)	0
Conv2DTranspose	(None, 8, 8, 128)	147,584
Conv2DTranspose	(None, 16, 16, 64)	73,792
Conv2DTranspose	(None, 32, 32, 32)	18,464
Conv2D	(None, 32, 32, 1)	289

Total params	246,273
Trainable params	246,273
Non-trainable params	0

Convolutional Transpose Layers

Standard convolutional layers allow us to halve the size of an input tensor in both dimensions (height and width), by setting `strides = 2`.

The convolutional transpose layer uses the same principle as a standard convolutional layer (passing a filter across the image), but is different in that setting `strides = 2` *doubles* the size of the input tensor in both dimensions.

In a convolutional transpose layer, the `strides` parameter determines the internal zero padding between pixels in the image, as shown in Figure 3-5. Here, a $3 \times 3 \times 1$ filter (gray) is being passed across a $3 \times 3 \times 1$ image (blue) with `strides = 2`, to produce a $6 \times 6 \times 1$ output tensor (green).

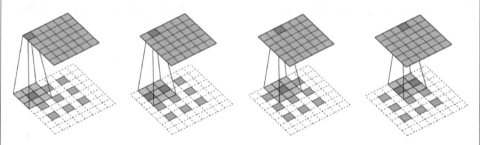

Figure 3-5. A convolutional transpose layer example (source: Dumoulin and Visin, 2018)[2]

In Keras, the `Conv2DTranspose` layer allows us to perform convolutional transpose operations on tensors. By stacking these layers, we can gradually expand the size of each layer, using strides of 2, until we get back to the original image dimension of 32×32.

Example 3-4 shows how we build the decoder in Keras.

Example 3-4. The decoder

```
decoder_input = layers.Input(shape=(2,), name="decoder_input") ❶
x = layers.Dense(np.prod(shape_before_flattening))(decoder_input) ❷
x = layers.Reshape(shape_before_flattening)(x) ❸
x = layers.Conv2DTranspose(
    128, (3, 3), strides=2, activation = 'relu', padding="same"
)(x) ❹
x = layers.Conv2DTranspose(
    64, (3, 3), strides=2, activation = 'relu', padding="same"
)(x)
x = layers.Conv2DTranspose(
    32, (3, 3), strides=2, activation = 'relu', padding="same"
)(x)
decoder_output = layers.Conv2D(
    1,
    (3, 3),
    strides = 1,
    activation="sigmoid",
    padding="same",
    name="decoder_output"
)(x)

decoder = models.Model(decoder_input, decoder_output) ❺
```

❶ Define the `Input` layer of the decoder (the embedding).

❷ Connect the input to a `Dense` layer.

❸ **Reshape** this vector into a tensor that can be fed as input into the first `Conv2DTranspose` layer.

❹ Stack `Conv2DTranspose` layers on top of each other.

❺ The Keras `Model` that defines the decoder—a model that takes an embedding in the latent space and decodes it into the original image domain.

Joining the Encoder to the Decoder

To train the encoder and decoder simultaneously, we need to define a model that will represent the flow of an image through the encoder and back out through the decoder. Luckily, Keras makes it extremely easy to do this, as you can see in Example 3-5. Notice the way in which we specify that the output from the autoencoder is simply the output from the encoder after it has been passed through the decoder.

Example 3-5. The full autoencoder

```
autoencoder = Model(encoder_input, decoder(encoder_output)) ❶
```

❶ The Keras `Model` that defines the full autoencoder—a model that takes an image and passes it through the encoder and back out through the decoder to generate a reconstruction of the original image.

Now that we've defined our model, we just need to compile it with a loss function and optimizer, as shown in Example 3-6. The loss function is usually chosen to be either the root mean squared error (RMSE) or binary cross-entropy between the individual pixels of the original image and the reconstruction.

Example 3-6. Compiling the autoencoder

```
# Compile the autoencoder
autoencoder.compile(optimizer="adam", loss="binary_crossentropy")
```

Choosing the Loss Function

Optimizing for RMSE means that your generated output will be symmetrically distributed around the average pixel values (because an overestimation is penalized equivalently to an underestimation).

On the other hand, binary cross-entropy loss is asymmetrical—it penalizes errors toward the extremes more heavily than errors toward the center. For example, if the true pixel value is high (say 0.7), then generating a pixel with value 0.8 is penalized more heavily than generating a pixel with value 0.6. If the true pixel value is low (say 0.3), then generating a pixel with value 0.2 is penalized more heavily than generating a pixel with value 0.4.

This has the effect of binary cross-entropy loss producing slightly blurrier images than RMSE loss (as it tends to push predictions toward 0.5), but sometimes this is desirable as RMSE can lead to obviously pixelized edges.

There is no right or wrong choice—you should choose whichever works best for your use case after experimentation.

We can now train the autoencoder by passing in the input images as both the input and output, as shown in Example 3-7.

Example 3-7. Training the autoencoder

```
autoencoder.fit(
    x_train,
    x_train,
    epochs=5,
    batch_size=100,
    shuffle=True,
    validation_data=(x_test, x_test),
)
```

Now that our autoencoder is trained, the first thing we need to check is that it is able to accurately reconstruct the input images.

Reconstructing Images

We can test the ability to reconstruct images by passing images from the test set through the autoencoder and comparing the output to the original images. The code for this is shown in Example 3-8.

Example 3-8. Reconstructing images using the autoencoder

```
example_images = x_test[:5000]
predictions = autoencoder.predict(example_images)
```

In Figure 3-6 you can see some examples of original images (top row), the 2D vectors after encoding, and the reconstructed items after decoding (bottom row).

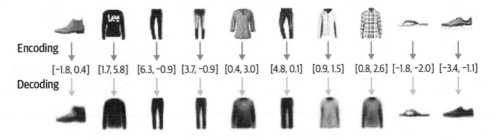

Figure 3-6. Examples of encoding and decoding items of clothing

Notice how the reconstruction isn't perfect—there are still some details of the original images that aren't captured by the decoding process, such as logos. This is because by reducing each image to just two numbers, we naturally lose some information.

Let's now investigate how the encoder is representing images in the latent space.

Visualizing the Latent Space

We can visualize how images are embedded into the latent space by passing the test set through the encoder and plotting the resulting embeddings, as shown in Example 3-9.

Example 3-9. Embedding images using the encoder

```
embeddings = encoder.predict(example_images)

plt.figure(figsize=(8, 8))
plt.scatter(embeddings[:, 0], embeddings[:, 1], c="black", alpha=0.5, s=3)
plt.show()
```

The resulting plot is the scatter plot shown in Figure 3-2—each black point represents an image that has been embedded into the latent space.

In order to better understand how this latent space is structured, we can make use of the labels that come with the Fashion-MNIST dataset, describing the type of item in each image. There are 10 groups altogether, shown in Table 3-3.

Table 3-3. The Fashion-MNIST labels

ID	Clothing label
0	T-shirt/top
1	Trouser
2	Pullover
3	Dress
4	Coat
5	Sandal
6	Shirt
7	Sneaker
8	Bag
9	Ankle boot

We can color each point based on the label of the corresponding image to produce the plot in Figure 3-7. Now the structure becomes very clear! Even though the clothing labels were never shown to the model during training, the autoencoder has naturally grouped items that look alike into the same parts of the latent space. For example, the dark blue cloud of points in the bottom-right corner of the latent space are all different images of trousers and the red cloud of points toward the center are all ankle boots.

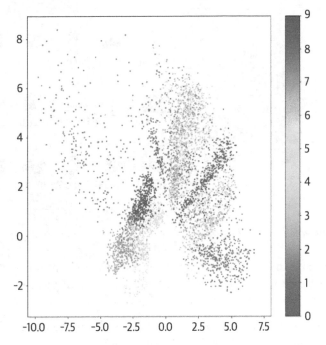

Figure 3-7. Plot of the latent space, colored by clothing label

Generating New Images

We can generate novel images by sampling some points in the latent space and using the decoder to convert these back into pixel space, as shown in Example 3-10.

Example 3-10. Generating novel images using the decoder

```
mins, maxs = np.min(embeddings, axis=0), np.max(embeddings, axis=0)
sample = np.random.uniform(mins, maxs, size=(18, 2))
reconstructions = decoder.predict(sample)
```

Some examples of generated images are shown in Figure 3-8, alongside their embeddings in the latent space.

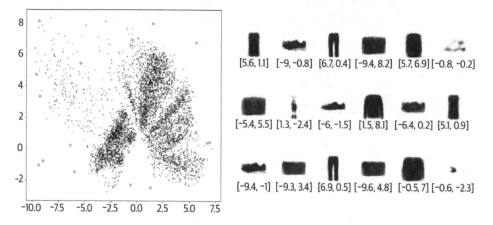

Figure 3-8. Generated items of clothing

Each blue dot maps to one of the images shown on the right of the diagram, with the embedding vector shown underneath. Notice how some of the generated items are more realistic than others. Why is this?

To answer this, let's first make a few observations about the overall distribution of points in the latent space, referring back to Figure 3-7:

- Some clothing items are represented over a very small area and others over a much larger area.
- The distribution is not symmetrical about the point (0, 0), or bounded. For example, there are far more points with positive y-axis values than negative, and some points even extend to a y-axis value > 8.
- There are large gaps between colors containing few points.

These observations actually make sampling from the latent space quite challenging. If we overlay the latent space with images of decoded points on a grid, as shown in Figure 3-9, we can begin to understand why the decoder may not always generate images to a satisfactory standard.

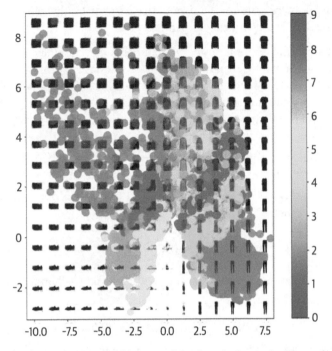

Figure 3-9. A grid of decoded embeddings, overlaid with the embeddings from the original images in the dataset, colored by item type

Firstly, we can see that if we pick points uniformly in a bounded space that we define, we're more likely to sample something that decodes to look like a bag (ID 8) than an ankle boot (ID 9) because the part of the latent space carved out for bags (orange) is larger than the ankle boot area (red).

Secondly, it is not obvious how we should go about choosing a *random* point in the latent space, since the distribution of these points is undefined. Technically, we would be justified in choosing any point in the 2D plane! It's not even guaranteed that points will be centered around (0, 0). This makes sampling from our latent space problematic.

Lastly, we can see holes in the latent space where none of the original images are encoded. For example, there are large white spaces at the edges of the domain—the autoencoder has no reason to ensure that points here are decoded to recognizable clothing items as very few images in the training set are encoded here.

Even points that are central may not be decoded into well-formed images. This is because the autoencoder is not forced to ensure that the space is continuous. For example, even though the point (−1, −1) might be decoded to give a satisfactory image of a sandal, there is no mechanism in place to ensure that the point (–1.1, –1.1) also produces a satisfactory image of a sandal.

In two dimensions this issue is subtle; the autoencoder only has a small number of dimensions to work with, so naturally it has to squash clothing groups together, resulting in the space between clothing groups being relatively small. However, as we start to use more dimensions in the latent space to generate more complex images such as faces, this problem becomes even more apparent. If we give the autoencoder free rein over how it uses the latent space to encode images, there will be huge gaps between groups of similar points with no incentive for the spaces in between to generate well-formed images.

In order to solve these three problems, we need to convert our autoencoder into a *variational autoencoder*.

Variational Autoencoders

To explain, let's revisit the infinite wardrobe and make a few changes…

Revisiting the Infinite Wardrobe

Suppose now, instead of placing every item of clothing at a single point in the wardrobe, you decide to allocate a general area where the item is more likely to be found. You reason that this more relaxed approach to item location will help to solve the current issue around local discontinuities in the wardrobe.

Also, in order to ensure you do not become too careless with the new placement system, you agree with Brian that you will try to place the center of each item's area as close to the middle of the wardrobe as possible and that deviation of the item from the center should be as close to one meter as possible (not smaller and not larger). The further you stray from this rule, the more you have to pay Brian as your stylist.

After several months of operating with these two simple changes, you step back and admire the new wardrobe layout, alongside some examples of new clothing items that Brian has generated. Much better! There is plenty of diversity in the generated items, and this time there are no examples of poor-quality garments. It seems the two changes have made all the difference!

Let's now try to understand what we need to do to our autoencoder model to convert it into a variational autoencoder and thus make it a more sophisticated generative model.

The two parts that we need to change are the encoder and the loss function.

The Encoder

In an autoencoder, each image is mapped directly to one point in the latent space. In a variational autoencoder, each image is instead mapped to a multivariate normal distribution around a point in the latent space, as shown in Figure 3-10.

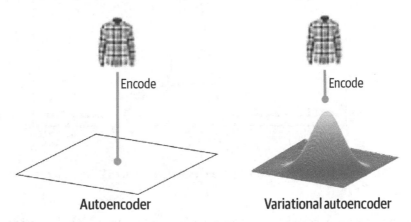

Figure 3-10. *The difference between the encoders in an autoencoder and a variational autoencoder*

The Multivariate Normal Distribution

A *normal distribution* (or *Gaussian distribution*) $\mathcal{N}(\mu, \sigma)$ is a probability distribution characterized by a distinctive *bell curve* shape, defined by two variables: the *mean* (μ) and the *variance* (σ^2). The *standard deviation* (σ) is the square root of the variance.

The probability density function of the normal distribution in one dimension is:

$$f\left(x \mid \mu, \sigma^2\right) = \frac{1}{\sqrt{2\pi\sigma^2}} e^{-\frac{(x-\mu)^2}{2\sigma^2}}$$

Figure 3-11 shows several normal distributions in one dimension, for different values of the mean and variance. The red curve is the *standard normal* (or *unit normal*) $\mathcal{N}(0, 1)$—the normal distribution with mean equal to 0 and variance equal to 1.

We can sample a point z from a normal distribution with mean μ and standard deviation σ using the following equation:

$$z = \mu + \sigma\epsilon$$

where ϵ is sampled from a standard normal distribution.

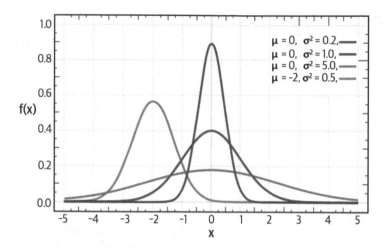

Figure 3-11. The normal distribution in one dimension (source: Wikipedia (https://oreil.ly/gWwKV))

The concept of a normal distribution extends to more than one dimension—the probability density function for a *multivariate normal distribution* (or *multivariate Gaussian distribution*) $\mathcal{N}(\mu, \Sigma)$ in k dimensions with mean vector μ and symmetric covariance matrix Σ is as follows:

$$f(x_1, ..., x_k) = \frac{\exp\left(-\frac{1}{2}(\mathbf{x} - \mu)^{\mathrm{T}}\Sigma^{-1}(\mathbf{x} - \mu)\right)}{\sqrt{(2\pi)^k |\Sigma|}}$$

In this book, we will typically be using *isotropic* multivariate normal distributions, where the covariance matrix is diagonal. This means that the distribution is independent in each dimension (i.e., we can sample a vector where each element is normally distributed with independent mean and variance). This is the case for the multivariate normal distribution that we will use in our variational autoencoder.

A *multivariate standard normal distribution* $\mathcal{N}(0, \mathbf{I})$ is a multivariate distribution with a zero-valued mean vector and identity covariance matrix.

Normal Versus Gaussian

In this book, the terms *normal* and *Gaussian* are used interchangeably and the isotropic and multivariate nature of the distribution is usually implied. For example, "we sample from a Gaussian distribution" can be interpreted to mean "we sample from an isotropic, multivariate Gaussian distribution."

The encoder only needs to map each input to a mean vector and a variance vector and does not need to worry about covariance between dimensions. Variational autoencoders assume that there is no correlation between dimensions in the latent space.

Variance values are always positive, so we actually choose to map to the *logarithm* of the variance, as this can take any real number in the range $(-\infty, \infty)$. This way we can use a neural network as the encoder to perform the mapping from the input image to the mean and log variance vectors.

To summarize, the encoder will take each input image and encode it to two vectors that together define a multivariate normal distribution in the latent space:

z_mean
  The mean point of the distribution

z_log_var
  The logarithm of the variance of each dimension

We can sample a point z from the distribution defined by these values using the following equation:

```
z = z_mean + z_sigma * epsilon
```

where:

```
z_sigma = exp(z_log_var * 0.5)
epsilon ~ N(0,I)
```

 The derivation of the relationship between z_sigma (σ) and z_log_var ($\log\left(\sigma^2\right)$) is as follows:

$$\sigma = \exp\left(\log\left(\sigma\right)\right) = \exp\left(2\log\left(\sigma\right)/2\right) = \exp\left(\log\left(\sigma^2\right)/2\right)$$

The decoder of a variational autoencoder is identical to the decoder of a plain autoencoder, giving the overall architecture shown in Figure 3-12.

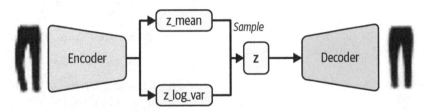

Figure 3-12. VAE architecture diagram

Why does this small change to the encoder help?

Previously, we saw that there was no requirement for the latent space to be continuous—even if the point (–2, 2) decodes to a well-formed image of a sandal, there's no requirement for (–2.1, 2.1) to look similar. Now, since we are sampling a random point from an area around z_mean, the decoder must ensure that all points in the same neighborhood produce very similar images when decoded, so that the reconstruction loss remains small. This is a very nice property that ensures that even when we choose a point in the latent space that has never been seen by the decoder, it is likely to decode to an image that is well formed.

Building the VAE encoder

Let's now see how we build this new version of the encoder in Keras.

Running the Code for This Example

The code for this example can be found in the Jupyter notebook located at *notebooks/03_vae/02_vae_fashion/vae_fashion.ipynb* in the book repository.

The code has been adapted from the excellent VAE tutorial (*https://oreil.ly/A7yqJ*) created by Francois Chollet, available on the Keras website.

First, we need to create a new type of `Sampling` layer that will allow us to sample from the distribution defined by z_mean and z_log_var, as shown in Example 3-11.

Example 3-11. The Sampling layer

```
class Sampling(layers.Layer): ❶
    def call(self, inputs):
        z_mean, z_log_var = inputs
        batch = tf.shape(z_mean)[0]
        dim = tf.shape(z_mean)[1]
        epsilon = K.random_normal(shape=(batch, dim))
        return z_mean + tf.exp(0.5 * z_log_var) * epsilon ❷
```

❶ We create a new layer by subclassing the Keras base `Layer` class (see the "Subclassing the Layer Class" sidebar).

❷ We use the reparameterization trick (see "The Reparameterization Trick" sidebar) to build a sample from the normal distribution parameterized by z_mean and z_log_var.

The complete code for the encoder, including the new Sampling layer, is shown in Example 3-12.

Example 3-12. The encoder

```
encoder_input = layers.Input(
    shape=(32, 32, 1), name="encoder_input"
)
x = layers.Conv2D(32, (3, 3), strides=2, activation="relu", padding="same")(
    encoder_input
)
x = layers.Conv2D(64, (3, 3), strides=2, activation="relu", padding="same")(x)
x = layers.Conv2D(128, (3, 3), strides=2, activation="relu", padding="same")(x)
shape_before_flattening = K.int_shape(x)[1:]

x = layers.Flatten()(x)
z_mean = layers.Dense(2, name="z_mean")(x)          ❶
z_log_var = layers.Dense(2, name="z_log_var")(x)
z = Sampling()([z_mean, z_log_var])                 ❷
```

```
encoder = models.Model(encoder_input, [z_mean, z_log_var, z], name="encoder") ❸
```

❶ Instead of connecting the Flatten layer directly to the 2D latent space, we connect it to layers z_mean and z_log_var.

❷ The Sampling layer samples a point z in the latent space from the normal distribution defined by the parameters z_mean and z_log_var.

❸ The Keras Model that defines the encoder—a model that takes an input image and outputs z_mean, z_log_var, and a sampled point z from the normal distribution defined by these parameters.

A summary of the encoder is shown in Table 3-4.

Table 3-4. Model summary of the VAE encoder

Layer (type)	Output shape	Param #	Connected to
InputLayer (input)	(None, 32, 32, 1)	0	[]
Conv2D (conv2d_1)	(None, 16, 16, 32)	320	[input]
Conv2D (conv2d_2)	(None, 8, 8, 64)	18,496	[conv2d_1]
Conv2D (conv2d_3)	(None, 4, 4, 128)	73,856	[conv2d_2]
Flatten (flatten)	(None, 2048)	0	[conv2d_3]
Dense (z_mean)	(None, 2)	4,098	[flatten]
Dense (z_log_var)	(None, 2)	4,098	[flatten]
Sampling (z)	(None, 2)	0	[z_mean, z_log_var]

Total params	100,868
Trainable params	100,868
Non-trainable params	0

The only other part of the original autoencoder that we need to change is the loss function.

The Loss Function

Previously, our loss function only consisted of the *reconstruction loss* between images and their attempted copies after being passed through the encoder and decoder. The reconstruction loss also appears in a variational autoencoder, but we now require one extra component: the *Kullback–Leibler (KL) divergence* term.

KL divergence is a way of measuring how much one probability distribution differs from another. In a VAE, we want to measure how much our normal distribution with parameters z_mean and z_log_var differs from a standard normal distribution. In this special case, it can be shown that the KL divergence has the following closed form:

```
kl_loss = -0.5 * sum(1 + z_log_var - z_mean ^ 2 - exp(z_log_var))
```

or in mathematical notation:

$$D_{KL}[N(\mu, \sigma \parallel N(0, 1)] = -\frac{1}{2}\sum\left(1 + log(\sigma^2) - \mu^2 - \sigma^2\right)$$

The sum is taken over all the dimensions in the latent space. kl_loss is minimized to 0 when z_mean = 0 and z_log_var = 0 for all dimensions. As these two terms start to differ from 0, kl_loss increases.

In summary, the KL divergence term penalizes the network for encoding observations to z_mean and z_log_var variables that differ significantly from the parameters of a standard normal distribution, namely z_mean = 0 and z_log_var = 0.

Why does this addition to the loss function help?

Firstly, we now have a well-defined distribution that we can use for choosing points in the latent space—the standard normal distribution. Secondly, since this term tries to force all encoded distributions toward the standard normal distribution, there is less chance that large gaps will form between point clusters. Instead, the encoder will try to use the space around the origin symmetrically and efficiently.

In the original VAE paper, the loss function for a VAE was simply the addition of the reconstruction loss and the KL divergence loss term. A variant on this (the β-VAE) includes a factor that weights the KL divergence to ensure that it is well balanced with the reconstruction loss. If we weight the reconstruction loss too heavily, the KL loss will not have the desired regulatory effect and we will see the same problems that we experienced with the plain autoencoder. If the KL divergence term is weighted too heavily, the KL divergence loss will dominate and the reconstructed images will be poor. This weighting term is one of the parameters to tune when you're training your VAE.

Training the Variational Autoencoder

Example 3-13 shows how we build the overall VAE model as a subclass of the abstract Keras `Model` class. This allows us to include the calculation of the KL divergence term of the loss function in a custom `train_step` method.

Example 3-13. Training the VAE

```python
class VAE(models.Model):
    def __init__(self, encoder, decoder, **kwargs):
        super(VAE, self).__init__(**kwargs)
        self.encoder = encoder
        self.decoder = decoder
        self.total_loss_tracker = metrics.Mean(name="total_loss")
        self.reconstruction_loss_tracker = metrics.Mean(
            name="reconstruction_loss"
        )
        self.kl_loss_tracker = metrics.Mean(name="kl_loss")

    @property
    def metrics(self):
        return [
            self.total_loss_tracker,
            self.reconstruction_loss_tracker,
            self.kl_loss_tracker,
        ]

    def call(self, inputs):  ❶
        z_mean, z_log_var, z = encoder(inputs)
        reconstruction = decoder(z)
        return z_mean, z_log_var, reconstruction

    def train_step(self, data):  ❷
        with tf.GradientTape() as tape:
            z_mean, z_log_var, reconstruction = self(data)
            reconstruction_loss = tf.reduce_mean(
                500
                * losses.binary_crossentropy(
                    data, reconstruction, axis=(1, 2, 3)
                )
            )  ❸
            kl_loss = tf.reduce_mean(
                tf.reduce_sum(
                    -0.5
                    * (1 + z_log_var - tf.square(z_mean) - tf.exp(z_log_var)),
                    axis = 1,
                )
            )
            total_loss = reconstruction_loss + kl_loss  ❹

        grads = tape.gradient(total_loss, self.trainable_weights)
```

```
        self.optimizer.apply_gradients(zip(grads, self.trainable_weights))

        self.total_loss_tracker.update_state(total_loss)
        self.reconstruction_loss_tracker.update_state(reconstruction_loss)
        self.kl_loss_tracker.update_state(kl_loss)

        return {m.name: m.result() for m in self.metrics}
vae = VAE(encoder, decoder)
vae.compile(optimizer="adam")
vae.fit(
    train,
    epochs=5,
    batch_size=100
)
```

❶ This function describes what we would like returned what we call the VAE on a particular input image.

❷ This function describes one training step of the VAE, including the calculation of the loss function.

❸ A beta value of 500 is used in the reconstruction loss.

❹ The total loss is the sum of the reconstruction loss and the KL divergence loss.

Gradient Tape

TensorFlow's *Gradient Tape* is a mechanism that allows the computation of gradients of operations executed during a forward pass of a model. To use it, you need to wrap the code that performs the operations you want to differentiate in a `tf.GradientTape()` context. Once you have recorded the operations, you can compute the gradient of the loss function with respect to some variables by calling `tape.gradient()`. The gradients can then be used to update the variables with the optimizer.

This mechanism is useful for calculating the gradient of custom loss functions (as we have done here) and also for creating custom training loops, as we shall see in Chapter 4.

Analysis of the Variational Autoencoder

Now that we have trained our VAE, we can use the encoder to encode the images in the test set and plot the z_mean values in the latent space. We can also sample from a standard normal distribution to generate points in the latent space and use the decoder to decode these points back into pixel space to see how the VAE performs.

Figure 3-13 shows the structure of the new latent space, alongside some sampled points and their decoded images. We can immediately see several changes in how the latent space is organized.

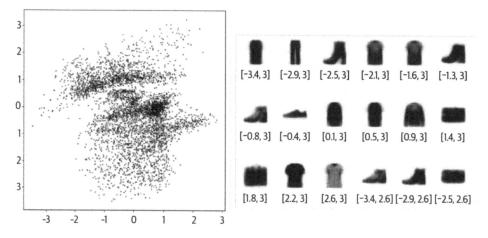

Figure 3-13. The new latent space: the black dots show the z_mean value of each encoded image, while blue dots show some sampled points in the latent space (with their decoded images on the right)

Firstly, the KL divergence loss term ensures that the z_mean and z_log_var values of the encoded images never stray too far from a standard normal distribution. Secondly, there are not so many poorly formed images as the latent space is now much more continuous, due to fact that the encoder is now stochastic, rather than deterministic.

Finally, by coloring points in the latent space by clothing type (Figure 3-14), we can see that there is no preferential treatment of any one type. The righthand plot shows the space transformed into *p*-values—we can see that each color is approximately equally represented. Again, it's important to remember that the labels were not used at all during training; the VAE has learned the various forms of clothing by itself in order to help minimize reconstruction loss.

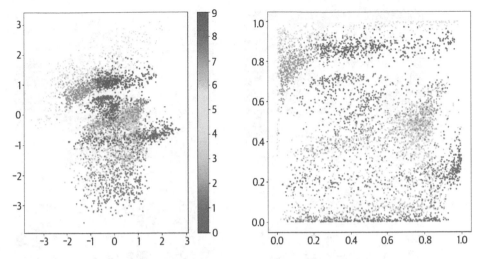

Figure 3-14. The latent space of the VAE colored by clothing type

Exploring the Latent Space

So far, all of our work on autoencoders and variational autoencoders has been limited to a latent space with two dimensions. This has helped us to visualize the inner workings of a VAE on the page and understand why the small tweaks that we made to the architecture of the autoencoder helped transform it into a more powerful class of network that can be used for generative modeling.

Let's now turn our attention to a more complex dataset and see the amazing things that variational autoencoders can achieve when we increase the dimensionality of the latent space.

Running the Code for This Example

The code for this example can be found in the Jupyter notebook located at *notebooks/03_vae/03_faces/vae_faces.ipynb* in the book repository.

The CelebA Dataset

We shall be using the CelebFaces Attributes (CelebA) dataset (*https://oreil.ly/tEUnh*) to train our next variational autoencoder. This is a collection of over 200,000 color images of celebrity faces, each annotated with various labels (e.g., *wearing hat, smiling*, etc.). A few examples are shown in Figure 3-15.

Figure 3-15. Some examples from the CelebA dataset (source: Liu et al., 2015)[3]

Of course, we don't need the labels to train the VAE, but these will be useful later when we start exploring how these features are captured in the multidimensional latent space. Once our VAE is trained, we can sample from the latent space to generate new examples of celebrity faces.

The CelebA dataset is also available through Kaggle, so you can download the dataset by running the Kaggle dataset downloader script in the book repository, as shown in Example 3-14. This will save the images and accompanying metadata locally to the */data* folder.

Example 3-14. Downloading the CelebA dataset

```
bash scripts/download_kaggle_data.sh jessicali9530 celeba-dataset
```

We use the Keras function `image_dataset_from_directory` to create a TensorFlow Dataset pointed at the directory where the images are stored, as shown in Example 3-15. This allows us to read batches of images into memory only when required (e.g., during training), so that we can work with large datasets and not worry about having to fit the entire dataset into memory. It also resizes the images to 32 × 32, interpolating between pixel values.

Example 3-15. Preprocessing the CelebA dataset

```
train_data = utils.image_dataset_from_directory(
    "/app/data/celeba-dataset/img_align_celeba/img_align_celeba",
    labels=None,
    color_mode="rgb",
    image_size=(32, 32),
    batch_size=128,
    shuffle=True,
    seed=42,
    interpolation="bilinear",
)
```

The original data is scaled in the range [0, 255] to denote the pixel intensity, which we rescale to the range [0, 1] as shown in Example 3-16.

Example 3-16. Preprocessing the CelebA dataset

```
def preprocess(img):
    img = tf.cast(img, "float32") / 255.0
    return img

train = train_data.map(lambda x: preprocess(x))
```

Training the Variational Autoencoder

The network architecture for the faces model is similar to the Fashion-MNIST example, with a few slight differences:

- Our data now has three input channels (RGB) instead of one (grayscale). This means we need to change the number of channels in the final convolutional transpose layer of the decoder to 3.

- We shall be using a latent space with 200 dimensions instead of 2. Since faces are much more complex than the Fashion-MNIST images, we increase the dimensionality of the latent space so that the network can encode a satisfactory amount of detail from the images.

- There are batch normalization layers after each convolutional layer to stabilize training. Even though each batch takes a longer time to run, the number of batches required to reach the same loss is greatly reduced.

- We increase the β factor for the KL divergence to 2,000. This is a parameter that requires tuning; for this dataset and architecture this value was found to generate good results.

The full architectures of the encoder and decoder are shown in Tables 3-5 and 3-6, respectively.

Table 3-5. Model summary of the VAE faces encoder

Layer (type)	Output shape	Param #	Connected to
InputLayer (input)	(None, 32, 32, 3)	0	[]
Conv2D (conv2d_1)	(None, 16, 16, 128)	3,584	[input]
BatchNormalization (bn_1)	(None, 16, 16, 128)	512	[conv2d_1]
LeakyReLU (lr_1)	(None, 16, 16, 128)	0	[bn_1]
Conv2D (conv2d_2)	(None, 8, 8, 128)	147,584	[lr_1]
BatchNormalization (bn_2)	(None, 8, 8, 128)	512	[conv2d_2]
LeakyReLU (lr_2)	(None, 8, 8, 128)	0	[bn_2]
Conv2D (conv2d_3)	(None, 4, 4, 128)	147,584	[lr_2]
BatchNormalization (bn_3)	(None, 4, 4, 128)	512	[conv2d_3]
LeakyReLU (lr_3)	(None, 4, 4, 128)	0	[bn_3]
Conv2D (conv2d_4)	(None, 2, 2, 128)	147,584	[lr_3]
BatchNormalization (bn_4)	(None, 2, 2, 128)	512	[conv2d_4]
LeakyReLU (lr_4)	(None, 2, 2, 128)	0	[bn_4]
Flatten (flatten)	(None, 512)	0	[lr_4]
Dense (z_mean)	(None, 200)	102,600	[flatten]
Dense (z_log_var)	(None, 200)	102,600	[flatten]
Sampling (z)	(None, 200)	0	[z_mean, z_log_var]

Total params	653,584
Trainable params	652,560
Non-trainable params	1,024

Table 3-6. Model summary of the VAE faces decoder

Layer (type)	Output shape	Param #
InputLayer	(None, 200)	0
Dense	(None, 512)	102,912
BatchNormalization	(None, 512)	2,048
LeakyReLU	(None, 512)	0
Reshape	(None, 2, 2, 128)	0
Conv2DTranspose	(None, 4, 4, 128)	147,584
BatchNormalization	(None, 4, 4, 128)	512
LeakyReLU	(None, 4, 4, 128)	0
Conv2DTranspose	(None, 8, 8, 128)	147,584

Layer (type)	Output shape	Param #
BatchNormalization	(None, 8, 8, 128)	512
LeakyReLU	(None, 8, 8, 128)	0
Conv2DTranspose	(None, 16, 16, 128)	147,584
BatchNormalization	(None, 16, 16, 128)	512
LeakyReLU	(None, 16, 16, 128)	0
Conv2DTranspose	(None, 32, 32, 128)	147,584
BatchNormalization	(None, 32, 32, 128)	512
LeakyReLU	(None, 32, 32, 128)	0
Conv2DTranspose	(None, 32, 32, 3)	3,459

Total params	700,803	
Trainable params	698,755	
Non-trainable params	2,048	

After around five epochs of training, our VAE should be able to produce novel images of celebrity faces!

Analysis of the Variational Autoencoder

First, let's take a look at a sample of reconstructed faces. The top row in Figure 3-16 shows the original images and the bottom row shows the reconstructions once they have passed through the encoder and decoder.

Figure 3-16. Reconstructed faces, after passing through the encoder and decoder

We can see that the VAE has successfully captured the key features of each face—the angle of the head, the hairstyle, the expression, etc. Some of the fine detail is missing, but it is important to remember that the aim of building variational autoencoders isn't to achieve perfect reconstruction loss. Our end goal is to sample from the latent space in order to generate new faces.

For this to be possible we must check that the distribution of points in the latent space approximately resembles a multivariate standard normal distribution. If we see any dimensions that are significantly different from a standard normal distribution, we should probably reduce the reconstruction loss factor, since the KL divergence term isn't having enough effect.

The first 50 dimensions in our latent space are shown in Figure 3-17. There aren't any distributions that stand out as being significantly different from the standard normal, so we can move on to generating some faces!

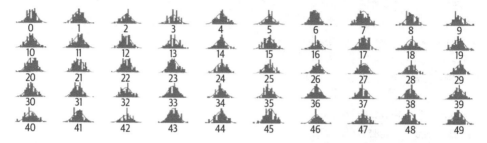

Figure 3-17. Distributions of points for the first 50 dimensions in the latent space

Generating New Faces

To generate new faces, we can use the code in Example 3-17.

Example 3-17. Generating new faces from the latent space

```
grid_width, grid_height = (10,3)
z_sample = np.random.normal(size=(grid_width * grid_height, 200)) ❶

reconstructions = decoder.predict(z_sample) ❷

fig = plt.figure(figsize=(18, 5))
fig.subplots_adjust(hspace=0.4, wspace=0.4)
for i in range(grid_width * grid_height):
    ax = fig.add_subplot(grid_height, grid_width, i + 1)
    ax.axis("off")
    ax.imshow(reconstructions[i, :, :]) ❸
```

❶ Sample 30 points from a standard multivariate normal distribution with 200 dimensions.

❷ Decode the sampled points.

❸ Plot the images!

The output is shown in Figure 3-18.

Figure 3-18. New generated faces

Amazingly, the VAE is able to take the set of points that we sampled from a standard normal distribution and convert each into a convincing image of a person's face. This is our first glimpse of the true power of generative models!

Next, let's see if we can start to use the latent space to perform some interesting operations on generated images.

Latent Space Arithmetic

One benefit of mapping images into a lower-dimensional latent space is that we can perform arithmetic on vectors in this latent space that has a visual analogue when decoded back into the original image domain.

For example, suppose we want to take an image of somebody who looks sad and give them a smile. To do this we first need to find a vector in the latent space that points in the direction of increasing smile. Adding this vector to the encoding of the original image in the latent space will give us a new point which, when decoded, should give us a more smiley version of the original image.

So how can we find the *smile* vector? Each image in the CelebA dataset is labeled with attributes, one of which is Smiling. If we take the average position of encoded images in the latent space with the attribute Smiling and subtract the average position of encoded images that do not have the attribute Smiling, we will obtain the vector that points in the direction of Smiling, which is exactly what we need.

Conceptually, we are performing the following vector arithmetic in the latent space, where alpha is a factor that determines how much of the feature vector is added or subtracted:

```
z_new = z + alpha * feature_vector
```

Let's see this in action. Figure 3-19 shows several images that have been encoded into the latent space. We then add or subtract multiples of a certain vector (e.g., Smiling, Black_Hair, Eyeglasses, Young, Male, Blond_Hair) to obtain different versions of the image, with only the relevant feature changed.

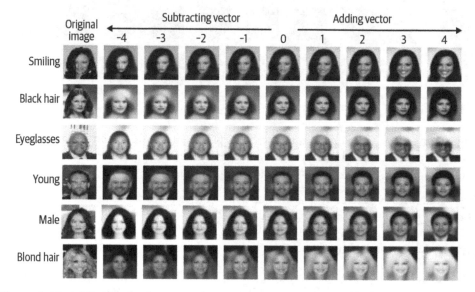

Figure 3-19. Adding and subtracting features to and from faces

It is remarkable that even though we are moving the point a significantly large distance in the latent space, the core image remains approximately the same, except for the one feature that we want to manipulate. This demonstrates the power of variational autoencoders for capturing and adjusting high-level features in images.

Morphing Between Faces

We can use a similar idea to morph between two faces. Imagine two points in the latent space, A and B, that represent two images. If you started at point A and walked toward point B in a straight line, decoding each point on the line as you went, you would see a gradual transition from the starting face to the end face.

Mathematically, we are traversing a straight line, which can be described by the following equation:

```
z_new = z_A * (1- alpha) + z_B * alpha
```

Here, alpha is a number between 0 and 1 that determines how far along the line we are, away from point A.

Figure 3-20 shows this process in action. We take two images, encode them into the latent space, and then decode points along the straight line between them at regular intervals.

Image A
0

Alpha

Image B
1

Figure 3-20. Morphing between two faces

It is worth noting the smoothness of the transition—even where there are multiple features to change simultaneously (e.g., removal of glasses, hair color, gender), the VAE manages to achieve this fluidly, showing that the latent space of the VAE is truly a continuous space that can be traversed and explored to generate a multitude of different human faces.

Summary

In this chapter we have seen how variational autoencoders are a powerful tool in the generative modeling toolbox. We started by exploring how plain autoencoders can be used to map high-dimensional images into a low-dimensional latent space, so that high-level features can be extracted from the individually uninformative pixels. However, we quickly found that there were some drawbacks to using plain autoencoders as a generative model—sampling from the learned latent space was problematic, for example.

Variational autoencoders solve these problems by introducing randomness into the model and constraining how points in the latent space are distributed. We saw that with a few minor adjustments, we can transform our autoencoder into a variational autoencoder, thus giving it the power to be a true generative model.

Finally, we applied our new technique to the problem of face generation and saw how we can simply decode points from a standard normal distribution to generate new faces. Moreover, by performing vector arithmetic within the latent space, we can achieve some amazing effects, such as face morphing and feature manipulation.

In the next chapter, we shall explore a different kind of model that remains a popular choice for generative image modeling: the generative adversarial network.

References

1. Diederik P. Kingma and Max Welling, "Auto-Encoding Variational Bayes," December 20, 2013, *https://arxiv.org/abs/1312.6114*.

2. Vincent Dumoulin and Francesco Visin, "A Guide to Convolution Arithmetic for Deep Learning," January 12, 2018, *https://arxiv.org/abs/1603.07285*.

3. Ziwei Liu et al., "Large-Scale CelebFaces Attributes (CelebA) Dataset," 2015, *http://mmlab.ie.cuhk.edu.hk/projects/CelebA.html*.

CHAPTER 4

Generative Adversarial Networks

Chapter Goals

In this chapter you will:

- Learn about the architectural design of a generative adversarial network (GAN).
- Build and train a deep convolutional GAN (DCGAN) from scratch using Keras.
- Use the DCGAN to generate new images.
- Understand some of the common problems faced when training a DCGAN.
- Learn how the Wasserstein GAN (WGAN) architecture addresses these problems.
- Understand additional enhancements that can be made to the WGAN, such as incorporating a gradient penalty (GP) term into the loss function.
- Build a WGAN-GP from scratch using Keras.
- Use the WGAN-GP to generate faces.
- Learn how a conditional GAN (CGAN) gives you the ability to condition generated output on a given label.
- Build and train a CGAN in Keras and use it to manipulate a generated image.

In 2014, Ian Goodfellow et al. presented a paper entitled "Generative Adversarial Nets"[1] at the Neural Information Processing Systems conference (NeurIPS) in Montreal. The introduction of generative adversarial networks (or GANs, as they are more commonly known) is now regarded as a key turning point in the history of generative modeling, as the core ideas presented in this paper have spawned some of the most successful and impressive generative models ever created.

This chapter will first lay out the theoretical underpinning of GANs, then we will see how to build our own GAN using Keras.

Introduction

Let's start with a short story to illustrate some of the fundamental concepts used in the GAN training process.

Brickki Bricks and the Forgers

It's your first day at your new job as head of quality control for Brickki, a company that specializes in producing high-quality building blocks of all shapes and sizes (Figure 4-1).

Figure 4-1. The production line of a company making bricks of many different shapes and sizes (created with Midjourney)

You are immediately alerted to a problem with some of the items coming off the production line. A competitor has started to make counterfeit copies of Brickki bricks and has found a way to mix them into the bags received by your customers. You decide to become an expert at telling the difference between the counterfeit bricks and the real thing, so that you can intercept the forged bricks on the production line before they are given to customers. Over time, by listening to customer feedback, you gradually become more adept at spotting the fakes.

The forgers are not happy about this—they react to your improved detection abilities by making some changes to their forgery process so that now, the difference between the real bricks and the fakes is even harder for you to spot.

Not one to give up, you retrain yourself to identify the more sophisticated fakes and try to keep one step ahead of the forgers. This process continues, with the forgers iteratively updating their brick creation technologies while you try to become increasingly more accomplished at intercepting their fakes.

With every week that passes, it becomes more and more difficult to tell the difference between the real Brickki bricks and those created by the forgers. It seems that this simple game of cat and mouse is enough to drive significant improvement in both the quality of the forgery and the quality of the detection.

The story of Brickki bricks and the forgers describes the training process of a generative adversarial network.

A GAN is a battle between two adversaries, the *generator* and the *discriminator*. The generator tries to convert random noise into observations that look as if they have been sampled from the original dataset, and the discriminator tries to predict whether an observation comes from the original dataset or is one of the generator's forgeries. Examples of the inputs and outputs to the two networks are shown in Figure 4-2.

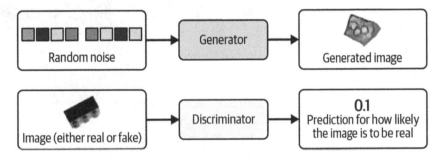

Figure 4-2. Inputs and outputs of the two networks in a GAN

At the start of the process, the generator outputs noisy images and the discriminator predicts randomly. The key to GANs lies in how we alternate the training of the two networks, so that as the generator becomes more adept at fooling the discriminator, the discriminator must adapt in order to maintain its ability to correctly identify which observations are fake. This drives the generator to find new ways to fool the discriminator, and so the cycle continues.

Deep Convolutional GAN (DCGAN)

To see this in action, let's start building our first GAN in Keras, to generate pictures of bricks.

We will be closely following one of the first major papers on GANs, "Unsupervised Representation Learning with Deep Convolutional Generative Adversarial

Networks."[2] In this 2015 paper, the authors show how to build a deep convolutional GAN to generate realistic images from a variety of datasets. They also introduce several changes that significantly improve the quality of the generated images.

Running the Code for This Example

The code for this example can be found in the Jupyter notebook located at *notebooks/04_gan/01_dcgan/dcgan.ipynb* in the book repository.

The Bricks Dataset

First, you'll need to download the training data. We'll be using the Images of LEGO Bricks dataset (*https://oreil.ly/3vp9f*) that is available through Kaggle. This is a computer-rendered collection of 40,000 photographic images of 50 different toy bricks, taken from multiple angles. Some example images of Brickki products are shown in Figure 4-3.

Figure 4-3. Examples of images from the Bricks dataset

You can download the dataset by running the Kaggle dataset downloader script in the book repository, as shown in Example 4-1. This will save the images and accompanying metadata locally to the */data* folder.

Example 4-1. Downloading the Bricks dataset

```
bash scripts/download_kaggle_data.sh joosthazelzet lego-brick-images
```

We use the Keras function `image_dataset_from_directory` to create a TensorFlow Dataset pointed at the directory where the images are stored, as shown in Example 4-2. This allows us to read batches of images into memory only when required (e.g., during training), so that we can work with large datasets and not worry about having to fit the entire dataset into memory. It also resizes the images to 64 × 64, interpolating between pixel values.

Example 4-2. Creating a TensorFlow Dataset from image files in a directory

```
train_data = utils.image_dataset_from_directory(
    "/app/data/lego-brick-images/dataset/",
    labels=None,
    color_mode="grayscale",
```

```
    image_size=(64, 64),
    batch_size=128,
    shuffle=True,
    seed=42,
    interpolation="bilinear",
)
```

The original data is scaled in the range [0, 255] to denote the pixel intensity. When training GANs we rescale the data to the range [−1, 1] so that we can use the tanh activation function on the final layer of the generator, which tends to provide stronger gradients than the sigmoid function (Example 4-3).

Example 4-3. Preprocessing the Bricks dataset

```
def preprocess(img):
    img = (tf.cast(img, "float32") - 127.5) / 127.5
    return img

train = train_data.map(lambda x: preprocess(x))
```

Let's now take a look at how we build the discriminator.

The Discriminator

The goal of the discriminator is to predict if an image is real or fake. This is a supervised image classification problem, so we can use a similar architecture to those we worked with in Chapter 2: stacked convolutional layers, with a single output node.

The full architecture of the discriminator we will be building is shown in Table 4-1.

Table 4-1. Model summary of the discriminator

Layer (type)	Output shape	Param #
InputLayer	(None, 64, 64, 1)	0
Conv2D	(None, 32, 32, 64)	1,024
LeakyReLU	(None, 32, 32, 64)	0
Dropout	(None, 32, 32, 64)	0
Conv2D	(None, 16, 16, 128)	131,072
BatchNormalization	(None, 16, 16, 128)	512
LeakyReLU	(None, 16, 16, 128)	0
Dropout	(None, 16, 16, 128)	0
Conv2D	(None, 8, 8, 256)	524,288
BatchNormalization	(None, 8, 8, 256)	1,024
LeakyReLU	(None, 8, 8, 256)	0
Dropout	(None, 8, 8, 256)	0

Layer (type)	Output shape	Param #
Conv2D	(None, 4, 4, 512)	2,097,152
BatchNormalization	(None, 4, 4, 512)	2,048
LeakyReLU	(None, 4, 4, 512)	0
Dropout	(None, 4, 4, 512)	0
Conv2D	(None, 1, 1, 1)	8,192
Flatten	(None, 1)	0

Total params	2,765,312
Trainable params	2,763,520
Non-trainable params	1,792

The Keras code to build the discriminator is provided in Example 4-4.

Example 4-4. The discriminator

```
discriminator_input = layers.Input(shape=(64, 64, 1)) ❶
x = layers.Conv2D(64, kernel_size=4, strides=2, padding="same", use_bias = False)(
    discriminator_input
) ❷
x = layers.LeakyReLU(0.2)(x)
x = layers.Dropout(0.3)(x)
x = layers.Conv2D(
    128, kernel_size=4, strides=2, padding="same", use_bias = False
)(x)
x = layers.BatchNormalization(momentum = 0.9)(x)
x = layers.LeakyReLU(0.2)(x)
x = layers.Dropout(0.3)(x)
x = layers.Conv2D(
    256, kernel_size=4, strides=2, padding="same", use_bias = False
)(x)
x = layers.BatchNormalization(momentum = 0.9)(x)
x = layers.LeakyReLU(0.2)(x)
x = layers.Dropout(0.3)(x)
x = layers.Conv2D(
    512, kernel_size=4, strides=2, padding="same", use_bias = False
)(x)
x = layers.BatchNormalization(momentum = 0.9)(x)
x = layers.LeakyReLU(0.2)(x)
x = layers.Dropout(0.3)(x)
x = layers.Conv2D(
    1,
    kernel_size=4,
    strides=1,
    padding="valid",
    use_bias = False,
    activation = 'sigmoid'
```

```
)(x)
discriminator_output = layers.Flatten()(x)  ❸

discriminator = models.Model(discriminator_input, discriminator_output)  ❹
```

❶ Define the `Input` layer of the discriminator (the image).

❷ Stack `Conv2D` layers on top of each other, with `BatchNormalization`, `LeakyReLU` activation, and `Dropout` layers sandwiched in between.

❸ Flatten the last convolutional layer—by this point, the shape of the tensor is $1 \times 1 \times 1$, so there is no need for a final `Dense` layer.

❹ The Keras model that defines the discriminator—a model that takes an input image and outputs a single number between 0 and 1.

Notice how we use a stride of 2 in some of the `Conv2D` layers to reduce the spatial shape of the tensor as it passes through the network (64 in the original image, then 32, 16, 8, 4, and finally 1), while increasing the number of channels (1 in the grayscale input image, then 64, 128, 256, and finally 512), before collapsing to a single prediction.

We use a sigmoid activation on the final `Conv2D` layer to output a number between 0 and 1.

The Generator

Now let's build the generator. The input to the generator will be a vector drawn from a multivariate standard normal distribution. The output is an image of the same size as an image in the original training data.

This description may remind you of the decoder in a variational autoencoder. In fact, the generator of a GAN fulfills exactly the same purpose as the decoder of a VAE: converting a vector in the latent space to an image. The concept of mapping from a latent space back to the original domain is very common in generative modeling, as it gives us the ability to manipulate vectors in the latent space to change high-level features of images in the original domain.

The architecture of the generator we will be building is shown in Table 4-2.

Table 4-2. Model summary of the generator

Layer (type)	Output shape	Param #
InputLayer	(None, 100)	0
Reshape	(None, 1, 1, 100)	0
Conv2DTranspose	(None, 4, 4, 512)	819,200

Layer (type)	Output shape	Param #
BatchNormalization	(None, 4, 4, 512)	2,048
ReLU	(None, 4, 4, 512)	0
Conv2DTranspose	(None, 8, 8, 256)	2,097,152
BatchNormalization	(None, 8, 8, 256)	1,024
ReLU	(None, 8, 8, 256)	0
Conv2DTranspose	(None, 16, 16, 128)	524,288
BatchNormalization	(None, 16, 16, 128)	512
ReLU	(None, 16, 16, 128)	0
Conv2DTranspose	(None, 32, 32, 64)	131,072
BatchNormalization	(None, 32, 32, 64)	256
ReLU	(None, 32, 32, 64)	0
Conv2DTranspose	(None, 64, 64, 1)	1,024

Total params	3,576,576
Trainable params	3,574,656
Non-trainable params	1,920

The code for building the generator is given in Example 4-5.

Example 4-5. The generator

```
generator_input = layers.Input(shape=(100,)) ❶
x = layers.Reshape((1, 1, 100))(generator_input) ❷
x = layers.Conv2DTranspose(
    512, kernel_size=4, strides=1, padding="valid", use_bias = False
)(x) ❸
x = layers.BatchNormalization(momentum=0.9)(x)
x = layers.LeakyReLU(0.2)(x)
x = layers.Conv2DTranspose(
    256, kernel_size=4, strides=2, padding="same", use_bias = False
)(x)
x = layers.BatchNormalization(momentum=0.9)(x)
x = layers.LeakyReLU(0.2)(x)
x = layers.Conv2DTranspose(
    128, kernel_size=4, strides=2, padding="same", use_bias = False
)(x)
x = layers.BatchNormalization(momentum=0.9)(x)
x = layers.LeakyReLU(0.2)(x)
x = layers.Conv2DTranspose(
    64, kernel_size=4, strides=2, padding="same", use_bias = False
)(x)
x = layers.BatchNormalization(momentum=0.9)(x)
x = layers.LeakyReLU(0.2)(x)
generator_output = layers.Conv2DTranspose(
```

```
    1,
    kernel_size=4,
    strides=2,
    padding="same",
    use_bias = False,
    activation = 'tanh'
)(x) ❹
generator = models.Model(generator_input, generator_output) ❺
```

❶ Define the `Input` layer of the generator—a vector of length 100.

❷ We use a `Reshape` layer to give a $1 \times 1 \times 100$ tensor, so that we can start applying convolutional transpose operations.

❸ We pass this through four `Conv2DTranspose` layers, with `BatchNormalization` and `LeakyReLU` layers sandwiched in between.

❹ The final `Conv2DTranspose` layer uses a tanh activation function to transform the output to the range $[-1, 1]$, to match the original image domain.

❺ The Keras model that defines the generator—a model that accepts a vector of length 100 and outputs a tensor of shape [`64, 64, 1`].

Notice how we use a stride of 2 in some of the `Conv2DTranspose` layers to increase the spatial shape of the tensor as it passes through the network (1 in the original vector, then 4, 8, 16, 32, and finally 64), while decreasing the number of channels (512 then 256, 128, 64, and finally 1 to match the grayscale output).

Upsampling Versus Conv2DTranspose

An alternative to using `Conv2DTranspose` layers is to instead use an `UpSampling2D` layer followed by a normal `Conv2D` layer with stride 1, as shown in Example 4-6.

Example 4-6. Upsampling example

```
x = layers.UpSampling2D(size = 2)(x)
x = layers.Conv2D(256, kernel_size=4, strides=1, padding="same")(x)
```

The `UpSampling2D` layer simply repeats each row and column of its input in order to double the size. The `Conv2D` layer with stride 1 then performs the convolution operation. It is a similar idea to convolutional transpose, but instead of filling the gaps between pixels with zeros, upsampling just repeats the existing pixel values.

It has been shown that the `Conv2DTranspose` method can lead to *artifacts*, or small checkerboard patterns in the output image (see Figure 4-4) that spoil the quality of the output. However, they are still used in many of the most impressive GANs in the

---

literature and have proven to be a powerful tool in the deep learning practitioner's toolbox.

Radford et al., 2015   Salimans et al., 2016   Donahue et al., 2019   Dumoulin et al., 2016

Figure 4-4. Artifacts when using convolutional transpose layers (source: Odena et al., 2016)[3]

Both of these methods—`UpSampling2D` + `Conv2D` and `Conv2DTranspose`—are acceptable ways to transform back to the original image domain. It really is a case of testing both methods in your own problem setting and seeing which produces better results.

Training the DCGAN

As we have seen, the architectures of the generator and discriminator in a DCGAN are very simple and not so different from the VAE models that we looked at in Chapter 3. The key to understanding GANs lies in understanding the training process for the generator and discriminator.

We can train the discriminator by creating a training set where some of the images are *real* observations from the training set and some are *fake* outputs from the generator. We then treat this as a supervised learning problem, where the labels are 1 for the real images and 0 for the fake images, with binary cross-entropy as the loss function.

How should we train the generator? We need to find a way of scoring each generated image so that it can optimize toward high-scoring images. Luckily, we have a discriminator that does exactly that! We can generate a batch of images and pass these through the discriminator to get a score for each image. The loss function for the generator is then simply the binary cross-entropy between these probabilities and a vector of ones, because we want to train the generator to produce images that the discriminator thinks are real.

Crucially, we must alternate the training of these two networks, making sure that we only update the weights of one network at a time. For example, during the generator training process, only the generator's weights are updated. If we allowed the discriminator's weights to change as well, the discriminator would just adjust so that it is more likely to predict the generated images to be real, which is not the desired outcome. We want generated images to be predicted close to 1 (real) because the generator is strong, not because the discriminator is weak.

A diagram of the training process for the discriminator and generator is shown in Figure 4-5.

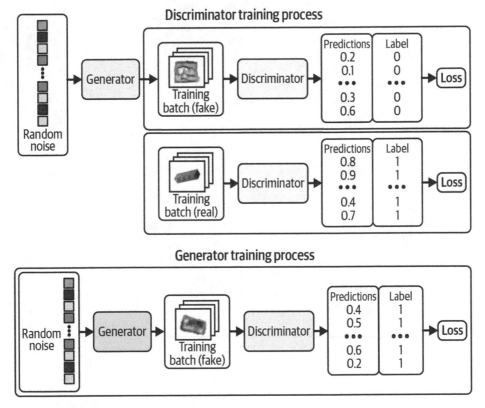

Figure 4-5. Training the DCGAN—gray boxes indicate that the weights are frozen during training

Keras provides us with the ability to create a custom `train_step` function to implement this logic. Example 4-7 shows the full DCGAN model class.

Example 4-7. Compiling the DCGAN

```python
class DCGAN(models.Model):
    def __init__(self, discriminator, generator, latent_dim):
        super(DCGAN, self).__init__()
        self.discriminator = discriminator
        self.generator = generator
        self.latent_dim = latent_dim

    def compile(self, d_optimizer, g_optimizer):
        super(DCGAN, self).compile()
        self.loss_fn = losses.BinaryCrossentropy()  ❶
        self.d_optimizer = d_optimizer
        self.g_optimizer = g_optimizer
        self.d_loss_metric = metrics.Mean(name="d_loss")
        self.g_loss_metric = metrics.Mean(name="g_loss")

    @property
    def metrics(self):
        return [self.d_loss_metric, self.g_loss_metric]

    def train_step(self, real_images):
        batch_size = tf.shape(real_images)[0]
        random_latent_vectors = tf.random.normal(
            shape=(batch_size, self.latent_dim)
        )  ❷

        with tf.GradientTape() as gen_tape, tf.GradientTape() as disc_tape:
            generated_images = self.generator(
                random_latent_vectors, training = True
            )  ❸
            real_predictions = self.discriminator(real_images, training = True)  ❹
            fake_predictions = self.discriminator(
                generated_images, training = True
            )  ❺

            real_labels = tf.ones_like(real_predictions)
            real_noisy_labels = real_labels + 0.1 * tf.random.uniform(
                tf.shape(real_predictions)
            )
            fake_labels = tf.zeros_like(fake_predictions)
            fake_noisy_labels = fake_labels - 0.1 * tf.random.uniform(
                tf.shape(fake_predictions)
            )

            d_real_loss = self.loss_fn(real_noisy_labels, real_predictions)
            d_fake_loss = self.loss_fn(fake_noisy_labels, fake_predictions)
            d_loss = (d_real_loss + d_fake_loss) / 2.0  ❻

            g_loss = self.loss_fn(real_labels, fake_predictions)  ❼

        gradients_of_discriminator = disc_tape.gradient(
```

```
        d_loss, self.discriminator.trainable_variables
    )
    gradients_of_generator = gen_tape.gradient(
        g_loss, self.generator.trainable_variables
    )

    self.d_optimizer.apply_gradients(
        zip(gradients_of_discriminator, discriminator.trainable_variables)
    ) ❽
    self.g_optimizer.apply_gradients(
        zip(gradients_of_generator, generator.trainable_variables)
    )

    self.d_loss_metric.update_state(d_loss)
    self.g_loss_metric.update_state(g_loss)

    return {m.name: m.result() for m in self.metrics}
dcgan = DCGAN(
    discriminator=discriminator, generator=generator, latent_dim=100
)

dcgan.compile(
    d_optimizer=optimizers.Adam(
        learning_rate=0.0002, beta_1 = 0.5, beta_2 = 0.999
    ),
    g_optimizer=optimizers.Adam(
        learning_rate=0.0002, beta_1 = 0.5, beta_2 = 0.999
    ),
)

dcgan.fit(train, epochs=300)
```

❶ The loss function for the generator and discriminator is `BinaryCrossentropy`.

❷ To train the network, first sample a batch of vectors from a multivariate standard normal distribution.

❸ Next, pass these through the generator to produce a batch of generated images.

❹ Now ask the discriminator to predict the realness of the batch of real images…

❺ …and the batch of generated images.

❻ The discriminator loss is the average binary cross-entropy across both the real images (with label 1) and the fake images (with label 0).

❼ The generator loss is the binary cross-entropy between the discriminator predictions for the generated images and a label of 1.

❽ Update the weights of the discriminator and generator separately.

The discriminator and generator are constantly fighting for dominance, which can make the DCGAN training process unstable. Ideally, the training process will find an equilibrium that allows the generator to learn meaningful information from the discriminator and the quality of the images will start to improve. After enough epochs, the discriminator tends to end up dominating, as shown in Figure 4-6, but this may not be a problem as the generator may have already learned to produce sufficiently high-quality images by this point.

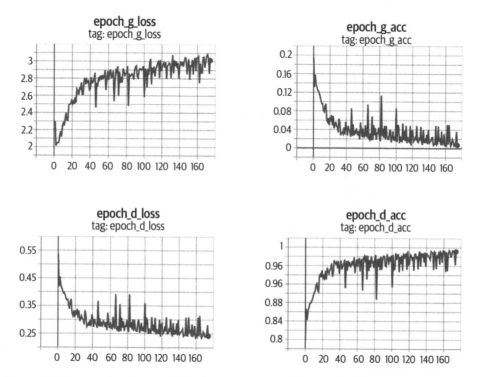

Figure 4-6. Loss and accuracy of the discriminator and generator during training

Adding Noise to the Labels

A useful trick when training GANs is to add a small amount of random noise to the training labels. This helps to improve the stability of the training process and sharpen the generated images. This *label smoothing* acts as way to tame the discriminator, so that it is presented with a more challenging task and doesn't overpower the generator.

Analysis of the DCGAN

By observing images produced by the generator at specific epochs during training (Figure 4-7), it is clear that the generator is becoming increasingly adept at producing images that could have been drawn from the training set.

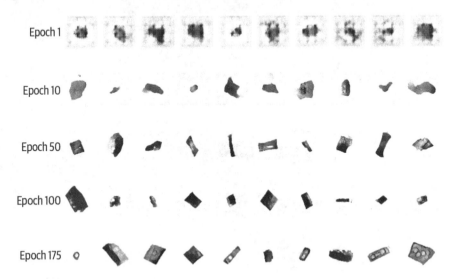

Figure 4-7. Output from the generator at specific epochs during training

It is somewhat miraculous that a neural network is able to convert random noise into something meaningful. It is worth remembering that we haven't provided the model with any additional features beyond the raw pixels, so it has to work out high-level concepts such as how to draw shadows, cuboids, and circles entirely by itself.

Another requirement of a successful generative model is that it doesn't only reproduce images from the training set. To test this, we can find the image from the training set that is closest to a particular generated example. A good measure for distance is the *L1 distance*, defined as:

```
def compare_images(img1, img2):
    return np.mean(np.abs(img1 - img2))
```

Figure 4-8 shows the closest observations in the training set for a selection of generated images. We can see that while there is some degree of similarity between the generated images and the training set, they are not identical. This shows that the generator has understood these high-level features and can generate examples that are distinct from those it has already seen.

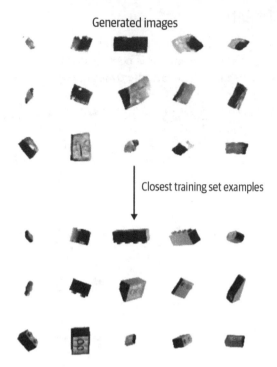

Figure 4-8. Closest matches of generated images from the training set

GAN Training: Tips and Tricks

While GANs are a major breakthrough for generative modeling, they are also notoriously difficult to train. We will explore some of the most common problems and challenges encountered when training GANs in this section, alongside potential solutions. In the next section, we will look at some more fundamental adjustments to the GAN framework that we can make to remedy many of these problems.

Discriminator overpowers the generator

If the discriminator becomes too strong, the signal from the loss function becomes too weak to drive any meaningful improvements in the generator. In the worst-case scenario, the discriminator perfectly learns to separate real images from fake images and the gradients vanish completely, leading to no training whatsoever, as can be seen in Figure 4-9.

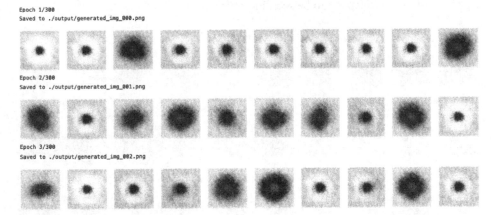

Figure 4-9. Example output when the discriminator overpowers the generator

If you find your discriminator loss function collapsing, you need to find ways to weaken the discriminator. Try the following suggestions:

- Increase the `rate` parameter of the `Dropout` layers in the discriminator to dampen the amount of information that flows through the network.
- Reduce the learning rate of the discriminator.
- Reduce the number of convolutional filters in the discriminator.
- Add noise to the labels when training the discriminator.
- Flip the labels of some images at random when training the discriminator.

Generator overpowers the discriminator

If the discriminator is not powerful enough, the generator will find ways to easily trick the discriminator with a small sample of nearly identical images. This is known as *mode collapse*.

For example, suppose we were to train the generator over several batches without updating the discriminator in between. The generator would be inclined to find a single observation (also known as a *mode*) that always fools the discriminator and would start to map every point in the latent input space to this image. Moreover, the gradients of the loss function would collapse to near 0, so it wouldn't be able to recover from this state.

Even if we then tried to retrain the discriminator to stop it being fooled by this one point, the generator would simply find another mode that fools the discriminator, since it has already become numb to its input and therefore has no incentive to diversify its output.

The effect of mode collapse can be seen in Figure 4-10.

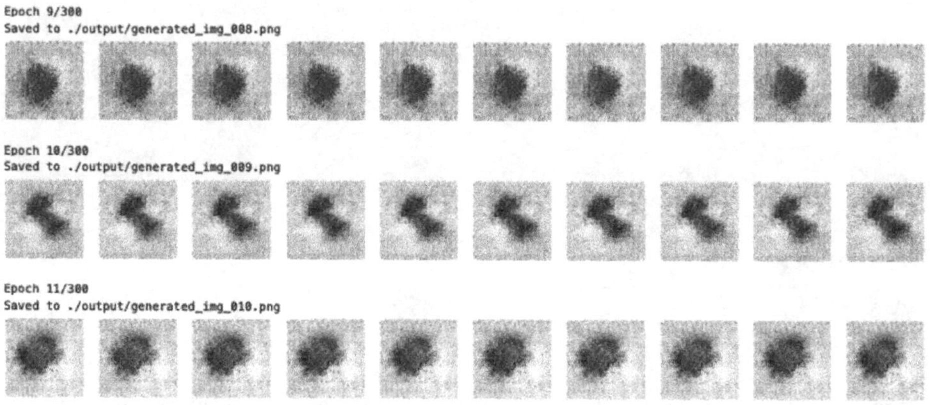

Figure 4-10. Example of mode collapse when the generator overpowers the discriminator

If you find that your generator is suffering from mode collapse, you can try strengthening the discriminator using the opposite suggestions to those listed in the previous section. Also, you can try reducing the learning rate of both networks and increasing the batch size.

Uninformative loss

Since the deep learning model is compiled to minimize the loss function, it would be natural to think that the smaller the loss function of the generator, the better the quality of the images produced. However, since the generator is only graded against the current discriminator and the discriminator is constantly improving, we cannot compare the loss function evaluated at different points in the training process. Indeed, in Figure 4-6, the loss function of the generator actually increases over time, even though the quality of the images is clearly improving. This lack of correlation between the generator loss and image quality sometimes makes GAN training difficult to monitor.

Hyperparameters

As we have seen, even with simple GANs, there are a large number of hyperparameters to tune. As well as the overall architecture of both the discriminator and the generator, there are the parameters that govern batch normalization, dropout, learning rate, activation layers, convolutional filters, kernel size, striding, batch size, and latent space size to consider. GANs are highly sensitive to very slight changes in all of these parameters, and finding a set of parameters that works is often a case of educated trial and error, rather than following an established set of guidelines.

This is why it is important to understand the inner workings of the GAN and know how to interpret the loss function—so that you can identify sensible adjustments to the hyperparameters that might improve the stability of the model.

Tackling GAN challenges

In recent years, several key advancements have drastically improved the overall stability of GAN models and diminished the likelihood of some of the problems listed earlier, such as mode collapse.

In the remainder of this chapter we shall examine the Wasserstein GAN with Gradient Penalty (WGAN-GP), which makes several key adjustments to the GAN framework we have explored thus far to improve the stability and quality of the image generation process.

Wasserstein GAN with Gradient Penalty (WGAN-GP)

In this section we will build a WGAN-GP to generate faces from the CelebA dataset that we utilized in Chapter 3.

Running the Code for This Example

The code for this example can be found in the Jupyter notebook located at *notebooks/04_gan/02_wgan_gp/wgan_gp.ipynb* in the book repository.

The code has been adapted from the excellent WGAN-GP tutorial (*https://oreil.ly/dHYbC*) created by Aakash Kumar Nain, available on the Keras website.

The Wasserstein GAN (WGAN), introduced in a 2017 paper by Arjovsky et al.,[4] was one of the first big steps toward stabilizing GAN training. With a few changes, the authors were able to show how to train GANs that have the following two properties (quoted from the paper):

- A meaningful loss metric that correlates with the generator's convergence and sample quality
- Improved stability of the optimization process

Specifically, the paper introduces the *Wasserstein loss function* for both the discriminator and the generator. Using this loss function instead of binary cross-entropy results in a more stable convergence of the GAN.

In this section we'll define the Wasserstein loss function and then see what other changes we need to make to the model architecture and training process to incorporate our new loss function.

You can find the full model class in the Jupyter notebook located at *chapter05/wgan-gp/faces/train.ipynb* in the book repository.

Wasserstein Loss

Let's first remind ourselves of the definition of binary cross-entropy loss—the function that we are currently using to train the discriminator and generator of the GAN (Equation 4-1).

Equation 4-1. Binary cross-entropy loss

$$-\frac{1}{n}\sum_{i=1}^{n}\left(y_i \log\left(p_i\right) + \left(1 - y_i\right)\log\left(1 - p_i\right)\right)$$

To train the GAN discriminator D, we calculate the loss when comparing predictions for real images $p_i = D(x_i)$ to the response $y_i = 1$ and predictions for generated images $p_i = D(G(z_i))$ to the response $y_i = 0$. Therefore, for the GAN discriminator, minimizing the loss function can be written as shown in Equation 4-2.

Equation 4-2. GAN discriminator loss minimization

$$\min_{D} -\left(\mathbb{E}_{x \sim p_X}[\log D(x)] + \mathbb{E}_{z \sim p_Z}[\log (1 - D(G(z)))]\right)$$

To train the GAN generator G, we calculate the loss when comparing predictions for generated images $p_i = D(G(z_i))$ to the response $y_i = 1$. Therefore, for the GAN generator, minimizing the loss function can be written as shown in Equation 4-3.

Equation 4-3. GAN generator loss minimization

$$\min_{G} -\left(\mathbb{E}_{z \sim p_Z}[\log D(G(z))]\right)$$

Now let's compare this to the Wasserstein loss function.

First, the Wasserstein loss requires that we use $y_i = 1$ and $y_i = -1$ as labels, rather than 1 and 0. We also remove the sigmoid activation from the final layer of the discriminator, so that predictions p_i are no longer constrained to fall in the range [0, 1] but instead can now be any number in the range $(-\infty, \infty)$. For this reason, the discriminator in a WGAN is usually referred to as a *critic* that outputs a *score* rather than a probability.

The Wasserstein loss function is defined as follows:

$$-\frac{1}{n}\sum_{i=1}^{n}(y_i p_i)$$

To train the WGAN critic D, we calculate the loss when comparing predictions for real images $p_i = D(x_i)$ to the response $y_i = 1$ and predictions for generated images $p_i = D(G(z_i))$ to the response $y_i = -1$. Therefore, for the WGAN critic, minimizing the loss function can be written as follows:

$$\min_{D} -\left(\mathbb{E}_{x \sim p_X}[D(x)] - \mathbb{E}_{z \sim p_Z}[D(G(z))]\right)$$

In other words, the WGAN critic tries to maximize the difference between its predictions for real images and generated images.

To train the WGAN generator, we calculate the loss when comparing predictions for generated images $p_i = D(G(z_i))$ to the response $y_i = 1$. Therefore, for the WGAN generator, minimizing the loss function can be written as follows:

$$\min_{G} -\left(\mathbb{E}_{z \sim p_Z}[D(G(z))]\right)$$

In other words, the WGAN generator tries to produce images that are scored as highly as possible by the critic (i.e., the critic is fooled into thinking they are real).

The Lipschitz Constraint

It may surprise you that we are now allowing the critic to output any number in the range $(-\infty, \infty)$, rather than applying a sigmoid function to restrict the output to the usual [0, 1] range. The Wasserstein loss can therefore be very large, which is unsettling—usually, large numbers in neural networks are to be avoided!

In fact, the authors of the WGAN paper show that for the Wasserstein loss function to work, we also need to place an additional constraint on the critic. Specifically, it is required that the critic is a *1-Lipschitz continuous function*. Let's pick this apart to understand what it means in more detail.

The critic is a function D that converts an image into a prediction. We say that this function is 1-Lipschitz if it satisfies the following inequality for any two input images, x_1 and x_2:

$$\frac{\left|D(x_1) - D(x_2)\right|}{\left|x_1 - x_2\right|} \leq 1$$

Here, $\left|x_1 - x_2\right|$ is the average pixelwise absolute difference between two images and $\left|D(x_1) - D(x_2)\right|$ is the absolute difference between the critic predictions. Essentially, we require a limit on the rate at which the predictions of the critic can change between two images (i.e., the absolute value of the gradient must be at most 1 everywhere). We can see this applied to a Lipschitz continuous 1D function in Figure 4-11 —at no point does the line enter the cone, wherever you place the cone on the line. In other words, there is a limit on the rate at which the line can rise or fall at any point.

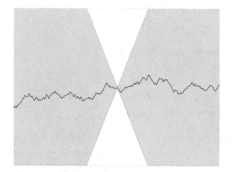

Figure 4-11. A Lipschitz continuous function (source: Wikipedia (https://oreil.ly/Ki7ds))

For those who want to delve deeper into the mathematical rationale behind why the Wasserstein loss only works when this constraint is enforced, Jonathan Hui offers an excellent explanation (*https://oreil.ly/devy5*).

Enforcing the Lipschitz Constraint

In the original WGAN paper, the authors show how it is possible to enforce the Lipschitz constraint by clipping the weights of the critic to lie within a small range, [−0.01, 0.01], after each training batch.

One of the criticisms of this approach is that the capacity of the critic to learn is greatly diminished, since we are clipping its weights. In fact, even in the original WGAN paper the authors write, "Weight clipping is a clearly terrible way to enforce a Lipschitz constraint." A strong critic is pivotal to the success of a WGAN, since without accurate gradients, the generator cannot learn how to adapt its weights to produce better samples.

Therefore, other researchers have looked for alternative ways to enforce the Lipschitz constraint and improve the capacity of the WGAN to learn complex features. One such method is the Wasserstein GAN with Gradient Penalty.

In the paper introducing this variant,[5] the authors show how the Lipschitz constraint can be enforced directly by including a *gradient penalty* term in the loss function for the critic that penalizes the model if the gradient norm deviates from 1. This results in a far more stable training process.

In the next section, we'll see how to build this extra term into the loss function for our critic.

The Gradient Penalty Loss

Figure 4-12 is a diagram of the training process for the critic of a WGAN-GP. If we compare this to the original discriminator training process from Figure 4-5, we can see that the key addition is the gradient penalty loss included as part of the overall loss function, alongside the Wasserstein loss from the real and fake images.

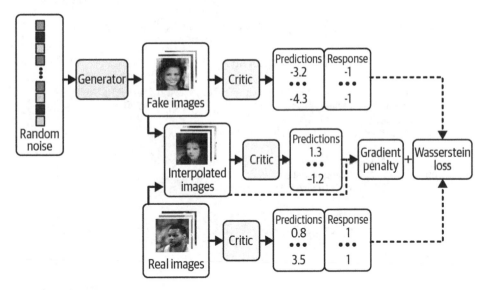

Figure 4-12. The WGAN-GP critic training process

The gradient penalty loss measures the squared difference between the norm of the gradient of the predictions with respect to the input images and 1. The model will naturally be inclined to find weights that ensure the gradient penalty term is minimized, thereby encouraging the model to conform to the Lipschitz constraint.

It is intractable to calculate this gradient everywhere during the training process, so instead the WGAN-GP evaluates the gradient at only a handful of points. To ensure a balanced mix, we use a set of interpolated images that lie at randomly chosen points along lines connecting the batch of real images to the batch of fake images pairwise, as shown in Figure 4-13.

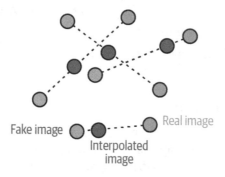

Figure 4-13. Interpolating between images

In Example 4-8, we show how the gradient penalty is calculated in code.

Example 4-8. The gradient penalty loss function

```
def gradient_penalty(self, batch_size, real_images, fake_images):
    alpha = tf.random.normal([batch_size, 1, 1, 1], 0.0, 1.0) ❶
    diff = fake_images - real_images
    interpolated = real_images + alpha * diff ❷

    with tf.GradientTape() as gp_tape:
        gp_tape.watch(interpolated)
        pred = self.critic(interpolated, training=True) ❸

    grads = gp_tape.gradient(pred, [interpolated])[0] ❹
    norm = tf.sqrt(tf.reduce_sum(tf.square(grads), axis=[1, 2, 3])) ❺
    gp = tf.reduce_mean((norm - 1.0) ** 2) ❻
    return gp
```

❶ Each image in the batch gets a random number, between 0 and 1, stored as the vector `alpha`.

❷ A set of interpolated images is calculated.

❸ The critic is asked to score each of these interpolated images.

❹ The gradient of the predictions is calculated with respect to the input images.

⑤ The L2 norm of this vector is calculated.

⑥ The function returns the average squared distance between the L2 norm and 1.

Training the WGAN-GP

A key benefit of using the Wasserstein loss function is that we no longer need to worry about balancing the training of the critic and the generator—in fact, when using the Wasserstein loss, the critic must be trained to convergence before updating the generator, to ensure that the gradients for the generator update are accurate. This is in contrast to a standard GAN, where it is important not to let the discriminator get too strong.

Therefore, with Wasserstein GANs, we can simply train the critic several times between generator updates, to ensure it is close to convergence. A typical ratio used is three to five critic updates per generator update.

We have now introduced both of the key concepts behind the WGAN-GP—the Wasserstein loss and the gradient penalty term that is included in the critic loss function. The training step of the WGAN model that incorporates all of these ideas is shown in Example 4-9.

Example 4-9. Training the WGAN-GP

```
def train_step(self, real_images):
    batch_size = tf.shape(real_images)[0]

    for i in range(3): ❶
        random_latent_vectors = tf.random.normal(
            shape=(batch_size, self.latent_dim)
        )

        with tf.GradientTape() as tape:
            fake_images = self.generator(
                random_latent_vectors, training = True
            )
            fake_predictions = self.critic(fake_images, training = True)
            real_predictions = self.critic(real_images, training = True)

            c_wass_loss = tf.reduce_mean(fake_predictions) - tf.reduce_mean(
                real_predictions
            ) ❷
            c_gp = self.gradient_penalty(
                batch_size, real_images, fake_images
            ) ❸
            c_loss = c_wass_loss + c_gp * self.gp_weight ❹

        c_gradient = tape.gradient(c_loss, self.critic.trainable_variables)
```

```
        self.c_optimizer.apply_gradients(
            zip(c_gradient, self.critic.trainable_variables)
        ) ❺

    random_latent_vectors = tf.random.normal(
        shape=(batch_size, self.latent_dim)
    )
    with tf.GradientTape() as tape:
        fake_images = self.generator(random_latent_vectors, training=True)
        fake_predictions = self.critic(fake_images, training=True)
        g_loss = -tf.reduce_mean(fake_predictions) ❻

    gen_gradient = tape.gradient(g_loss, self.generator.trainable_variables)
    self.g_optimizer.apply_gradients(
        zip(gen_gradient, self.generator.trainable_variables)
    ) ❼

    self.c_loss_metric.update_state(c_loss)
    self.c_wass_loss_metric.update_state(c_wass_loss)
    self.c_gp_metric.update_state(c_gp)
    self.g_loss_metric.update_state(g_loss)

    return {m.name: m.result() for m in self.metrics}
```

❶ Perform three critic updates.

❷ Calculate the Wasserstein loss for the critic—the difference between the average prediction for the fake images and the real images.

❸ Calculate the gradient penalty term (see Example 4-8).

❹ The critic loss function is a weighted sum of the Wasserstein loss and the gradient penalty.

❺ Update the weights of the critic.

❻ Calculate the Wasserstein loss for the generator.

❼ Update the weights of the generator.

Batch Normalization in a WGAN-GP

One last consideration we should note before training a WGAN-GP is that batch normalization shouldn't be used in the critic. This is because batch normalization creates correlation between images in the same batch, which makes the gradient penalty loss less effective. Experiments have shown that WGAN-GPs can still produce excellent results even without batch normalization in the critic.

We have now covered all of the key differences between a standard GAN and a WGAN-GP. To recap:

- A WGAN-GP uses the Wasserstein loss.
- The WGAN-GP is trained using labels of 1 for real and −1 for fake.
- There is no sigmoid activation in the final layer of the critic.
- Include a gradient penalty term in the loss function for the critic.
- Train the critic multiple times for each update of the generator.
- There are no batch normalization layers in the critic.

Analysis of the WGAN-GP

Let's take a look at some example outputs from the generator, after 25 epochs of training (Figure 4-14).

Figure 4-14. WGAN-GP face examples

The model has learned the significant high-level attributes of a face, and there is no sign of mode collapse.

We can also see how the loss functions of the model evolve over time (Figure 4-15)— the loss functions of both the critic and generator are highly stable and convergent.

If we compare the WGAN-GP output to the VAE output from the previous chapter, we can see that the GAN images are generally sharper—especially the definition between the hair and the background. This is true in general; VAEs tend to produce softer images that blur color boundaries, whereas GANs are known to produce sharper, more well-defined images.

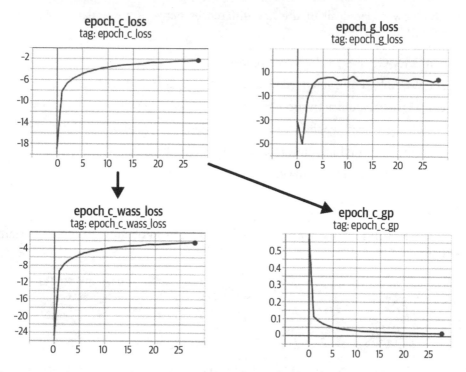

Figure 4-15. WGAN-GP loss curves: the critic loss (`epoch_c_loss`) is broken down into the Wasserstein loss (`epoch_c_wass`) and the gradient penalty loss (`epoch_c_gp`)

It is also true that GANs are generally more difficult to train than VAEs and take longer to reach a satisfactory quality. However, many state-of-the-art generative models today are GAN-based, as the rewards for training large-scale GANs on GPUs over a longer period of time are significant.

Conditional GAN (CGAN)

So far in this chapter, we have built GANs that are able to generate realistic images from a given training set. However, we haven't been able to control the type of image we would like to generate—for example, a male or female face, or a large or small brick. We can sample a random point from the latent space, but we do not have the ability to easily understand what kind of image will be produced given the choice of latent variable.

In the final part of this chapter we shall turn our attention to building a GAN where we are able to control the output—a so called *conditional GAN*. This idea, first introduced in "Conditional Generative Adversarial Nets" by Mirza and Osindero in 2014,[6] is a relatively simple extension to the GAN architecture.

Running the Code for This Example

The code for this example can be found in the Jupyter notebook located at *notebooks/04_gan/03_cgan/cgan.ipynb* in the book repository.

The code has been adapted from the excellent CGAN tutorial (*https://oreil.ly/Ey1lI*) created by Sayak Paul, available on the Keras website.

CGAN Architecture

In this example, we will condition our CGAN on the *blond hair* attribute of the faces dataset. That is, we will be able to explicitly specify whether we want to generate an image with blond hair or not. This label is provided as part of the CelebA dataset.

The high-level CGAN architecture is shown in Figure 4-16.

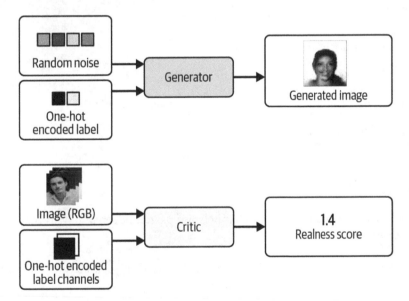

Figure 4-16. Inputs and outputs of the generator and critic in a CGAN

The key difference between a standard GAN and a CGAN is that in a CGAN we pass in extra information to the generator and critic relating to the label. In the generator, this is simply appended to the latent space sample as a one-hot encoded vector. In the critic, we add the label information as extra channels to the RGB image. We do this by repeating the one-hot encoded vector to fill the same shape as the input images.

CGANs work because the critic now has access to extra information regarding the content of the image, so the generator must ensure that its output agrees with the provided label, in order to keep fooling the critic. If the generator produced perfect images that disagreed with the image label the critic would be able to tell that they were fake simply because the images and labels did not match.

 In our example, our one-hot encoded label will have length 2, because there are two classes (Blonde and Not Blond). However, you can have as many labels as you like—for example, you could train a CGAN on the Fashion-MNIST dataset to output one of the 10 different fashion items, by incorporating a one-hot encoded label vector of length 10 into the input of the generator and 10 additional one-hot encoded label channels into the input of the critic.

The only change we need to make to the architecture is to concatenate the label information to the existing inputs of the generator and the critic, as shown in Example 4-10.

Example 4-10. Input layers in the CGAN

```
critic_input = layers.Input(shape=(64, 64, 3)) ❶
label_input = layers.Input(shape=(64, 64, 2))
x = layers.Concatenate(axis = -1)([critic_input, label_input])
...
generator_input = layers.Input(shape=(32,)) ❷
label_input = layers.Input(shape=(2,))
x = layers.Concatenate(axis = -1)([generator_input, label_input])
x = layers.Reshape((1,1, 34))(x)
...
```

❶ The image channels and label channels are passed in separately to the critic and concatenated.

❷ The latent vector and the label classes are passed in separately to the generator and concatenated before being reshaped.

Training the CGAN

We must also make some changes to the `train_step` of the CGAN to match the new input formats of the generator and critic, as shown in Example 4-11.

Example 4-11. The `train_step` of the CGAN

```
def train_step(self, data):
    real_images, one_hot_labels = data ❶
```

```
image_one_hot_labels = one_hot_labels[:, None, None, :]  ❷
image_one_hot_labels = tf.repeat(
    image_one_hot_labels, repeats=64, axis = 1
)
image_one_hot_labels = tf.repeat(
    image_one_hot_labels, repeats=64, axis = 2
)

batch_size = tf.shape(real_images)[0]

for i in range(self.critic_steps):
    random_latent_vectors = tf.random.normal(
        shape=(batch_size, self.latent_dim)
    )

    with tf.GradientTape() as tape:
        fake_images = self.generator(
            [random_latent_vectors, one_hot_labels], training = True
        )  ❸

        fake_predictions = self.critic(
            [fake_images, image_one_hot_labels], training = True
        )  ❹
        real_predictions = self.critic(
            [real_images, image_one_hot_labels], training = True
        )

        c_wass_loss = tf.reduce_mean(fake_predictions) - tf.reduce_mean(
            real_predictions
        )
        c_gp = self.gradient_penalty(
            batch_size, real_images, fake_images, image_one_hot_labels
        )  ❺
        c_loss = c_wass_loss + c_gp * self.gp_weight

    c_gradient = tape.gradient(c_loss, self.critic.trainable_variables)
    self.c_optimizer.apply_gradients(
        zip(c_gradient, self.critic.trainable_variables)
    )

random_latent_vectors = tf.random.normal(
    shape=(batch_size, self.latent_dim)
)

with tf.GradientTape() as tape:
    fake_images = self.generator(
        [random_latent_vectors, one_hot_labels], training=True
    )  ❻
    fake_predictions = self.critic(
        [fake_images, image_one_hot_labels], training=True
    )
    g_loss = -tf.reduce_mean(fake_predictions)
```

```
gen_gradient = tape.gradient(g_loss, self.generator.trainable_variables)
self.g_optimizer.apply_gradients(
    zip(gen_gradient, self.generator.trainable_variables)
)
```

❶ The images and labels are unpacked from the input data.

❷ The one-hot encoded vectors are expanded to one-hot encoded images that have
the same spatial size as the input images (64 × 64).

❸ The generator is now fed with a list of two inputs—the random latent vectors and
the one-hot encoded label vectors.

❹ The critic is now fed with a list of two inputs—the fake/real images and the one-
hot encoded label channels.

❺ The gradient penalty function also requires the one-hot encoded label channels
to be passed through as it uses the critic.

❻ The changes made to the critic training step also apply to the generator training
step.

Analysis of the CGAN

We can control the CGAN output by passing a particular one-hot encoded label into
the input of the generator. For example, to generate a face with nonblond hair, we
pass in the vector [1, 0]. To generate a face with blond hair, we pass in the vector
[0, 1].

The output from the CGAN can be seen in Figure 4-17. Here, we keep the random
latent vectors the same across the examples and change only the conditional label
vector. It is clear that the CGAN has learned to use the label vector to control only the
hair color attribute of the images. It is impressive that the rest of the image barely
changes—this is proof that GANs are able to organize points in the latent space in
such a way that individual features can be decoupled from each other.

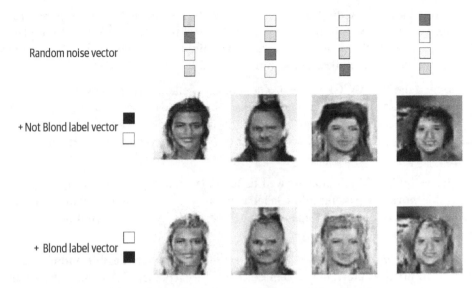

Figure 4-17. Output from the CGAN when the Blond and Not Blond vectors are appended to the latent sample

 If labels are available for your dataset, it is generally a good idea to include them as input to your GAN even if you do not necessarily need to condition the generated output on the label, as they tend to improve the quality of images generated. You can think of the labels as just a highly informative extension to the pixel input.

Summary

In this chapter we explored three different generative adversarial network (GAN) models: the deep convolutional GAN (DCGAN), the more sophisticated Wasserstein GAN with Gradient Penalty (WGAN-GP), and the conditional GAN (CGAN).

All GANs are characterized by a generator versus discriminator (or critic) architecture, with the discriminator trying to "spot the difference" between real and fake images and the generator aiming to fool the discriminator. By balancing how these two adversaries are trained, the GAN generator can gradually learn how to produce similar observations to those in the training set.

We first saw how to train a DCGAN to generate images of toy bricks. It was able to learn how to realistically represent 3D objects as images, including accurate representations of shadow, shape, and texture. We also explored the different ways in which GAN training can fail, including mode collapse and vanishing gradients.

We then explored how the Wasserstein loss function remedied many of these problems and made GAN training more predictable and reliable. The WGAN-GP places the 1-Lipschitz requirement at the heart of the training process by including a term in the loss function to pull the gradient norm toward 1.

We applied the WGAN-GP to the problem of face generation and saw how by simply choosing points from a standard normal distribution, we can generate new faces. This sampling process is very similar to a VAE, though the faces produced by a GAN are quite different—often sharper, with greater distinction between different parts of the image.

Finally, we built a CGAN that allowed us to control the type of image that is generated. This works by passing in the label as input to the critic and generator, thereby giving the network the additional information it needs in order to condition the generated output on a given label.

Overall, we have seen how the GAN framework is extremely flexible and able to be adapted to many interesting problem domains. In particular, GANs have driven significant progress in the field of image generation with many interesting extensions to the underlying framework, as we shall see in Chapter 10.

In the next chapter, we will explore a different family of generative model that is ideal for modeling sequential data—autoregressive models.

References

1. Ian J. Goodfellow et al., "Generative Adversarial Nets," June 10, 2014, *https://arxiv.org/abs/1406.2661*

2. Alec Radford et al., "Unsupervised Representation Learning with Deep Convolutional Generative Adversarial Networks," January 7, 2016, *https://arxiv.org/abs/1511.06434*.

3. Augustus Odena et al., "Deconvolution and Checkerboard Artifacts," October 17, 2016, *https://distill.pub/2016/deconv-checkerboard*.

4. Martin Arjovsky et al., "Wasserstein GAN," January 26, 2017, *https://arxiv.org/abs/1701.07875*.

5. Ishaan Gulrajani et al., "Improved Training of Wasserstein GANs," March 31, 2017, *https://arxiv.org/abs/1704.00028*.

6. Mehdi Mirza and Simon Osindero, "Conditional Generative Adversarial Nets," November 6, 2014, *https://arxiv.org/abs/1411.1784*.

CHAPTER 5

Autoregressive Models

Chapter Goals

In this chapter you will:

- Learn why autoregressive models are well suited to generating sequential data such as text.
- Learn how to process and tokenize text data.
- Learn about the architectural design of recurrent neural networks (RNNs).
- Build and train a long short-term memory network (LSTM) from scratch using Keras.
- Use the LSTM to generate new text.
- Learn about other variations of RNNs, including gated recurrent units (GRUs) and bidirectional cells.
- Understand how image data can be treated as a sequence of pixels.
- Learn about the architectural design of a PixelCNN.
- Build a PixelCNN from scratch using Keras.
- Use the PixelCNN to generate images.

So far, we have explored two different families of generative models that have both involved latent variables—variational autoencoders (VAEs) and generative adversarial networks (GANs). In both cases, a new variable is introduced with a distribution that is easy to sample from and the model learns how to *decode* this variable back into the original domain.

We will now turn our attention to *autoregressive models*—a family of models that simplify the generative modeling problem by treating it as a sequential process. Autoregressive models condition predictions on previous values in the sequence, rather than on a latent random variable. Therefore, they attempt to explicitly model the data-generating distribution rather than an approximation of it (as in the case of VAEs).

In this chapter we shall explore two different autoregressive models: long short-term memory networks and PixelCNN. We will apply the LSTM to text data and the PixelCNN to image data. We will cover another highly successful autoregressive model, the Transformer, in detail in Chapter 9.

Introduction

To understand how an LSTM works, we will first pay a visit to a strange prison, where the inmates have formed a literary society…

The Literary Society for Troublesome Miscreants

Edward Sopp hated his job as a prison warden. He spent his days watching over the prisoners and had no time to follow his true passion of writing short stories. He was running low on inspiration and needed to find a way to generate new content.

One day, he came up with a brilliant idea that would allow him to produce new works of fiction in his style, while also keeping the inmates occupied—he would get the inmates to collectively write the stories for him! He branded the new society the Literary Society for Troublesome Miscreants, or LSTM (Figure 5-1).

Figure 5-1. A large cell of prisoners reading books (created with Midjourney)

The prison is particularly strange because it only consists of one large cell, containing 256 prisoners. Each prisoner has an opinion on how Edward's current story should continue. Every day, Edward posts the latest word from his novel into the cell, and it is the job of the inmates to individually update their opinions on the current state of the story, based on the new word and the opinions of the inmates from the previous day.

Each prisoner uses a specific thought process to update their own opinion, which involves balancing information from the new incoming word and other prisoners' opinions with their own prior beliefs. First, they decide how much of yesterday's opinion they wish to forget, taking into account the information from the new word and the opinions of other prisoners in the cell. They also use this information to form new thoughts and decide to what extent they want to mix these into the old beliefs that they have chosen to carry forward from the previous day. This then forms the prisoner's new opinion for the day.

However, the prisoners are secretive and don't always tell their fellow inmates all of their opinions. They each also use the latest chosen word and the opinions of the other inmates to decide how much of their opinion they wish to disclose.

When Edward wants the cell to generate the next word in the sequence, the prisoners each tell their disclosable opinions to the guard at the door, who combines this information to ultimately decide on the next word to be appended to the end of the novel. This new word is then fed back into the cell, and the process continues until the full story is completed.

To train the inmates and the guard, Edward feeds short sequences of words that he has written previously into the cell and monitors whether the inmates' chosen next word is correct. He updates them on their accuracy, and gradually they begin to learn how to write stories in his own unique style.

After many iterations of this process, Edward finds that the system has become quite accomplished at generating realistic-looking text. Satisfied with the results, he publishes a collection of the generated tales in his new book, entitled *E. Sopp's Fables*.

The story of Mr. Sopp and his crowdsourced fables is an analogy for one of the most notorious autoregressive techniques for sequential data such as text: the long short-term memory network.

Long Short-Term Memory Network (LSTM)

An LSTM is a particular type of recurrent neural network (RNN). RNNs contain a recurrent layer (or *cell*) that is able to handle sequential data by making its own output at a particular timestep form part of the input to the next timestep.

When RNNs were first introduced, recurrent layers were very simple and consisted solely of a tanh operator that ensured that the information passed between timesteps was scaled between –1 and 1. However, this approach was shown to suffer from the vanishing gradient problem and didn't scale well to long sequences of data.

LSTM cells were first introduced in 1997 in a paper by Sepp Hochreiter and Jürgen Schmidhuber.[1] In the paper, the authors describe how LSTMs do not suffer from the same vanishing gradient problem experienced by vanilla RNNs and can be trained on sequences that are hundreds of timesteps long. Since then, the LSTM architecture has been adapted and improved, and variations such as gated recurrent units (discussed later in this chapter) are now widely utilized and available as layers in Keras.

LSTMs have been applied to a wide range of problems involving sequential data, including time series forecasting, sentiment analysis, and audio classification. In this chapter we will be using LSTMs to tackle the challenge of text generation.

Running the Code for This Example

The code for this example can be found in the Jupyter notebook located at *notebooks/05_autoregressive/01_lstm/lstm.ipynb* in the book repository.

The Recipes Dataset

We'll be using the Epicurious Recipes dataset (*https://oreil.ly/laNUt*) that is available through Kaggle. This is a set of over 20,000 recipes, with accompanying metadata such as nutritional information and ingredient lists.

You can download the dataset by running the Kaggle dataset downloader script in the book repository, as shown in Example 5-1. This will save the recipes and accompanying metadata locally to the */data* folder.

Example 5-1. Downloading the Epicurious Recipe dataset

```
bash scripts/download_kaggle_data.sh hugodarwood epirecipes
```

Example 5-2 shows how the data can be loaded and filtered so that only recipes with a title and a description remain. An example of a recipe text string is given in Example 5-3.

Example 5-2. Loading the data

```
with open('/app/data/epirecipes/full_format_recipes.json') as json_data:
    recipe_data = json.load(json_data)

filtered_data = [
```

```
'Recipe for ' + x['title']+ ' | ' + ' '.join(x['directions'])
for x in recipe_data
if 'title' in x
and x['title'] is not None
and 'directions' in x
and x['directions'] is not None
]
```

Example 5-3. A text string from the Recipes dataset

```
Recipe for Ham Persillade with Mustard Potato Salad and Mashed Peas  | Chop enough
parsley leaves to measure 1 tablespoon; reserve. Chop remaining leaves and stems
and simmer with broth and garlic in a small saucepan, covered, 5 minutes.
Meanwhile, sprinkle gelatin over water in a medium bowl and let soften 1 minute.
Strain broth through a fine-mesh sieve into bowl with gelatin and stir to dissolve.
Season with salt and pepper. Set bowl in an ice bath and cool to room temperature,
stirring. Toss ham with reserved parsley and divide among jars. Pour gelatin on top
and chill until set, at least 1 hour. Whisk together mayonnaise, mustard, vinegar,
1/4 teaspoon salt, and 1/4 teaspoon pepper in a large bowl. Stir in celery,
cornichons, and potatoes. Pulse peas with marjoram, oil, 1/2 teaspoon pepper, and
1/4 teaspoon salt in a food processor to a coarse mash. Layer peas, then potato
salad, over ham.
```

Before taking a look at how to build an LSTM network in Keras, we must first take a quick detour to understand the structure of text data and how it is different from the image data that we have seen so far in this book.

Working with Text Data

There are several key differences between text and image data that mean that many of the methods that work well for image data are not so readily applicable to text data. In particular:

- Text data is composed of discrete chunks (either characters or words), whereas pixels in an image are points in a continuous color spectrum. We can easily make a green pixel more blue, but it is not obvious how we should go about making the word *cat* more like the word *dog*, for example. This means we can easily apply backpropagation to image data, as we can calculate the gradient of our loss function with respect to individual pixels to establish the direction in which pixel colors should be changed to minimize the loss. With discrete text data, we can't obviously apply backpropagation in the same way, so we need to find a way around this problem.

- Text data has a time dimension but no spatial dimension, whereas image data has two spatial dimensions but no time dimension. The order of words is highly important in text data and words wouldn't make sense in reverse, whereas images can usually be flipped without affecting the content. Furthermore, there are often long-term sequential dependencies between words that need to be captured by the model: for example, the answer to a question or carrying forward the context of a pronoun. With image data, all pixels can be processed simultaneously.

- Text data is highly sensitive to small changes in the individual units (words or characters). Image data is generally less sensitive to changes in individual pixel units—a picture of a house would still be recognizable as a house even if some pixels were altered—but with text data, changing even a few words can drastically alter the meaning of the passage, or make it nonsensical. This makes it very difficult to train a model to generate coherent text, as every word is vital to the overall meaning of the passage.

- Text data has a rules-based grammatical structure, whereas image data doesn't follow set rules about how the pixel values should be assigned. For example, it wouldn't make grammatical sense in any context to write "The cat sat on the having." There are also semantic rules that are extremely difficult to model; it wouldn't make sense to say "I am in the beach," even though grammatically, there is nothing wrong with this statement.

Advances in Text-Based Generative Deep Learning

Until recently, most of the most sophisticated generative deep learning models have focused on image data, because many of the challenges presented in the preceding list were beyond the reach of even the most advanced techniques. However, in the last five years astonishing progress has been made in the field of text-based generative deep learning, thanks to the introduction of the Transformer model architecture, which we will explore in Chapter 9.

With these points in mind, let's now take a look at the steps we need to take in order to get the text data into the right shape to train an LSTM network.

Tokenization

The first step is to clean up and tokenize the text. *Tokenization* is the process of splitting the text up into individual units, such as words or characters.

How you tokenize your text will depend on what you are trying to achieve with your text generation model. There are pros and cons to using both word and character tokens, and your choice will affect how you need to clean the text prior to modeling and the output from your model.

If you use word tokens:

- All text can be converted to lowercase, to ensure capitalized words at the start of sentences are tokenized the same way as the same words appearing in the middle of a sentence. In some cases, however, this may not be desirable; for example, some proper nouns, such as names or places, may benefit from remaining capitalized so that they are tokenized independently.

- The text *vocabulary* (the set of distinct words in the training set) may be very large, with some words appearing very sparsely or perhaps only once. It may be wise to replace sparse words with a token for *unknown word*, rather than including them as separate tokens, to reduce the number of weights the neural network needs to learn.

- Words can be *stemmed*, meaning that they are reduced to their simplest form, so that different tenses of a verb remained tokenized together. For example, *browse, browsing, browses*, and *browsed* would all be stemmed to *brows*.

- You will need to either tokenize the punctuation, or remove it altogether.

- Using word tokenization means that the model will never be able to predict words outside of the training vocabulary.

If you use character tokens:

- The model may generate sequences of characters that form new words outside of the training vocabulary—this may be desirable in some contexts, but not in others.

- Capital letters can either be converted to their lowercase counterparts, or remain as separate tokens.

- The vocabulary is usually much smaller when using character tokenization. This is beneficial for model training speed as there are fewer weights to learn in the final output layer.

For this example, we'll use lowercase word tokenization, without word stemming. We'll also tokenize punctuation marks, as we would like the model to predict when it should end sentences or use commas, for example.

The code in Example 5-4 cleans and tokenizes the text.

Example 5-4. Tokenization

```
def pad_punctuation(s):
    s = re.sub(f"([{string.punctuation}])", r' \1 ', s)
    s = re.sub(' +', ' ', s)
    return s
```

```
text_data = [pad_punctuation(x) for x in filtered_data] ❶

text_ds = tf.data.Dataset.from_tensor_slices(text_data).batch(32).shuffle(1000) ❷

vectorize_layer = layers.TextVectorization( ❸
    standardize = 'lower',
    max_tokens = 10000,
    output_mode = "int",
    output_sequence_length = 200 + 1,
)

vectorize_layer.adapt(text_ds) ❹
vocab = vectorize_layer.get_vocabulary() ❺
```

❶ Pad the punctuation marks, to treat them as separate words.

❷ Convert to a TensorFlow Dataset.

❸ Create a Keras `TextVectorization` layer to convert text to lowercase, give the most prevalent 10,000 words a corresponding integer token, and trim or pad the sequence to 201 tokens long.

❹ Apply the `TextVectorization` layer to the training data.

❺ The `vocab` variable stores a list of the word tokens.

An example of a recipe after tokenization is shown in Example 5-5. The sequence length that we use to train the model is a parameter of the training process. In this example we choose to use a sequence length of 200, so we pad or clip the recipe to one more than this length, to allow us to create the target variable (more on this in the next section). To achieve this desired length, the end of the vector is padded with zeros.

Stop Tokens

The 0 token is known as a the *stop token*, signifying that the text string has come to an end.

Example 5-5. The recipe from Example 5-3 tokenized

```
[  26   16  557    1    8  298  335  189    4 1054  494   27  332  228
  235  262    5  594   11  133   22  311    2  332   45  262    4  671
    4   70    8  171    4   81    6    9   65   80    3  121    3   59
   12    2  299    3   88  650   20   39    6    9   29   21    4   67
  529   11  164    2  320  171  102    9  374   13  643  306   25   21
    8  650    4   42    5  931    2   63    8   24    4   33    2  114
   21    6  178  181 1245    4   60    5  140  112    3   48    2  117
```

```
557     8   285   235     4   200   292   980     2   107   650    28    72     4
108    10   114     3    57   204    11   172     2    73   110   482     3   298
  3   190     3    11    23    32   142    24     3     4    11    23    32   142
 33     6     9    30    21     2    42     6   353     3  3224     3     4   150
  2   437   494     8  1281     3    37     3    11    23    15   142    33     3
  4    11    23    32   142    24     6     9   291   188     5     9   412   572
  2   230   494     3    46   335   189     3    20   557     2     0     0     0
  0     0     0     0     0]
```

In Example 5-6, we can see a subset of the list of tokens mapped to their respective indices. The layer reserves the 0 token for padding (i.e., it is the stop token) and the 1 token for unknown words that fall outside the top 10,000 words (e.g., persillade). The other words are assigned tokens in order of frequency. The number of words to include in the vocabulary is also a parameter of the training process. The more words included, the fewer *unknown* tokens you will see in the text; however, your model will need to be larger to accommodate the larger vocabulary size.

Example 5-6. The vocabulary of the TextVectorization layer

```
0:
1: [UNK]
2: .
3: ,
4: and
5: to
6: in
7: the
8: with
9: a
```

Creating the Training Set

Our LSTM will be trained to predict the next word in a sequence, given a sequence of words preceding this point. For example, we could feed the model the tokens for *grilled chicken with boiled* and would expect the model to output a suitable next word (e.g., *potatoes*, rather than *bananas*).

We can therefore simply shift the entire sequence by one token in order to create our target variable.

The dataset generation step can be achieved with the code in Example 5-7.

Example 5-7. Creating the training dataset

```
def prepare_inputs(text):
    text = tf.expand_dims(text, -1)
    tokenized_sentences = vectorize_layer(text)
    x = tokenized_sentences[:, :-1]
```

```
    y = tokenized_sentences[:, 1:]
    return x, y

train_ds = text_ds.map(prepare_inputs) ❶
```

❶ Create the training set consisting of recipe tokens (the input) and the same vector shifted by one token (the target).

The LSTM Architecture

The architecture of the overall LSTM model is shown in Table 5-1. The input to the model is a sequence of integer tokens and the output is the probability of each word in the 10,000-word vocabulary appearing next in the sequence. To understand how this works in detail, we need to introduce two new layer types, Embedding and LSTM.

Table 5-1. Model summary of the LSTM

Layer (type)	Output shape	Param #
InputLayer	(None, None)	0
Embedding	(None, None, 100)	1,000,000
LSTM	(None, None, 128)	117,248
Dense	(None, None, 10000)	1,290,000

Total params	2,407,248
Trainable params	2,407,248
Non-trainable params	0

The Input Layer of the LSTM

Notice that the Input layer does not need us to specify the sequence length in advance. Both the batch size and the sequence length are flexible (hence the (None, None) shape). This is because all downstream layers are agnostic to the length of the sequence being passed through.

The Embedding Layer

An *embedding layer* is essentially a lookup table that converts each integer token into a vector of length embedding_size, as shown in Figure 5-2. The lookup vectors are learned by the model as *weights*. Therefore, the number of weights learned by this layer is equal to the size of the vocabulary multiplied by the dimension of the embedding vector (i.e., 10,000 × 100 = 1,000,000).

Token	Embedding				
0	-0.13	0.45	...	0.13	-0.04
1	0.22	0.56	...	0.24	-0.63
...	...	...	...	...	...
9998	0.16	-0.70	...	-0.35	1.02
9999	-0.98	-0.45	...	-0.15	-0.52

Vocabulary size (10,000)

Embedding size (100)

Figure 5-2. An embedding layer is a lookup table for each integer token

We embed each integer token into a continuous vector because it enables the model to learn a representation for each word that is able to be updated through backpropagation. We could also just one-hot encode each input token, but using an embedding layer is preferred because it makes the embedding itself trainable, thus giving the model more flexibility in deciding how to embed each token to improve its performance.

Therefore, the Input layer passes a tensor of integer sequences of shape [batch_size, seq_length] to the Embedding layer, which outputs a tensor of shape [batch_size, seq_length, embedding_size]. This is then passed on to the LSTM layer (Figure 5-3).

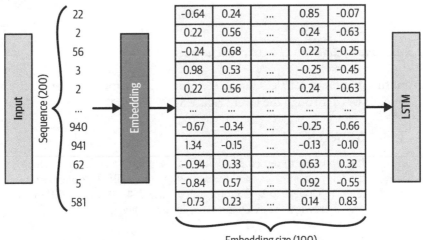

Embedding size (100)

Figure 5-3. A single sequence as it flows through an embedding layer

The LSTM Layer

To understand the LSTM layer, we must first look at how a general recurrent layer works.

A recurrent layer has the special property of being able to process sequential input data $x_1, \cdots, x_n$. It consists of a cell that updates its *hidden state*, h_t, as each element of the sequence x_t is passed through it, one timestep at a time.

The hidden state is a vector with length equal to the number of *units* in the cell—it can be thought of as the cell's current understanding of the sequence. At timestep t, the cell uses the previous value of the hidden state, h_{t-1}, together with the data from the current timestep x_t to produce an updated hidden state vector, h_t. This recurrent process continues until the end of the sequence. Once the sequence is finished, the layer outputs the final hidden state of the cell, h_n, which is then passed on to the next layer of the network. This process is shown in Figure 5-4.

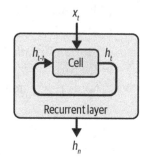

Figure 5-4. A simple diagram of a recurrent layer

To explain this in more detail, let's unroll the process so that we can see exactly how a single sequence is fed through the layer (Figure 5-5).

Cell Weights

It's important to remember that all of the cells in this diagram share the same weights (as they are really the same cell). There is no difference between this diagram and Figure 5-4; it's just a different way of drawing the mechanics of a recurrent layer.

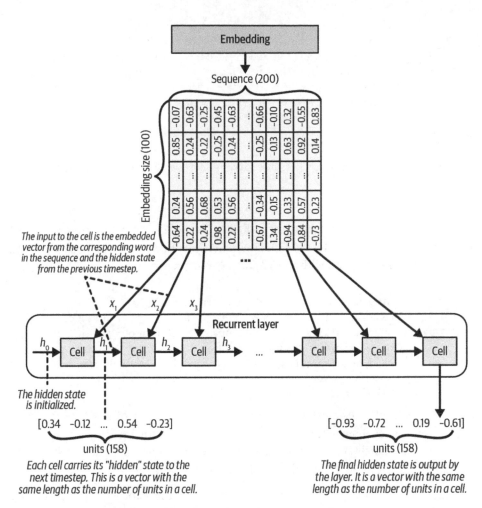

Figure 5-5. How a single sequence flows through a recurrent layer

Here, we represent the recurrent process by drawing a copy of the cell at each timestep and show how the hidden state is constantly being updated as it flows through the cells. We can clearly see how the previous hidden state is blended with the current sequential data point (i.e., the current embedded word vector) to produce the next hidden state. The output from the layer is the final hidden state of the cell, after each word in the input sequence has been processed.

The fact that the output from the cell is called a *hidden* state is an unfortunate naming convention—it's not really hidden, and you shouldn't think of it as such. Indeed, the last hidden state is the overall output from the layer, and we will be making use of the fact that we can access the hidden state at each individual timestep later in this chapter.

The LSTM Cell

Now that we have seen how a generic recurrent layer works, let's take a look inside an individual LSTM cell.

The job of the LSTM cell is to output a new hidden state, h_t, given its previous hidden state, h_{t-1}, and the current word embedding, x_t. To recap, the length of h_t is equal to the number of units in the LSTM. This is a parameter that is set when you define the layer and has nothing to do with the length of the sequence.

Make sure you do not confuse the term *cell* with *unit*. There is one cell in an LSTM layer that is defined by the number of units it contains, in the same way that the prisoner cell from our earlier story contained many prisoners. We often draw a recurrent layer as a chain of cells unrolled, as it helps to visualize how the hidden state is updated at each timestep.

An LSTM cell maintains a cell state, C_t, which can be thought of as the cell's internal beliefs about the current status of the sequence. This is distinct from the hidden state, h_t, which is ultimately output by the cell after the final timestep. The cell state is the same length as the hidden state (the number of units in the cell).

Let's look more closely at a single cell and how the hidden state is updated (Figure 5-6).

The hidden state is updated in six steps:

1. The hidden state of the previous timestep, h_{t-1}, and the current word embedding, x_t, are concatenated and passed through the *forget* gate. This gate is simply a dense layer with weights matrix W_f, bias b_f, and a sigmoid activation function. The resulting vector, f_t, has length equal to the number of units in the cell and contains values between 0 and 1 that determine how much of the previous cell state, C_{t-1}, should be retained.

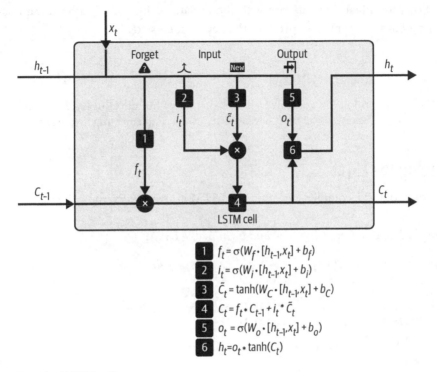

$$1 \quad f_t = \sigma(W_f \cdot [h_{t-1}, x_t] + b_f)$$
$$2 \quad i_t = \sigma(W_i \cdot [h_{t-1}, x_t] + b_i)$$
$$3 \quad \tilde{C}_t = \tanh(W_C \cdot [h_{t-1}, x_t] + b_C)$$
$$4 \quad C_t = f_t * C_{t-1} + i_t * \tilde{C}_t$$
$$5 \quad o_t = \sigma(W_o \cdot [h_{t-1}, x_t] + b_o)$$
$$6 \quad h_t = o_t * \tanh(C_t)$$

Figure 5-6. An LSTM cell

2. The concatenated vector is also passed through an *input* gate that, like the forget gate, is a dense layer with weights matrix W_i, bias b_i, and a sigmoid activation function. The output from this gate, i_t, has length equal to the number of units in the cell and contains values between 0 and 1 that determine how much new information will be added to the previous cell state, C_{t-1}.

3. The concatenated vector is passed through a dense layer with weights matrix W_C, bias b_C, and a tanh activation function to generate a vector $\tilde{C}_t$ that contains the new information that the cell wants to consider keeping. It also has length equal to the number of units in the cell and contains values between –1 and 1.

4. f_t and C_{t-1} are multiplied element-wise and added to the element-wise multiplication of i_t and $\tilde{C}_t$. This represents forgetting parts of the previous cell state and then adding new relevant information to produce the updated cell state, C_t.

5. The concatenated vector is passed through an *output* gate: a dense layer with weights matrix W_o, bias b_o, and a sigmoid activation. The resulting vector, o_t, has length equal to the number of units in the cell and stores values between 0 and 1 that determine how much of the updated cell state, C_t, to output from the cell.

6. o_t is multiplied element-wise with the updated cell state, C_t, after a tanh activation has been applied to produce the new hidden state, h_t.

The Keras LSTM Layer

All of this complexity is wrapped up within the LSTM layer type in Keras, so you don't have to worry about implementing it yourself!

Training the LSTM

The code to build, compile, and train the LSTM is given in Example 5-8.

Example 5-8. Building, compiling, and training the LSTM

```
inputs = layers.Input(shape=(None,), dtype="int32") ❶
x = layers.Embedding(10000, 100)(inputs) ❷
x = layers.LSTM(128, return_sequences=True)(x) ❸
outputs = layers.Dense(10000, activation = 'softmax')(x) ❹
lstm = models.Model(inputs, outputs) ❺

loss_fn = losses.SparseCategoricalCrossentropy()
lstm.compile("adam", loss_fn) ❻
lstm.fit(train_ds, epochs=25) ❼
```

❶ The Input layer does not need us to specify the sequence length in advance (it can be flexible), so we use None as a placeholder.

❷ The Embedding layer requires two parameters, the size of the vocabulary (10,000 tokens) and the dimensionality of the embedding vector (100).

❸ The LSTM layers require us to specify the dimensionality of the hidden vector (128). We also choose to return the full sequence of hidden states, rather than just the hidden state at the final timestep.

❹ The Dense layer transforms the hidden states at each timestep into a vector of probabilities for the next token.

❺ The overall Model predicts the next token, given an input sequence of tokens. It does this for each token in the sequence.

❻ The model is compiled with SparseCategoricalCrossentropy loss—this is the same as categorical cross-entropy, but is used when the labels are integers rather than one-hot encoded vectors.

⑦ The model is fit to the training dataset.

In Figure 5-7 you can see the first few epochs of the LSTM training process—notice how the example output becomes more comprehensible as the loss metric falls. Figure 5-8 shows the cross-entropy loss metric falling throughout the training process.

```
Epoch 1/25
628/629 [===========================>.] – ETA: 0s – loss: 4.4536
generated text:
recipe for mold salad are high 8 pickled to fold cook the dish into and warm in baking reduced but halves beans
and cut

629/629 [============================] – 29s 43ms/step – loss: 4.4527
Epoch 2/25
628/629 [===========================>.] – ETA: 0s – loss: 3.2339
generated text:
recipe for racks – up–don with herb fizz | serve checking thighs onto sanding butter and baking surface in a hea
vy heavy large saucepan over blender ; stand overnight . [UNK] over moderate heat until very blended , garlic ,
about 8 minutes . cook airtight until cooked are soft seeds , about 1 45 minutes . sugar , until s is brown , 5
to sliced , parmesan , until browned and add extract . wooden crumb to outside of out sheets . flatten and prehe
ated return to the paste . add in pecans oval and let transfer day .

629/629 [============================] – 30s 48ms/step – loss: 3.2336
Epoch 3/25
629/629 [============================] – ETA: 0s – loss: 2.6229
generated text:
recipe for grilled chicken | preheat oven to 400°f . cook in large 8 – caramel grinder or until desired are firm
, about 6 minutes

629/629 [============================] – 27s 42ms/step – loss: 2.6229
Epoch 4/25
629/629 [============================] – ETA: 0s – loss: 2.3426
generated text:
recipe for pizza salad with sweet red pepper and star fruit | combine all ingredients except lowest ingredients
in a large skillet . working with batches and deglaze , cook until just cooked through , about 1 minute . meanwh
ile , boil potatoes and paprika in a little oil over medium – high heat , stirring it just until crisp , about 3
minutes . stir in bell pepper , onion and cooked paste and jalapeño until clams well after most – reggiano , abo
ut 5 minutes . transfer warm 2 tablespoons flesh of eggplants to medium bowl . serve .
```

Figure 5-7. The first few epochs of the LSTM training process

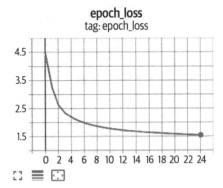

Figure 5-8. The cross-entropy loss metric of the LSTM training process by epoch

Analysis of the LSTM

Now that we have compiled and trained the LSTM, we can start to use it to generate long strings of text by applying the following process:

1. Feed the network with an existing sequence of words and ask it to predict the following word.

2. Append this word to the existing sequence and repeat.

The network will output a set of probabilities for each word that we can sample from. Therefore, we can make the text generation stochastic, rather than deterministic. Moreover, we can introduce a *temperature* parameter to the sampling process to indicate how deterministic we would like the process to be.

The Temperature Parameter

A temperature close to 0 makes the sampling more deterministic (i.e., the word with the highest probability is very likely to be chosen), whereas a temperature of 1 means each word is chosen with the probability output by the model.

This is achieved with the code in Example 5-9, which creates a callback function that can be used to generate text at the end of each training epoch.

Example 5-9. The TextGenerator callback function

```python
class TextGenerator(callbacks.Callback):
    def __init__(self, index_to_word, top_k=10):
        self.index_to_word = index_to_word
        self.word_to_index = {
            word: index for index, word in enumerate(index_to_word)
        } ❶

    def sample_from(self, probs, temperature): ❷
        probs = probs ** (1 / temperature)
        probs = probs / np.sum(probs)
        return np.random.choice(len(probs), p=probs), probs

    def generate(self, start_prompt, max_tokens, temperature):
        start_tokens = [
            self.word_to_index.get(x, 1) for x in start_prompt.split()
        ] ❸
        sample_token = None
        info = []
        while len(start_tokens) < max_tokens and sample_token != 0: ❹
            x = np.array([start_tokens])
            y = self.model.predict(x) ❺
```

```
                sample_token, probs = self.sample_from(y[0][-1], temperature)  ❻
                info.append({'prompt': start_prompt , 'word_probs': probs})
                start_tokens.append(sample_token)  ❼
                start_prompt = start_prompt + ' ' + self.index_to_word[sample_token]
            print(f"\ngenerated text:\n{start_prompt}\n")
            return info

    def on_epoch_end(self, epoch, logs=None):
        self.generate("recipe for", max_tokens = 100, temperature = 1.0)
```

❶ Create an inverse vocabulary mapping (from word to token).

❷ This function updates the probabilities with a `temperature` scaling factor.

❸ The start prompt is a string of words that you would like to give the model to start the generation process (for example, *recipe for*). The words are first converted to a list of tokens.

❹ The sequence is generated until it is `max_tokens` long or a stop token (0) is produced.

❺ The model outputs the probabilities of each word being next in the sequence.

❻ The probabilities are passed through the sampler to output the next word, parameterized by `temperature`.

❼ We append the new word to the prompt text, ready for the next iteration of the generative process.

Let's take a look at this in action, at two different temperature values (Figure 5-9).

```
temperature = 1.0

generated text:
recipe for sour japanese potatoes julienne | in a bowl stir together the yeast mixture with the milk and the
peanut butter crumbs , the sour cream , and the butter mixture with a fork , gently fold in the prunes gently
or until incorporated . lightly stir the oil and yeast until it just holds soft peaks , but not runny , on bo
ttom of a 7 - sided sheet of aluminum foil , top it with a round , and a pinch of each brownies into a goblet
, or with the baking dish . serve each with sorbet
```

```
temperature = 0.2

generated text:
recipe for grilled chicken with mustard - herb sauce | combine first 6 ingredients in medium bowl . add chick
en to pot . add chicken and turn to coat . cover and refrigerate at least 1 hour and up to 1 day . preheat ov
en to 450°f . place turkey on rock in roasting pan . roast until thermometer inserted into thickest part of t
high registers 175°f , about 1 hour longer . transfer to rack in center of oven and preheat to 450°f . brush
chicken with oil . sprinkle with salt and pepper . roast until thermometer inserted into
```

Figure 5-9. Generated outputs at `temperature = 1.0` and `temperature = 0.2`

There are a few things to note about these two passages. First, both are stylistically similar to a recipe from the original training set. They both open with a recipe title and contain generally grammatically correct constructions. The difference is that the generated text with a temperature of 1.0 is more adventurous and therefore less accurate than the example with a temperature of 0.2. Generating multiple samples with a temperature of 1.0 will therefore lead to more variety, as the model is sampling from a probability distribution with greater variance.

To demonstrate this, Figure 5-10 shows the top five tokens with the highest probabilities for a range of prompts, for both temperature values.

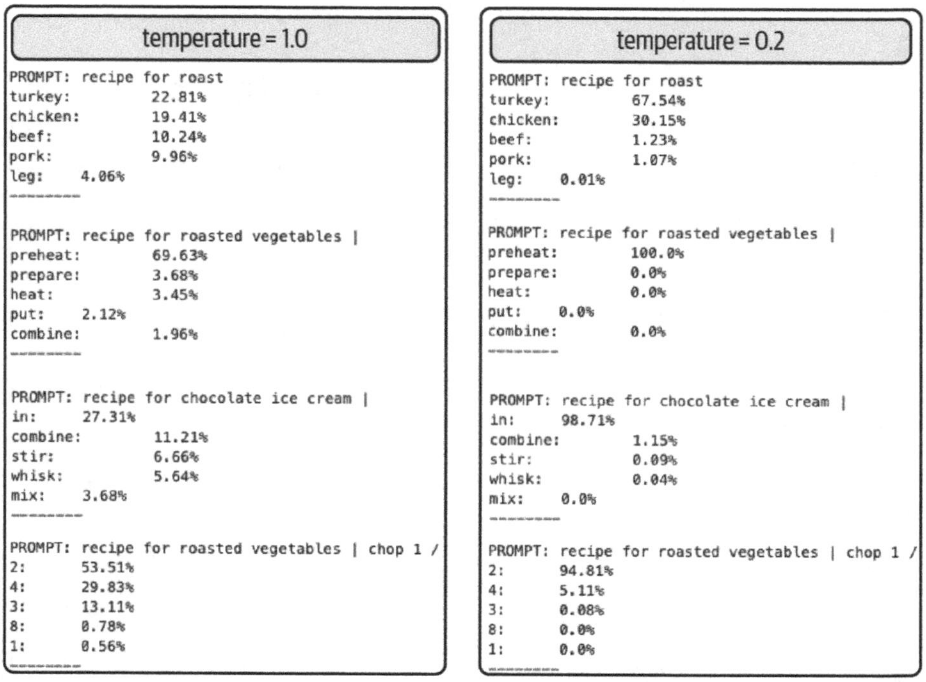

```
┌──────────────────────────────────┐   ┌──────────────────────────────────┐
│         temperature = 1.0        │   │         temperature = 0.2        │
├──────────────────────────────────┤   ├──────────────────────────────────┤
PROMPT: recipe for roast               PROMPT: recipe for roast
turkey:        22.81%                  turkey:        67.54%
chicken:       19.41%                  chicken:       30.15%
beef:          10.24%                  beef:          1.23%
pork:          9.96%                   pork:          1.07%
leg:     4.06%                         leg:     0.01%
--------                               --------

PROMPT: recipe for roasted vegetables |   PROMPT: recipe for roasted vegetables |
preheat:       69.63%                  preheat:       100.0%
prepare:       3.68%                   prepare:       0.0%
heat:          3.45%                   heat:          0.0%
put:     2.12%                         put:     0.0%
combine:       1.96%                   combine:       0.0%
--------                               --------

PROMPT: recipe for chocolate ice cream |   PROMPT: recipe for chocolate ice cream |
in:      27.31%                        in:      98.71%
combine:       11.21%                  combine:       1.15%
stir:          6.66%                   stir:          0.09%
whisk:         5.64%                   whisk:         0.04%
mix:     3.68%                         mix:     0.0%
--------                               --------

PROMPT: recipe for roasted vegetables | chop 1 /   PROMPT: recipe for roasted vegetables | chop 1 /
2:       53.51%                        2:       94.81%
4:       29.83%                        4:       5.11%
3:       13.11%                        3:       0.08%
8:       0.78%                         8:       0.0%
1:       0.56%                         1:       0.0%
--------                               --------
```

Figure 5-10. Distribution of word probabilities following various sequences, for temperature values of 1.0 and 0.2

The model is able to generate a suitable distribution for the next most likely word across a range of contexts. For example, even though the model was never told about parts of speech such as nouns, verbs, or numbers, it is generally able to separate words into these classes and use them in a way that is grammatically correct.

Moreover, the model is able to select an appropriate verb to begin the recipe instructions, depending on the preceding title. For roasted vegetables, it selects preheat, prepare, heat, put, or combine as the most likely possibilities, whereas for ice cream it selects in, combine, stir, whisk, and mix. This shows that the model has some contextual understanding of the differences between recipes depending on their ingredients.

Notice also how the probabilities for the temperature = 0.2 examples are much more heavily weighted toward the first choice token. This is the reason why there is generally less variety in generations when the temperature is lower.

While our basic LSTM model is doing a great job at generating realistic text, it is clear that it still struggles to grasp some of the semantic meaning of the words that it is generating. It introduces ingredients that are not likely to work well together (for example, sour Japanese potatoes, pecan crumbs, and sorbet)! In some cases, this may be desirable—say, if we want our LSTM to generate interesting and unique patterns of words—but in other cases, we will need our model to have a deeper understanding of the ways in which words can be grouped together and a longer memory of ideas introduced earlier in the text.

In the next section, we'll explore some of the ways that we can improve our basic LSTM network. In Chapter 9, we'll take a look at a new kind of autoregressive model, the Transformer, which takes language modeling to the next level.

Recurrent Neural Network (RNN) Extensions

The model in the preceding section is a simple example of how an LSTM can be trained to learn how to generate text in a given style. In this section we will explore several extensions to this idea.

Stacked Recurrent Networks

The network we just looked at contained a single LSTM layer, but we can also train networks with stacked LSTM layers, so that deeper features can be learned from the text.

To achieve this, we simply introduce another LSTM layer after the first. The second LSTM layer can then use the hidden states from the first layer as its input data. This is shown in Figure 5-11, and the overall model architecture is shown in Table 5-2.

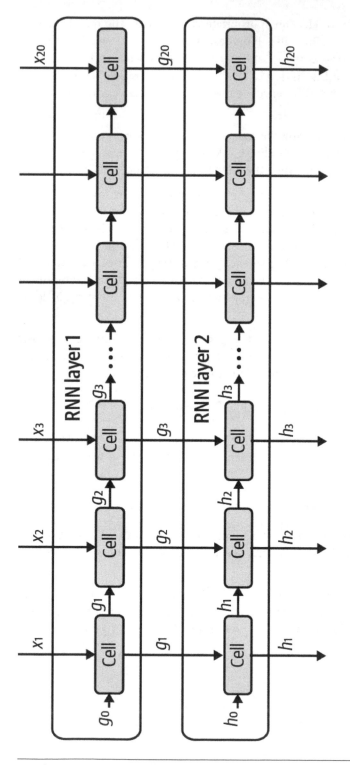

Figure 5-11. Diagram of a multilayer RNN: g_t denotes hidden states of the first layer and h_t denotes hidden states of the second layer

Table 5-2. Model summary of the stacked LSTM

Layer (type)	Output shape	Param #
InputLayer	(None, None)	0
Embedding	(None, None, 100)	1,000,000
LSTM	(None, None, 128)	117,248
LSTM	(None, None, 128)	131,584
Dense	(None, None, 10000)	1,290,000

Total params	2,538,832
Trainable params	2,538,832
Non-trainable params	0

The code to build the stacked LSTM is given in Example 5-10.

Example 5-10. Building a stacked LSTM

```
text_in = layers.Input(shape = (None,))
embedding = layers.Embedding(total_words, embedding_size)(text_in)
x = layers.LSTM(n_units, return_sequences = True)(x)
x = layers.LSTM(n_units, return_sequences = True)(x)
probabilites = layers.Dense(total_words, activation = 'softmax')(x)
model = models.Model(text_in, probabilites)
```

Gated Recurrent Units

Another type of commonly used RNN layer is the *gated recurrent unit* (GRU).[2] The key differences from the LSTM unit are as follows:

1. The *forget* and *input* gates are replaced by *reset* and *update* gates.
2. There is no *cell state* or *output* gate, only a *hidden state* that is output from the cell.

The hidden state is updated in four steps, as illustrated in Figure 5-12.

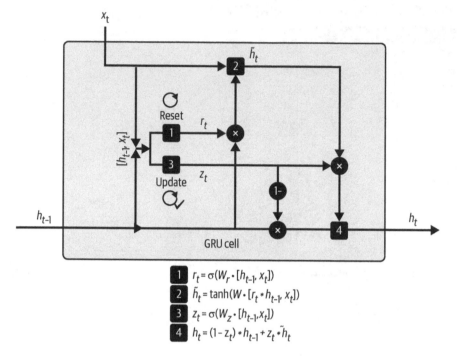

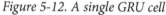

1 $r_t = \sigma(W_r \cdot [h_{t-1}, x_t])$

2 $\tilde{h}_t = \tanh(W \cdot [r_t \ast h_{t-1}, x_t])$

3 $z_t = \sigma(W_z \cdot [h_{t-1}, x_t])$

4 $h_t = (1 - z_t) \ast h_{t-1} + z_t \ast \tilde{h}_t$

Figure 5-12. A single GRU cell

The process is as follows:

1. The hidden state of the previous timestep, h_{t-1}, and the current word embedding, x_t, are concatenated and used to create the *reset* gate. This gate is a dense layer, with weights matrix W_r and a sigmoid activation function. The resulting vector, r_t, has length equal to the number of units in the cell and stores values between 0 and 1 that determine how much of the previous hidden state, h_{t-1}, should be carried forward into the calculation for the new beliefs of the cell.

2. The reset gate is applied to the hidden state, h_{t-1}, and concatenated with the current word embedding, x_t. This vector is then fed to a dense layer with weights matrix W and a tanh activation function to generate a vector, $\tilde{h}_t$, that stores the new beliefs of the cell. It has length equal to the number of units in the cell and stores values between −1 and 1.

3. The concatenation of the hidden state of the previous timestep, h_{t-1}, and the current word embedding, x_t, are also used to create the *update* gate. This gate is a dense layer with weights matrix W_z and a sigmoid activation. The resulting vector, z_t, has length equal to the number of units in the cell and stores values

between 0 and 1, which are used to determine how much of the new beliefs, $\tilde{h}_t$, to blend into the current hidden state, h_{t-1}.

4. The new beliefs of the cell, $\tilde{h}_t$, and the current hidden state, h_{t-1}, are blended in a proportion determined by the update gate, z_t, to produce the updated hidden state, h_t, that is output from the cell.

Bidirectional Cells

For prediction problems where the entire text is available to the model at inference time, there is no reason to process the sequence only in the forward direction—it could just as well be processed backward. A Bidirectional layer takes advantage of this by storing two sets of hidden states: one that is produced as a result of the sequence being processed in the usual forward direction and another that is produced when the sequence is processed backward. This way, the layer can learn from information both preceding and succeeding the given timestep.

In Keras, this is implemented as a wrapper around a recurrent layer, as shown in Example 5-11.

Example 5-11. Building a bidirectional GRU layer

```
layer = layers.Bidirectional(layers.GRU(100))
```

Hidden State

The hidden states in the resulting layer are vectors of length equal to double the number of units in the wrapped cell (a concatenation of the forward and backward hidden states). Thus, in this example the hidden states of the layer are vectors of length 200.

So far, we have only applied autoregressive models (LSTMs) to text data. In the next section, we will see how autoregressive models can also be used to generate images.

PixelCNN

In 2016, van den Oord et al.[3] introduced a model that generates images pixel by pixel by predicting the likelihood of the next pixel based on the pixels before it. The model is called *PixelCNN*, and it can be trained to generate images autoregressively.

There are two new concepts that we need to introduce to understand the PixelCNN— *masked convolutional layers* and *residual blocks*.

Masked Convolutional Layers

As we saw in Chapter 2, a convolutional layer can be used to extract features from an image by applying a series of filters. The output of the layer at a particular pixel is a weighted sum of the filter weights multiplied by the preceding layer values over a small square centered on the pixel. This method can detect edges and textures and, at deeper layers, shapes and higher-level features.

Whilst convolutional layers are extremely useful for feature detection, they cannot directly be used in an autoregressive sense, because there is no ordering placed on the pixels. They rely on the fact that all pixels are treated equally—no pixel is treated as the *start* or *end* of the image. This is in contrast to the text data that we have already seen in this chapter, where there is a clear ordering to the tokens so recurrent models such as LSTMs can be readily applied.

For us to be able to apply convolutional layers to image generation in an autoregressive sense, we must first place an ordering on the pixels and ensure that the filters are only able to see pixels that precede the pixel in question. We can then generate images one pixel at a time, by applying convolutional filters to the current image to predict the value of the next pixel from all preceding pixels.

We first need to choose an ordering for the pixels—a sensible suggestion is to order the pixels from top left to bottom right, moving first along the rows and then down the columns.

We then mask the convolutional filters so that the output of the layer at each pixel is only influenced by pixel values that precede the pixel in question. This is achieved by multiplying a mask of ones and zeros with the filter weights matrix, so that the values of any pixels that are after the target pixel are zeroed.

There are actually two different kinds of masks in a PixelCNN, as shown in Figure 5-13:

- Type A, where the value of the central pixel is masked
- Type B, where the value of the central pixel is *not* masked

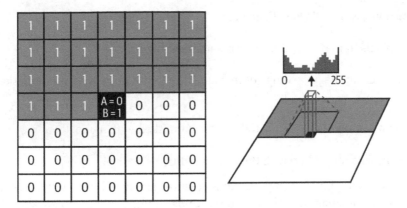

Figure 5-13. Left: a convolutional filter mask; right: a mask applied to a set of pixels to predict the distribution of the central pixel value (source: van den Oord et al., 2016)

The initial masked convolutional layer (i.e., the one that is applied directly to the input image) cannot use the central pixel, because this is precisely the pixel we want the network to guess! However, subsequent layers can use the central pixel because this will have been calculated only as a result of information from preceding pixels in the original input image.

We can see in Example 5-12 how a `MaskedConvLayer` can be built using Keras.

Example 5-12. A `MaskedConvLayer` in Keras

```python
class MaskedConvLayer(layers.Layer):
    def __init__(self, mask_type, **kwargs):
        super(MaskedConvLayer, self).__init__()
        self.mask_type = mask_type
        self.conv = layers.Conv2D(**kwargs) ❶

    def build(self, input_shape):
        self.conv.build(input_shape)
        kernel_shape = self.conv.kernel.get_shape()
        self.mask = np.zeros(shape=kernel_shape) ❷
        self.mask[: kernel_shape[0] // 2, ...] = 1.0 ❸
        self.mask[kernel_shape[0] // 2, : kernel_shape[1] // 2, ...] = 1.0 ❹
        if self.mask_type == "B":
            self.mask[kernel_shape[0] // 2, kernel_shape[1] // 2, ...] = 1.0 ❺

    def call(self, inputs):
        self.conv.kernel.assign(self.conv.kernel * self.mask) ❻
        return self.conv(inputs)
```

❶ The `MaskedConvLayer` is based on the normal `Conv2D` layer.

❷ The mask is initialized with all zeros.

❸ The pixels in the preceding rows are unmasked with ones.

❹ The pixels in the preceding columns that are in the same row are unmasked with ones.

❺ If the mask type is B, the central pixel is unmasked with a one.

❻ The mask is multiplied with the filter weights.

Note that this simplified example assumes a grayscale image (i.e., with one channel). If we have color images, we'll have three color channels that we can also place an ordering on so that, for example, the red channel precedes the blue channel, which precedes the green channel.

Residual Blocks

Now that we have seen how to mask the convolutional layer, we can start to build our PixelCNN. The core building block that we will use is the residual block.

A *residual block* is a set of layers where the output is added to the input before being passed on to the rest of the network. In other words, the input has a *fast-track* route to the output, without having to go through the intermediate layers—this is called a *skip connection*. The rationale behind including a skip connection is that if the optimal transformation is just to keep the input the same, this can be achieved by simply zeroing the weights of the intermediate layers. Without the skip connection, the network would have to find an identity mapping through the intermediate layers, which is much harder.

A diagram of the residual block in our PixelCNN is shown in Figure 5-14.

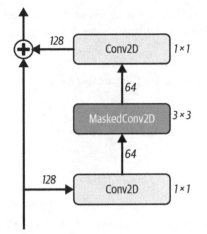

Figure 5-14. A PixelCNN residual block (the numbers of filters are next to the arrows and the filter sizes are next to the layers)

We can build a `ResidualBlock` using the code shown in Example 5-13.

Example 5-13. A `ResidualBlock`

```python
class ResidualBlock(layers.Layer):
    def __init__(self, filters, **kwargs):
        super(ResidualBlock, self).__init__(**kwargs)
        self.conv1 = layers.Conv2D(
            filters=filters // 2, kernel_size=1, activation="relu"
        ) ❶
        self.pixel_conv = MaskedConv2D(
            mask_type="B",
            filters=filters // 2,
            kernel_size=3,
            activation="relu",
            padding="same",
        ) ❷
        self.conv2 = layers.Conv2D(
            filters=filters, kernel_size=1, activation="relu"
        ) ❸

    def call(self, inputs):
        x = self.conv1(inputs)
        x = self.pixel_conv(x)
        x = self.conv2(x)
        return layers.add([inputs, x]) ❹
```

❶ The initial `Conv2D` layer halves the number of channels.

❷ The Type B `MaskedConv2D` layer with kernel size of 3 only uses information from five pixels—three pixels in the row above the focus pixel, one to the left, and the focus pixel itself.

❸ The final `Conv2D` layer doubles the number of channels to again match the input shape.

❹ The output from the convolutional layers is added to the input—this is the skip connection.

Training the PixelCNN

In Example 5-14 we put together the whole PixelCNN network, approximately following the structure laid out in the original paper. In the original paper, the output layer is a 256-filter `Conv2D` layer, with softmax activation. In other words, the network tries to re-create its input by predicting the correct pixel values, a bit like an autoencoder. The difference is that the PixelCNN is constrained so that no information from earlier pixels can flow through to influence the prediction for each pixel, due to the way that network is designed, using `MaskedConv2D` layers.

A challenge with this approach is that the network has no way to understand that a pixel value of, say, 200 is very close to a pixel value of 201. It must learn every pixel output value independently, which means training can be very slow, even for the simplest datasets. Therefore, in our implementation, we instead simplify the input so that each pixel can take only one of four values. This way, we can use a 4-filter `Conv2D` output layer instead of 256.

Example 5-14. The PixelCNN architecture

```
inputs = layers.Input(shape=(16, 16, 1)) ❶
x = MaskedConv2D(mask_type="A"
                    , filters=128
                    , kernel_size=7
                    , activation="relu"
                    , padding="same")(inputs)❷

for _ in range(5):
    x = ResidualBlock(filters=128)(x) ❸

for _ in range(2):
    x = MaskedConv2D(
        mask_type="B",
        filters=128,
        kernel_size=1,
        strides=1,
        activation="relu",
```

```
        padding="valid",
    )(x) ❹

out = layers.Conv2D(
    filters=4, kernel_size=1, strides=1, activation="softmax", padding="valid"
)(x) ❺

pixel_cnn = models.Model(inputs, out) ❻

adam = optimizers.Adam(learning_rate=0.0005)
pixel_cnn.compile(optimizer=adam, loss="sparse_categorical_crossentropy")

pixel_cnn.fit(
    input_data
    , output_data
    , batch_size=128
    , epochs=150
) ❼
```

❶ The model `Input` is a grayscale image of size $16 \times 16 \times 1$, with inputs scaled between 0 and 1.

❷ The first Type A `MaskedConv2D` layer with a kernel size of 7 uses information from 24 pixels—21 pixels in the three rows above the focus pixel and 3 to the left (the focus pixel itself is not used).

❸ Five `ResidualBlock` layer groups are stacked sequentially.

❹ Two Type B `MaskedConv2D` layers with a kernel size of 1 act as `Dense` layers across the number of channels for each pixel.

❺ The final `Conv2D` layer reduces the number of channels to four—the number of pixel levels for this example.

❻ The `Model` is built to accept an image and output an image of the same dimensions.

❼ Fit the model—`input_data` is scaled in the range [0, 1] (floats); `output_data` is scaled in the range [0, 3] (integers).

Analysis of the PixelCNN

We can train our PixelCNN on images from the Fashion-MNIST dataset that we encountered in Chapter 3. To generate new images, we need to ask the model to predict the next pixel given all preceding pixels, one pixel at a time. This is a very slow process compared to a model such as a variational autoencoder! For a 32×32

grayscale image, we need to make 1,024 predictions sequentially using the model, compared to the single prediction that we need to make for a VAE. This is one of the major downsides to autoregressive models such as a PixelCNN—they are slow to sample from, because of the sequential nature of the sampling process.

For this reason, we use an image size of 16 × 16, rather than 32 × 32, to speed up the generation of new images. The generation callback class is shown in Example 5-15.

Example 5-15. Generating new images using the PixelCNN

```
class ImageGenerator(callbacks.Callback):
    def __init__(self, num_img):
        self.num_img = num_img

    def sample_from(self, probs, temperature):
        probs = probs ** (1 / temperature)
        probs = probs / np.sum(probs)
        return np.random.choice(len(probs), p=probs)

    def generate(self, temperature):
        generated_images = np.zeros(
            shape=(self.num_img,) + (pixel_cnn.input_shape)[1:]
        ) ❶
        batch, rows, cols, channels = generated_images.shape

        for row in range(rows):
            for col in range(cols):
                for channel in range(channels):
                    probs = self.model.predict(generated_images)[
                        :, row, col, :
                    ] ❷
                    generated_images[:, row, col, channel] = [
                        self.sample_from(x, temperature) for x in probs
                    ] ❸
                    generated_images[:, row, col, channel] /= 4 ❹
        return generated_images

    def on_epoch_end(self, epoch, logs=None):
        generated_images = self.generate(temperature = 1.0)
        display(
            generated_images,
            save_to = "./output/generated_img_%03d.png" % (epoch)
        )

img_generator_callback = ImageGenerator(num_img=10)
```

❶ Start with a batch of empty images (all zeros).

❷ Loop over the rows, columns, and channels of the current image, predicting the distribution of the next pixel value.

❸ Sample a pixel level from the predicted distribution (for our example, a level in the range [0, 3]).

❹ Convert the pixel level to the range [0, 1] and overwrite the pixel value in the current image, ready for the next iteration of the loop.

In Figure 5-15, we can see several images from the original training set, alongside images that have been generated by the PixelCNN.

Figure 5-15. Example images from the training set and generated images created by the PixelCNN model

The model does a great job of re-creating the overall shape and style of the original images! It is quite amazing that we can treat images as a series of tokens (pixel values) and apply autoregressive models such as a PixelCNN to produce realistic samples.

As mentioned previously, one of the downsides to autoregressive models is that they are slow to sample from, which is why a simple example of their application is presented in this book. However, as we shall see in Chapter 10, more complex forms of autoregressive model can be applied to images to produce state-of-the-art outputs. In such cases, the slow generation speed is a necessary price to pay in return for exceptional-quality outputs.

Since the original paper was published, several improvements have been made to the architecture and training process of the PixelCNN. The following section introduces one of those changes—using mixture distributions—and demonstrates how to train a PixelCNN model with this improvement using a built-in TensorFlow function.

Mixture Distributions

For our previous example, we reduced the output of the PixelCNN to just 4 pixel levels to ensure the network didn't have to learn a distribution over 256 independent pixel values, which would slow the training process. However, this is far from ideal—for color images, we wouldn't want our canvas to be restricted to only a handful of possible colors.

To get around this problem, we can make the output of the network a *mixture distribution*, instead of a softmax over 256 discrete pixel values, following the ideas presented by Salimans et al.[4] A mixture distribution is quite simply a mixture of two or more other probability distributions. For example, we could have a mixture distribution of five logistic distributions, each with different parameters. The mixture distribution also requires a discrete categorical distribution that denotes the probability of choosing each of the distributions included in the mix. An example is shown in Figure 5-16.

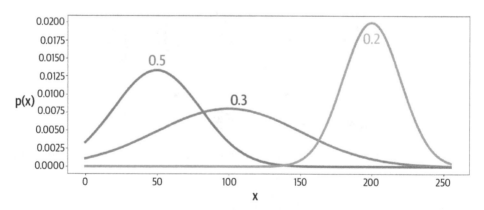

Figure 5-16. A mixture distribution of three normal distributions with different parameters—the categorical distribution over the three normal distributions is [0.5, 0.3, 0.2]

To sample from a mixture distribution, we first sample from the categorical distribution to choose a particular subdistribution and then sample from this in the usual way. This way, we can create complex distributions with relatively few parameters.

For example, the mixture distribution in Figure 5-16 only requires eight parameters —two for the categorical distribution and a mean and variance for each of the three normal distributions. This is compared to the 255 parameters that would define a categorical distribution over the entire pixel range.

Conveniently, the TensorFlow Probability library provides a function that allows us to create a PixelCNN with mixture distribution output in a single line. Example 5-16 illustrates how to build a PixelCNN using this function.

Running the Code for This Example

The code for this example can be found in the Jupyter notebook in *notebooks/05_autoregressive/03_pixelcnn_md/pixelcnn_md.ipynb* in the book repository.

Example 5-16. Building a PixelCNN using the TensorFlow function

```python
import tensorflow_probability as tfp

dist = tfp.distributions.PixelCNN(
    image_shape=(32, 32, 1),
    num_resnet=1,
    num_hierarchies=2,
    num_filters=32,
    num_logistic_mix=5,
    dropout_p=.3,
) ❶

image_input = layers.Input(shape=(32, 32, 1)) ❷

log_prob = dist.log_prob(image_input)

model = models.Model(inputs=image_input, outputs=log_prob) ❸
model.add_loss(-tf.reduce_mean(log_prob)) ❹
```

❶ Define the PixelCNN as a distribution—i.e., the output layer is a mixture distribution made up of five logistic distributions.

❷ The input is a grayscale image of size 32 × 32 × 1.

❸ The Model takes a grayscale image as input and outputs the log-likelihood of the image under the mixture distribution calculated by the PixelCNN.

❹ The loss function is the mean negative log-likelihood over the batch of input images.

The model is trained in the same way as before, but this time accepting integer pixel values as input, in the range [0, 255]. Outputs can be generated from the distribution using the `sample` function, as shown in Example 5-17.

Example 5-17. Sampling from the PixelCNN mixture distribution

```
dist.sample(10).numpy()
```

Example generated images are shown in Figure 5-17. The difference from our previous examples is that now the full range of pixel values is being utilized.

Figure 5-17. Outputs from the PixelCNN using a mixture distribution output

Summary

In this chapter we have seen how autoregressive models such as recurrent neural networks can be applied to generate text sequences that mimic a particular style of writing, and also how a PixelCNN can generate images in a sequential fashion, one pixel at a time.

We explored two different types of recurrent layers—long short-term memory (LSTM) and gated recurrent unit (GRU)—and saw how these cells can be stacked or made bidirectional to form more complex network architectures. We built an LSTM to generate realistic recipes using Keras and saw how to manipulate the temperature of the sampling process to increase or decrease the randomness of the output.

We also saw how images can be generated in an autoregressive manner, using a PixelCNN. We built a PixelCNN from scratch using Keras, coding the masked convolutional layers and residual blocks to allow information to flow through the network so that only preceding pixels could be used to generate the current pixel. Finally, we discussed how the TensorFlow Probability library provides a standalone `PixelCNN` function that implements a mixture distribution as the output layer, allowing us to further improve the learning process.

In the next chapter we will explore another generative modeling family that explicitly models the data-generating distribution—normalizing flow models.

References

1. Sepp Hochreiter and Jürgen Schmidhuber, "Long Short-Term Memory," *Neural Computation* 9 (1997): 1735–1780, *https://www.bioinf.jku.at/publications/older/2604.pdf.*

2. Kyunghyun Cho et al., "Learning Phrase Representations Using RNN Encoder-Decoder for Statistical Machine Translation," June 3, 2014, *https://arxiv.org/abs/1406.1078.*

3. Aaron van den Oord et al., "Pixel Recurrent Neural Networks," August 19, 2016, *https://arxiv.org/abs/1601.06759.*

4. Tim Salimans et al., "PixelCNN++: Improving the PixelCNN with Discretized Logistic Mixture Likelihood and Other Modifications," January 19, 2017, *http://arxiv.org/abs/1701.05517.*

CHAPTER 6

Normalizing Flow Models

Chapter Goals

In this chapter you will:

- Learn how normalizing flow models utilize the change of variables equation.
- See how the Jacobian determinant plays a vital role in our ability to compute an explicit density function.
- Understand how we can restrict the form of the Jacobian using coupling layers.
- See how the neural network is designed to be invertible.
- Build a RealNVP model—a particular example of a normalizing flow to generate points in 2D.
- Use the RealNVP model to generate new points that appear to have been drawn from the data distribution.
- Learn about two key extensions of the RealNVP model, GLOW and FFJORD.

So far, we have discussed three families of generative models: variational autoencoders, generative adversarial networks, and autoregressive models. Each presents a different way to address the challenge of modeling the distribution $p(x)$, either by introducing a latent variable that can be easily sampled (and transformed using the decoder in VAEs or generator in GANs), or by tractably modeling the distribution as a function of the values of preceding elements (autoregressive models).

In this chapter, we will cover a new family of generative models—normalizing flow models. As we shall see, normalizing flows share similarities with both autoregressive models and variational autoencoders. Like autoregressive models, normalizing flows are able to explicitly and tractably model the data-generating distribution $p(x)$. Like

VAEs, normalizing flows attempt to map the data into a simpler distribution, such as a Gaussian distribution. The key difference is that normalizing flows place a constraint on the form of the mapping function, so that it is invertible and can therefore be used to generate new data points.

We will dig into this definition in detail in the first section of this chapter before implementing a normalizing flow model called RealNVP using Keras. We will also see how normalizing flows can be extended to create more powerful models, such as GLOW and FFJORD.

Introduction

We will begin with a short story to illustrate the key concepts behind normalizing flows.

Jacob and the F.L.O.W. Machine

Upon visiting a small village, you notice a mysterious-looking shop with a sign above the door that says *JACOB'S*. Intrigued, you cautiously enter and ask the old man standing behind the counter what he sells (Figure 6-1).

Figure 6-1. Inside a steampunk shop, with a large metallic bell (created with Midjourney)

He replies that he offers a service for digitizing paintings, with a difference. After a brief moment rummaging around the back of the shop, he brings out a silver box, embossed with the letters F.L.O.W. He tells you that this stands for Finding Likenesses Of Watercolors, which approximately describes what the machine does. You decide to give the machine a try.

You come back the next day and hand the shopkeeper a set of your favorite paintings, and he passes them through the machine. The F.L.O.W. machine begins to hum and whistle and after a while outputs a set of numbers that appear randomly generated. The shopkeeper hands you the list and begins to walk to the till to calculate how much you owe him for the digitization process and the F.L.O.W. box. Distinctly unimpressed, you ask the shopkeeper what you should do with this long list of numbers, and how you can get your favorite paintings back.

The shopkeeper rolls his eyes, as if the answer should be obvious. He walks back to the machine and passes in the long list of numbers, this time from the opposite side. You hear the machine whir again and wait, puzzled, until finally your original paintings drop out from where they entered.

Relieved to finally have your paintings back, you decide that it might be best to just store them in the attic instead. However, before you have a chance to leave, the shopkeeper ushers you across to a different corner of the shop, where a giant bell hangs from the rafters. He hits the bell curve with a huge stick, sending vibrations around the store.

Instantly, the F.L.O.W. machine under your arm begins to hiss and whirr in reverse, as if a new set of numbers had just been passed in. After a few moments, more beautiful watercolor paintings begin to fall out of the F.L.O.W. machine, but they are not the same as the ones you originally digitized. They resemble the style and form of your original set of paintings, but each one is completely unique!

You ask the shopkeeper how this incredible device works. He explains that the magic lies in the fact that he has developed a special process that ensures the transformation is extremely fast and simple to calculate while still being sophisticated enough to convert the vibrations produced by the bell into the complex patterns and shapes present in the paintings.

Realizing the potential of this contraption, you hurriedly pay for the device and exit the store, happy that you now have a way to generate new paintings in your favorite style, simply by visiting the shop, chiming the bell, and waiting for your F.L.O.W. machine to work its magic!

The story of Jacob and the F.L.O.W. machine is a depiction of a normalizing flow model. Let's now explore the theory of normalizing flows in more detail, before we implement a practical example using Keras.

Normalizing Flows

The motivation of normalizing flow models is similar to that of variational autoencoders, which we explored in Chapter 3. To recap, in a variational autoencoder, we learn an *encoder* mapping function between a complex distribution and a much simpler distribution that we can sample from. We then also learn a *decoder* mapping function from the simpler distribution to the complex distribution, so that we can generate a new data point by sampling a point z from the simpler distribution and applying the learned transformation. Probabilistically speaking, the decoder models $p(x|z)$ but the encoder is only an approximation $q(z|x)$ of the true $p(z|x)$—the encoder and decoder are two completely distinct neural networks.

In a normalizing flow model, the decoding function is designed to be the exact inverse of the encoding function and quick to calculate, giving normalizing flows the property of tractability. However, neural networks are not by default invertible functions. This raises the question of how we can create an invertible process that converts between a complex distribution (such as the data generation distribution of a set of watercolor paintings) and a much simpler distribution (such as a bell-shaped Gaussian distribution) while still making use of the flexibility and power of deep learning.

To answer this question, we first need to understand a technique known as *change of variables*. For this section, we will work with a simple example in just two dimensions, so that you can see exactly how normalizing flows work in fine detail. More complex examples are just extensions of the basic techniques presented here.

Change of Variables

Suppose we have a probability distribution $p_X(x)$ defined over a rectangle X in two dimensions $(x = (x_1, x_2))$, as shown in Figure 6-2.

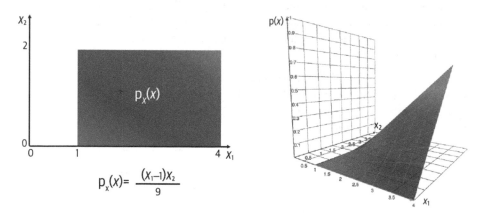

$$p_X(x) = \frac{(x_1 - 1)x_2}{9}$$

Figure 6-2. A probability distribution $p_X(x)$ defined over two dimensions, shown in 2D (left) and 3D (right)

This function integrates to 1 over the domain of the distribution (i.e., x_1 in the range [1, 4] and x_2 in the range [0, 2]), so it represents a well-defined probability distribution. We can write this as follows:

$$\int_0^2 \int_1^4 p_X(x)\,dx_1\,dx_2 = 1$$

Let's say that we want to shift and scale this distribution so that it is instead defined over a unit square Z. We can achieve this by defining a new variable $z = (z_1, z_2)$ and a function f that maps each point in X to exactly one point in Z as follows:

$$z = f(x)$$
$$z_1 = \frac{x_1 - 1}{3}$$
$$z_2 = \frac{x_2}{2}$$

Note that this function is *invertible*. That is, there is a function g that maps every z back to its corresponding x. This is essential for a change of variables, as otherwise we cannot consistently map backward and forward between the two spaces. We can find g simply by rearranging the equations that define f, as shown in Figure 6-3.

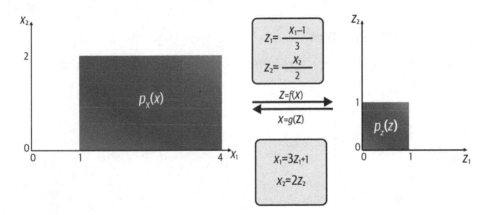

Figure 6-3. Changing variables between X and Z

We now need to see how the change of variables from X to Z affects the probability distribution $p_X(x)$. We can do this by plugging the equations that define g into $p_X(x)$ to transform it into a function $p_Z(z)$ that is defined in terms of z:

$$p_Z(z) = \frac{((3z_1 + 1) - 1)(2z_2)}{9}$$
$$= \frac{2z_1 z_2}{3}$$

However, if we now integrate $p_Z(z)$ over the unit square, we can see that we have a problem!

$$\int_0^1 \int_0^1 \frac{2z_1 z_2}{3} dz_1 dz_2 = \frac{1}{6}$$

The transformed function $p_Z(z)$ is now no longer a valid probability distribution, because it only integrates to 1/6. If we want to transform our complex probability distribution over the data into a simpler distribution that we can sample from, we must ensure that it integrates to 1.

The missing factor of 6 is due to the fact that the domain of our transformed probability distribution is six times smaller than the original domain—the original rectangle X had area 6, and this has been compressed into a unit square Z that only has area 1. Therefore, we need to multiply the new probability distribution by a normalization factor that is equal to the relative change in area (or volume in higher dimensions).

Luckily, there is a way to calculate this volume change for a given transformation—it is the absolute value of the Jacobian determinant of the transformation. Let's unpack that!

The Jacobian Determinant

The *Jacobian* of a function $z = f(x)$ is the matrix of its first-order partial derivatives, as shown here:

$$J = \frac{\partial z}{\partial x} = \begin{bmatrix} \frac{\partial z_1}{\partial x_1} & \cdots & \frac{\partial z_1}{\partial x_n} \\ \ddots & \vdots \\ \frac{\partial z_m}{\partial x_1} & \cdots & \frac{\partial z_m}{\partial x_n} \end{bmatrix}$$

The best way to explain this is with our example. If we take the partial derivative of z_1 with respect to x_1, we obtain $\frac{1}{3}$. If we take the partial derivative of z_1 with respect to x_2, we obtain 0. Similarly, if we take the partial derivative of z_2 with respect to x_1, we obtain 0. Lastly, if we take the partial derivative of z_2 with respect to x_2, we obtain $\frac{1}{2}$.

Therefore, the Jacobian matrix for our function $f(x)$ is as follows:

$$J = \begin{pmatrix} \frac{1}{3} & 0 \\ 0 & \frac{1}{2} \end{pmatrix}$$

The *determinant* is only defined for square matrices and is equal to the signed volume of the parallelepiped created by applying the transformation represented by the matrix to the unit (hyper)cube. In two dimensions, this is therefore just the signed area of the parallelogram created by applying the transformation represented by the matrix to the unit square.

There is a general formula (*https://oreil.ly/FuDCf*) for calculating the determinant of a matrix with n dimensions, which runs in $\mathcal{O}(n^3)$ time. For our example, we only need the formula for two dimensions, which is simply as follows:

$$\det\begin{pmatrix} a & b \\ c & d \end{pmatrix} = ad - bc$$

Therefore, for our example, the determinant of the Jacobian is $\frac{1}{3} \times \frac{1}{2} - 0 \times 0 = \frac{1}{6}$. This is the scaling factor of 1/6 that we need to ensure that the probability distribution after transformation still integrates to 1!

> By definition, the determinant is signed—that is, it can be negative. Therefore we need to take the absolute value of the Jacobian determinant in order to obtain the relative change of volume.

The Change of Variables Equation

We can now write down a single equation that describes the process for changing variables between X and Z. This is known as the *change of variables equation* (Equation 6-1).

Equation 6-1. The change of variables equation

$$p_X(x) = p_Z(z) \left| \det\left(\frac{\partial z}{\partial x}\right) \right|$$

How does this help us build a generative model? The key is understanding that if $p_Z(z)$ is a simple distribution from which we can easily sample (e.g., a Gaussian), then in theory, all we need to do is find an appropriate invertible function $f(x)$ that can map from the data X into Z and the corresponding inverse function $g(z)$ that can be used to map a sampled z back to a point x in the original domain. We can use the preceding equation involving the Jacobian determinant to find an exact, tractable formula for the data distribution $p(x)$.

However, there are two major issues when applying this in practice that we first need to address!

Firstly, calculating the determinant of a high-dimensional matrix is computationally extremely expensive—specifically, it is $\mathcal{O}(n^3)$. This is completely impractical to implement in practice, as even small 32×32–pixel grayscale images have 1,024 dimensions.

Secondly, it is not immediately obvious how we should go about calculating the invertible function $f(x)$. We could use a neural network to find some function $f(x)$ but we cannot necessarily invert this network—neural networks only work in one direction!

To solve these two problems, we need to use a special neural network architecture that ensures that the change of variables function f is invertible and has a determinant that is easy to calculate.

We shall see how to do this in the following section using a technique called *real-valued non-volume preserving (RealNVP) transformations*.

RealNVP

RealNVP was first introduced by Dinh et al. in 2017.[1] In this paper the authors show how to construct a neural network that can transform a complex data distribution into a simple Gaussian, while also possessing the desired properties of being invertible and having a Jacobian that can be easily calculated.

Running the Code for This Example

The code for this example can be found in the Jupyter notebook located at *notebooks/06_normflow/01_realnvp/realnvp.ipynb* in the book repository.

The code has been adapted from the excellent RealNVP tutorial (*https://oreil.ly/ZjjwP*) created by Mandolini Giorgio Maria et al. available on the Keras website.

The Two Moons Dataset

The dataset we will use for this example is created by the make_moons function from the Python library sklearn. This creates a noisy dataset of points in 2D that resemble two crescents, as shown in Figure 6-4.

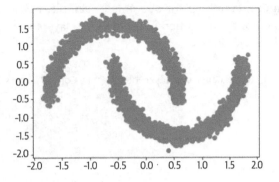

Figure 6-4. The two moons dataset in two dimensions

The code for creating this dataset is given in Example 6-1.

Example 6-1. Creating a moons dataset

```
data = datasets.make_moons(3000, noise=0.05)[0].astype("float32")  ❶
norm = layers.Normalization()
norm.adapt(data)
normalized_data = norm(data)  ❷
```

❶ Make a noisy, unnormalized moons dataset of 3,000 points.

❷ Normalize the dataset to have mean 0 and standard deviation 1.

We will build a RealNVP model that can generate points in 2D that follow a similar distribution to the two moons dataset. Whilst this is a very simple example, it will help us understand how a normalizing flow model works in practice, in fine detail.

First, however, we need to introduce a new type of layer, called a coupling layer.

Coupling Layers

A *coupling layer* produces a scale and translation factor for each element of its input. In other words, it produces two tensors that are exactly the same size as the input, one for the scale factor and one for the translation factor, as shown in Figure 6-5.

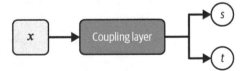

Figure 6-5. A coupling layer outputs two tensors that are the same shape as the input: a scaling factor (s) and a translation factor (t)

To build a custom `Coupling` layer for our simple example, we can stack `Dense` layers to create the scale output and a different set of `Dense` layers to create the translation output, as shown in Example 6-2.

 For images, `Coupling` layer blocks use `Conv2D` layers instead of `Dense` layers.

Example 6-2. A `Coupling` layer in Keras

```python
def Coupling():
    input_layer = layers.Input(shape=2) ❶

    s_layer_1 = layers.Dense(
        256, activation="relu", kernel_regularizer=regularizers.l2(0.01)
    )(input_layer) ❷
    s_layer_2 = layers.Dense(
        256, activation="relu", kernel_regularizer=regularizers.l2(0.01)
    )(s_layer_1)
    s_layer_3 = layers.Dense(
        256, activation="relu", kernel_regularizer=regularizers.l2(0.01)
    )(s_layer_2)
    s_layer_4 = layers.Dense(
        256, activation="relu", kernel_regularizer=regularizers.l2(0.01)
    )(s_layer_3)
    s_layer_5 = layers.Dense(
        2, activation="tanh", kernel_regularizer=regularizers.l2(0.01)
    )(s_layer_4) ❸

    t_layer_1 = layers.Dense(
        256, activation="relu", kernel_regularizer=regularizers.l2(0.01)
    )(input_layer) ❹
    t_layer_2 = layers.Dense(
        256, activation="relu", kernel_regularizer=regularizers.l2(0.01)
    )(t_layer_1)
    t_layer_3 = layers.Dense(
        256, activation="relu", kernel_regularizer=regularizers.l2(0.01)
    )(t_layer_2)
    t_layer_4 = layers.Dense(
        256, activation="relu", kernel_regularizer=regularizers.l2(0.01)
    )(t_layer_3)
    t_layer_5 = layers.Dense(
        2, activation="linear", kernel_regularizer=regularizers.l2(0.01)
    )(t_layer_4) ❺

    return models.Model(inputs=input_layer, outputs=[s_layer_5, t_layer_5]) ❻
```

❶ The input to the `Coupling` layer block in our example has two dimensions.

❷ The *scaling* stream is a stack of Dense layers of size 256.

❸ The final scaling layer is of size 2 and has tanh activation.

❹ The *translation* stream is a stack of Dense layers of size 256.

❺ The final translation layer is of size 2 and has linear activation.

❻ The Coupling layer is constructed as a Keras Model with two outputs (the scaling and translation factors).

Notice how the number of channels is temporarily increased to allow for a more complex representation to be learned, before being collapsed back down to the same number of channels as the input. In the original paper, the authors also use regularizers on each layer to penalize large weights.

Passing data through a coupling layer

The architecture of a coupling layer is not particularly interesting—what makes it unique is the way the input data is masked and transformed as it is fed through the layer, as shown in Figure 6-6.

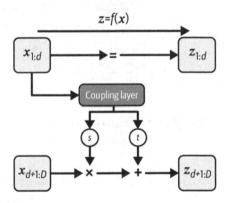

Figure 6-6. The process of transforming the input x through a coupling layer

Notice how only the first d dimensions of the data are fed through to the first coupling layer—the remaining $D - d$ dimensions are completely masked (i.e., set to zero). In our simple example with $D = 2$, choosing $d = 1$ means that instead of the coupling layer seeing two values, (x_1, x_2), the layer sees $(x_1, 0)$.

The outputs from the layer are the scale and translation factors. These are again masked, but this time with the *inverse* mask to previously, so that only the second halves are let through—i.e., in our example, we obtain $(0, s_2)$ and $(0, t_2)$. These are then applied element-wise to the second half of the input x_2 and the first half of the input x_1 is simply passed straight through, without being updated at all. In summary, for a vector with dimension D where $d < D$, the update equations are as follows:

$$z_{1:d} = x_{1:d}$$

$$z_{d+1:D} = x_{d+1:D} \odot \exp(s(x_{1:d})) + t(x_{1:d})$$

You may be wondering why we go to the trouble of building a layer that masks so much information. The answer is clear if we investigate the structure of the Jacobian matrix of this function:

$$\frac{\partial z}{\partial x} = \begin{bmatrix} \mathbf{I} & 0 \\ \dfrac{\partial z_{d+1:D}}{\partial x_{1:d}} & \mathrm{diag}(\exp[s(x_{1:d})]) \end{bmatrix}$$

The top-left $d \times d$ submatrix is simply the identity matrix, because $z_{1:d} = x_{1:d}$. These elements are passed straight through without being updated. The top-right submatrix is therefore 0, because $z_{1:d}$ is not dependent on $x_{d+1:D}$.

The bottom-left submatrix is complex, and we do not seek to simplify this. The bottom-right submatrix is simply a diagonal matrix, filled with the elements of $\exp(s(x_{1:d}))$, because $z_{d+1:D}$ is linearly dependent on $x_{d+1:D}$ and the gradient is dependent only on the scaling factor (not on the translation factor). Figure 6-7 shows a diagram of this matrix form, where only the nonzero elements are filled in with color.

Notice how there are no nonzero elements above the diagonal—for this reason, this matrix form is called *lower triangular*. Now we see the benefit of structuring the matrix in this way—the determinant of a lower-triangular matrix is just equal to the product of the diagonal elements. In other words, the determinant is not dependent on any of the complex derivatives in the bottom-left submatrix!

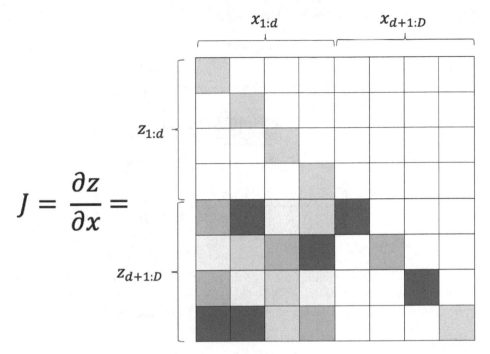

$$J = \frac{\partial z}{\partial x} =$$

Figure 6-7. The Jacobian matrix of the transformation—a lower triangular matrix, with determinant equal to the product of the elements along the diagonal

Therefore, we can write the determinant of this matrix as follows:

$$\det(J) = \exp\left[\sum_j s(x_{1:d})_j\right]$$

This is easily computable, which was one of the two original goals of building a normalizing flow model.

The other goal was that the function must be easily invertible. We can see that this is true as we can write down the invertible function just by rearranging the forward equations, as follows:

$$x_{1:d} = z_{1:d}$$
$$x_{d+1:D} = (z_{d+1:D} - t(x_{1:d})) \odot \exp(-s(x_{1:d}))$$

The equivalent diagram is shown in Figure 6-8.

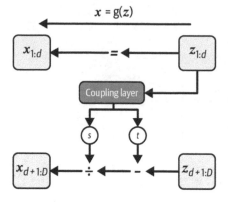

Figure 6-8. The inverse function x = g(z)

We now have almost everything we need to build our RealNVP model. However, there is one issue that still remains—how should we update the first d elements of the input? Currently they are left completely unchanged by the model!

Stacking coupling layers

To resolve this problem, we can use a really simple trick. If we stack coupling layers on top of each other but alternate the masking pattern, the layers that are left unchanged by one layer will be updated in the next. This architecture has the added benefit of being able to learn more complex representations of the data, as it is a deeper neural network.

The Jacobian of this composition of coupling layers will still be simple to compute, because linear algebra tells us that the determinant of a matrix product is the product of the determinants. Similarly, the inverse of the composition of two functions is just the composition of the inverses, as shown in the following equations:

$$\det(A \cdot B) = \det(A)\det(B)$$
$$\left(f_b \circ f_a\right)^{-1} = f_a^{-1} \circ f_b^{-1}$$

Therefore, if we stack coupling layers, flipping the masking each time, we can build a neural network that is able to transform the whole input tensor, while retaining the essential properties of having a simple Jacobian determinant and being invertible. Figure 6-9 shows the overall structure.

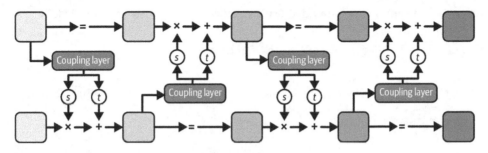

Figure 6-9. Stacking coupling layers, alternating the masking with each layer

Training the RealNVP Model

Now that we have built the RealNVP model, we can train it to learn the complex distribution of the two moons dataset. Remember, we want to minimize the negative log-likelihood of the data under the model $- \log p_X(x)$. Using Equation 6-1, we can write this as follows:

$$- \log p_X(x) = - \log p_Z(z) - \log \left| \det\left(\frac{\partial z}{\partial x}\right) \right|$$

We choose the target output distribution $p_Z(z)$ of the forward process f to be a standard Gaussian, because we can easily sample from this distribution. We can then transform a point sampled from the Gaussian back into the original image domain by applying the inverse process g, as shown in Figure 6-10.

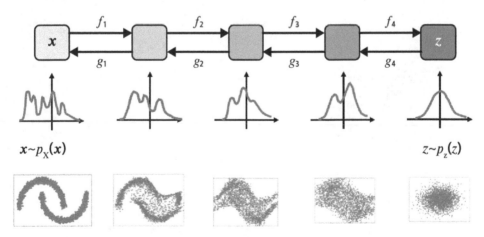

Figure 6-10. Transforming between the complex distribution $p_X(x)$ and a simple Gaussian $p_Z(z)$ in 1D (middle row) and 2D (bottom row)

Example 6-3 shows how to build a RealNVP network, as a custom Keras `Model`.

Example 6-3. Building the RealNVP model in Keras

```
class RealNVP(models.Model):
    def __init__(self, input_dim, coupling_layers, coupling_dim, regularization):
        super(RealNVP, self).__init__()
        self.coupling_layers = coupling_layers
        self.distribution = tfp.distributions.MultivariateNormalDiag(
            loc=[0.0, 0.0], scale_diag=[1.0, 1.0]
        ) ❶
        self.masks = np.array(
            [[0, 1], [1, 0]] * (coupling_layers // 2), dtype="float32"
        ) ❷
        self.loss_tracker = metrics.Mean(name="loss")
        self.layers_list = [
            Coupling(input_dim, coupling_dim, regularization)
            for i in range(coupling_layers)
        ] ❸

    @property
    def metrics(self):
        return [self.loss_tracker]

    def call(self, x, training=True):
        log_det_inv = 0
        direction = 1
        if training:
            direction = -1
        for i in range(self.coupling_layers)[::direction]: ❹
            x_masked = x * self.masks[i]
            reversed_mask = 1 - self.masks[i]
            s, t = self.layers_list[i](x_masked)
            s *= reversed_mask
            t *= reversed_mask
            gate = (direction - 1) / 2
            x = (
                reversed_mask
                * (x * tf.exp(direction * s) + direction * t * tf.exp(gate * s))
                + x_masked
            ) ❺
            log_det_inv += gate * tf.reduce_sum(s, axis = 1) ❻
        return x, log_det_inv

    def log_loss(self, x):
        y, logdet = self(x)
        log_likelihood = self.distribution.log_prob(y) + logdet ❼
        return -tf.reduce_mean(log_likelihood)

    def train_step(self, data):
        with tf.GradientTape() as tape:
```

```
        loss = self.log_loss(data)
        g = tape.gradient(loss, self.trainable_variables)
        self.optimizer.apply_gradients(zip(g, self.trainable_variables))
        self.loss_tracker.update_state(loss)
        return {"loss": self.loss_tracker.result()}

    def test_step(self, data):
        loss = self.log_loss(data)
        self.loss_tracker.update_state(loss)
        return {"loss": self.loss_tracker.result()}

model = RealNVP(
    input_dim = 2
    , coupling_layers= 6
    , coupling_dim = 256
    , regularization = 0.01
)

model.compile(optimizer=optimizers.Adam(learning_rate=0.0001))

model.fit(
    normalized_data
    , batch_size=256
    , epochs=300
)
```

❶ The target distribution is a standard 2D Gaussian.

❷ Here, we create the alternating mask pattern.

❸ A list of `Coupling` layers that define the RealNVP network.

❹ In the main `call` function of the network, we loop over the `Coupling` layers. If `training=True`, then we move forward through the layers (i.e., from data to latent space). If `training=False`, then we move backward through the layers (i.e., from latent space to data).

❺ This line describes both the forward and backward equations dependent on the `direction` (try plugging in `direction = -1` and `direction = 1` to prove this to yourself!).

❻ The log determinant of the Jacobian, which we need to calculate the loss function, is simply the sum of the scaling factors.

❼ The loss function is the negative sum of the log probability of the transformed data, under our target Gaussian distribution and the log determinant of the Jacobian.

Analysis of the RealNVP Model

Once the model is trained, we can use it to transform the training set into the latent space (using the forward direction, f) and, more importantly, to transform a sampled point in the latent space into a point that looks like it could have been sampled from the original data distribution (using the backward direction, g).

Figure 6-11 shows the output from the network before any learning has taken place—the forward and backward directions just pass information straight through with hardly any transformation.

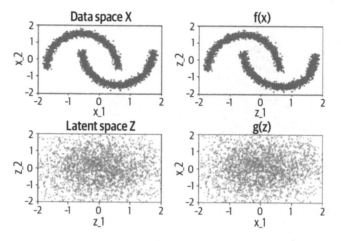

Figure 6-11. The RealNVP model inputs (left) and outputs (right) before training, for the forward process (top) and the reverse process (bottom)

After training (Figure 6-12), the forward process is able to convert the points from the training set into a distribution that resembles a Gaussian. Likewise, the backward process can take points sampled from a Gaussian distribution and map them back to a distribution that resembles the original data.

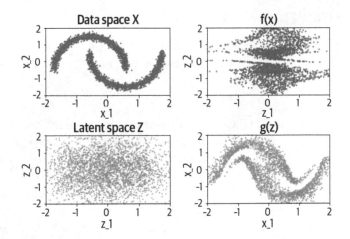

Figure 6-12. *The RealNVP model inputs (left) and outputs (right) after training, for the forward process (top) and the reverse process (bottom)*

The loss curve for the training process is shown in Figure 6-13.

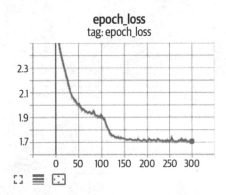

Figure 6-13. *The loss curve for the RealNVP training process*

This completes our discussion of RealNVP, a specific case of a normalizing flow generative model. In the next section, we'll cover some modern normalizing flow models that extend the ideas introduced in the RealNVP paper.

Other Normalizing Flow Models

Two other successful and important normalizing flow models are *GLOW* and *FFJORD*. The following sections describe the key advancements they made.

GLOW

Presented at NeurIPS 2018, GLOW was one of the first models to demonstrate the ability of normalizing flows to generate high-quality samples and produce a meaningful latent space that can be traversed to manipulate samples. The key step was to replace the reverse masking setup with invertible 1 × 1 convolutional layers. For example, with RealNVP applied to images, the ordering of the channels is flipped after each step, to ensure that the network gets the chance to transform all of the input. In GLOW a 1 × 1 convolution is applied instead, which effectively acts as a general method to produce any permutation of the channels that the model desires. The authors show that even with this addition, the distribution as a whole remains tractable, with determinants and inverses that are easy to compute at scale.

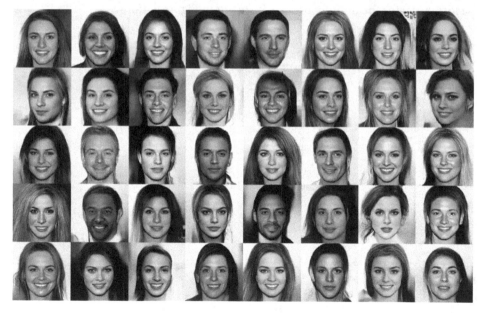

Figure 6-14. Random samples from the GLOW model (source: Kingma and Dhariwal, 2018)[2]

FFJORD

RealNVP and GLOW are discrete time normalizing flows—that is, they transform the input through a discrete set of coupling layers. FFJORD (Free-Form Continuous Dynamics for Scalable Reversible Generative Models), presented at ICLR 2019, shows how it is possible to model the transformation as a continuous time process (i.e., by taking the limit as the number of steps in the flow tends to infinity and the step size tends to zero). In this case, the dynamics are modeled using an ordinary differential equation (ODE) whose parameters are produced by a neural network (f_θ). A black-box solver is used to solve the ODE at time t_1—i.e., to find z_1 given some initial point z_0 sampled from a Gaussian at t_0, as described by the following equations:

$$z_0 \sim p(z_0)$$
$$\frac{\partial z(t)}{\partial t} = f_\theta(x(t), t)$$
$$x = z_1$$

A diagram of the transformation process is shown in Figure 6-15.

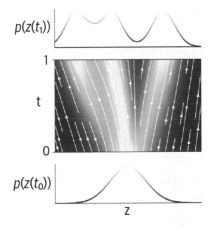

Figure 6-15. FFJORD models the transformation between the data distribution and a standard Gaussian via an ordinary differential equation, parameterized by a neural network (source: Will Grathwohl et al., 2018)[3]

Summary

In this chapter we explored normalizing flow models such as RealNVP, GLOW, and FFJORD.

A normalizing flow model is an invertible function defined by a neural network that allows us to directly model the data density via a change of variables. In the general case, the change of variables equation requires us to calculate a highly complex Jacobian determinant, which is impractical for all but the simplest of examples.

To sidestep this issue, the RealNVP model restricts the form of the neural network, such that it adheres to the two essential criteria: it is invertible and has a Jacobian determinant that is easy to compute.

It does this through stacking coupling layers, which produce scale and translation factors at each step. Importantly, the coupling layer masks the data as it flows through the network, in a way that ensures that the Jacobian is lower triangular and therefore has a simple-to-compute determinant. Full visibility of the input data is achieved through flipping the masks at each layer.

By design, the scale and translation operations can be easily inverted, so that once the model is trained it is possible to run data through the network in reverse. This means that we can target the forward transformation process toward a standard Gaussian, which we can easily sample from. We can then run the sampled points backward through the network to generate new observations.

The RealNVP paper also shows how it is possible to apply this technique to images, by using convolutions inside the coupling layers, rather than densely connected layers. The GLOW paper extended this idea to remove the necessity for any hardcoded permutation of the masks. The FFJORD model introduced the concept of continuous time normalizing flows, by modeling the transformation process as an ODE defined by a neural network.

Overall, we have seen how normalizing flows are a powerful generative modeling family that can produce high-quality samples, while maintaining the ability to tractably describe the data density function.

References

1. Laurent Dinh et al., "Density Estimation Using Real NVP," May 27, 2016, *https://arxiv.org/abs/1605.08803v3*.

2. Diedrick P. Kingma and Prafulla Dhariwal, "Glow: Generative Flow with Invertible 1x1 Convolutions," July 10, 2018, *https://arxiv.org/abs/1807.03039*.

3. Will Grathwohl et al., "FFJORD: Free-Form Continuous Dynamics for Scalable Reversible Generative Models," October 22, 2018, *https://arxiv.org/abs/1810.01367*.

CHAPTER 7

Energy-Based Models

Chapter Goals

In this chapter you will:

- Understand how to formulate a deep energy-based model (EBM).
- See how to sample from an EBM using Langevin dynamics.
- Train your own EBM using contrastive divergence.
- Analyze the EBM, including viewing snapshots of the Langevin dynamics sampling process.
- Learn about other types of EBM, such as restricted Boltzmann machines.

Energy-based models are a broad class of generative model that borrow a key idea from modeling physical systems—namely, that the probability of an event can be expressed using a Boltzmann distribution, a specific function that normalizes a real-valued energy function between 0 and 1. This distribution was originally formulated in 1868 by Ludwig Boltzmann, who used it to describe gases in thermal equilibrium.

In this chapter, we will see how we can use this idea to train a generative model that can be used to produce images of handwritten digits. We will explore several new concepts, including contrastive divergence for training the EBM and Langevin dynamics for sampling.

Introduction

We will begin with a short story to illustrate the key concepts behind energy-based models.

The Long-au-Vin Running Club

Diane Mixx was head coach of the long-distance running team in the fictional French town of Long-au-Vin. She was well known for her exceptional abilities as a trainer and had acquired a reputation for being able to turn even the most mediocre of athletes into world-class runners (Figure 7-1).

Figure 7-1. A running coach training some elite athletes (created with Midjourney)

Her methods were based around assessing the energy levels of each athlete. Over years of working with athletes of all abilities, she had developed an incredibly accurate sense of just how much energy a particular athlete had left after a race, just by looking at them. The lower an athlete's energy level, the better—elite athletes always gave everything they had during the race!

To keep her skills sharp, she regularly trained herself by measuring the contrast between her energy sensing abilities on known elite athletes and the best athletes from her club. She ensured that the divergence between her predictions for these two groups was as large as possible, so that people would take her seriously if she said that she had found a true elite athlete within her club.

The real magic was her ability to convert a mediocre runner into a top-class runner. The process was simple—she measured the current energy level of the athlete and worked out the optimal set of adjustments the athlete needed to make to improve their performance next time. Then, after making these adjustments, she measured the athlete's energy level again, looking for it to be slightly lower than before, explaining the improved performance on the track. This process of assessing the optimal adjustments and taking a small step in the right direction would continue until eventually the athlete was indistinguishable from a world-class runner.

After many years Diane retired from coaching and published a book on her methods for generating elite athletes—a system she branded the "Long-au-Vin, Diane Mixx" technique.

The story of Diane Mixx and the Long-au-Vin running club captures the key ideas behind energy-based modeling. Let's now explore the theory in more detail, before we implement a practical example using Keras.

Energy-Based Models

Energy-based models attempt to model the true data-generating distribution using a *Boltzmann distribution* (Equation 7-1) where $E(x)$ is know as the *energy function* (or *score*) of an observation x.

Equation 7-1. Boltzmann distribution

$$p(\mathbf{x}) = \frac{e^{-E(\mathbf{x})}}{\int_{\hat{\mathbf{x}} \in \mathbf{X}} e^{-E(\hat{\mathbf{x}})}}$$

In practice, this amounts to training a neural network $E(x)$ to output low scores for likely observations (so $p\mathbf{x}$ is close to 1) and high scores for unlikely observations (so $p\mathbf{x}$ is close to 0).

There are two challenges with modeling the data in this way. Firstly, it is not clear how we should use our model for sampling new observations—we can use it to generate a score given an observation, but how do we generate an observation that has a low score (i.e., a plausible observation)?

Secondly, the normalizing denominator of Equation 7-1 contains an integral that is intractable for all but the simplest of problems. If we cannot calculate this integral, then we cannot use maximum likelihood estimation to train the model, as this requires that $p\mathbf{x}$ is a valid probability distribution.

The key idea behind an energy-based model is that we can use approximation techniques to ensure we never need to calculate the intractable denominator. This is in contrast to, say, a normalizing flow, where we go to great lengths to ensure that the transformations that we apply to our standard Gaussian distribution do not change the fact that the output is still a valid probability distribution.

We sidestep the tricky intractable denominator problem by using a technique called contrastive divergence (for training) and a technique called Langevin dynamics (for sampling), following the ideas from Du and Mordatch's 2019 paper "Implicit

Generation and Modeling with Energy-Based Models."[1] We shall explore these techniques in detail while building our own EBM later in the chapter.

First, let's get set up with a dataset and design a simple neural network that will represent our real-valued energy function $E(x)$.

Running the Code for This Example

The code for this example can be found in the Jupyter notebook located at *notebooks/07_ebm/01_ebm/ebm.ipynb* in the book repository.

The code is adapted from the excellent tutorial on deep energy-based generative models (*https://oreil.ly/kyO9B*) by Phillip Lippe.

The MNIST Dataset

We'll be using the standard MNIST dataset (*https://oreil.ly/mSvhc*), consisting of grayscale images of handwritten digits. Some example images from the dataset are shown in Figure 7-2.

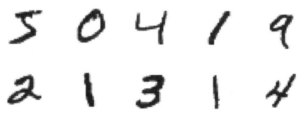

Figure 7-2. Examples of images from the MNIST dataset

The dataset comes prepackaged with TensorFlow, so it can be downloaded as shown in Example 7-1.

Example 7-1. Loading the MNIST dataset

```
from tensorflow.keras import datasets
(x_train, _), (x_test, _) = datasets.mnist.load_data()
```

As usual, we'll scale the pixel values to the range [-1, 1] and add some padding to make the images 32 × 32 pixels in size. We also convert it to a TensorFlow Dataset, as shown in Example 7-2.

Example 7-2. Preprocessing the MNIST dataset

```
def preprocess(imgs):
    imgs = (imgs.astype("float32") - 127.5) / 127.5
```

```
    imgs = np.pad(imgs , ((0,0), (2,2), (2,2)), constant_values= -1.0)
    imgs = np.expand_dims(imgs, -1)
    return imgs

x_train = preprocess(x_train)
x_test = preprocess(x_test)
x_train = tf.data.Dataset.from_tensor_slices(x_train).batch(128)
x_test = tf.data.Dataset.from_tensor_slices(x_test).batch(128)
```

Now that we have our dataset, we can build the neural network that will represent our energy function $E(x)$.

The Energy Function

The energy function $E_\theta(x)$ is a neural network with parameters θ that can transform an input image x into a scalar value. Throughout this network, we make use of an activation function called *swish*, as described in the following sidebar.

Swish Activation

Swish is an alternative to ReLU that was introduced by Google in 2017[2] and is defined as follows:

$$\text{swish}(x) = x \cdot \text{sigmoid}(x) = \frac{x}{e^{-x} + 1}$$

Swish is visually similar to ReLU, with the key difference being that it is smooth, which helps to alleviate the vanishing gradient problem. This is particularly important for energy-based models. A plot of the swish function is shown in Figure 7-3.

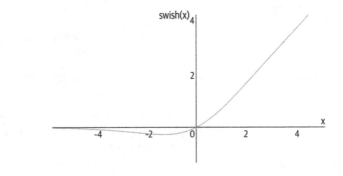

Figure 7-3. The swish activation function

The network is a set of stacked Conv2D layers that gradually reduce the size of the image while increasing the number of channels. The final layer is a single fully connected unit with linear activation, so the network can output values in the range $(-\infty, \infty)$. The code to build it is given in Example 7-3.

Example 7-3. Building the energy function E(x) neural network

```
ebm_input = layers.Input(shape=(32, 32, 1))
x = layers.Conv2D(
    16, kernel_size=5, strides=2, padding="same", activation = activations.swish
)(ebm_input) ❶
x = layers.Conv2D(
    32, kernel_size=3, strides=2, padding="same", activation = activations.swish
)(x)
x = layers.Conv2D(
    64, kernel_size=3, strides=2, padding="same", activation = activations.swish
)(x)
x = layers.Conv2D(
    64, kernel_size=3, strides=2, padding="same", activation = activations.swish
)(x)
x = layers.Flatten()(x)
x = layers.Dense(64, activation = activations.swish)(x)
ebm_output = layers.Dense(1)(x) ❷
model = models.Model(ebm_input, ebm_output) ❸
```

❶ The energy function is a set of stacked Conv2D layers, with swish activation.

❷ The final layer is a single fully connected unit, with a linear activation function.

❸ A Keras Model that converts the input image into a scalar energy value.

Sampling Using Langevin Dynamics

The energy function only outputs a score for a given input—how can we use this function to generate new samples that have a low energy score?

We will use a technique called *Langevin dynamics*, which makes use of the fact that we can compute the gradient of the energy function with respect to its input. If we start from a random point in the sample space and take small steps in the opposite direction of the calculated gradient, we will gradually reduce the energy function. If our neural network is trained correctly, then the random noise should transform into an image that resembles an observation from the training set before our eyes!

We can visualize this gradient descent as shown in Figure 7-4, for a two-dimensional space with the energy function value on the third dimension. The path is a noisy descent downhill, following the negative gradient of the energy function $E(x)$ with respect to the input x. In the MNIST image dataset, we have 1,024 pixels so are navigating a 1,024-dimensional space, but the same principles apply!

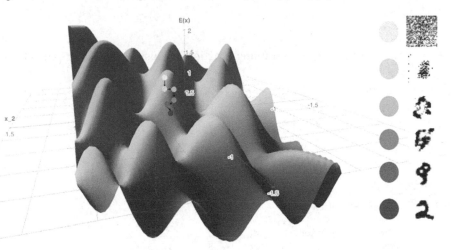

Figure 7-4. Gradient descent using Langevin dynamics

It is worth noting the difference between this kind of gradient descent and the kind of gradient descent we normally use to train a neural network.

When training a neural network, we calculate the gradient of the *loss function* with respect to the *parameters* of the network (i.e., the weights) using backpropagation. Then we update the parameters a small amount in the direction of the negative gradient, so that over many iterations, we gradually minimize the loss.

With Langevin dynamics, we keep the neural network weights *fixed* and calculate the gradient of the *output* with respect to the *input*. Then we update the input a small amount in the direction of the negative gradient, so that over many iterations, we gradually minimize the output (the energy score).

Both processes utilize the same idea (gradient descent), but are applied to different functions and with respect to different entities.

Formally, Langevin dynamics can be described by the following equation:

$$x^k = x^{k-1} - \eta \nabla_x E_\theta\left(x^{k-1}\right) + \omega$$

where $\omega \sim \mathcal{N}(0, \sigma)$ and $x^0 \sim \mathcal{U}(-1,1)$. η is the step size hyperparameter that must be tuned—too large and the steps jump over minima, too small and the algorithm will be too slow to converge.

$x^0 \sim \mathcal{U}(-1,1)$ is the uniform distribution on the range $[-1, 1]$.

We can code up our Langevin sampling function as illustrated in Example 7-4.

Example 7-4. The Langevin sampling function

```
def generate_samples(model, inp_imgs, steps, step_size, noise):
    imgs_per_step = []
    for _ in range(steps):  ❶
        inp_imgs += tf.random.normal(inp_imgs.shape, mean = 0, stddev = noise)  ❷
        inp_imgs = tf.clip_by_value(inp_imgs, -1.0, 1.0)
        with tf.GradientTape() as tape:
            tape.watch(inp_imgs)
            out_score = -model(inp_imgs)  ❸
        grads = tape.gradient(out_score, inp_imgs)  ❹
        grads = tf.clip_by_value(grads, -0.03, 0.03)
        inp_imgs += -step_size * grads  ❺
        inp_imgs = tf.clip_by_value(inp_imgs, -1.0, 1.0)
    return inp_imgs
```

❶ Loop over given number of steps.

❷ Add a small amount of noise to the image.

❸ Pass the image through the model to obtain the energy score.

❹ Calculate the gradient of the output with respect to the input.

❺ Add a small amount of the gradient to the input image.

Training with Contrastive Divergence

Now that we know how to sample a novel low-energy point from the sample space, let's turn our attention to training the model.

We cannot apply maximum likelihood estimation, because the energy function does not output a probability; it outputs a score that does not integrate to 1 across the sample space. Instead, we will apply a technique first proposed in 2002 by Geoffrey Hinton, called *contrastive divergence*, for training unnormalized scoring models.[4]

The value that we want to minimize (as always) is the negative log-likelihood of the data:

$$\mathcal{L} = -\mathbb{E}_{x \sim \text{data}}\left[\log p_\theta(\mathbf{x})\right]$$

When $p_\theta(\mathbf{x})$ has the form of a Boltzmann distribution, with energy function $E_\theta(\mathbf{x})$, it can be shown that the gradient of this value can be written as follows (Oliver Woodford's "Notes on Contrastive Divergence" for the full derivation):[5]

$$\nabla_\theta \mathcal{L} = \mathbb{E}_{x \sim \text{data}}\left[\nabla_\theta E_\theta(\mathbf{x})\right] - \mathbb{E}_{x \sim \text{model}}\left[\nabla_\theta E_\theta(\mathbf{x})\right]$$

This intuitively makes a lot of sense—we want to train the model to output large negative energy scores for real observations and large positive energy scores for generated fake observations so that the contrast between these two extremes is as large as possible.

In other words, we can calculate the difference between the energy scores of real and fake samples and use this as our loss function.

To calculate the energy scores of fake samples, we would need to be able to sample exactly from the distribution $p_\theta(\mathbf{x})$, which isn't possible due to the intractable denominator. Instead, we can use our Langevin sampling procedure to generate a set of observations with low energy scores. The process would need to run for infinitely many steps to produce a perfect sample (which is obviously impractical), so instead we run for some small number of steps, on the assumption that this is good enough to produce a meaningful loss function.

We also maintain a buffer of samples from previous iterations, so that we can use this as the starting point for the next batch, rather than pure random noise. The code to produce the sampling buffer is shown in Example 7-5.

Example 7-5. The Buffer

```python
class Buffer:
    def __init__(self, model):
        super().__init__()
        self.model = model
        self.examples = [
            tf.random.uniform(shape = (1, 32, 32, 1)) * 2 - 1
            for _ in range(128)
        ] ❶

    def sample_new_exmps(self, steps, step_size, noise):
        n_new = np.random.binomial(128, 0.05) ❷
        rand_imgs = (
            tf.random.uniform((n_new, 32, 32, 1)) * 2 - 1
        )
        old_imgs = tf.concat(
            random.choices(self.examples, k=128-n_new), axis=0
        ) ❸
        inp_imgs = tf.concat([rand_imgs, old_imgs], axis=0)
        inp_imgs = generate_samples(
            self.model, inp_imgs, steps=steps, step_size=step_size, noise = noise
        ) ❹
        self.examples = tf.split(inp_imgs, 128, axis = 0) + self.examples ❺
        self.examples = self.examples[:8192]
        return inp_imgs
```

❶ The sampling buffer is initialized with a batch of random noise.

❷ On average, 5% of observations are generated from scratch (i.e., random noise) each time.

❸ The rest are pulled at random from the existing buffer.

❹ The observations are concatenated and run through the Langevin sampler.

❺ The resulting sample is added to the buffer, which is trimmed to a max length of 8,192 observations.

Figure 7-5 shows one training step of contrastive divergence. The scores of real observations are pushed down by the algorithm and the scores of fake observations are pulled up, without caring about normalizing these scores after each step.

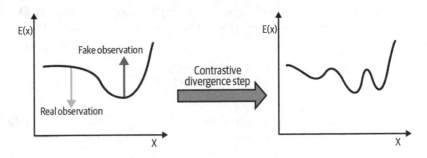

Figure 7-5. One step of contrastive divergence

We can code up the training step of the contrastive divergence algorithm within a custom Keras model as shown in Example 7-6.

Example 7-6. EBM trained using contrastive divergence

```python
class EBM(models.Model):
    def __init__(self):
        super(EBM, self).__init__()
        self.model = model
        self.buffer = Buffer(self.model)
        self.alpha = 0.1
        self.loss_metric = metrics.Mean(name="loss")
        self.reg_loss_metric = metrics.Mean(name="reg")
        self.cdiv_loss_metric = metrics.Mean(name="cdiv")
        self.real_out_metric = metrics.Mean(name="real")
        self.fake_out_metric = metrics.Mean(name="fake")

    @property
    def metrics(self):
        return [
            self.loss_metric,
            self.reg_loss_metric,
            self.cdiv_loss_metric,
            self.real_out_metric,
            self.fake_out_metric
        ]

    def train_step(self, real_imgs):
        real_imgs += tf.random.normal(
            shape=tf.shape(real_imgs), mean = 0, stddev = 0.005
        ) ❶
        real_imgs = tf.clip_by_value(real_imgs, -1.0, 1.0)
        fake_imgs = self.buffer.sample_new_exmps(
            steps=60, step_size=10, noise = 0.005
        ) ❷
        inp_imgs = tf.concat([real_imgs, fake_imgs], axis=0)
        with tf.GradientTape() as training_tape:
```

```
        real_out, fake_out = tf.split(self.model(inp_imgs), 2, axis=0) ❸
        cdiv_loss = tf.reduce_mean(fake_out, axis = 0) - tf.reduce_mean(
            real_out, axis = 0
        ) ❹
        reg_loss = self.alpha * tf.reduce_mean(
            real_out ** 2 + fake_out ** 2, axis = 0
        ) ❺
        loss = reg_loss + cdiv_loss
    grads = training_tape.gradient(loss, self.model.trainable_variables) ❻
    self.optimizer.apply_gradients(
        zip(grads, self.model.trainable_variables)
    )
    self.loss_metric.update_state(loss)
    self.reg_loss_metric.update_state(reg_loss)
    self.cdiv_loss_metric.update_state(cdiv_loss)
    self.real_out_metric.update_state(tf.reduce_mean(real_out, axis = 0))
    self.fake_out_metric.update_state(tf.reduce_mean(fake_out, axis = 0))
    return {m.name: m.result() for m in self.metrics}

def test_step(self, real_imgs): ❼
    batch_size = real_imgs.shape[0]
    fake_imgs = tf.random.uniform((batch_size, 32, 32, 1)) * 2 - 1
    inp_imgs = tf.concat([real_imgs, fake_imgs], axis=0)
    real_out, fake_out = tf.split(self.model(inp_imgs), 2, axis=0)
    cdiv = tf.reduce_mean(fake_out, axis = 0) - tf.reduce_mean(
        real_out, axis = 0
    )
    self.cdiv_loss_metric.update_state(cdiv)
    self.real_out_metric.update_state(tf.reduce_mean(real_out, axis = 0))
    self.fake_out_metric.update_state(tf.reduce_mean(fake_out, axis = 0))
    return {m.name: m.result() for m in self.metrics[2:]}

ebm = EBM()
ebm.compile(optimizer=optimizers.Adam(learning_rate=0.0001), run_eagerly=True)
ebm.fit(x_train, epochs=60, validation_data = x_test,)
```

❶ A small amount of random noise is added to the real images, to avoid the model overfitting to the training set.

❷ A set of fake images are sampled from the buffer.

❸ The real and fake images are run through the model to produce real and fake scores.

❹ The contrastive divergence loss is simply the difference between the scores of real and fake observations.

❺ A regularization loss is added to avoid the scores becoming too large.

❻ Gradients of the loss function with respect to the weights of the network are calculated for backpropagation.

❼ The `test_step` is used during validation and calculates the contrastive divergence between the scores of a set of random noise and data from the training set. It can be used as a measure for how well the model is training (see the following section).

Analysis of the Energy-Based Model

The loss curves and supporting metrics from the training process are shown in Figure 7-6.

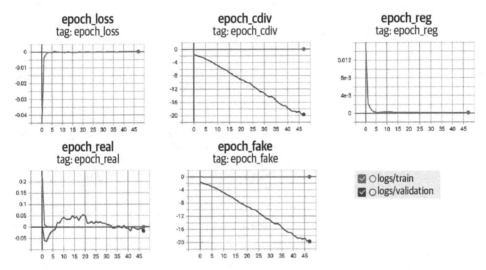

Figure 7-6. Loss curves and metrics for the training process of the EBM

Firstly, notice that the loss calculated during the training step is approximately constant and small across epochs. While the model is constantly improving, so is the quality of generated images in the buffer that it is required to compare against real images from the training set, so we shouldn't expect the training loss to fall significantly.

Therefore, to judge model performance, we also set up a validation process that doesn't sample from the buffer, but instead scores a sample of random noise and compares this against the scores of examples from the training set. If the model is improving, we should see that the contrastive divergence falls over the epochs (i.e., it is getting better at distinguishing random noise from real images), as can be seen in Figure 7-6.

Generating new samples from the EBM is simply a case of running the Langevin sampler for a large number of steps, from a standing start (random noise), as shown in Example 7-7. The observation is forced *downhill*, following the gradients of the scoring function with respect to the input, so that out of the noise, a plausible observation appears.

Example 7-7. Generating new observations using the EBM

```
start_imgs = np.random.uniform(size = (10, 32, 32, 1)) * 2 - 1
gen_img = generate_samples(
    ebm.model,
    start_imgs,
    steps=1000,
    step_size=10,
    noise = 0.005,
    return_img_per_step=True,
)
```

Some examples of observations produced by the sampler after 50 epochs of training are shown in Figure 7-7.

Figure 7-7. Examples produced by the Langevin sampler using the EBM model to direct the gradient descent

We can even show a replay of how a single observation is generated by taking snapshots of the current observations during the Langevin sampling process—this is shown in Figure 7-8.

| Step | 0 | 1 | 3 | 5 | 10 | 30 | 50 | 100 | 300 | 999 |

Figure 7-8. Snapshots of an observation at different steps of the Langevin sampling process

Other Energy-Based Models

In the previous example we made use of a deep EBM trained using contrastive divergence with a Langevin dynamics sampler. However, early EBM models did not make use of Langevin sampling, but instead relied on other techniques and architectures.

One of the earliest examples of an EBM was the *Boltzmann machine*.[6] This is a fully connected, undirected neural network, where binary units are either *visible* (*v*) or *hidden* (*h*). The energy of a given configuration of the network is defined as follows:

$$E_\theta(v, h) = -\frac{1}{2}\left(v^T L v + h^T J h + v^T W h\right)$$

where W, L, J are the weights matrices that are learned by the model. Training is achieved by contrastive divergence, but using Gibbs sampling to alternate between the visible and hidden layers until an equilibrium is found. In practice this is very slow and not scalable to large numbers of hidden units.

See Jessica Stringham's blog post "Gibbs Sampling in Python" (*https://oreil.ly/tXmOq*) for an excellent simple example of Gibbs sampling.

An extension to this model, the *restricted Boltzmann machine* (RBM), removes the connections between units of the same type, therefore creating a two-layer bipartite graph. This allows RBMs to be stacked into *deep belief networks* to model more complex distributions. However, modeling high-dimensional data with RBMs remains impractical, due to the fact that Gibbs sampling with long mixing times is still required.

It was only in the late 2000s that EBMs were shown to have potential for modeling more high-dimensional datasets and a framework for building deep EBMs was established.[7] Langevin dynamics became the preferred sampling method for EBMs, which later evolved into a training technique known as *score matching*. This further developed into a model class known as *Denoising Diffusion Probabilistic Models*, which power state-of-the-art generative models such as DALL.E 2 and ImageGen. We will explore diffusion models in more detail in Chapter 8.

Summary

Energy-based models are a class of generative model that make use of an energy scoring function—a neural network that is trained to output low scores for real observations and high scores for generated observations. Calculating the probability distribution given by this score function would require normalizing by an intractable denominator. EBMs avoid this problem by utilizing two tricks: contrastive divergence for training the network and Langevin dynamics for sampling new observations.

The energy function is trained by minimizing the difference between the generated sample scores and the scores of the training data, a technique known as contrastive divergence. This can be shown to be equivalent to minimizing the negative log-likelihood, as required by maximum likelihood estimation, but does not require us to calculate the intractable normalizing denominator. In practice, we approximate the sampling process for the fake samples to ensure the algorithm remains efficient.

Sampling of deep EBMs is achieved through Langevin dynamics, a technique that uses the gradient of the score with respect to the input image to gradually transform random noise into a plausible observation by updating the input in small steps, following the gradient downhill. This improves upon earlier methods such as Gibbs sampling, which is utilized by restricted Boltzmann machines.

References

1. Yilun Du and Igor Mordatch, "Implicit Generation and Modeling with Energy-Based Models," March 20, 2019, *https://arxiv.org/abs/1903.08689*.

2. Prajit Ramachandran et al., "Searching for Activation Functions," October 16, 2017, *https://arxiv.org/abs/1710.05941v2*.

3. Max Welling and Yee Whye Teh, "Bayesian Learning via Stochastic Gradient Langevin Dynamics," 2011, *https://www.stats.ox.ac.uk/~teh/research/compstats/WelTeh2011a.pdf*

4. Geoffrey E. Hinton, "Training Products of Experts by Minimizing Contrastive Divergence," 2002, *https://www.cs.toronto.edu/~hinton/absps/tr00-004.pdf*.

5. Oliver Woodford, "Notes on Contrastive Divergence," 2006, *https://www.robots.ox.ac.uk/~ojw/files/NotesOnCD.pdf*.

6. David H. Ackley et al., "A Learning Algorithm for Boltzmann Machines," 1985, *Cognitive Science* 9(1), 147-165.

7. Yann Lecun et al., "A Tutorial on Energy-Based Learning," 2006, *https://www.researchgate.net/publication/200744586_A_tutorial_on_energy-based_learning*.

CHAPTER 8

Diffusion Models

Chapter Goals

In this chapter you will:

- Learn the underlying principles and components that define a diffusion model.
- See how the forward process is used to add noise to the training set of images.
- Understand the reparameterization trick and why it is important.
- Explore different forms of forward diffusion scheduling.
- Understand the reverse diffusion process and how it relates to the forward noising process.
- Explore the architecture of the U-Net, which is used to parameterize the reverse diffusion process.
- Build your own denoising diffusion model (DDM) using Keras to generate images of flowers.
- Sample new images of flowers from your model.
- Explore the effect of the number of diffusion steps on image quality and interpolate between two images in the latent space.

Alongside GANs, diffusion models are one of the most influential and impactful generative modeling techniques for image generation to have been introduced over the last decade. Across many benchmarks, diffusion models now outperform previously state-of-the-art GANs and are quickly becoming the go-to choice for generative modeling practitioners, particularly for visual domains (e.g., OpenAI's DALL.E 2 and Google's ImageGen for text-to-image generation). Recently, there has been an explosion of diffusion models being applied across wide range of tasks, reminiscent of the GAN proliferation that took place between 2017–2020.

Many of the core ideas that underpin diffusion models share similarities with earlier types of generative models that we have already explored in this book (e.g., denoising autoencoders, energy-based models). Indeed, the name *diffusion* takes inspiration from the well-studied property of thermodynamic diffusion: an important link was made between this purely physical field and deep learning in 2015.[1]

Important progress was also being made in the field of score-based generative models,[2,3] a branch of energy-based modeling that directly estimates the gradient of the log distribution (also known as the score function) in order to train the model, as an alternative to using contrastive divergence. In particular, Yang Song and Stefano Ermon used multiple scales of noise perturbations applied to the raw data to ensure the model—a *noise conditional score network* (NCSN)—performs well on regions of low data density.

The breakthrough diffusion model paper came in the summer of 2020.[4] Standing on the shoulders of earlier works, the paper uncovers a deep connection between diffusion models and score-based generative models, and the authors use this fact to train a diffusion model that can rival GANs across several datasets, called the *Denoising Diffusion Probabilistic Model* (DDPM).

This chapter will walk through the theoretical requirements for understanding how a denoising diffusion model works. You will then learn how to build your own denoising diffusion model using Keras.

Introduction

To help explain the key ideas that underpin diffusion models, let's begin with a short story!

DiffuseTV

You are standing in an electronics store that sells television sets. However, this store is clearly very different from ones you have visited in the past. Instead of a wide variety of different brands, there are hundreds of identical copies of the same TV connected together in sequence, stretching into the back of the shop as far as you can see. What's more, the first few TV sets appear to be showing nothing but random static noise (Figure 8-1).

The shopkeeper comes over to ask if you need assistance. Confused, you ask her about the odd setup. She explains that this is the new DiffuseTV model that is set to revolutionize the entertainment industry and immediately starts telling you how it works, while walking deeper into the shop, alongside the line of TVs.

Figure 8-1. A long line of connected television sets stretching out along an aisle of a shop (created with Midjourney)

She explains that during the manufacturing process, the DiffuseTV is exposed to thousands of images of previous TV shows—but each of those images has been gradually corrupted with random static, until it is indistinguishable from pure random noise. The TVs are then designed to *undo* the random noise, in small steps, essentially trying to predict what the images looked like before the noise was added. You can see that as you walk further into the shop the images on each television set are indeed slightly clearer than the last.

You eventually reach the end of the long line of televisions, where you can see a perfect picture on the last set. While this is certainly clever technology, you are curious to understand how this is useful to the viewer. The shopkeeper continues with her explanation.

Instead of choosing a channel to watch, the viewer chooses a random initial configuration of static. Every configuration will lead to a different output image, and in some models can even be guided by a text prompt that you choose to input. Unlike a normal TV, with a limited range of channels to watch, the DiffuseTV gives the viewer unlimited choice and freedom to generate whatever they would like to appear on the screen!

You purchase a DiffuseTV right away and are relieved to hear that the long line of TVs in the shop is for demonstration purposes only, so you won't have to also buy a warehouse to store your new device!

The DiffuseTV story describes the general idea behind a diffusion model. Now let's dive into the technicalities of how we build such a model using Keras.

Denoising Diffusion Models (DDM)

The core idea behind a denoising diffusion model is simple—we train a deep learning model to denoise an image over a series of very small steps. If we start from pure random noise, in theory we should be able to keep applying the model until we obtain an image that looks as if it were drawn from the training set. What's amazing is that this simple concept works so well in practice!

Let's first get set up with a dataset and then walk through the forward (noising) and backward (denoising) diffusion processes.

Running the Code for This Example

The code for this example can be found in the Jupyter notebook located at *notebooks/08_diffusion/01_ddm/ddm.ipynb* in the book repository.

The code is adapted from the excellent tutorial on denoising diffusion implicit models (*https://oreil.ly/srPCe*) created by András Béres available on the Keras website.

The Flowers Dataset

We'll be using the Oxford 102 Flower dataset (*https://oreil.ly/HfrKV*) that is available through Kaggle. This is a set of over 8,000 color images of a variety of flowers.

You can download the dataset by running the Kaggle dataset downloader script in the book repository, as shown in Example 8-1. This will save the flower images to the */data* folder.

Example 8-1. Downloading the Oxford 102 Flower dataset

```
bash scripts/download_kaggle_data.sh nunenuh pytorch-challange-flower-dataset
```

As usual, we'll load the images in using the Keras `image_dataset_from_directory` function, resize the images to 64 × 64 pixels, and scale the pixel values to the range [0, 1]. We'll also repeat the dataset five times to increase the epoch length and batch the data into groups of 64 images, as shown in Example 8-2.

Example 8-2. Loading the Oxford 102 Flower dataset

```
train_data = utils.image_dataset_from_directory(
    "/app/data/pytorch-challange-flower-dataset/dataset",
    labels=None,
    image_size=(64, 64),
    batch_size=None,
    shuffle=True,
```

```
    seed=42,
    interpolation="bilinear",
) ❶

def preprocess(img):
    img = tf.cast(img, "float32") / 255.0
    return img

train = train_data.map(lambda x: preprocess(x)) ❷
train = train.repeat(5) ❸
train = train.batch(64, drop_remainder=True) ❹
```

❶   Load dataset (when required during training) using the Keras `image_data set_from_directory` function.

❷   Scale the pixel values to the range [0, 1].

❸   Repeat the dataset five times.

❹   Batch the dataset into groups of 64 images.

Example images from the dataset are shown in Figure 8-2.

Figure 8-2. Example images from the Oxford 102 Flower dataset

Now that we have our dataset we can explore how we should add noise to the images, using a forward diffusion process.

The Forward Diffusion Process

Suppose we have an image $\mathbf{x}_0$ that we want to corrupt gradually over a large number of steps (say, $T = 1,000$), so that eventually it is indistinguishable from standard Gaussian noise (i.e., $\mathbf{x}_T$ should have zero mean and unit variance). How should we go about doing this?

We can define a function q that adds a small amount of Gaussian noise with variance β_t to an image $\mathbf{x}_{t-1}$ to generate a new image $\mathbf{x}_t$. If we keep applying this function, we will generate a sequence of progressively noisier images $(\mathbf{x}_0, ..., \mathbf{x}_T)$, as shown in Figure 8-3.

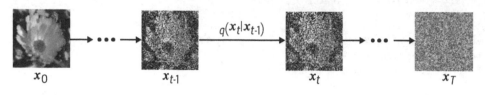

Figure 8-3. The forward diffusion process q

We can write this update process mathematically as follows (here, ϵ_{t-1} is a standard Gaussian with zero mean and unit variance):

$$\mathbf{x}_t = \sqrt{1 - \beta_t}\mathbf{x}_{t-1} + \sqrt{\beta_t}\epsilon_{t-1}$$

Note that we also scale the input image $\mathbf{x}_{t-1}$, to ensure that the variance of the output image $\mathbf{x}_t$ remains constant over time. This way, if we normalize our original image $\mathbf{x}_0$ to have zero mean and unit variance, then $\mathbf{x}_T$ will approximate a standard Gaussian distribution for large enough T, by induction, as follows.

If we assume that $\mathbf{x}_{t-1}$ has zero mean and unit variance then $\sqrt{1-\beta_t}\mathbf{x}_{t-1}$ will have variance $1 - \beta_t$ and $\sqrt{\beta_t}\epsilon_{t-1}$ will have variance β_t, using the rule that $Var(aX) = a^2 Var(X)$. Adding these together, we obtain a new distribution $\mathbf{x}_t$ with zero mean and variance $1 - \beta_t + \beta_t = 1$, using the rule that $Var(X + Y) = Var(X) + Var(Y)$ for independent X and Y. Therefore, if $\mathbf{x}_0$ is normalized to a zero mean and unit variance, then we guarantee that this is also true for all $\mathbf{x}_t$, including the final image $\mathbf{x}_T$, which will approximate a standard Gaussian distribution. This is exactly what we need, as we want to be able to easily sample $\mathbf{x}_T$ and then apply a reverse diffusion process through our trained neural network model!

In other words, our forward noising process q can also be written as follows:

$$q(\mathbf{x}_t | \mathbf{x}_{t-1}) = \mathcal{N}(\mathbf{x}_t; \sqrt{1 - \beta_t}\mathbf{x}_{t-1}, \beta_t \mathbf{I})$$

The Reparameterization Trick

It would also be useful to be able to jump straight from an image $\mathbf{x}_0$ to any noised version of the image $\mathbf{x}_t$ without having to go through t applications of q. Luckily, there is a reparameterization trick that we can use to do this.

If we define $\alpha_t = 1 - \beta_t$ and $\bar{\alpha}_t = \Pi_{i=1}^{t} \alpha_i$, then we can write the following:

$$
\begin{aligned}
\mathbf{x}_t &= \sqrt{\alpha_t}\mathbf{x}_{t-1} + \sqrt{1-\alpha_t}\epsilon_{t-1} \\
&= \sqrt{\alpha_t\alpha_{t-1}}\mathbf{x}_{t-2} + \sqrt{1-\alpha_t\alpha_{t-1}}\epsilon \\
&= \cdots \\
&= \sqrt{\bar{\alpha}_t}\mathbf{x}_0 + \sqrt{1-\bar{\alpha}_t}\epsilon
\end{aligned}
$$

Note that the second line uses the fact that we can add two Gaussians to obtain a new Gaussian. We therefore have a way to jump from the original image $\mathbf{x}_0$ to any step of the forward diffusion process $\mathbf{x}_t$. Moreover, we can define the diffusion schedule using the $\bar{\alpha}_t$ values, instead of the original β_t values, with the interpretation that $\bar{\alpha}_t$ is the variance due to the signal (the original image, $\mathbf{x}_0$) and $1 - \bar{\alpha}_t$ is the variance due to the noise (ϵ).

The forward diffusion process q can therefore also be written as follows:

$$
q(\mathbf{x}_t | \mathbf{x}_0) = \mathcal{N}\left(\mathbf{x}_t; \sqrt{\bar{\alpha}_t}\mathbf{x}_0, (1-\bar{\alpha}_t)\mathbf{I}\right)
$$

Diffusion Schedules

Notice that we are also free to choose a different β_t at each timestep—they don't all have be the same. How the β_t (or $\bar{\alpha}_t$) values change with t is called the *diffusion schedule*.

In the original paper (Ho et al., 2020), the authors chose a *linear diffusion schedule* for β_t—that is, β_t increases linearly with t, from $\beta_1 = 0.0001$ to $\beta_T = 0.02$. This ensures that in the early stages of the noising process we take smaller noising steps than in the later stages, when the image is already very noisy.

We can code up a linear diffusion schedule as shown in Example 8-3.

Example 8-3. The linear diffusion schedule

```
def linear_diffusion_schedule(diffusion_times):
    min_rate = 0.0001
    max_rate = 0.02
    betas = min_rate + tf.convert_to_tensor(diffusion_times) * (max_rate - min_rate)
    alphas = 1 - betas
    alpha_bars = tf.math.cumprod(alphas)
    signal_rates = alpha_bars
    noise_rates = 1 - alpha_bars
    return noise_rates, signal_rates
```

```
T = 1000
diffusion_times = [x/T for x in range(T)] ❶
linear_noise_rates, linear_signal_rates = linear_diffusion_schedule(
    diffusion_times
) ❷
```

❶   The diffusion times are equally spaced steps between 0 and 1.

❷   The linear diffusion schedule is applied to the diffusion times to produce the noise and signal rates.

In a later paper it was found that a *cosine diffusion schedule* outperformed the linear schedule from the original paper.[5] A cosine schedule defines the following values of $\bar{\alpha}_t$:

$$\bar{\alpha}_t = \cos^2\left(\frac{t}{T} \cdot \frac{\pi}{2}\right)$$

The updated equation is therefore as follows (using the trigonometric identity $\cos^2(x) + \sin^2(x) = 1$):

$$\mathbf{x}_t = \cos\left(\frac{t}{T} \cdot \frac{\pi}{2}\right)\mathbf{x}_0 + \sin\left(\frac{t}{T} \cdot \frac{\pi}{2}\right)\epsilon$$

This equation is a simplified version of the actual cosine diffusion schedule used in the paper. The authors also add an offset term and scaling to prevent the noising steps from being too small at the beginning of the diffusion process. We can code up the cosine and offset cosine diffusion schedules as shown in Example 8-4.

Example 8-4. The cosine and offset cosine diffusion schedules

```
def cosine_diffusion_schedule(diffusion_times): ❶
    signal_rates = tf.cos(diffusion_times * math.pi / 2)
    noise_rates = tf.sin(diffusion_times * math.pi / 2)
    return noise_rates, signal_rates

def offset_cosine_diffusion_schedule(diffusion_times): ❷
    min_signal_rate = 0.02
    max_signal_rate = 0.95
    start_angle = tf.acos(max_signal_rate)
    end_angle = tf.acos(min_signal_rate)

    diffusion_angles = start_angle + diffusion_times * (end_angle - start_angle)

    signal_rates = tf.cos(diffusion_angles)
    noise_rates = tf.sin(diffusion_angles)
```

```
return noise_rates, signal_rates
```

 The pure cosine diffusion schedule (without offset or rescaling).

❷ The offset cosine diffusion schedule that we will be using, which adjusts the schedule to ensure the noising steps are not too small at the start of the noising process.

We can compute the $\bar{\alpha}_t$ values for each t to show how much signal ($\bar{\alpha}_t$) and noise ($1 - \bar{\alpha}_t$) is let through at each stage of the process for the linear, cosine, and offset cosine diffusion schedules, as shown in Figure 8-4.

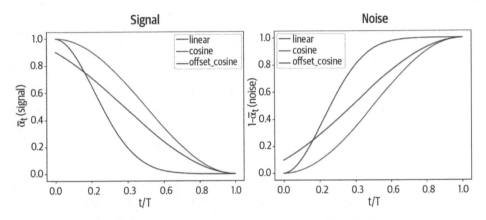

Figure 8-4. The signal and noise at each step of the noising process, for the linear, cosine, and offset cosine diffusion schedules

Notice how the noise level ramps up more slowly in the cosine diffusion schedule. A cosine diffusion schedule adds noise to the image more gradually than a linear diffusion schedule, which improves training efficiency and generation quality. This can also be seen in images that have been corrupted by the linear and cosine schedules (Figure 8-5).

Figure 8-5. An image being corrupted by the linear (top) and cosine (bottom) diffusion schedules, at equally spaced values of t from 0 to T (source: Ho et al., 2020)

The Reverse Diffusion Process

Now let's look at the reverse diffusion process. To recap, we are looking to build a neural network $p_\theta(\mathbf{x}_{t-1}|\mathbf{x}_t)$ that can *undo* the noising process—that is, approximate the reverse distribution $q(\mathbf{x}_{t-1}|\mathbf{x}_t)$. If we can do this, we can sample random noise from $\mathcal{N}(0, \mathbf{I})$ and then apply the reverse diffusion process multiple times in order to generate a novel image. This is visualized in Figure 8-6.

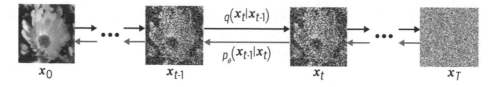

Figure 8-6. The reverse diffusion process $p_\theta \cdot (\mathbf{x}_{t-1}|\mathbf{x}_t)$ tries to undo the noise produced by the forward diffusion process

There are many similarities between the reverse diffusion process and the decoder of a variational autoencoder. In both, we aim to transform random noise into meaningful output using a neural network. The difference between diffusion models and VAEs is that in a VAE the forward process (converting images to noise) is part of the model (i.e., it is learned), whereas in a diffusion model it is unparameterized.

Therefore, it makes sense to apply the same loss function as in a variational autoencoder. The original DDPM paper derives the exact form of this loss function and shows that it can be optimized by training a network ϵ_θ to predict the noise ϵ that has been added to a given image $\mathbf{x}_0$ at timestep t.

In other words, we sample an image $\mathbf{x}_0$ and transform it by t noising steps to get the image $\mathbf{x}_t = \sqrt{\bar{\alpha}_t}\mathbf{x}_0 + \sqrt{1 - \bar{\alpha}_t}\epsilon$. We give this new image and the noising rate $\bar{\alpha}_t$ to the neural network and ask it to predict ϵ, taking a gradient step against the squared error between the prediction $\epsilon_\theta(\mathbf{x}_t)$ and the true ϵ.

We'll take a look at the structure of the neural network in the next section. It is worth noting here that the diffusion model actually maintains two copies of the network: one that is actively trained used gradient descent and another (the EMA network) that is an exponential moving average (EMA) of the weights of the actively trained network over previous training steps. The EMA network is not as susceptible to short-term fluctuations and spikes in the training process, making it more robust for generation than the actively trained network. We therefore use the EMA network whenever we want to produce generated output from the network.

The training process for the model is shown in Figure 8-7.

> **Algorithm 1** Training
>
> 1: **repeat**
> 2: $x_0 \sim q(x_0)$
> 3: $t \sim \text{Uniform}(\{1, \ldots, T\})$
> 4: $\epsilon \sim \mathcal{N}(0, I)$
> 5:   Take gradient descent step on
> $$\nabla_\theta \left\| \epsilon - \epsilon_\theta(\sqrt{\bar{\alpha}_t}x_0 + \sqrt{1 - \bar{\alpha}_t}\epsilon, t) \right\|^2$$
> 6: **until** converged

Figure 8-7. The training process for a denoising diffusion model (source: Ho et al., 2020)

In Keras, we can code up this training step as illustrated in Example 8-5.

Example 8-5. The `train_step` function of the Keras diffusion model

```python
class DiffusionModel(models.Model):
    def __init__(self):
        super().__init__()
        self.normalizer = layers.Normalization()
        self.network = unet
        self.ema_network = models.clone_model(self.network)
        self.diffusion_schedule = cosine_diffusion_schedule

    ...

    def denoise(self, noisy_images, noise_rates, signal_rates, training):
        if training:
            network = self.network
        else:
            network = self.ema_network
        pred_noises = network(
            [noisy_images, noise_rates**2], training=training
        )
        pred_images = (noisy_images - noise_rates * pred_noises) / signal_rates

        return pred_noises, pred_images

    def train_step(self, images):
        images = self.normalizer(images, training=True)   ❶
        noises = tf.random.normal(shape=tf.shape(images))   ❷
        batch_size = tf.shape(images)[0]
        diffusion_times = tf.random.uniform(
            shape=(batch_size, 1, 1, 1), minval=0.0, maxval=1.0
        )   ❸
        noise_rates, signal_rates = self.cosine_diffusion_schedule(
            diffusion_times
        )   ❹
        noisy_images = signal_rates * images + noise_rates * noises   ❺
```

```
with tf.GradientTape() as tape:
    pred_noises, pred_images = self.denoise(
        noisy_images, noise_rates, signal_rates, training=True
    ) ❻
    noise_loss = self.loss(noises, pred_noises) ❼
gradients = tape.gradient(noise_loss, self.network.trainable_weights)
self.optimizer.apply_gradients(
    zip(gradients, self.network.trainable_weights)
) ❽
self.noise_loss_tracker.update_state(noise_loss)

for weight, ema_weight in zip(
    self.network.weights, self.ema_network.weights
):
    ema_weight.assign(0.999 * ema_weight + (1 - 0.999) * weight) ❾

return {m.name: m.result() for m in self.metrics}

...
```

❶ We first normalize the batch of images to have zero mean and unit variance.

❷ Next, we sample noise to match the shape of the input images.

❸ We also sample random diffusion times...

❹ ...and use these to generate the noise and signal rates according to the cosine diffusion schedule.

❺ Then we apply the signal and noise weightings to the input images to generate the noisy images.

❻ Next, we denoise the noisy images by asking the network to predict the noise and then undoing the noising operation, using the provided `noise_rates` and `signal_rates`.

❼ We can then calculate the loss (mean absolute error) between the predicted noise and the true noise...

❽ ...and take a gradient step against this loss function.

❾ The EMA network weights are updated to a weighted average of the existing EMA weights and the trained network weights after the gradient step.

The U-Net Denoising Model

Now that we have seen the kind of neural network that we need to build (one that predicts the noise added to a given image), we can look at the architecture that makes this possible.

The authors of the DDPM paper used a type of architecture known as a *U-Net*. A diagram of this network is shown in Figure 8-8, explicitly showing the shape of the tensor as it passes through the network.

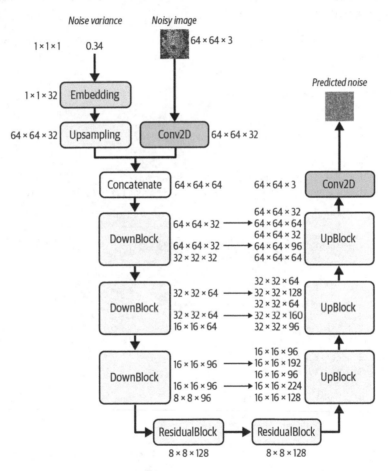

Figure 8-8. U-Net architecture diagram

In a similar manner to a variational autoencoder, a U-Net consists of two halves: the downsampling half, where input images are compressed spatially but expanded channel-wise, and the upsampling half, where representations are expanded spatially while the number of channels is reduced. However, unlike in a VAE, there are also *skip connections* between equivalent spatially shaped layers in the upsampling and downsampling parts of the network. A VAE is sequential; data flows through the network from input to output, one layer after another. A U-Net is different, because the skip connections allow information to shortcut parts of the network and flow through to later layers.

A U-Net is particularly useful when we want the output to have the same shape as the input. In our diffusion model example, we want to predict the noise added to an image, which has exactly the same shape as the image itself, so a U-Net is the natural choice for the network architecture.

First let's take a look at the code that builds this U-Net in Keras, shown in Example 8-6.

Example 8-6. A U-Net model in Keras

```
noisy_images = layers.Input(shape=(64, 64, 3)) ❶
x = layers.Conv2D(32, kernel_size=1)(noisy_images) ❷

noise_variances = layers.Input(shape=(1, 1, 1)) ❸
noise_embedding = layers.Lambda(sinusoidal_embedding)(noise_variances) ❹
noise_embedding = layers.UpSampling2D(size=64, interpolation="nearest")(
    noise_embedding
) ❺

x = layers.Concatenate()([x, noise_embedding]) ❻

skips = [] ❼

x = DownBlock(32, block_depth = 2)([x, skips]) ❽
x = DownBlock(64, block_depth = 2)([x, skips])
x = DownBlock(96, block_depth = 2)([x, skips])

x = ResidualBlock(128)(x) ❾
x = ResidualBlock(128)(x)

x = UpBlock(96, block_depth = 2)([x, skips]) ❿
x = UpBlock(64, block_depth = 2)([x, skips])
x = UpBlock(32, block_depth = 2)([x, skips])

x = layers.Conv2D(3, kernel_size=1, kernel_initializer="zeros")(x) ⓫

unet = models.Model([noisy_images, noise_variances], x, name="unet") ⓬
```

❶ The first input to the U-Net is the image that we wish to denoise.

❷ This image is passed through a Conv2D layer to increase the number of channels.

❸ The second input to the U-Net is the noise variance (a scalar).

❹ This is encoded using a sinusoidal embedding.

❺ This embedding is copied across spatial dimensions to match the size of the input image.

❻ The two input streams are concatenated across channels.

❼ The `skips` list will hold the output from the `DownBlock` layers that we wish to connect to `UpBlock` layers downstream.

❽ The tensor is passed through a series of `DownBlock` layers that reduce the size of the image, while increasing the number of channels.

❾ The tensor is then passed through two `ResidualBlock` layers that hold the image size and number of channels constant.

❿ Next, the tensor is passed through a series of `UpBlock` layers that increase the size of the image, while decreasing the number of channels. The skip connections incorporate output from the earlier `DownBlock` layers.

⓫ The final `Conv2D` layer reduces the number of channels to three (RGB).

⓬ The U-Net is a Keras `Model` that takes the noisy images and noise variances as input and outputs a predicted noise map.

To understand the U-Net in detail, we need to explore four more concepts: the sinusoidal embedding of the noise variance, the `ResidualBlock`, the `DownBlock`, and the `UpBlock`.

Sinusoidal embedding

Sinusoidal embedding was first introduced in a paper by Vaswani et al.[6] We will be using an adaptation of that original idea as utilized in Mildenhall et al.'s paper titled "NeRF: Representing Scenes as Neural Radiance Fields for View Synthesis."[7]

The idea is that we want to be able to convert a scalar value (the noise variance) into a distinct higher-dimensional vector that is able to provide a more complex representation, for use downstream in the network. The original paper used this idea to encode the discrete position of words in a sentence into vectors; the NeRF paper extends this idea to continuous values.

Specifically, a scalar value x is encoded as shown in the following equation:

$$\gamma(x) = \left(\sin\left(2\pi e^{0f}x\right), \cdots, \sin\left(2\pi e^{(L-1)f}x\right), \cos\left(2\pi e^{0f}x\right), \cdots, \cos\left(2\pi e^{(L-1)f}x\right)\right)$$

where we choose $L = 16$ to be half the size of our desired noise embedding length and $f = \frac{\ln(1000)}{L-1}$ to be the maximum scaling factor for the frequencies.

This produces the embedding pattern shown in Figure 8-9.

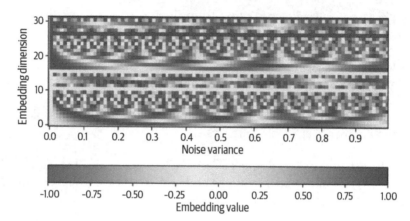

Figure 8-9. The pattern of sinusoidal embeddings for noise variances from 0 to 1

We can code this sinusoidal embedding function as shown in Example 8-7. This converts a single noise variance scalar value into a vector of length 32.

Example 8-7. The `sinusoidal_embedding` function that encodes the noise variance

```
def sinusoidal_embedding(x):
    frequencies = tf.exp(
        tf.linspace(
            tf.math.log(1.0),
            tf.math.log(1000.0),
            16,
        )
    )
    angular_speeds = 2.0 * math.pi * frequencies
    embeddings = tf.concat(
        [tf.sin(angular_speeds * x), tf.cos(angular_speeds * x)], axis=3
    )
    return embeddings
```

ResidualBlock

Both the `DownBlock` and the `UpBlock` contain `ResidualBlock` layers, so let's start with these. We already explored residual blocks in Chapter 5, when we built a PixelCNN, but we will recap here for completeness.

A *residual block* is a group of layers that contains a skip connection that adds the input to the output. Residual blocks help us to build deeper networks that can learn more complex patterns without suffering as greatly from vanishing gradient and degradation problems. The vanishing gradient problem is the assertion that as the network gets deeper, the gradient propagated through deeper layers is tiny and therefore learning is very slow. The degradation problem is the fact that as neural networks become deeper, they are not necessarily as accurate as their shallower counterparts—accuracy seems to become saturated at a certain depth and then degrade rapidly.

Degradation

The degradation problem is somewhat counterintuitive, but observed in practice as the deeper layers must at least learn the identity mapping, which is not trivial—especially considering other problems deeper networks face, such as the vanishing gradient problem.

The solution, first introduced in the ResNet paper by He et al. in 2015,[8] is very simple. By including a skip connection *highway* around the main weighted layers, the block has the option to bypass the complex weight updates and simply pass through the identity mapping. This allows the network to be trained to great depth without sacrificing gradient size or network accuracy.

A diagram of a `ResidualBlock` is shown in Figure 8-10. Note that in some residual blocks, we also include an extra `Conv2D` layer with kernel size 1 on the skip connection, to bring the number of channels in line with the rest of the block.

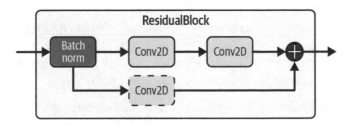

Figure 8-10. The `ResidualBlock` in the U-Net

We can code a `ResidualBlock` in Keras as shown in Example 8-8.

Example 8-8. Code for the `ResidualBlock` in the U-Net

```
def ResidualBlock(width):
    def apply(x):
        input_width = x.shape[3]
        if input_width == width:  ❶
            residual = x
        else:
            residual = layers.Conv2D(width, kernel_size=1)(x)
        x = layers.BatchNormalization(center=False, scale=False)(x)  ❷
        x = layers.Conv2D(
            width, kernel_size=3, padding="same", activation=activations.swish
        )(x)  ❸
        x = layers.Conv2D(width, kernel_size=3, padding="same")(x)
        x = layers.Add()([x, residual])  ❹
        return x

    return apply
```

❶ Check if the number of channels in the input matches the number of channels that we would like the block to output. If not, include an extra `Conv2D` layer on the skip connection to bring the number of channels in line with the rest of the block.

❷ Apply a `BatchNormalization` layer.

❸ Apply two `Conv2D` layers.

❹ Add the original block input to the output to provide the final output from the block.

DownBlocks and UpBlocks

Each successive `DownBlock` increases the number of channels via `block_depth` (=2 in our example) `ResidualBlocks`, while also applying a final `AveragePooling2D` layer in order to halve the size of the image. Each `ResidualBlock` is added to a list for use later by the `UpBlock` layers as skip connections across the U-Net.

An `UpBlock` first applies an `UpSampling2D` layer that doubles the size of the image, through bilinear interpolation. Each successive `UpBlock` decreases the number of channels via `block_depth` (=2) `ResidualBlocks`, while also concatenating the outputs from the `DownBlocks` through skip connections across the U-Net. A diagram of this process is shown in Figure 8-11.

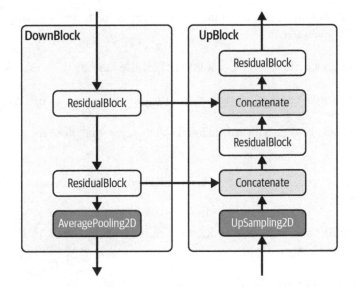

Figure 8-11. The `DownBlock` *and corresponding* `UpBlock` *in the U-Net*

We can code the `DownBlock` and `UpBlock` using Keras as illustrated in Example 8-9.

Example 8-9. Code for the `DownBlock` *and* `UpBlock` *in the U-Net model*

```
def DownBlock(width, block_depth):
    def apply(x):
        x, skips = x
        for _ in range(block_depth):
            x = ResidualBlock(width)(x)  ❶
            skips.append(x)  ❷
        x = layers.AveragePooling2D(pool_size=2)(x)  ❸
        return x

    return apply

def UpBlock(width, block_depth):
    def apply(x):
        x, skips = x
        x = layers.UpSampling2D(size=2, interpolation="bilinear")(x)  ❹
        for _ in range(block_depth):
            x = layers.Concatenate()([x, skips.pop()])  ❺
            x = ResidualBlock(width)(x)  ❻
        return x

    return apply
```

❶ The `DownBlock` increases the number of channels in the image using a `Residual Block` of a given `width`…

❷ …each of which are saved to a list (`skips`) for use later by the `UpBlocks`.

❸ A final `AveragePooling2D` layer reduces the dimensionality of the image by half.

❹ The `UpBlock` begins with an `UpSampling2D` layer that doubles the size of the image.

❺ The output from a `DownBlock` layer is glued to the current output using a `Concatenate` layer.

❻ A `ResidualBlock` is used to reduce the number of channels in the image as it passes through the `UpBlock`.

Training the Diffusion Model

We now have all the components in place to train our denoising diffusion model! Example 8-10 creates, compiles, and fits the diffusion model.

Example 8-10. Code for training the `DiffusionModel`

```
model = DiffusionModel() ❶
model.compile(
    optimizer=optimizers.experimental.AdamW(learning_rate=1e-3, weight_decay=1e-4),
    loss=losses.mean_absolute_error,
) ❷

model.normalizer.adapt(train) ❸

model.fit(
    train,
    epochs=50,
) ❹
```

❶ Instantiate the model.

❷ Compile the model, using the AdamW optimizer (similar to Adam but with weight decay, which helps stabilize the training process) and mean absolute error loss function.

❸ Calculate the normalization statistics using the training set.

❹ Fit the model over 50 epochs.

The loss curve (noise mean absolute error [MAE]) is shown in Figure 8-12.

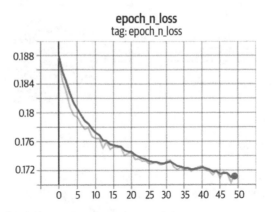

Figure 8-12. The noise mean absolute error loss curve, by epoch

Sampling from the Denoising Diffusion Model

In order to sample images from our trained model, we need to apply the reverse diffusion process—that is, we need to start with random noise and use the model to gradually undo the noise, until we are left with a recognizable picture of a flower.

We must bear in mind that our model is trained to predict the total amount of noise that has been added to a given noisy image from the training set, not just the noise that was added at the last timestep of the noising process. However, we do not want to undo the noise all in one go—predicting an image from pure random noise in one shot is clearly not going to work! We would rather mimic the forward process and undo the predicted noise gradually over many small steps, to allow the model to adjust to its own predictions.

To achieve this, we can jump from x_t to x_{t-1} in two steps—first by using our model's noise prediction to calculate an estimate for the original image x_0 and then by reapplying the predicted noise to this image, but only over $t-1$ timesteps, to produce x_{t-1}. This idea is shown in Figure 8-13.

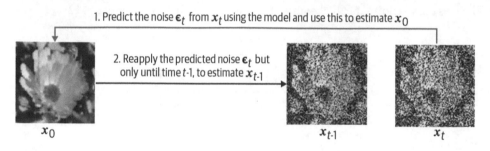

1. Predict the noise ϵ_t from x_t using the model and use this to estimate x_0

2. Reapply the predicted noise ϵ_t but only until time t-1, to estimate x_{t-1}

x_0

x_{t-1}

x_t

Figure 8-13. One step of the sampling process for our diffusion model

If we repeat this process over a number of steps, we'll eventually get back to an estimate for x_0 that has been guided gradually over many small steps. In fact, we are free to choose the number of steps we take, and crucially, it doesn't have to be the same as the large number of steps in the training noising process (i.e., 1,000). It can be much smaller—in this example we choose 20.

The following equation (Song et al., 2020) this process mathematically:

$$\mathbf{x}_{t-1} = \sqrt{\bar{\alpha}_{t-1}}\underbrace{\left(\frac{\mathbf{x}_t - \sqrt{1-\bar{\alpha}_t}\,\epsilon_\theta^{(t)}(\mathbf{x}_t)}{\sqrt{\bar{\alpha}_t}}\right)}_{\text{predicted } \mathbf{x}_0} + \underbrace{\sqrt{1-\bar{\alpha}_{t-1}-\sigma_t^2}\cdot\epsilon_\theta^{(t)}(\mathbf{x}_t)}_{\text{direction pointing to } \mathbf{x}_t} + \underbrace{\sigma_t\epsilon_t}_{\text{random noise}}$$

Let's break this down. The first term inside the brackets on the righthand side of the equation is the estimated image x_0, calculated using the noise predicted by our network $\epsilon_\theta^{(t)}$. We then scale this by the $t-1$ signal rate $\sqrt{\bar{\alpha}_{t-1}}$ and reapply the predicted noise, but this time scaled by the $t-1$ noise rate $\sqrt{1-\bar{\alpha}_{t-1}-\sigma_t^2}$. Additional Gaussian random noise $\sigma_t\epsilon_t$ is also added, with the factors σ_t determining how random we want our generation process to be.

The special case $\sigma_t = 0$ for all t corresponds to a type of model known as a *Denoising Diffusion Implicit Model* (DDIM), introduced by Song et al. in 2020.[9] With a DDIM, the generation process is entirely deterministic—that is, the same random noise input will always give the same output. This is desirable as then we have a well-defined mapping between samples from the latent space and the generated outputs in pixel space.

In our example, we will implement a DDIM, thus making our generation process deterministic. The code for the DDIM sampling process (reverse diffusion) is shown in Example 8-11.

Example 8-11. Sampling from the diffusion model

```python
class DiffusionModel(models.Model):

...

    def reverse_diffusion(self, initial_noise, diffusion_steps):
        num_images = initial_noise.shape[0]
        step_size = 1.0 / diffusion_steps
        current_images = initial_noise
        for step in range(diffusion_steps):  ❶
            diffusion_times = tf.ones((num_images, 1, 1, 1)) - step * step_size  ❷
            noise_rates, signal_rates = self.diffusion_schedule(diffusion_times)  ❸
            pred_noises, pred_images = self.denoise(
                current_images, noise_rates, signal_rates, training=False
            )  ❹
            next_diffusion_times = diffusion_times - step_size  ❺
            next_noise_rates, next_signal_rates = self.diffusion_schedule(
                next_diffusion_times
            )  ❻
            current_images = (
                next_signal_rates * pred_images + next_noise_rates * pred_noises
            )  ❼
        return pred_images  ❽
```

❶ Look over a fixed number of steps (e.g., 20).

❷ The diffusion times are all set to 1 (i.e., at the start of the reverse diffusion process).

❸ The noise and signal rates are calculated according to the diffusion schedule.

❹ The U-Net is used to predict the noise, allowing us to calculate the denoised image estimate.

❺ The diffusion times are reduced by one step.

❻ The new noise and signal rates are calculated.

❼ The t-1 images are calculated by reapplying the predicted noise to the predicted image, according to the t-1 diffusion schedule rates.

❽ After 20 steps, the final x_0 predicted images are returned.

Analysis of the Diffusion Model

We'll now take a look at three different ways that we can use our trained model: for generation of new images, testing how the number of reverse diffusion steps affects quality, and interpolating between two images in the latent space.

Generating images

In order to produce samples from our trained model, we can simply run the reverse diffusion process, ensuring that we denormalize the output at the end (i.e., take the pixel values back into the range [0, 1]). We can achieve this using the code in Example 8-12 inside the `DiffusionModel` class.

Example 8-12. Generating images using the diffusion model

```python
class DiffusionModel(models.Model):

...

    def denormalize(self, images):
        images = self.normalizer.mean + images * self.normalizer.variance**0.5  ❶
        return tf.clip_by_value(images, 0.0, 1.0)

    def generate(self, num_images, diffusion_steps):
        initial_noise = tf.random.normal(shape=(num_images, 64, 64, 3))  ❶
        generated_images = self.reverse_diffusion(initial_noise, diffusion_steps)  ❷
        generated_images = self.denormalize(generated_images)  ❸
        return generated_images
```

❶ Generate some initial noise maps.

❷ Apply the reverse diffusion process.

❸ The images output by the network will have mean zero and unit variance, so we need to denormalize by reapplying the mean and variance calculated from the training data.

In Figure 8-14 we can observe some samples from the diffusion model at different epochs of the training process.

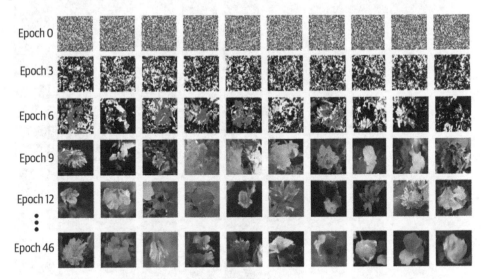

Figure 8-14. Samples from the diffusion model at different epochs of the training process

Adjusting the number of diffusion steps

We can also test to see how adjusting the number of diffusion steps in the reverse process affects image quality. Intuitively, the more steps taken by the process, the higher the quality of the image generation.

We can see in Figure 8-15 that the quality of the generations does indeed improve with the number of diffusion steps. With one giant leap from the initial sampled noise, the model can only predict a hazy blob of color. With more steps, the model is able to refine and sharpen its generations. However, the time taken to generate the images scales linearly with the number of diffusion steps, so there is a trade-off. There is minimal improvement between 20 and 100 diffusion steps, so we choose 20 as a reasonable compromise between quality and speed in this example.

Diffusion steps

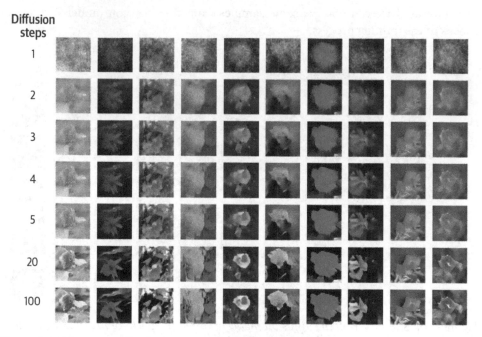

Figure 8-15. Image quality improves with the number of diffusion steps

Interpolating between images

Lastly, as we have seen previously with variational autoencoders, we can interpolate between points in the Gaussian latent space in order to smoothly transition between images in pixel space. Here we choose to use a form of spherical interpolation that ensures that the variance remains constant while blending the two Gaussian noise maps together. Specifically, the initial noise map at each step is given by $a \sin\left(\frac{\pi}{2}t\right) + b \cos\left(\frac{\pi}{2}t\right)$, where t ranges smoothly from 0 to 1 and a and b are the two randomly sampled Gaussian noise tensors that we wish to interpolate between.

The resulting images are shown in Figure 8-16.

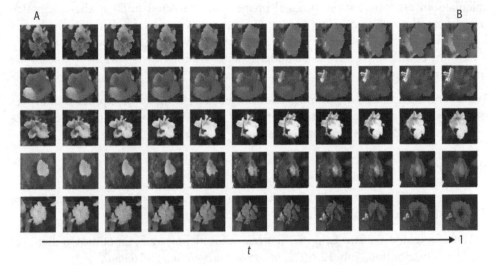

Figure 8-16. Interpolating between images using the denoising diffusion model

Summary

In this chapter we have explored one of the most exciting and promising areas of generative modeling in recent times: diffusion models. In particular, we implemented the ideas from a key paper on generative diffusion models (Ho et al., 2020) that introduced the original Denoising Diffusion Probabilistic Model (DDPM). We then extended this with the ideas from the Denoising Diffusion Implicit Model (DDIM) paper to make the generation process fully deterministic.

We have seen how diffusion models are formed of a forward diffusion process and a reverse diffusion process. The forward diffusion process adds noise to the training data through a series of small steps, while the reverse diffusion process consists of a model that tries to predict the noise added.

We make use of a reparameterization trick in order to calculate the noised images at any step of the forward process without having to go through multiple noising steps. We have seen how the chosen schedule of parameters used to add noise to the data plays an important part in the overall success of the model.

The reverse diffusion process is parameterized by a U-Net that tries to predict the noise at each timestep, given the noised image and the noise rate at that step. A U-Net consists of `DownBlocks` that increase the number of channels while reducing the size of the image and `UpBlocks` that decrease the number of channels while increasing the size. The noise rate is encoded using sinusoidal embedding.

Sampling from the diffusion model is conducted over a series of steps. The U-Net is used to predict the noise added to a given noised image, which is then used to calculate an estimate for the original image. The predicted noise is then reapplied using a smaller noise rate. This process is repeated over a series of steps (which may be significantly smaller than the number of steps used during training), starting from a random point sampled from a standard Gaussian noise distribution, to obtain the final generation.

We saw how increasing the number of diffusion steps in the reverse process improves the image generation quality, at the expense of speed. We also performed latent space arithmetic in order to interpolate between two images.

References

1. Jascha Sohl-Dickstein et al., "Deep Unsupervised Learning Using Nonequilibrium Thermodynamics," March 12, 2015, *https://arxiv.org/abs/1503.03585*

2. Yang Song and Stefano Ermon, "Generative Modeling by Estimating Gradients of the Data Distribution," July 12, 2019, *https://arxiv.org/abs/1907.05600*.

3. Yang Song and Stefano Ermon, "Improved Techniques for Training Score-Based Generative Models," June 16, 2020, *https://arxiv.org/abs/2006.09011*.

4. Jonathon Ho et al., "Denoising Diffusion Probabilistic Models," June 19, 2020, *https://arxiv.org/abs/2006.11239*.

5. Alex Nichol and Prafulla Dhariwal, "Improved Denoising Diffusion Probabilistic Models," February 18, 2021, *https://arxiv.org/abs/2102.09672*.

6. Ashish Vaswani et al., "Attention Is All You Need," June 12, 2017, *https://arxiv.org/abs/1706.03762*.

7. Ben Mildenhall et al., "NeRF: Representing Scenes as Neural Radiance Fields for View Synthesis," March 1, 2020, *https://arxiv.org/abs/2003.08934*.

8. Kaiming He et al., "Deep Residual Learning for Image Recognition," December 10, 2015, *https://arxiv.org/abs/1512.03385*.

9. Jiaming Song et al., "Denoising Diffusion Implicit Models," October 6, 2020, *https://arxiv.org/abs/2010.02502*

Applications

In Part III, we will explore some of the key applications of the generative modeling techniques that we have seen so far, across images, text, music, and games. We will also see how these domains can be traversed using state-of-the-art multimodal models.

In Chapter 9 we shall turn our attention to Transformers, a start-of-the-art architecture that powers most modern-day text generation models. In particular, we shall explore the inner workings of GPT and build our own version using Keras, and we'll see how it forms the foundation of tools such as ChatGPT.

In Chapter 10 we will look at some of the most important GAN architectures that have influenced image generation, including ProGAN, StyleGAN, StyleGAN2, SAGAN, BigGAN, VQ-GAN, and ViT VQ-GAN. We shall explore the key contributions of each and look to understand how the technique has evolved over time.

Chapter 11 looks at music generation, which presents additional challenges such as modeling musical pitch and rhythm. We'll see that many of the techniques that work for text generation (such as Transformers) can also be applied in this domain, but we'll also explore a deep learning architecture known as MuseGAN that applies a GAN-based approach to generating music.

Chapter 12 shows how generative models can be used within other machine learning domains, such as reinforcement learning. We will focus on the "World Models" paper, which shows how a generative model can be used as the environment in which the agent trains, allowing it to train within a hallucinated dream version of the environment rather than the real thing.

In Chapter 13 we will explore state-of-the-art multimodal models that cross over domains such as images and text. This includes text-to-image models such as DALL.E 2, Imagen, and Stable Diffusion, as well as visual language models such as Flamingo.

Finally, Chapter 14 summarizes the generative AI journey so far, the current generative AI landscape, and where we may be heading in the future. We will explore how generative AI may change the way we live and work, as well as considering whether it has the potential to unlock deeper forms of artificial intelligence in the years to come.

CHAPTER 9

Transformers

Chapter Goals

In this chapter you will:

- Learn about the origins of GPT, a powerful decoder Transformer model for text generation.
- Learn conceptually how an attention mechanism mimics our way of attaching more importance to some words in a sentence than others.
- Delve into how the attention mechanism works from first principles, including how queries, keys, and values are created and manipulated.
- See the importance of causal masking for text generation tasks.
- Understand how attention heads can be grouped into a multihead attention layer.
- See how multihead attention layers form one part of a Transformer block that also includes layer normalization and skip connections.
- Create positional encodings that capture the position of each token as well as the word token embedding.
- Build a GPT model in Keras to generate the text contained in wine reviews.
- Analyze the output from the GPT model, including interrogating the attention scores to inspect where the model is looking.
- Learn about the different types of Transformers, including examples of the types of tasks that can be tackled by each and descriptions of the most famous state-of-the-art implementations.
- Understand how encoder-decoder architectures work, like Google's T5 model.
- Explore the training process behind OpenAI's ChatGPT.

We saw in Chapter 5 how we can build generative models on text data using recurrent neural networks (RNNs), such as LSTMs and GRUs. These autoregressive models process sequential data one token at a time, constantly updating a hidden vector that captures the current latent representation of the input. The RNN can be designed to predict the next word in a sequence by applying a dense layer and softmax activation over the hidden vector. This was considered the most sophisticated way to generatively produce text until 2017, when one paper changed the landscape of text generation forever.

Introduction

The Google Brain paper, confidently entitled "Attention Is All You Need,"[1] is famous for popularizing the concept of *attention*—a mechanism that now powers most state-of-the-art text generation models.

The authors show how it is possible to create powerful neural networks called *Transformers* for sequential modeling that do not require complex recurrent or convolutional architectures but instead only rely on attention mechanisms. This approach overcomes a key downside to the RNN approach, which is that it is challenging to parallelize, as it must process sequences one token as a time. Transformers are highly paralellizable, allowing them to be trained on massive datasets.

In this chapter, we are going to delve into how modern text generation models make use of the Transformer architecture to reach state-of-the-art performance on text generation challenges. In particular, we will explore a type of autoregressive model known as the *generative pre-trained transformer* (GPT), which powers OpenAI's GPT-4 model, widely considered to be the current state of the art for text generation.

GPT

OpenAI introduced GPT in June 2018, in the paper "Improving Language Understanding by Generative Pre-Training,"[2] almost exactly a year after the appearance of the original Transformer paper.

In this paper, the authors show how a Transformer architecture can be trained on a huge amount of text data to predict the next word in a sequence and then subsequently fine-tuned to specific downstream tasks.

The pre-training process of GPT involves training the model on a large corpus of text called BookCorpus (4.5 GB of text from 7,000 unpublished books of different genres). During pre-training, the model is trained to predict the next word in a sequence given the previous words. This process is known as *language modeling* and is used to teach the model to understand the structure and patterns of natural language.

After pre-training, the GPT model can be fine-tuned for a specific task by providing it with a smaller, task-specific dataset. Fine-tuning involves adjusting the parameters of the model to better fit the task at hand. For example, the model can be fine-tuned for tasks such as classification, similarity scoring, or question answering.

The GPT architecture has since been improved and extended by OpenAI with the release of subsequent models such as GPT-2, GPT-3, GPT-3.5, and GPT-4. These models are trained on larger datasets and have larger capacities, so they can generate more complex and coherent text. The GPT models have been widely adopted by researchers and industry practitioners and have contributed to significant advancements in natural language processing tasks.

In this chapter, we will build our own variation of the original GPT model, trained on less data, but still utilizing the same components and underlying principles.

Running the Code for This Example

The code for this example can be found in the Jupyter notebook located at *notebooks/09_transformer/01_gpt/gpt.ipynb* in the book repository.

The code is adapted from the excellent GPT tutorial (*https://oreil.ly/J86pg*) created by Apoorv Nandan available on the Keras website.

The Wine Reviews Dataset

We'll be using the Wine Reviews dataset (*https://oreil.ly/DC9EG*) that is available through Kaggle. This is a set of over 130,000 reviews of wines, with accompanying metadata such as description and price.

You can download the dataset by running the Kaggle dataset downloader script in the book repository, as shown in Example 9-1. This will save the wine reviews and accompanying metadata locally to the */data* folder.

Example 9-1. Downloading the Wine Reviews dataset

```
bash scripts/download_kaggle_data.sh zynicide wine-reviews
```

The data preparation steps are identical to the steps used in Chapter 5 for preparing data for input into an LSTM, so we will not repeat them in detail here. The steps, as shown in Figure 9-1, are as follows:

1. Load the data and create a list of text string descriptions of each wine.

2. Pad punctuation with spaces, so that each punctuation mark is treated as a separate word.

3. Pass the strings through a `TextVectorization` layer that tokenizes the data and pads/clips each string to a fixed length.

4. Create a training set where the inputs are the tokenized text strings and the outputs to predict are the same strings shifted by one token.

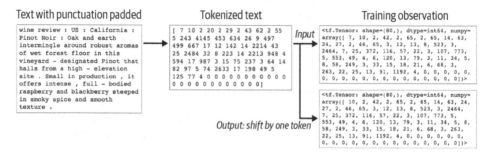

Figure 9-1. Data processing for the Transformer

Attention

The first step to understanding how GPT works is to understand how the *attention mechanism* works. This mechanism is what makes the Transformer architecture unique and distinct from recurrent approaches to language modeling. When we have developed a solid understanding of attention, we will then see how it is used within Transformer architectures such as GPT.

When you write, the choice that you make for the next word in the sentence is influenced by other words that you have already written. For example, suppose you start a sentence as follows:

```
The pink elephant tried to get into the car but it was too
```

Clearly, the next word should be something synonymous with *big*. How do we know this?

Certain other words in the sentence are important for helping us to make our decision. For example, the fact that it is an elephant, rather than a sloth, means that we prefer *big* rather than *slow*. If it were a swimming pool, rather than a car, we might choose *scared* as a possible alternative to *big*. Lastly, the action of *getting into* the car implies that size is the problem—if the elephant was trying to *squash* the car instead, we might choose *fast* as the final word, with *it* now referring to the car.

Other words in the sentence are not important at all. For example, the fact that the elephant is pink has no influence on our choice of final word. Equally, the minor words in the sentence (*the*, *but*, *it*, etc.) give the sentence grammatical form, but here aren't important to determine the required adjective.

In other words, we are *paying attention* to certain words in the sentence and largely ignoring others. Wouldn't it be great if our model could do the same thing?

An attention mechanism (also know as an *attention head*) in a Transformer is designed to do exactly this. It is able to decide where in the input it wants to pull information from, in order to efficiently extract useful information without being clouded by irrelevant details. This makes it highly adaptable to a range of circumstances, as it can decide where it wants to look for information at inference time.

In contrast, a recurrent layer tries to build up a generic hidden state that captures an overall representation of the input at each timestep. A weakness of this approach is that many of the words that have already been incorporated into the hidden vector will not be directly relevant to the immediate task at hand (e.g., predicting the next word), as we have just seen. Attention heads do not suffer from this problem, because they can pick and choose how to combine information from nearby words, depending on the context.

Queries, Keys, and Values

So how does an attention head decide where it wants to look for information? Before we get into the details, let's explore how it works at a high level, using our *pink elephant* example.

Imagine that we want to predict what follows the word *too*. To help with this task, other preceding words chime in with their opinions, but their contributions are weighted by how confident they are in their own expertise in predicting words that follow *too*. For example, the word *elephant* might confidently contribute that it is more likely to be a word related to size or loudness, whereas the word *was* doesn't have much to offer to narrow down the possibilities.

In other words, we can think of an attention head as a kind of information retrieval system, where a *query* ("What word follows *too*?") is made into a *key/value* store (other words in the sentence) and the resulting output is a sum of the values, weighted by the *resonance* between the query and each key.

We will now walk through the process in detail (Figure 9-2), again with reference to our *pink elephant* sentence.

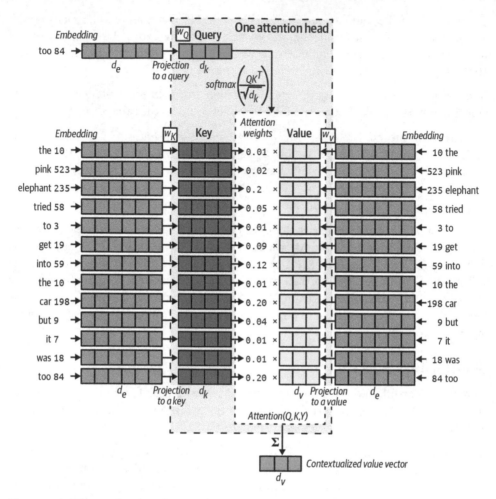

Figure 9-2. The mechanics of an attention head

The *query* (Q) can be thought of as a representation of the current task at hand (e.g., "What word follows *too*?"). In this example, it is derived from the embedding of the word *too*, by passing it through a weights matrix W_Q to change the dimensionality of the vector from d_e to d_k.

The *key* vectors (K) are representations of each word in the sentence—you can think of these as descriptions of the kinds of prediction tasks that each word can help with. They are derived in a similar fashion to the query, by passing each embedding through a weights matrix W_K to change the dimensionality of each vector from d_e to d_k. Notice that the keys and the query are the same length (d_k).

Inside the attention head, each key is compared to the query using a dot product between each pair of vectors (QK^T). This is why the keys and the query have to be the same length. The higher this number is for a particular key/query pair, the more the key resonates with the query, so it is allowed to make more of a contribution to the output of the attention head. The resulting vector is scaled by $\sqrt{d_k}$ to keep the variance of the vector sum stable (approximately equal to 1), and a softmax is applied to ensure the contributions sum to 1. This is a vector of *attention weights*.

The *value* vectors (V) are also representations of the words in the sentence—you can think of these as the unweighted contributions of each word. They are derived by passing each embedding through a weights matrix W_V to change the dimensionality of each vector from d_e to d_v. Notice that the value vectors do not necessarily have to have the same length as the keys and query (but often do, for simplicity).

The value vectors are multiplied by the attention weights to give the *attention* for a given Q, K, and V, as shown in Equation 9-1.

Equation 9-1. Attention equation

$$Attention(Q, K, V) = softmax\left(\frac{QK^T}{\sqrt{d_k}}\right)V$$

To obtain the final output vector from the attention head, the attention is summed to give a vector of length d_v. This *context vector* captures a blended opinion from words in the sentence on the task of predicting what word follows *too*.

Multihead Attention

There's no reason to stop at just one attention head! In Keras, we can build a `Multi HeadAttention` layer that concatenates the output from multiple attention heads, allowing each to learn a distinct attention mechanism so that the layer as a whole can learn more complex relationships.

The concatenated outputs are passed through one final weights matrix W_O to project the vector into the desired output dimension, which in our case is the same as the input dimension of the query (d_e), so that the layers can be stacked sequentially on top of each other.

Figure 9-3 shows how the output from a `MultiHeadAttention` layer is constructed. In Keras we can simply write the line shown in Example 9-2 to create such a layer.

Example 9-2. Creating a `MultiHeadAttention` layer in Keras

```
layers.MultiHeadAttention(
    num_heads = 4, ❶
    key_dim = 128, ❷
    value_dim = 64, ❸
    output_shape = 256 ❹
    )
```

❶ This multihead attention layer has four heads.

❷ The keys (and query) are vectors of length 128.

❸ The values (and therefore also the output from each head) are vectors of length 64.

❹ The output vector has length 256.

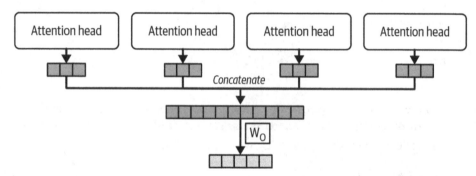

Figure 9-3. A multihead attention layer with four heads

Causal Masking

So far, we have assumed that the query input to our attention head is a single vector. However, for efficiency during training, we would ideally like the attention layer to be able to operate on every word in the input at once, predicting for each what the subsequent word will be. In other words, we want our GPT model to be able to handle a group of query vectors in parallel (i.e., a matrix).

You might think that we can just batch the vectors together into a matrix and let linear algebra handle the rest. This is true, but we need one extra step—we need to apply a mask to the query/key dot product, to avoid information from future words leaking through. This is known as *causal masking* and is shown in Figure 9-4.

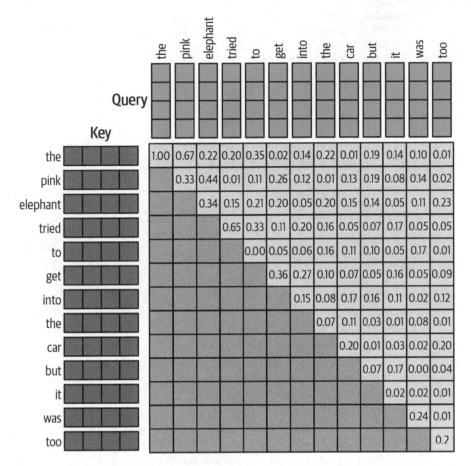

Figure 9-4. Matrix calculation of the attention scores for a batch of input queries, using a causal attention mask to hide keys that are not available to the query (because they come later in the sentence)

Without this mask, our GPT model would be able to perfectly guess the next word in the sentence, because it would be using the key from the word itself as a feature! The code for creating a causal mask is shown in Example 9-3, and the resulting numpy array (transposed to match the diagram) is shown in Figure 9-5.

Example 9-3. The causal mask function

```
def causal_attention_mask(batch_size, n_dest, n_src, dtype):
    i = tf.range(n_dest)[:, None]
    j = tf.range(n_src)
    m = i >= j - n_src + n_dest
    mask = tf.cast(m, dtype)
    mask = tf.reshape(mask, [1, n_dest, n_src])
```

```
    mult = tf.concat(
        [tf.expand_dims(batch_size, -1), tf.constant([1, 1], dtype=tf.int32)], 0
    )
    return tf.tile(mask, mult)

np.transpose(causal_attention_mask(1, 10, 10, dtype = tf.int32)[0])

array([[1, 1, 1, 1, 1, 1, 1, 1, 1, 1],
       [0, 1, 1, 1, 1, 1, 1, 1, 1, 1],
       [0, 0, 1, 1, 1, 1, 1, 1, 1, 1],
       [0, 0, 0, 1, 1, 1, 1, 1, 1, 1],
       [0, 0, 0, 0, 1, 1, 1, 1, 1, 1],
       [0, 0, 0, 0, 0, 1, 1, 1, 1, 1],
       [0, 0, 0, 0, 0, 0, 1, 1, 1, 1],
       [0, 0, 0, 0, 0, 0, 0, 1, 1, 1],
       [0, 0, 0, 0, 0, 0, 0, 0, 1, 1],
       [0, 0, 0, 0, 0, 0, 0, 0, 0, 1]], dtype=int32)
```

Figure 9-5. The causal mask as a numpy array—1 means unmasked and 0 means masked

Causal masking is only required in *decoder Transformers* such as GPT, where the task is to sequentially generate tokens given previous tokens. Masking out future tokens during training is therefore essential.

Other flavors of Transformer (e.g., *encoder Transformers*) do not need causal masking, because they are not trained to predict the next token. For example Google's BERT predicts masked words within a given sentence, so it can use context from both before and after the word in question.[3]

We will explore the different types of Transformers in more detail at the end of the chapter.

This concludes our explanation of the multihead attention mechanism that is present in all Transformers. It is remarkable that the learnable parameters of such an influential layer consist of nothing more than three densely connected weights matrices for each attention head (W_Q, W_K, W_V) and one further weights matrix to reshape the output (W_O). There are no convolutions or recurrent mechanisms at all in a multihead attention layer!

Next, we shall take a step back and see how the multihead attention layer forms just one part of a larger component known as a *Transformer block*.

The Transformer Block

A *Transformer block* is a single component within a Transformer that applies some skip connections, feed-forward (dense) layers, and normalization around the multi-head attention layer. A diagram of a Transformer block is shown in Figure 9-6.

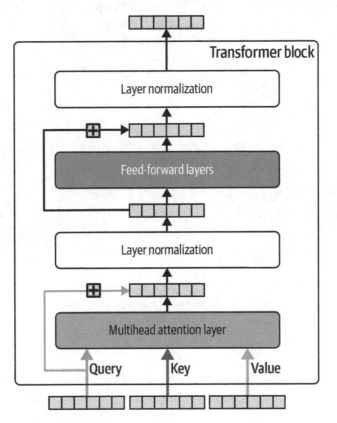

Figure 9-6. A Transformer block

Firstly, notice how the query is passed around the multihead attention layer to be added to the output—this is a skip connection and is common in modern deep learning architectures. It means we can build very deep neural networks that do not suffer as much from the vanishing gradient problem, because the skip connection provides a gradient-free *highway* that allows the network to transfer information forward uninterrupted.

Secondly, *layer normalization* is used in the Transformer block to provide stability to the training process. We have already seen the batch normalization layer in action throughout this book, where the output from each channel is normalized to have a mean of 0 and standard deviation of 1. The normalization statistics are calculated across the batch and spatial dimensions.

In contrast, layer normalization in a Transformer block normalizes each position of each sequence in the batch by calculating the normalizing statistics across the channels. It is the complete opposite of batch normalization, in terms of how the normalization statistics are calculated. A diagram showing the difference between batch normalization and layer normalization is shown in Figure 9-7.

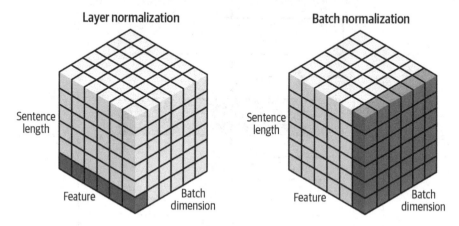

Figure 9-7. Layer normalization versus batch normalization—the normalization statistics are calculated across the red cells (source: Sheng et al., 2020)[4]

Layer Normalization Versus Batch Normalization

Layer normalization was used in the original GPT paper and is commonly used for text-based tasks to avoid creating normalization dependencies across sequences in the batch. However, recent work such as Shen et al.s challenges this assumption, showing that with some tweaks a form of batch normalization can still be used within Transformers, outperforming more traditional layer normalization.

Lastly, a set of feed-forward (i.e., densely connected) layers is included in the Transformer block, to allow the component to extract higher-level features as we go deeper into the network.

A Keras implementation of a Transformer block is shown in Example 9-4.

Example 9-4. A `TransformerBlock` layer in Keras

```python
class TransformerBlock(layers.Layer):
    def __init__(self, num_heads, key_dim, embed_dim, ff_dim, dropout_rate=0.1):  ❶
        super(TransformerBlock, self).__init__()
        self.num_heads = num_heads
        self.key_dim = key_dim
        self.embed_dim = embed_dim
        self.ff_dim = ff_dim
        self.dropout_rate = dropout_rate
        self.attn = layers.MultiHeadAttention(
            num_heads, key_dim, output_shape = embed_dim
        )
        self.dropout_1 = layers.Dropout(self.dropout_rate)
        self.ln_1 = layers.LayerNormalization(epsilon=1e-6)
        self.ffn_1 = layers.Dense(self.ff_dim, activation="relu")
        self.ffn_2 = layers.Dense(self.embed_dim)
        self.dropout_2 = layers.Dropout(self.dropout_rate)
        self.ln_2 = layers.LayerNormalization(epsilon=1e-6)

    def call(self, inputs):
        input_shape = tf.shape(inputs)
        batch_size = input_shape[0]
        seq_len = input_shape[1]
        causal_mask = causal_attention_mask(
            batch_size, seq_len, seq_len, tf.bool
        )  ❷
        attention_output, attention_scores = self.attn(
            inputs,
            inputs,
            attention_mask=causal_mask,
            return_attention_scores=True
        )  ❸
        attention_output = self.dropout_1(attention_output)
        out1 = self.ln_1(inputs + attention_output)  ❹
        ffn_1 = self.ffn_1(out1)  ❺
        ffn_2 = self.ffn_2(ffn_1)
        ffn_output = self.dropout_2(ffn_2)
        return (self.ln_2(out1 + ffn_output), attention_scores)  ❻
```

❶ The sublayers that make up the `TransformerBlock` layer are defined within the initialization function.

❷ The causal mask is created to hide future keys from the query.

❸ The multihead attention layer is created, with the attention masks specified.

❹ The first *add and normalization* layer.

❺ The feed-forward layers.

❻ The second *add and normalization* layer.

Positional Encoding

There is one final step to cover before we can put everything together to train our GPT model. You may have noticed that in the multihead attention layer, there is nothing that cares about the ordering of the keys. The dot product between each key and the query is calculated in parallel, not sequentially, like in a recurrent neural network. This is a strength (because of the parallelization efficiency gains) but also a problem, because we clearly need the attention layer to be able to predict different outputs for the following two sentences:

• The dog looked at the boy and … (barked?)
• The boy looked at the dog and … (smiled?)

To solve this problem, we use a technique called *positional encoding* when creating the inputs to the initial Transformer block. Instead of only encoding each token using a *token embedding*, we also encode the position of the token, using a *position embedding*.

The *token embedding* is created using a standard `Embedding` layer to convert each token into a learned vector. We can create the *positional embedding* in the same way, using a standard `Embedding` layer to convert each integer position into a learned vector.

While GPT uses an `Embedding` layer to embed the position, the original Transformer paper used trigonometric functions—we'll cover this alternative in Chapter 11, when we explore music generation.

To construct the joint token–position encoding, the token embedding is added to the positional embedding, as shown in Figure 9-8. This way, the meaning and position of each word in the sequence are captured in a single vector.

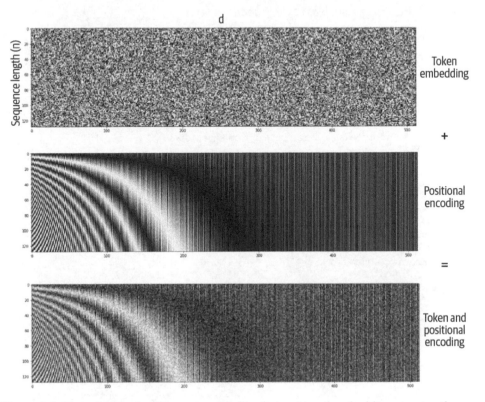

Figure 9-8. The token embeddings are added to the positional embeddings to give the token position encoding

The code that defines our TokenAndPositionEmbedding layer is shown in Example 9-5.

Example 9-5. The TokenAndPositionEmbedding layer

```python
class TokenAndPositionEmbedding(layers.Layer):
    def __init__(self, maxlen, vocab_size, embed_dim):
        super(TokenAndPositionEmbedding, self).__init__()
        self.maxlen = maxlen
        self.vocab_size =vocab_size
        self.embed_dim = embed_dim
        self.token_emb = layers.Embedding(
            input_dim=vocab_size, output_dim=embed_dim
        ) ❶
        self.pos_emb = layers.Embedding(input_dim=maxlen, output_dim=embed_dim) ❷

    def call(self, x):
        maxlen = tf.shape(x)[-1]
        positions = tf.range(start=0, limit=maxlen, delta=1)
        positions = self.pos_emb(positions)
        x = self.token_emb(x)
        return x + positions ❸
```

❶ The tokens are embedded using an Embedding layer.

❷ The positions of the tokens are also embedded using an Embedding layer.

❸ The output from the layer is the sum of the token and position embeddings.

Training GPT

Now we are ready to build and train our GPT model! To put everything together, we need to pass our input text through the token and position embedding layer, then through our Transformer block. The final output of the network is a simple Dense layer with softmax activation over the number of words in the vocabulary.

For simplicity, we will use just one Transformer block, rather than the 12 in the paper.

The overall architecture is shown in Figure 9-9 and the equivalent code is provided in Example 9-6.

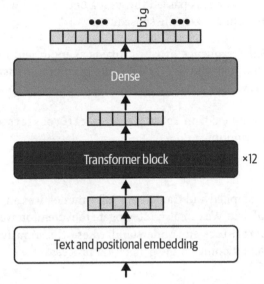

Figure 9-9. The simplified GPT model architecture

Example 9-6. A GPT model in Keras

```
MAX_LEN = 80
VOCAB_SIZE = 10000
EMBEDDING_DIM = 256
N_HEADS = 2
KEY_DIM = 256
FEED_FORWARD_DIM = 256

inputs = layers.Input(shape=(None,), dtype=tf.int32) ❶
x = TokenAndPositionEmbedding(MAX_LEN, VOCAB_SIZE, EMBEDDING_DIM)(inputs) ❷
x, attention_scores = TransformerBlock(
    N_HEADS, KEY_DIM, EMBEDDING_DIM, FEED_FORWARD_DIM
)(x) ❸
outputs = layers.Dense(VOCAB_SIZE, activation = 'softmax')(x) ❹
gpt = models.Model(inputs=inputs, outputs=[outputs, attention_scores]) ❺
gpt.compile("adam", loss=[losses.SparseCategoricalCrossentropy(), None]) ❻
gpt.fit(train_ds, epochs=5)
```

❶ The input is padded (with zeros).

❷ The text is encoded using a TokenAndPositionEmbedding layer.

❸ The encoding is passed through a `TransformerBlock`.

❹ The transformed output is passed through a `Dense` layer with softmax activation to predict a distribution over the subsequent word.

❺ The `Model` takes a sequence of word tokens as input and outputs the predicted subsequent word distribution. The output from the Transformer block is also returned so that we can inspect how the model is directing its attention.

❻ The model is compiled with `SparseCategoricalCrossentropy` loss over the predicted word distribution.

Analysis of GPT

Now that we have compiled and trained our GPT model, we can start to use it to generate long strings of text. We can also interrogate the attention weights that are output from the `TransformerBlock`, to understand where the Transformer is looking for information at different points in the generation process.

Generating text

We can generate new text by applying the following process:

1. Feed the network with an existing sequence of words and ask it to predict the following word.

2. Append this word to the existing sequence and repeat.

The network will output a set of probabilities for each word that we can sample from, so we can make the text generation stochastic, rather than deterministic.

We will use the same `TextGenerator` class introduced in Chapter 5 for LSTM text generation, including the `temperature` parameter that specifies how deterministic we would like the sampling process to be. Let's take a look at this in action, at two different temperature values (Figure 9-10).

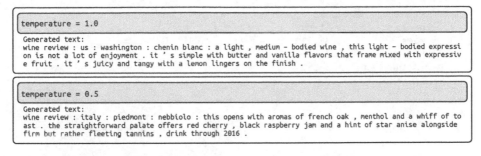

```
temperature = 1.0
Generated text:
wine review : us : washington : chenin blanc : a light , medium - bodied wine , this light - bodied expressi
on is not a lot of enjoyment . it ' s simple with butter and vanilla flavors that frame mixed with expressiv
e fruit . it ' s juicy and tangy with a lemon lingers on the finish .
```

```
temperature = 0.5
Generated text:
wine review : italy : piedmont : nebbiolo : this opens with aromas of french oak , menthol and a whiff of to
ast . the straightforward palate offers red cherry , black raspberry jam and a hint of star anise alongside
firm but rather fleeting tannins , drink through 2016 .
```

Figure 9-10. Generated outputs at `temperature = 1.0` *and* `temperature = 0.5`.

There are a few things to note about these two passages. First, both are stylistically similar to a wine review from the original training set. They both open with the region and type of wine, and the wine type stays consistent throughout the passage (for example, it doesn't switch color halfway through). As we saw in Chapter 5, the generated text with temperature 1.0 is more adventurous and therefore less accurate than the example with temperature 0.5. Generating multiple samples with temperature 1.0 will therefore lead to more variety as the model is sampling from a probability distribution with greater variance.

Viewing the attention scores

We can also ask the model to tell us how much attention is being placed on each word, when deciding on the next word in the sentence. The `TransformerBlock` outputs the attention weights for each head, which are a softmax distribution over the preceding words in the sentence.

To demonstrate this, Figure 9-11 shows the top five tokens with the highest probabilities for three different input prompts, as well as the average attention across both heads, against each preceding word. The preceding words are colored according to their attention score, averaged across the two attention heads. Darker blue indicates more attention is being placed on the word.

```
wine review : germany :
    pfalz:           51.53%
    mosel:           41.21%
    rheingau:        4.27%
    rheinhessen:     2.16%
    franken:         0.44%
    --------
```

```
wine review : germany : rheingau : riesling : this is a ripe , full - bodied
    riesling:        46.56%
    ,:        27.78%
    wine:            16.88%
    and:      4.58%
    yet:      1.33%
    --------
```

```
wine review : germany : rheingau : riesling : this is a ripe , full - bodied riesling
with a touch of residual sugar . it ' s a slightly
    sweet:           94.23%
    oily:            1.25%
    viscous:         1.09%
    bitter:          0.88%
    honeyed:         0.66%
    --------
```

Figure 9-11. Distribution of word probabilities following various sequences

In the first example, the model attends closely to the country (*germany*) in order to decide on the word that relates to the region. This makes sense! To pick a region, it needs to take lots of information from the words that relate to the country, to ensure they match. It doesn't need to pay as much attention to the first two tokens (*wine review*) because they don't hold any useful information regarding the region.

In the second example, it needs to refer back to the grape (*riesling*), so it pays attention to the first time that it was mentioned. It can pull this information by directly attending to the word, no matter how far back it is in the sentence (within the upper limit of 80 words). Notice that this is very different from a recurrent neural network, which relies on a hidden state to maintain all interesting information over the length of the sequence so that it can be drawn upon if required—a much less efficient approach.

The final sequence shows an example of how our GPT model can choose an appropriate adjective based on a combination of information. Here the attention is again on the grape (*riesling*), but also on the fact that it contains *residual sugar*. As Riesling is typically a sweet wine, and sugar is already mentioned, it makes sense that it should be described as *slightly sweet* rather than *slightly earthy*, for example.

It is incredibly informative to be able to interrogate the network in this way, to understand exactly where it is pulling information from in order to make accurate decisions about each subsequent word. I highly recommend playing around with the input prompts to see if you can get the model to attend to words really far back in the sentence, to convince yourself of the power of attention-based models over more traditional recurrent models!

Other Transformers

Our GPT model is a *decoder Transformer*—it generates a text string one token at a time and uses causal masking to only attend to previous words in the input string. There are also *encoder Transformers*, which do not use causal masking—instead, they attend to the entire input string in order to extract a meaningful contextual representation of the input. For other tasks, such as language translation, there are also *encoder-decoder Transformers* that can translate from one text string to another; this type of model contains both encoder Transformer blocks and decoder Transformer blocks.

Table 9-1 summarizes the three types of Transformers, with the best examples of each architecture and typical use cases.

Table 9-1. The three Transformer architectures

Type	Examples	Use cases
Encoder	BERT (Google)	Sentence classification, named entity recognition, extractive question answering
Encoder-decoder	T5 (Google)	Summarization, translation, question answering
Decoder	GPT-3 (OpenAI)	Text generation

A well-known example of an encoder Transformer is the *Bidirectional Encoder Representations from Transformers* (BERT) model, developed by Google (Devlin et al., 2018) that predicts missing words from a sentence, given context from both before and after the missing word in all layers.

Encoder Transformers

Encoder Transformers are typically used for tasks that require an understanding of the input as a whole, such as sentence classification, named entity recognition, and extractive question answering. They are not used for text generation tasks, so we will not explore them in detail in this book—see Lewis Tunstall et al.'s *Natural Language Processing with Transformers* (O'Reilly) for more information.

In the following sections we will explore how encoder-decoder transformers work and discuss extensions of the original GPT model architecture released by OpenAI, including ChatGPT, which has been specifically designed for conversational applications.

T5

An example of a modern Transformer that uses the encoder-decoder structure is the T5 model from Google.[5] This model reframes a range of tasks into a text-to-text framework, including translation, linguistic acceptability, sentence similarity, and document summarization, as shown in Figure 9-12.

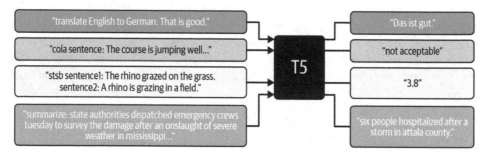

Figure 9-12. Examples of how T5 reframes a range of tasks into a text-to-text framework, including translation, linguistic acceptability, sentence similarity, and document summarization (source: Raffel et al., 2019)

The T5 model architecture closely matches the encoder-decoder architecture used in the original Transformer paper, shown in Figure 9-13. The key difference is that T5 is trained on an enormous 750 GB corpus of text (the Colossal Clean Crawled Corpus, or C4), whereas the original Transformer paper was focused only on language translation, so it was trained on 1.4 GB of English–German sentence pairs.

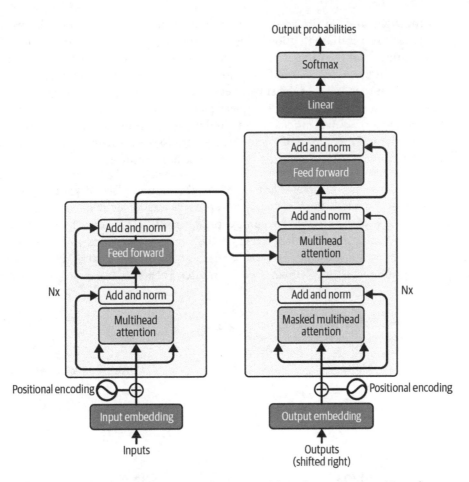

Figure 9-13. *An encoder-decoder Transformer model: each gray box is a Transformer block (source: Vaswani et al., 2017)*

Much of this diagram is already familiar to us—we can see the Transformer blocks being repeated and positional embedding being used to capture the ordering of the input sequences. The two key differences between this model and the GPT model that we built earlier in the chapter are as follows:

- On the lefthand side, a set of *encoder* Transformer blocks encode the sequence to be translated. Notice that there is no causal masking on the attention layer. This is because we are not generating further text to extend the sequence to be translated; we just want to learn a good representation of the sequence as a whole that can be fed to the decoder. Therefore, the attention layers in the encoder can be completely unmasked to capture all the cross-dependencies between words, no matter the order.

- On the righthand side, a set of *decoder* Transformer blocks generate the translated text. The initial attention layer is *self-referential* (i.e., the key, value, and
  query come from the same input) and causal masking is used to ensure information from future tokens is not leaked to the current word to be predicted. However, we can then see that the subsequent attention layer pulls the key and value
  from the encoder, leaving only the query passed through from the decoder itself.
  This is called *cross-referential* attention and means that the decoder can attend to
  the encoder representation of the input sequence to be translated. This is how the
  decoder knows what meaning the translation needs to convey!

Figure 9-14 shows an example of cross-referential attention. Two attention heads of
the decoder layer are able to work together to provide the correct German translation
for the word *the*, when used in the context of *the street*. In German, there are three
definite articles (*der, die, das*) depending on the gender of the noun, but the Transformer knows to choose *die* because one attention head is able to attend to the word
street (a feminine word in German), while another attends to the word to translate
(*the*).

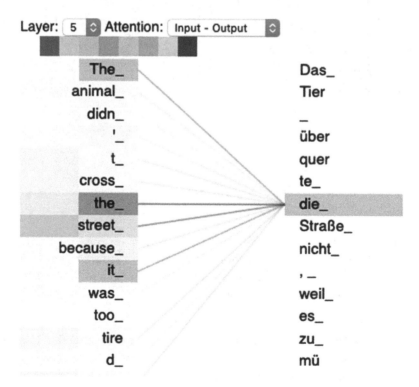

*Figure 9-14. An example of how one attention head attends to the word "the" and
another attends to the word "street" in order to correctly translate the word "the" to the
German word "die" as the feminine definite article of "Straße"*

This example is from the Tensor2Tensor GitHub repository (*https://oreil.ly/84lIA*), which contains a Colab notebook that allows you to play around with a trained encoder-decoder Transformer model and see how the attention mechanisms of the encoder and decoder impact the translation of a given sentence into German.

GPT-3 and GPT-4

Since the original 2018 publication of GPT, OpenAI has released multiple updated versions that improve upon the original model, as shown in Table 9-2.

Table 9-2. The evolution of OpenAI's GPT collection of models

Model	Date	Layers	Attention heads	Word embedding size	Context window	# parameters	Training data
GPT	Jun 2018	12	12	768	512	120,000,000	BookCorpus: 4.5 GB of text from unpublished books
GPT-2	Feb 2019	48	48	1,600	1,024	1,500,000,000	WebText: 40 GB of text from outbound Reddit links
GPT-3	May 2020	96	96	12,888	2,048	175,000,000,000	CommonCrawl, WebText, English Wikipedia, book corpora and others: 570 GB
GPT-4	Mar 2023	-	-	-	-	-	-

The model architecture of GPT-3 is fairly similar to the original GPT model, except it is much larger and trained on much more data. At the time of writing, GPT-4 is in limited beta—OpenAI has not publicly released details of the model's structure and size, though we do know that it is able to accept images as input, so crosses over into being a multimodal model for the first time. The model weights of GPT-3 and GPT-4 are not open source, though the models are available through a commercial tool and API (*https://platform.openai.com*).

GPT-3 can also be fine-tuned to your own training data (*https://oreil.ly/B-Koo*)—this allows you to provide multiple examples of how it should react to a given style of prompt by physically updating the weights of the network. In many cases this may not be necessary, as GPT-3 can be told how to react to a given style of prompt simply by providing a few examples in the prompt itself (this is known as *few-shot learning*). The benefit of fine-tuning is that you do not need to provide these examples as part of every single input prompt, saving costs in the long run.

An example of the output from GPT-3, given a system prompt sentence, is shown in Figure 9-15.

Write me a short story about a unicorn who defeats an evil dragon.

Luna was out for a leisurely stroll through the forest when she heard a loud, ferocious roar. She immediately knew it was a dragon and ran as fast as she could in the opposite direction.

As she ran, she could feel the dragon's hot breath on her back and knew she wouldn't be able to outrun it for long. She had to think of a plan, and fast.

Just as the dragon was about to snatch her up in its teeth, Luna turned around and stabbed it in the eye with her horn. The dragon screeched in pain and flew into a rage, but Luna was ready for it.

She dodged its fire breath and claws until she finally had an opportunity to strike. She impaled the dragon with her horn and it fell to the ground with a thud, dead.

Luna breathed a sigh of relief and trotted away, knowing that she had saved the forest from the evil dragon.

Figure 9-15. An example of how GPT-3 can extend a given system prompt

Language models such as GPT benefit hugely from scaling—both in terms of number of model weights and dataset size. The ceiling of large language model capability has yet to be reached, with researchers continuing to push the boundaries of what is possible with increasingly larger models and datasets.

ChatGPT

A few months before the beta release of GPT-4, OpenAI announced *ChatGPT* (*https://chat.openai.com*)—a tool that allows users to interact with their suite of large language models through a conversational interface. The original release in November 2022 was powered by *GPT-3.5*, a version of the model that was more powerful that GPT-3 and was fine-tuned to conversational responses.

Example dialogue is shown in Figure 9-16. Notice how the agent is able to maintain state between inputs, understanding that the *attention* mentioned in the second question refers to attention in the context of Transformers, rather than a person's ability to focus.

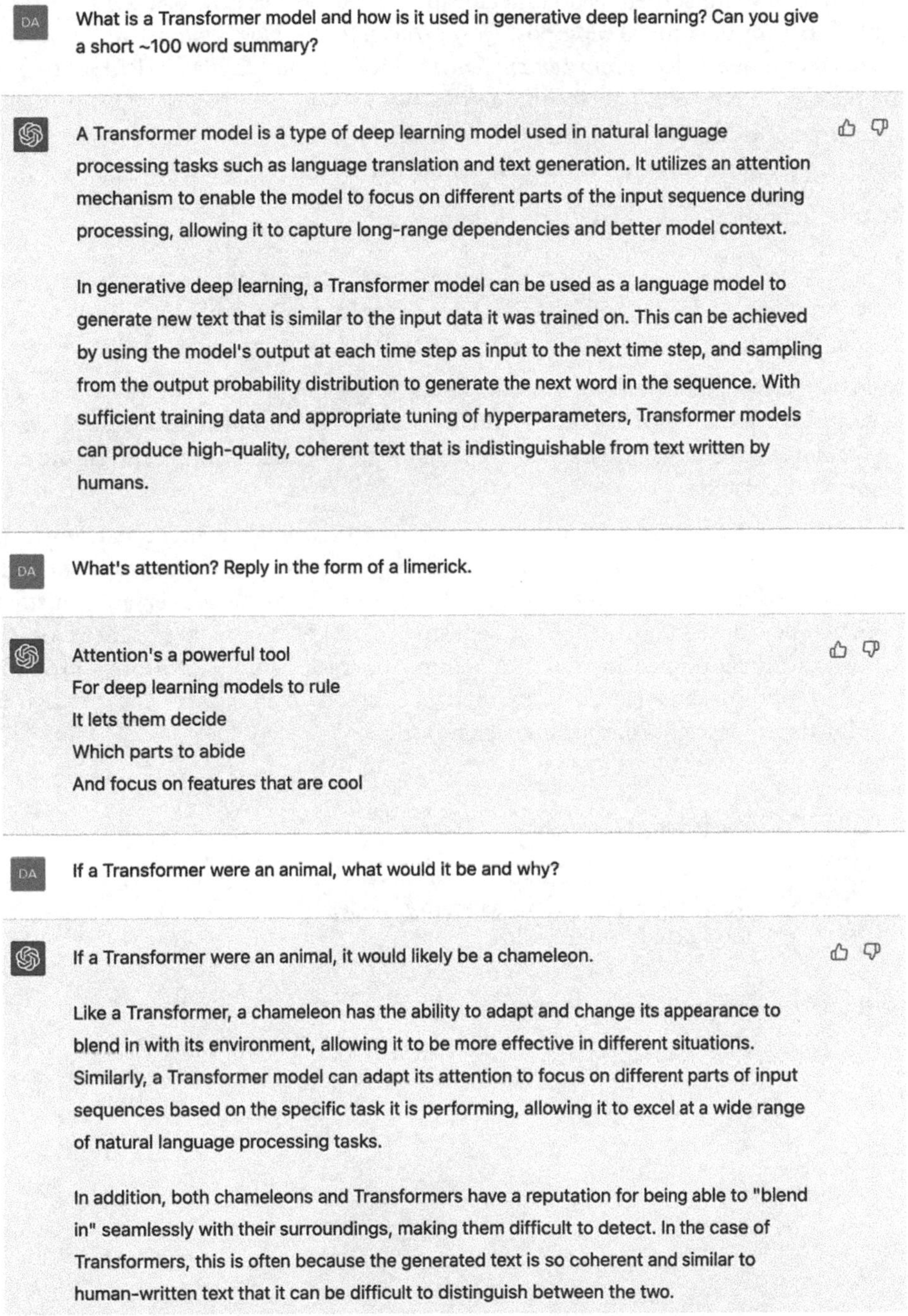

DA What is a Transformer model and how is it used in generative deep learning? Can you give a short ~100 word summary?

A Transformer model is a type of deep learning model used in natural language processing tasks such as language translation and text generation. It utilizes an attention mechanism to enable the model to focus on different parts of the input sequence during processing, allowing it to capture long-range dependencies and better model context.

In generative deep learning, a Transformer model can be used as a language model to generate new text that is similar to the input data it was trained on. This can be achieved by using the model's output at each time step as input to the next time step, and sampling from the output probability distribution to generate the next word in the sequence. With sufficient training data and appropriate tuning of hyperparameters, Transformer models can produce high-quality, coherent text that is indistinguishable from text written by humans.

DA What's attention? Reply in the form of a limerick.

Attention's a powerful tool
For deep learning models to rule
It lets them decide
Which parts to abide
And focus on features that are cool

DA If a Transformer were an animal, what would it be and why?

If a Transformer were an animal, it would likely be a chameleon.

Like a Transformer, a chameleon has the ability to adapt and change its appearance to blend in with its environment, allowing it to be more effective in different situations. Similarly, a Transformer model can adapt its attention to focus on different parts of input sequences based on the specific task it is performing, allowing it to excel at a wide range of natural language processing tasks.

In addition, both chameleons and Transformers have a reputation for being able to "blend in" seamlessly with their surroundings, making them difficult to detect. In the case of Transformers, this is often because the generated text is so coherent and similar to human-written text that it can be difficult to distinguish between the two.

Figure 9-16. An example of ChatGPT answering questions about Transformers

At the time of writing, there is no official paper that describes how ChatGPT works in detail, but from the official blog post (*https://openai.com/blog/chatgpt*) we know that it uses a technique called *reinforcement learning from human feedback* (RLHF) to fine-tune the GPT-3.5 model. This technique was also used in the ChatGPT group's earlier paper[6] that introduced the *InstructGPT* model, a fine-tuned GPT-3 model that is specifically designed to more accurately follow written instructions.

The training process for ChatGPT is as follows:

1. *Supervised fine-tuning*: Collect a demonstration dataset of conversational inputs (prompts) and desired outputs that have been written by humans. This is used to fine-tune the underlying language model (GPT-3.5) using supervised learning.

2. *Reward modeling*: Present a human labeler with examples of prompts and several sampled model outputs and ask them to rank the outputs from best to worst. Train a reward model that predicts the score given to each output, given the conversation history.

3. *Reinforcement learning*: Treat the conversation as a reinforcement learning environment where the *policy* is the underlying language model, initialized to the fine-tuned model from step 1. Given the current *state* (the conversation history) the policy outputs an *action* (a sequence of tokens), which is scored by the reward model trained in step 2. A reinforcement learning algorithm—proximal policy optimization (PPO)—can then be trained to maximize the reward, by adjusting the weights of the language model.

Reinforcement Learning

For an introduction to reinforcement learning see Chapter 12, where we explore how generative models can be used in a reinforcement learning setting.

The RLHF process is shown in Figure 9-17.

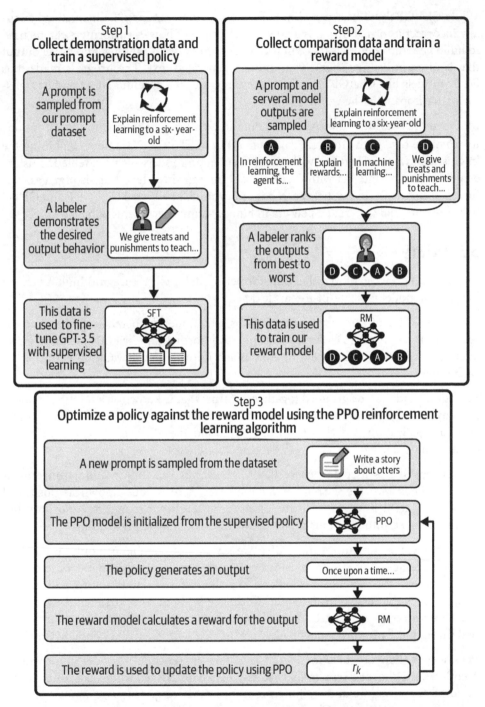

Figure 9-17. The reinforcement learning from human feedback fine-tuning process used in ChatGPT (source: OpenAI)

While ChatGPT still has many limitations (such as sometimes "hallucinating" factually incorrect information), it is a powerful example of how Transformers can be used to build generative models that can produce complex, long-ranging, and novel output that is often indistinguishable from human-generated text. The progress made thus far by models like ChatGPT serves as a testament to the potential of AI and its transformative impact on the world.

Moreover, it is evident that AI-driven communication and interaction will continue to rapidly evolve in the future. Projects like *Visual ChatGPT*[7] are now combining the linguistic power of ChatGPT with visual foundation models such as Stable Diffusion, enabling users to interact with ChatGPT not only through text, but also images. The fusion of linguistic and visual capabilities in projects like Visual ChatGPT and GPT-4 have the potential to herald a new era in human–computer interaction.

Summary

In this chapter, we explored the Transformer model architecture and built a version of GPT—a model for state-of-the-art text generation.

GPT makes use of a mechanism known as attention, which removes the need for recurrent layers (e.g., LSTMs). It works like an information retrieval system, utilizing queries, keys, and values to decide how much information it wants to extract from each input token.

Attention heads can be grouped together to form what is known as a multihead attention layer. These are then wrapped up inside a Transformer block, which includes layer normalization and skip connections around the attention layer. Transformer blocks can be stacked to create very deep neural networks.

Causal masking is used to ensure that GPT cannot leak information from downstream tokens into the current prediction. Also, a technique known as positional encoding is used to ensure that the ordering of the input sequence is not lost, but instead is baked into the input alongside the traditional word embedding.

When analyzing the output from GPT, we saw it was possible not only to generate new text passages, but also to interrogate the attention layer of the network to understand where in the sentence it is looking to gather information to improve its prediction. GPT can access information at a distance without loss of signal, because the attention scores are calculated in parallel and do not rely on a hidden state that is carried through the network sequentially, as is the case with recurrent neural networks.

We saw how there are three families of Transformers (encoder, decoder, and encoder-decoder) and the different tasks that can be accomplished with each. Finally, we explored the structure and training process of other large language models such as Google's T5 and OpenAI's ChatGPT.

References

1. Ashish Vaswani et al., "Attention Is All You Need," June 12, 2017, *https://arxiv.org/abs/1706.03762*.

2. Alec Radford et al., "Improving Language Understanding by Generative Pre-Training," June 11, 2018, *https://openai.com/research/language-unsupervised*.

3. Jacob Devlin et al., "BERT: Pre-Training of Deep Bidirectional Transformers for Language Understanding," October 11, 2018, *https://arxiv.org/abs/1810.04805*.

4. Sheng Shen et al., "PowerNorm: Rethinking Batch Normalization in Transformers," June 28, 2020, *https://arxiv.org/abs/2003.07845*.

5. Colin Raffel et al., "Exploring the Limits of Transfer Learning with a Unified Text-to-Text Transformer," October 23, 2019, *https://arxiv.org/abs/1910.10683*.

6. Long Ouyang et al., "Training Language Models to Follow Instructions with Human Feedback," March 4, 2022, *https://arxiv.org/abs/2203.02155*.

7. Chenfei Wu et al., "Visual ChatGPT: Talking, Drawing and Editing with Visual Foundation Models," March 8, 2023, *https://arxiv.org/abs/2303.04671*.

CHAPTER 10

Advanced GANs

Chapter Goals

In this chapter you will:

- See how a ProGAN model progressively trains a GAN to generate high-resolution images.

- Understand how ProGAN was adapted to build StyleGAN, a high-performing GAN for image synthesis.

- Explore how StyleGAN was adjusted to create StyleGAN2, a state-of-the-art model that improves further upon the original work.

- Learn about the key contributions of these models, including progressive training, adaptive instance normalization, weight modulation and demodulation, and path length regularization.

- Walk through the architecture of the Self-Attention GAN (SAGAN), which incorporates the attention mechanism into the GAN framework.

- See how BigGAN expands upon the ideas in the SAGAN paper to produce high-quality images.

- Learn how VQ-GAN uses a codebook to encode images into a discrete sequence of tokens that can be modeled using a Transformer.

- See how ViT VQ-GAN adapts the VQ-GAN architecture to use Transformers instead of convolutional layers in the encoder and decoder.

Chapter 4 introduced generative adversarial networks (GANs), a class of generative model that has produced state-of-the-art results across a wide variety of image generation tasks. The flexibility in the model architecture and training process has led academics and deep learning practitioners to find new ways to design and train GANs, leading to many different advanced *flavors* of the architecture that we shall explore in this chapter.

Introduction

Explaining all GAN developments and their repercussions in detail could easily fill another book. The GAN Zoo repository (*https://oreil.ly/Oy6bR*) on GitHub contains over 500 distinct examples of GANs with linked papers, ranging from ABC-GAN to ZipNet-GAN!

In this chapter we will cover the main GANs that have been influential in the field, including a detailed explanation of the model architecture and training process for each.

We will first explore three important models from NVIDIA that have pushed the boundaries of image generation: ProGAN, StyleGAN, and StyleGAN2. We will analyze each of these models in enough detail to understand the fundamental concepts that underpin the architectures and see how they have each built on ideas from earlier papers.

We will also explore two other important GAN architectures that incorporate attention: the Self-Attention GAN (SAGAN) and BigGAN, which built on many of the ideas in the SAGAN paper. We have already seen the power of the attention mechanism in the context of Transformers in Chapter 9.

Lastly, we will cover VQ-GAN and ViT VQ-GAN, which incorporate a blend of ideas from variational autoencoders, Transformers, and GANs. VQ-GAN is a key component of Google's state-of-the-art text-to-image generation model Muse.[1] We will explore so-called multimodal models in more detail in Chapter 13.

 Training Your Own Models

For conciseness I have chosen not to include code to directly build these models in the code repository for this book, but instead will point to publicly available implementations where possible, so that you can train your own versions if you wish.

ProGAN

ProGAN is a technique developed by NVIDIA Labs in 2017[2] to improve both the speed and stability of GAN training. Instead of immediately training a GAN on full-resolution images, the ProGAN paper suggests first training the generator and discriminator on low-resolution images of, say, 4 × 4 pixels and then incrementally adding layers throughout the training process to increase the resolution.

Let's take a look at the concept of *progressive training* in more detail.

 Training Your Own ProGAN

There is an excellent tutorial by Bharath K on training your own ProGAN using Keras available on the Paperspace blog (*https://oreil.ly/b2CJm*). Bear in mind that training a ProGAN to achieve the results from the paper requires a significant amount of computing power.

Progressive Training

As always with GANs, we build two independent networks, the generator and discriminator, with a fight for dominance taking place during the training process.

In a normal GAN, the generator always outputs full-resolution images, even in the early stages of training. It is reasonable to think that this strategy might not be optimal—the generator might be slow to learn high-level structures in the early stages of training, because it is immediately operating over complex, high-resolution images. Wouldn't it be better to first train a lightweight GAN to output accurate low-resolution images and then see if we can build on this to gradually increase the resolution?

This simple idea leads us to *progressive training*, one of the key contributions of the ProGAN paper. The ProGAN is trained in stages, starting with a training set that has been condensed down to 4 × 4–pixel images using interpolation, as shown in Figure 10-1.

Figure 10-1. Images in the dataset can be compressed to lower resolution using interpolation

We can then initially train the generator to transform a latent input noise vector z (say, of length 512) into an image of shape $4 \times 4 \times 3$. The matching discriminator will need to transform an input image of size $4 \times 4 \times 3$ into a single scalar prediction. The network architectures for this first step are shown in Figure 10-2.

The blue box in the generator represents the convolutional layer that converts the set of feature maps into an RGB image (toRGB), and the blue box in the discriminator represents the convolutional layer that converts the RGB images into a set of feature maps (fromRGB).

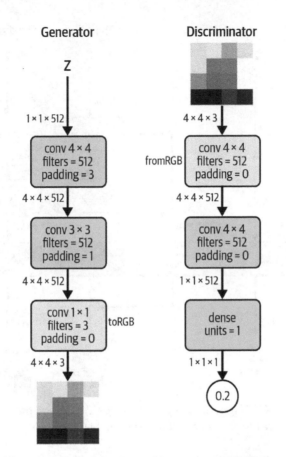

Figure 10-2. The generator and discriminator architectures for the first stage of the Pro-GAN training process

In the paper, the authors train this pair of networks until the discriminator has seen 800,000 real images. We now need to understand how the generator and discriminator are expanded to work with 8 × 8–pixel images.

To expand the generator and discriminator, we need to blend in additional layers. This is managed in two phases, transition and stabilization, as shown in Figure 10-3.

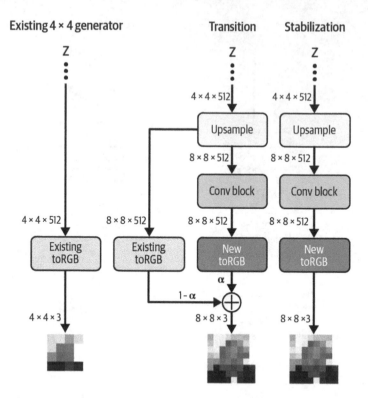

Figure 10-3. The ProGAN generator training process, expanding the network from 4 × 4 images to 8 × 8 (dotted lines represent the rest of the network, not shown)

Let's first look at the generator. During the *transition phase*, new upsampling and convolutional layers are appended to the existing network, with a residual connection set up to maintain the output from the existing trained toRGB layer. Crucially, the new layers are initially masked using a parameter α that is gradually increased from 0 to 1 throughout the transition phase to allow more of the new toRGB output through and less of the existing toRGB layer. This is to avoid a *shock* to the network as the new layers take over.

Eventually, there is no flow through the old toRGB layer and the network enters the *stabilization phase*—a further period of training where the network can fine-tune the output, without any flow through the old toRGB layer.

The discriminator uses a similar process, as shown in Figure 10-4.

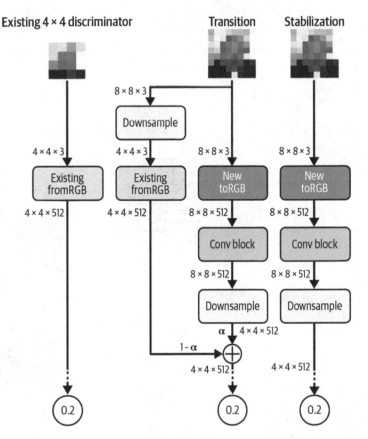

Figure 10-4. The ProGAN discriminator training process, expanding the network from 4 × 4 images to 8 × 8 (dotted lines represent the rest of the network, not shown)

Here, we need to blend in additional downscaling and convolutional layers. Again, the layers are injected into the network—this time at the start of the network, just after the input image. The existing `fromRGB` layer is connected via a residual connection and gradually phased out as the new layers take over during the transition phase. The stabilization phase allows the discriminator to fine-tune using the new layers.

All transition and stabilization phases last until the discriminator has been shown 800,000 real images. Note that even through the network is trained progressively, no layers are *frozen*. Throughout the training process, all layers remain fully trainable.

This process continues, growing the GAN from 4 × 4 images to 8 × 8, then 16 × 16, 32 × 32, and so on, until it reaches full resolution (1,024 × 1,024), as shown in Figure 10-5.

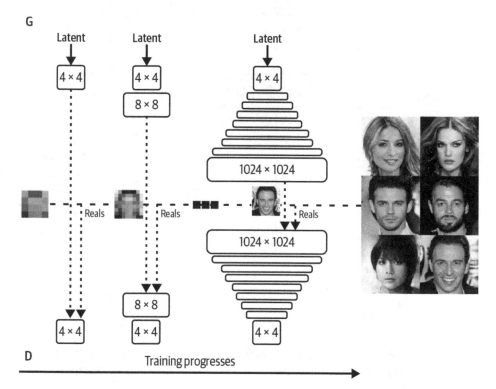

Figure 10-5. The ProGAN training mechanism, and some example generated faces (source: Karras et al., 2017)

The overall structure of the generator and discriminator after the full progressive training process is complete is shown in Figure 10-6.

Generator	Act.	Output shape			Params
Latent vector	–	512 ×	1 ×	1	–
Conv 4 × 4	LReLU	512 ×	4 ×	4	4.2M
Conv 3 × 3	LReLU	512 ×	4 ×	4	2.4M
Upsample	–	512 ×	8 ×	8	–
Conv 3 × 3	LReLU	512 ×	8 ×	8	2.4M
Conv 3 × 3	LReLU	512 ×	8 ×	8	2.4M
Upsample	–	512 ×	16 ×	16	–
Conv 3 × 3	LReLU	512 ×	16 ×	16	2.4M
Conv 3 × 3	LReLU	512 ×	16 ×	16	2.4M
Upsample	–	512 ×	32 ×	32	–
Conv 3 × 3	LReLU	512 ×	32 ×	32	2.4M
Conv 3 × 3	LReLU	512 ×	32 ×	32	2.4M
Upsample	–	512 ×	64 ×	64	–
Conv 3 × 3	LReLU	256 ×	64 ×	64	1.2M
Conv 3 × 3	LReLU	256 ×	64 ×	64	590k
Upsample	–	256 ×	128 ×	128	–
Conv 3 × 3	LReLU	128 ×	128 ×	128	295k
Conv 3 × 3	LReLU	128 ×	128 ×	128	148k
Upsample	–	128 ×	256 ×	256	–
Conv 3 × 3	LReLU	64 ×	256 ×	256	74k
Conv 3 × 3	LReLU	64 ×	256 ×	256	37k
Upsample	–	64 ×	512 ×	512	–
Conv 3 × 3	LReLU	32 ×	512 ×	512	18k
Conv 3 × 3	LReLU	32 ×	512 ×	512	9.2k
Upsample	–	32 ×	1024 ×	1024	–
Conv 3 × 3	LReLU	16 ×	1024 ×	1024	4.6k
Conv 3 × 3	LReLU	16 ×	1024 ×	1024	2.3k
Conv 1 × 1	linear	3 ×	1024 ×	1024	51
Total trainable parameters					23.1M

Discriminator	Act.	Output shape			Params
Input image	–	3 ×	1024 ×	1024	–
Conv 1 × 1	LReLU	16 ×	1024 ×	1024	64
Conv 3 × 3	LReLU	16 ×	1024 ×	1024	2.3k
Conv 3 × 3	LReLU	32 ×	1024 ×	1024	4.6k
Downsample	–	32 ×	512 ×	512	–
Conv 3 × 3	LReLU	32 ×	512 ×	512	9.2k
Conv 3 × 3	LReLU	64 ×	512 ×	512	18k
Downsample	–	64 ×	256 ×	256	–
Conv 3 × 3	LReLU	64 ×	256 ×	256	37k
Conv 3 × 3	LReLU	128 ×	256 ×	256	74k
Downsample	–	128 ×	128 ×	128	–
Conv 3 × 3	LReLU	128 ×	128 ×	128	148k
Conv 3 × 3	LReLU	256 ×	128 ×	128	295k
Downsample	–	256 ×	64 ×	64	–
Conv 3 × 3	LReLU	256 ×	64 ×	64	590k
Conv 3 × 3	LReLU	512 ×	64 ×	64	1.2M
Downsample	–	512 ×	32 ×	32	–
Conv 3 × 3	LReLU	512 ×	32 ×	32	2.4M
Conv 3 × 3	LReLU	512 ×	32 ×	32	2.4M
Downsample	–	512 ×	16 ×	16	–
Conv 3 × 3	LReLU	512 ×	16 ×	16	2.4M
Conv 3 × 3	LReLU	512 ×	16 ×	16	2.4M
Downsample	–	512 ×	8 ×	8	–
Conv 3 × 3	LReLU	512 ×	8 ×	8	2.4M
Conv 3 × 3	LReLU	512 ×	8 ×	8	2.4M
Downsample	–	512 ×	4 ×	4	–
Minibatch stddev	–	513 ×	4 ×	4	–
Conv 3 × 3	LReLU	512 ×	4 ×	4	2.4M
Conv 4 × 4	LReLU	512 ×	1 ×	1	4.2M
Fully-connected	linear	1 ×	1 ×	1	513
Total trainable parameters					23.1M

Figure 10-6. The ProGAN generator and discriminator used to generate 1,024 × 1,024–pixel CelebA faces (source: Karras et al., 2018)

The paper also makes several other important contributions, namely minibatch standard deviation, equalized learning rates, and pixelwise normalization, which are described briefly in the following sections.

Minibatch standard deviation

The *minibatch standard deviation* layer is an extra layer in the discriminator that appends the standard deviation of the feature values, averaged across all pixels and across the minibatch as an additional (constant) feature. This helps to ensure the generator creates more variety in its output—if variety is low across the minibatch, then the standard deviation will be small, and the discriminator can use this feature to distinguish the fake batches from the real batches! Therefore, the generator is incentivized to ensure it generates a similar amount of variety as is present in the real training data.

Equalized learning rates

All dense and convolutional layers in ProGAN use *equalized learning rates*. Usually, weights in a neural network are initialized using a method such as *He initialization*—a Gaussian distribution where the standard deviation is scaled to be inversely proportional to the square root of the number of inputs to the layer. This way, layers with a greater number of inputs will be initialized with weights that have a smaller deviation from zero, which generally improves the stability of the training process.

The authors of the ProGAN paper found that this was causing problems when used in combination with modern optimizers such as Adam or RMSProp. These methods normalize the gradient update for each weight, so that the size of the update is independent of the scale (magnitude) of the weight. However, this means that weights with a larger dynamic range (i.e., layers with fewer inputs) will take comparatively longer to adjust than weights with a smaller dynamic range (i.e., layers with more inputs). It was found that this causes an imbalance between the speed of training of the different layers of the generator and discriminator in ProGAN, so they used *equalized learning rates* to solve this problem.

In ProGAN, weights are initialized using a simple standard Gaussian, regardless of the number of inputs to the layer. The normalization is applied dynamically, as part of the call to the layer, rather than only at initialization. This way, the optimizer sees each weight as having approximately the same dynamic range, so it applies the same learning rate. It is only when the layer is called that the weight is scaled by the factor from the He initializer.

Pixelwise normalization

Lastly, in ProGAN *pixelwise normalization* is used in the generator, rather than batch normalization. This normalizes the feature vector in each pixel to a unit length and helps to prevent the signal from spiraling out of control as it propagates through the network. The pixelwise normalization layer has no trainable weights.

Outputs

In addition to the CelebA dataset, ProGAN was also applied to images from the Large-scale Scene Understanding (LSUN) dataset with excellent results, as shown in Figure 10-7. This demonstrated the power of ProGAN over earlier GAN architectures and paved the way for future iterations such as StyleGAN and StyleGAN2, which we shall explore in the next sections.

| POTTEDPLANT | HORSE | SOFA | BUS | CHURCHOUTDOOR | BICYCLE | TVMONITOR |

Figure 10-7. Generated examples from a ProGAN trained progressively on the LSUN dataset at 256 × 256 resolution (source: Karras et al., 2017)

StyleGAN

StyleGAN[3] is a GAN architecture from 2018 that builds on the earlier ideas in the ProGAN paper. In fact, the discriminator is identical; only the generator is changed.

Often when training GANs it is difficult to separate out vectors in the latent space corresponding to high-level attributes—they are frequently *entangled*, meaning that adjusting an image in the latent space to give a face more freckles, for example, might also inadvertently change the background color. While ProGAN generates fantastically realistic images, it is no exception to this general rule. We would ideally like to have full control of the style of the image, and this requires a disentangled separation of features in the latent space.

StyleGAN achieves this by explicitly injecting style vectors into the network at different points: some that control high-level features (e.g., face orientation) and some that control low-level details (e.g., the way the hair falls across the forehead).

The overall architecture of the StyleGAN generator is shown in Figure 10-8. Let's walk through this architecture step by step, starting with the mapping network.

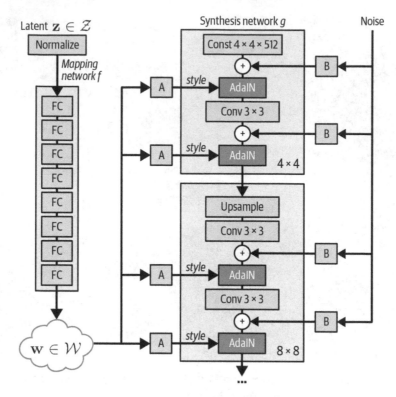

Figure 10-8. The StyleGAN generator architecture (source: Karras et al., 2018)

Training Your Own StyleGAN

There is an excellent tutorial by Soon-Yau Cheong on training your own StyleGAN using Keras available on the Keras website (*https://oreil.ly/MooSe*). Bear in mind that training a StyleGAN to achieve the results from the paper requires a significant amount of computing power.

The Mapping Network

The *mapping network* f is a simple feed-forward network that converts the input noise $z \in \mathcal{Z}$ into a different latent space $w \in \mathcal{W}$. This gives the generator the opportunity to disentangle the noisy input vector into distinct factors of variation, which can be easily picked up by the downstream style-generating layers.

The point of doing this is to separate out the process of choosing a style for the image (the mapping network) from the generation of an image with a given style (the synthesis network).

The Synthesis Network

The synthesis network is the generator of the actual image with a given style, as provided by the mapping network. As can be seen from Figure 10-8, the style vector $\mathbf{w}$ is injected into the synthesis network at different points, each time via a differently densely connected layer A_i, which generates two vectors: a bias vector $\mathbf{y}_{b,i}$ and a scaling vector $\mathbf{y}_{s,i}$. These vectors define the specific style that should be injected at this point in the network—that is, they tell the synthesis network how to adjust the feature maps to move the generated image in the direction of the specified style.

This adjustment is achieved through *adaptive instance normalization* (AdaIN) layers.

Adaptive instance normalization

An AdaIN layer is a type of neural network layer that adjusts the mean and variance of each feature map $\mathbf{x}_i$ with a reference style bias $\mathbf{y}_{b,i}$ and scale $\mathbf{y}_{s,i}$, respectively.[4] Both vectors are of length equal to the number of channels output from the preceding convolutional layer in the synthesis network. The equation for adaptive instance normalization is as follows:

$$\text{AdaIN}(\mathbf{x}_i, \mathbf{y}) = \mathbf{y}_{s,i} \frac{\mathbf{x}_i - \mu(\mathbf{x}_i)}{\sigma(\mathbf{x}_i)} + \mathbf{y}_{b,i}$$

The adaptive instance normalization layers ensure that the style vectors that are injected into each layer only affect features at that layer, by preventing any style information from leaking through between layers. The authors show that this results in the latent vectors $\mathbf{w}$ being significantly more disentangled than the original $\mathbf{z}$ vectors.

Since the synthesis network is based on the ProGAN architecture, it is trained progressively. The style vectors at earlier layers in the synthesis network (when the resolution of the image is lowest—4 × 4, 8 × 8) will affect coarser features than those later in the network (64 × 64 to 1,024 × 1,024–pixel resolution). This means that not only do we have complete control over the generated image through the latent vector $\mathbf{w}$, but we can also switch the $\mathbf{w}$ vector at different points in the synthesis network to change the style at a variety of levels of detail.

Style mixing

The authors use a trick known as *style mixing* to ensure that the generator cannot utilize correlations between adjacent styles during training (i.e., the styles injected at each layer are as disentangled as possible). Instead of sampling only a single latent vector $\mathbf{z}$, two are sampled $(\mathbf{z}_1, \mathbf{z}_2)$, corresponding to two style vectors $(\mathbf{w}_1, \mathbf{w}_2)$. Then, at each layer, either $(\mathbf{w}_1$ or $\mathbf{w}_2)$ is chosen at random, to break any possible correlation between the vectors.

Stochastic variation

The synthesizer network adds noise (passed through a learned broadcasting layer *B*) after each convolution to account for stochastic details such as the placement of individual hairs, or the background behind the face. Again, the depth at which the noise is injected affects the coarseness of the impact on the image.

This also means that the initial input to the synthesis network can simply be a learned constant, rather than additional noise. There is enough stochasticity already present in the style inputs and the noise inputs to generate sufficient variation in the images.

Outputs from StyleGAN

Figure 10-9 shows StyleGAN in action.

Figure 10-9. Merging styles between two generated images at different levels of detail (source: Karras et al., 2018)

Here, two images, source A and source B, are generated from two different **w** vectors. To generate a merged image, the source A **w** vector is passed through the synthesis network but, at some point, switched for the source B **w** vector. If this switch happens early on (4 × 4 or 8 × 8 resolution), coarse styles such as pose, face shape, and glasses from source B are carried across onto source A. However, if the switch happens later, only fine-grained detail is carried across from source B, such as colors and microstructure of the face, while the coarse features from source A are preserved.

StyleGAN2

The final contribution in this chain of important GAN papers is StyleGAN2.[5] This builds further upon the StyleGAN architecture, with some key changes that improve the quality of the generated output. In particular, StyleGAN2 generations do not suffer as greatly from *artifacts*—water droplet–like areas of the image that were found to be caused by the adaptive instance normalization layers in StyleGAN, as shown in Figure 10-10.

Figure 10-10. An artifact in a StyleGAN-generated image of a face (source: Karras et al., 2019)

Both the generator and the discriminator in StyleGAN2 are different from the StyleGAN. In the next sections we will explore the key differences between the architectures.

Weight Modulation and Demodulation

The artifact problem is solved by removing the AdaIN layers in the generator and replacing them with weight modulation and demodulation steps, as shown in Figure 10-11. **w** represents the weights of the convolutional layer, which are directly updated by the modulation and demodulation steps in StyleGAN2 at runtime. In comparison, the AdaIN layers of StyleGAN operate on the image tensor as it flows through the network.

The AdaIN layer in StyleGAN is simply an instance normalization followed by style modulation (scaling and bias). The idea in StyleGAN2 is to apply style modulation and normalization (demodulation) directly to the weights of the convolutional layers at runtime, rather than the output from the convolutional layers, as shown in Figure 10-11. The authors show how this removes the artifact issue while retaining control of the image style.

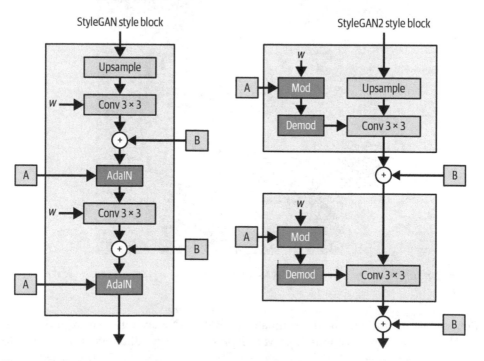

Figure 10-11. A comparison between the StyleGAN and StyleGAN2 style blocks

In StyleGAN2, each dense layer A outputs a single style vector s_i, where i indexes the number of input channels in the corresponding convolutional layer. This style vector is then applied to the weights of the convolutional layer as follows:

$$w'_{i,j,k} = s_i \cdot w_{i,j,k}$$

Here, j indexes the output channels of the layer and k indexes the spatial dimensions. This is the *modulation* step of the process.

Then, we need to normalize the weights so that they again have a unit standard deviation, to ensure stability in the training process. This is the *demodulation* step:

$$w''_{i,j,k} = \frac{w'_{i,j,k}}{\sqrt{\Sigma_{i,k} {w'_{i,j,k}}^2 + \varepsilon}}$$

where ϵ is a small constant value that prevents division by zero.

In the paper, the authors show how this simple change is enough to prevent water-droplet artifacts, while retaining control over the generated images via the style vectors and ensuring the quality of the output remains high.

Path Length Regularization

Another change made to the StyleGAN architecture is the inclusion of an additional penalty term in the loss function—*this is known as path length regularization.*

We would like the latent space to be as smooth and uniform as possible, so that a fixed-size step in the latent space in any direction results in a fixed-magnitude change in the image.

To encourage this property, StyleGAN2 aims to minimize the following term, alongside the usual Wasserstein loss with gradient penalty:

$$\mathbb{E}_{w,y}\left(\| \mathbf{J}_w^\top y \|_2 - a\right)^2$$

Here, w is a set of style vectors created by the mapping network, y is a set of noisy images drawn from $\mathcal{N}(0, \mathbf{I})$, and $\mathbf{J}_w = \frac{\partial g}{\partial w}$ is the Jacobian of the generator network with respect to the style vectors.

The term $\| \mathbf{J}_w^\top y \|_2$ measures the magnitude of the images y after transformation by the gradients given in the Jacobian. We want this to be close to a constant a, which is calculated dynamically as the exponential moving average of $\| \mathbf{J}_w^{\top} y \|_2$ as the training progresses.

The authors find that this additional term makes exploring the latent space more reliable and consistent. Moreover, the regularization terms in the loss function are only applied once every 16 minibatches, for efficiency. This technique, called *lazy regularization*, does not cause a measurable drop in performance.

No Progressive Growing

Another major update is in how StyleGAN2 is trained. Rather than adopting the usual progressive training mechanism, StyleGAN2 utilizes skip connections in the generator and residual connections in the discriminator to train the entire network as one. It no longer requires different resolutions to be trained independently and blended as part of the training process.

Figure 10-12 shows the generator and discriminator blocks in StyleGAN2.

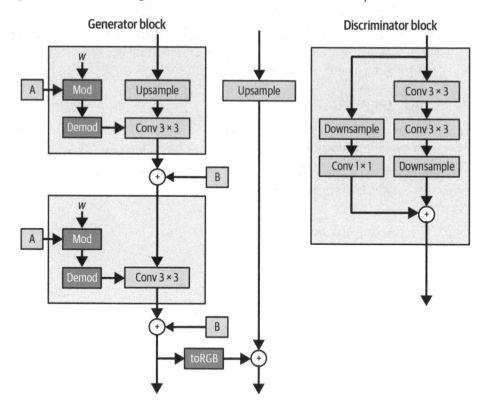

Figure 10-12. The generator and discriminator blocks in StyleGAN2

The crucial property that we would like to be able to preserve is that the StyleGAN2 starts by learning low-resolution features and gradually refines the output as training progresses. The authors show that this property is indeed preserved using this architecture. Each network benefits from refining the convolutional weights in the lower-resolution layers in the earlier stages of training, with the skip and residual connections used to pass the output through the higher-resolution layers mostly unaffected. As training progresses, the higher-resolution layers begin to dominate, as the generator discovers more intricate ways to improve the realism of the images in order to fool the discriminator. This process is demonstrated in Figure 10-13.

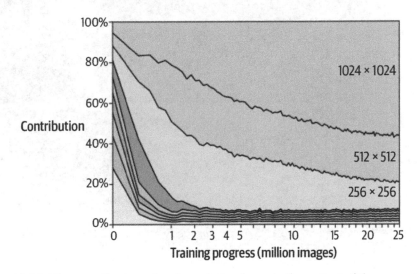

Figure 10-13. The contribution of each resolution layer to the output of the generator, by training time (adapted from Karras et al., 2019)

Outputs from StyleGAN2

Some examples of StyleGAN2 output are shown in Figure 10-14. To date, the Style-GAN2 architecture (and scaled variations such as StyleGAN-XL[6]) remain state of the art for image generation on datasets such as Flickr-Faces-HQ (FFHQ) and CIFAR-10, according to the benchmarking website Papers with Code (*https://oreil.ly/VwH2r*).

Figure 10-14. Uncurated StyleGAN2 output for the FFHQ face dataset and LSUN car dataset (source: Karras et al., 2019)

Other Important GANs

In this section, we will explore two more architectures that have also contributed significantly to the development of GANs—SAGAN and BigGAN.

Self-Attention GAN (SAGAN)

The Self-Attention GAN (SAGAN)[7] is a key development for GANs as it shows how the attention mechanism that powers sequential models such as the Transformer can also be incorporated into GAN-based models for image generation. Figure 10-15 shows the self-attention mechanism from the paper introducing this architecture.

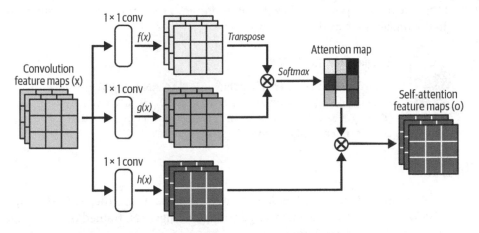

Figure 10-15. The self-attention mechanism within the SAGAN model (source: Zhang et al., 2018)

The problem with GAN-based models that do not incorporate attention is that convolutional feature maps are only able to process information locally. Connecting pixel information from one side of an image to the other requires multiple convolutional layers that reduce the size of the image, while increasing the number of channels. Precise positional information is reduced throughout this process in favor of capturing higher-level features, making it computationally inefficient for the model to learn long-range dependencies between distantly connected pixels. SAGAN solves this problem by incorporating the attention mechanism that we explored earlier in this chapter into the GAN. The effect of this inclusion is shown in Figure 10-16.

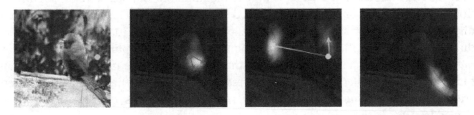

Figure 10-16. A SAGAN-generated image of a bird (leftmost cell) and the attention maps of the final attention-based generator layer for the pixels covered by the three colored dots (rightmost cells) (source: Zhang et al., 2018)

The red dot is a pixel that is part of the bird's body, and so attention naturally falls on the surrounding body cells. The green dot is part of the background, and here the attention actually falls on the other side of the bird's head, on other background pixels. The blue dot is part of the bird's long tail and so attention falls on other tail pixels, some of which are distant from the blue dot. It would be difficult to maintain this long-range dependency for pixels without attention, especially for long, thin structures in the image (such as the tail in this case).

Training Your Own SAGAN

The official code for training your own SAGAN using TensorFlow is available on GitHub (*https://oreil.ly/rvej0*). Bear in mind that training a SAGAN to achieve the results from the paper requires a significant amount of computing power.

BigGAN

BigGAN,[8] developed at DeepMind, extends the ideas from the SAGAN paper. Figure 10-17 shows some of the images generated by BigGAN, trained on the ImageNet dataset at 128 × 128 resolution.

Figure 10-17. Examples of images generated by BigGAN (source: Brock et al., 2018)

As well as some incremental changes to the base SAGAN model, there are also several innovations outlined in the paper that take the model to the next level of sophistication. One such innovation is the so-called *truncation trick*. This is where the latent distribution used for sampling is different from the $z \sim \mathcal{N}(0, \mathbf{I})$ distribution used during training. Specifically, the distribution used during sampling is a *truncated normal distribution* (resampling values of z that have magnitude greater than a certain threshold). The smaller the truncation threshold, the greater the believability of generated samples, at the expense of reduced variability. This concept is shown in Figure 10-18.

Figure 10-18. The truncation trick: from left to right, the threshold is set to 2, 1, 0.5, and 0.04 (source: Brock et al., 2018)

Also, as the name suggests, BigGAN is an improvement over SAGAN in part simply by being *bigger*. BigGAN uses a batch size of 2,048—8 times larger than the batch size of 256 used in SAGAN—and a channel size that is increased by 50% in each layer. However, BigGAN additionally shows that SAGAN can be improved structurally by the inclusion of a shared embedding, by orthogonal regularization, and by incorporating the latent vector z into each layer of the generator, rather than just the initial layer.

For a full description of the innovations introduced by BigGAN, I recommend reading the original paper and accompanying presentation material (*https://oreil.ly/vPn8T*).

Using BigGAN

A tutorial for generating images using a pre-trained BigGAN is available on the TensorFlow website (*https://oreil.ly/YLbLb*).

VQ-GAN

Another important type of GAN is the Vector Quantized GAN (VQ-GAN), introduced in 2020.[9] This model architecture builds upon an idea introduced in the 2017 paper "Neural Discrete Representation Learning"[10]—namely, that the representations learned by a VAE can be discrete, rather than continuous. This new type of model, the Vector Quantized VAE (VQ-VAE), was shown to generate high-quality images while avoiding some of the issues often seen with traditional continuous latent space VAEs, such as *posterior collapse* (where the learned latent space becomes uninformative due to an overly powerful decoder).

The first version of DALL.E, a text-to-image model released by OpenAI in 2021 (see Chapter 13), utilized a VAE with a discrete latent space, similar to VQ-VAE.

By a *discrete latent space*, we mean a learned list of vectors (the *codebook*), each associated with a corresponding index. The job of the encoder in a VQ-VAE is to collapse the input image to a smaller grid of vectors that can then be compared to the codebook. The closest codebook vector to each grid square vector (by Euclidean distance) is then taken forward to be decoded by the decoder, as shown in Figure 10-19. The codebook is a list of learned vectors of length d (the embedding size) that matches the number of channels in the output of the encoder and input to the decoder. For example, e_1 is a vector that can be interpreted as *background*.

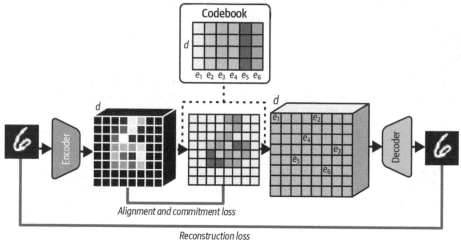

Figure 10-19. A diagram of a VQ-VAE

The codebook can be thought of as a set of learned discrete concepts that are shared by the encoder and decoder in order to describe the contents of a given image. The VQ-VAE must find a way to make this set of discrete concepts as informative as possible so that the encoder can accurately *label* each grid square with a particular code vector that is meaningful to the decoder. The loss function for a VQ-VAE is therefore the reconstruction loss added to two terms (alignment and commitment loss) that ensure that the output vectors from the encoder are as close as possible to vectors in the codebook. These terms replace the the KL divergence term between the encoded distribution and the standard Gaussian prior in a typical VAE.

However, this architecture poses a question—how do we sample novel code grids to pass to the decoder to generate new images? Clearly, using a uniform prior (picking each code with equal probability for each grid square) will not work. For example in the MNIST dataset, the top-left grid square is highly likely to be coded as *background*, whereas grid squares toward the center of the image are not as likely to be coded as such. To solve this problem, the authors used another model, an autoregressive PixelCNN (see Chapter 5), to predict the next code vector in the grid, given previous code vectors. In other words, the prior is learned by the model, rather than static as in the case of the vanilla VAE.

Training Your Own VQ-VAE

There is an excellent tutorial by Sayak Paul on training your own VQ-VAE using Keras available on the Keras website (*https://oreil.ly/dmcb4*).

The VQ-GAN paper details several key changes to the VQ-VAE architecture, as shown in Figure 10-20.

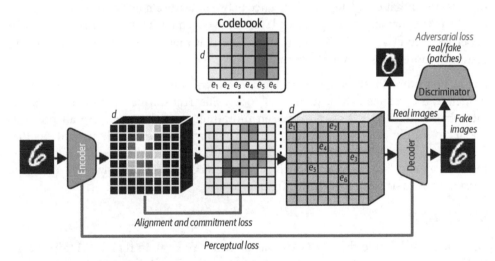

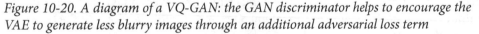

Figure 10-20. A diagram of a VQ-GAN: the GAN discriminator helps to encourage the VAE to generate less blurry images through an additional adversarial loss term

Firstly, as the name suggests, the authors include a GAN discriminator that tries to distinguish between the output from the VAE decoder and real images, with an accompanying adversarial term in the loss function. GANs are known to produce sharper images than VAEs, so this addition improves the overall image quality. Notice that despite the name, the VAE is still present in a VQ-GAN model—the GAN discriminator is an additional component rather than a replacement of the VAE. The idea of combining a VAE with a GAN discriminator (VAE-GAN) was first introduced by Larsen et al. in their 2015 paper.[11]

Secondly, the GAN discriminator predicts if small patches of the images are real or fake, rather than the entire image at once. This idea (*PatchGAN*) was applied in the successful *pix2pix* image-to-image model introduced in 2016 by Isola et al.[12] and was also successfully applied as part of *CycleGAN*,[13] another image-to-image style transfer model. The PatchGAN discriminator outputs a prediction vector (a prediction for each patch), rather than a single prediction for the overall image. The benefit of using a PatchGAN discriminator is that the loss function can then measure how good the discriminator is at distinguishing images based on their *style*, rather than their *content*. Since each individual element of the discriminator prediction is based on a small square of the image, it must use the style of the patch, rather than its content, to make its decision. This is useful as we know that VAEs produce images that are stylistically more blurry than real images, so the PatchGAN discriminator can encourage the VAE decoder to generate sharper images than it would naturally produce.

Thirdly, rather than use a single MSE reconstruction loss that compares the input image pixels with the output pixels from the VAE decoder, VQ-GAN uses a *perceptual loss* term that calculates the difference between feature maps at intermediate layers of the encoder and corresponding layers of the decoder. This idea is from the 2016 paper by Hou et al.,[14] where the authors show that this change to the loss function results in more realistic image generations.

Lastly, instead of PixelCNN, a Transformer is used as the autoregressive part of the model, trained to generate sequences of codes. The Transformer is trained in a separate phase, after the VQ-GAN has been fully trained. Rather than use all previous tokens in a fully autoregressive manner, the authors choose to only use tokens that fall within a sliding window around the token to be predicted. This ensures that the model scales to larger images, which require a larger latent grid size and therefore more tokens to be generated by the Transformer.

ViT VQ-GAN

One final extension to the VQ-GAN was made by Yu et al. in their 2021 paper entitled "Vector-Quantized Image Modeling with Improved VQGAN."[15] Here, the authors show how the convolutional encoder and decoder of the VQ-GAN can be replaced with Transformers as shown in Figure 10-21.

For the encoder, the authors use a *Vision Transformer* (ViT).[16] A ViT is a neural network architecture that applies the Transformer model, originally designed for natural language processing, to image data. Instead of using convolutional layers to extract features from an image, a ViT divides the image into a sequence of patches, which are tokenized and then fed as input to an encoder Transformer.

Specifically, in the ViT VQ-GAN, the nonoverlapping input patches (each of size 8 × 8) are first flattened, then projected into a low-dimensional embedding space, where positional embeddings are added. This sequence is then fed to a standard encoder Transformer and the resulting embeddings are quantized according to a learned codebook. These integer codes are then processed by a decoder Transformer model, with the overall output being a sequence of patches that can be stitched back together to form the original image. The overall encoder-decoder model is trained end-to-end as an autoencoder.

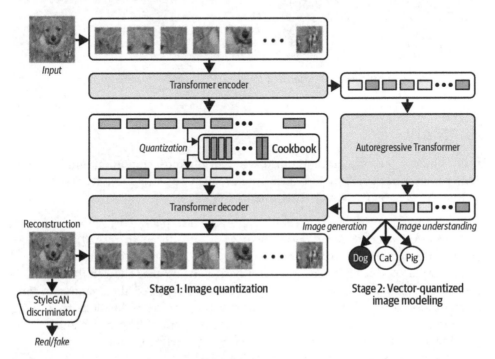

Figure 10-21. A diagram of a ViT VQ-GAN: the GAN discriminator helps to encourage the VAE to generate less blurry images through an additional adversarial loss term (source: Yu and Koh, 2022)[17]

As with the original VQ-GAN model, the second phase of training involves using an autoregressive decoder Transformer to generate sequences of codes. Therefore in total, there are three Transformers in a ViT VQ-GAN, in addition to the GAN discriminator and learned codebook. Examples of images generated by the ViT VQ-GAN from the paper are shown in Figure 10-22.

Figure 10-22. Example images generated by a ViT VQ-GAN trained on ImageNet (source: Yu et al., 2021)

Summary

In this chapter, we have taken a tour of some of the most important and influential GAN papers since 2017. In particular, we have explored ProGAN, StyleGAN, StyleGAN2, SAGAN, BigGAN, VQ-GAN, and ViT VQ-GAN.

We started by exploring the concept of progressive training that was pioneered in the 2017 ProGAN paper. Several key changes were introduced in the 2018 StyleGAN paper that gave greater control over the image output, such as the mapping network for creating a specific style vector and synthesis network that allowed the style to be injected at different resolutions. Finally, StyleGAN2 replaced the adaptive instance normalization of StyleGAN with weight modulation and demodulation steps, alongside additional enhancements such as path regularization. The paper also showed how the desirable property of gradual resolution refinement could be retained without having to the train the network progressively.

We also saw how the concept of attention could be built into a GAN, with the introduction of SAGAN in 2018. This allows the network to capture long-range dependencies, such as similar background colors over opposite sides of an image, without relying on deep convolutional maps to spread the information over the spatial dimensions of the image. BigGAN was an extension of this idea that made several key changes and trained a larger network to improve the image quality further.

In the VQ-GAN paper, the authors show how several different types of generative models can be combined to great effect. Building on the original VQ-VAE paper that introduced the concept of a VAE with a discrete latent space, VQ-GAN additionally includes a discriminator that encourages the VAE to generate less blurry images through an additional adversarial loss term. An autoregressive Transformer is used to construct a novel sequence of code tokens that can be decoded by the VAE decoder to produce novel images. The ViT VQ-GAN paper extends this idea even further, by replacing the convolutional encoder and decoder of VQ-GAN with Transformers.

References

1. Huiwen Chang et al., "Muse: Text-to-Image Generation via Masked Generative Transformers," January 2, 2023, *https://arxiv.org/abs/2301.00704*.

2. Tero Karras et al., "Progressive Growing of GANs for Improved Quality, Stability, and Variation," October 27, 2017, *https://arxiv.org/abs/1710.10196*.

3. Tero Karras et al., "A Style-Based Generator Architecture for Generative Adversarial Networks," December 12, 2018, *https://arxiv.org/abs/1812.04948*.

4. Xun Huang and Serge Belongie, "Arbitrary Style Transfer in Real-Time with Adaptive Instance Normalization," March 20, 2017, *https://arxiv.org/abs/1703.06868*.

5. Tero Karras et al., "Analyzing and Improving the Image Quality of StyleGAN," December 3, 2019, *https://arxiv.org/abs/1912.04958*.

6. Axel Sauer et al., "StyleGAN-XL: Scaling StyleGAN to Large Diverse Datasets," February 1, 2022, *https://arxiv.org/abs/2202.00273v2*.

7. Han Zhang et al., "Self-Attention Generative Adversarial Networks," May 21, 2018, *https://arxiv.org/abs/1805.08318*.

8. Andrew Brock et al., "Large Scale GAN Training for High Fidelity Natural Image Synthesis," September 28, 2018, *https://arxiv.org/abs/1809.11096*.

9. Patrick Esser et al., "Taming Transformers for High-Resolution Image Synthesis," December 17, 2020, *https://arxiv.org/abs/2012.09841*.

10. Aaron van den Oord et al., "Neural Discrete Representation Learning," November 2, 2017, *https://arxiv.org/abs/1711.00937v2*.

11. Anders Boesen Lindbo Larsen et al., "Autoencoding Beyond Pixels Using a Learned Similarity Metric," December 31, 2015, *https://arxiv.org/abs/1512.09300*.

12. Phillip Isola et al., "Image-to-Image Translation with Conditional Adversarial Networks," November 21, 2016, *https://arxiv.org/abs/1611.07004v3*.

13. Jun-Yan Zhu et al., "Unpaired Image-to-Image Translation using Cycle-Consistent Adversarial Networks," March 30, 2017, *https://arxiv.org/abs/1703.10593*.

14. Xianxu Hou et al., "Deep Feature Consistent Variational Autoencoder," October 2, 2016, *https://arxiv.org/abs/1610.00291*.

15. Jiahui Yu et al., "Vector-Quantized Image Modeling with Improved VQGAN," October 9, 2021, *https://arxiv.org/abs/2110.04627*.

16. Alexey Dosovitskiy et al., "An Image Is Worth 16x16 Words: Transformers for Image Recognition at Scale," October 22, 2020, *https://arxiv.org/abs/2010.11929v2*.

17. Jiahui Yu and Jing Yu Koh, "Vector-Quantized Image Modeling with Improved VQGAN," May 18, 2022, *https://ai.googleblog.com/2022/05/vector-quantized-image-modeling-with.html*.

CHAPTER 11

Music Generation

Chapter Goals

In this chapter you will:

- Understand how we can treat music generation as a sequence prediction problem, so we can apply autoregressive models such as Transformers.

- See how to parse and tokenize MIDI files using the `music21` package to create a training set.

- Learn how to use sine positional encoding.

- Train a music-generating Transformer, with multiple inputs and outputs to handle note and duration.

- Understand how to handle polyphonic music, including grid tokenization and event-based tokenization.

- Train a MuseGAN model to generate multitrack music.

- Use the MuseGAN to adjust different properties of the generated bars.

Musical composition is a complex and creative process that involves combining different musical elements such as melody, harmony, rhythm, and timbre. While this is traditionally seen as a uniquely human activity, recent advancements have made it possible to generate music that both is pleasing to the ear and has long-term structure.

One of the most popular techniques for music generation is the Transformer, as music can be thought of as a sequence prediction problem. These models have been adapted to generate music by treating musical notes as a sequence of tokens, similar to words in a sentence. The Transformer model learns to predict the next note in the sequence based on the previous notes, resulting in a generated piece of music.

MuseGAN takes a totally different approach to generating music. Unlike Transformers, which generate music note by note, MuseGAN generates entire musical tracks at once by treating music as an *image*, consisting of a pitch axis and a time axis. Moreover, MuseGAN separates out different musical components such as chords, style, melody, and groove so that they can be controlled independently.

In this chapter we will learn how to process music data and apply both a Transformer and MuseGAN to generate music that is stylistically similar to a given training set.

Introduction

For a machine to compose music that is pleasing to our ear, it must master many of the same technical challenges that we saw in Chapter 9 in relation to text. In particular, our model must be able to learn from and re-create the sequential structure of music and be able to choose from a discrete set of possibilities for subsequent notes.

However, music generation presents additional challenges that are not present for text generation, namely pitch and rhythm. Music is often polyphonic—that is, there are several streams of notes played simultaneously on different instruments, which combine to create harmonies that are either dissonant (clashing) or consonant (harmonious). Text generation only requires us to handle a single stream of text, in contrast to the parallel streams of chords that are present in music.

Also, text generation can be handled one word at a time. Unlike text data, music is a multipart, interwoven tapestry of sounds that are not necessarily delivered at the same time—much of the interest that stems from listening to music is in the interplay between different rhythms across the ensemble. For example, a guitarist might play a flurry of quicker notes while the pianist holds a longer sustained chord. Therefore, generating music note by note is complex, because we often do not want all the instruments to change notes simultaneously.

We will start this chapter by simplifying the problem to focus on music generation for a single (monophonic) line of music. Many of the techniques from Chapter 9 for text generation can also be used for music generation, as the two tasks share many common themes. We will start by training a Transformer to generate music in the style of the J.S. Bach cello suites and see how the attention mechanism allows the model to focus on previous notes in order to determine the most natural subsequent note. We'll then tackle the task of polyphonic music generation and explore how we can deploy an architecture based around GANs to create music for multiple voices.

Transformers for Music Generation

The model we will be building here is a decoder Transformer, taking inspiration from OpenAI's *MuseNet* (*https://oreil.ly/OaCDY*), which also utilizes a decoder Transformer (similar to GPT-3) trained to predict the next note given a sequence of previous notes.

In music generation tasks, the length of the sequence N grows large as the music progresses, and this means that the $N \times N$ attention matrix for each head becomes expensive to store and compute. We ideally do not want to clip the input sequence to a short number of tokens, as we would like the model to construct the piece around a long-term structure and repeat motifs and phrases from several minutes ago, as a human composer would.

To tackle this problem, MuseNet utilizes a form of Transformer known as a *Sparse Transformer* (*https://oreil.ly/euQiL*). Each output position in the attention matrix only computes weights for a subset of input positions, thereby reducing the computational complexity and memory required to train the model. MuseNet can therefore operate with full attention over 4,096 tokens and can learn long-term structure and melodic structure across a range of styles. (See, for example, OpenAI's Chopin (*https://oreil.ly/cmwsO*) and Mozart (*https://oreil.ly/-T-Je*) recordings on SoundCloud.)

To see how the continuation of a musical phrase is often influenced by notes from several bars ago, take a look at the opening bars of the Prelude to Bach's Cello Suite No. 1 (Figure 11-1).

Figure 11-1. The opening of Bach's Cello Suite No. 1 (Prelude)

Bars

Bars (or *measures*) are small units of music that contain a fixed, small number of beats and are marked out by vertical lines that cross the staff. If you can count 1, 2, 1, 2 along to a piece of music, then there are two beats in each bar and you're probably listening to a march. If you can count 1, 2, 3, 1, 2, 3, then there are three beats to each bar and you may be listening to a waltz.

What note do you think comes next? Even if you have no musical training you may still be able to guess. If you said G (the same as the very first note of the piece), then you'd be correct. How did you know this? You may have been able to see that every bar and half bar starts with the same note and used this information to inform your decision. We want our model to be able to perform the same trick—in particular, we want it to pay attention to a particular note from the previous half bar, when the previous low G was registered. An attention-based model such as a Transformer will be able to incorporate this long-term look-back without having to maintain a hidden state across many bars, as is the case with a recurrent neural network.

Anyone tackling the task of music generation must first have a basic understanding of musical theory. In the next section we'll go through the essential knowledge required to read music and how we can represent this numerically, in order to transform music into the input data required to train our Transformer.

Running the Code for This Example

The code for this example can be found in the Jupyter notebook located at *notebooks/11_music/01_transformer/transformer.ipynb* in the book repository.

The Bach Cello Suite Dataset

The raw dataset that we shall be using is a set of MIDI files for the Cello Suites by J.S. Bach. You can download the dataset by running the dataset downloader script in the book repository, as shown in Example 11-1. This will save the MIDI files locally to the */data* folder.

Example 11-1. Downloading the J.S. Bach Cello Suites dataset

```bash
bash scripts/download_music_data.sh
```

To view and listen to the music generated by the model, you'll need some software that can produce musical notation. MuseScore (*https://musescore.org*) is a great tool for this purpose and can be downloaded for free.

Parsing MIDI Files

We'll be using the Python library music21 to load the MIDI files into Python for processing. Example 11-2 shows how to load a MIDI file and visualize it (Figure 11-2), both as a score and as structured data.

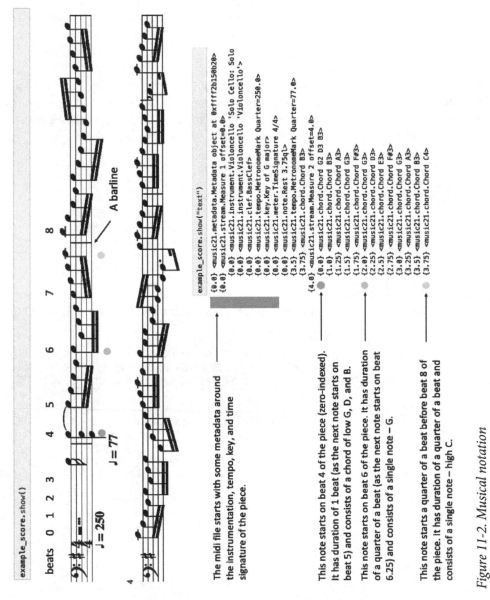

Figure 11-2. Musical notation

Example 11-2. Importing a MIDI file

```
import music21

file = "/app/data/bach-cello/cs1-2all.mid"
example_score = music21.converter.parse(file).chordify()
```

Octaves

The number after each note name indicates the *octave* that the note is in—since the note names (A to G) repeat, this is needed to uniquely identify the pitch of the note. For example, G2 is an octave below G3.

Now it's time to convert the scores into something that looks more like text! We start by looping over each score and extracting the note and duration of each element in the piece into two separate text strings, with elements separated by spaces. We encode the key and time signature of the piece as special symbols, with zero duration.

Monophonic Versus Polyphonic Music

In this first example, we will treat the music as *monophonic* (one single line), taking just the top note of any chords. Sometimes we may wish to keep the parts separate to generate music that is *polyphonic* in nature. This presents additional challenges that we shall tackle later on in this chapter.

The output from this process is shown in Figure 11-3—compare this to Figure 11-2 so that you can see how the raw music data has been transformed into the two strings.

```
Notes string
 START G:major 4/4TS rest B3 B3 B3 A3 G3 F#3 G3 D3 E3 F#3 G
3 A3 B3 C4 D4 B3 G3 F#3 G3 E3 D3 C3 B2 C3 D3 E3 F#3 G3 A3 B
3 C4 A3 G3 F#3 G3 E3 F#3 G3 A2 D3 F#3 G3 A3 B3 C4 A3 B3 ...

Duration string
 0.0 0.0 0.0 3.75 0.25 1.0 0.25 0.25 0.25 0.25 0.25 0.25 0.
25 0.25 0.25 0.25 0.25 0.25 0.25 0.25 0.25 0.25 0.25 0.25
 0.25 0.25 0.25 0.25 0.25 0.25 0.25 0.25 0.25 0.25 0.25 0.25
 0.25 0.25 0.25 0.25 0.25 0.25 0.25 0.25 0.25 0.25 0.25 0.25
 0.25 0.25 0.25 ...
```

Figure 11-3. Samples of the notes text string and the duration text string, corresponding to Figure 11-2

This looks a lot more like the text data that we have dealt with previously. The *words* are the note–duration combinations, and we should try to build a model that predicts the next note and duration, given a sequence of previous notes and durations. A key difference between music and text generation is that we need to build a model that can handle the note and duration prediction simultaneously—i.e., there are two streams of information that we need to handle, compared to the single streams of text that we saw in Chapter 9.

Tokenization

To create the dataset that will train the model, we first need to tokenize each note and duration, exactly as we did previously for each word in a text corpus. We can achieve this by using a `TextVectorization` layer, applied to the notes and durations separately, as shown in Example 11-3.

Example 11-3. Tokenizing the notes and durations

```
def create_dataset(elements):
    ds = (
        tf.data.Dataset.from_tensor_slices(elements)
        .batch(BATCH_SIZE, drop_remainder = True)
        .shuffle(1000)
    )
    vectorize_layer = layers.TextVectorization(
        standardize = None, output_mode="int"
    )
    vectorize_layer.adapt(ds)
    vocab = vectorize_layer.get_vocabulary()
    return ds, vectorize_layer, vocab

notes_seq_ds, notes_vectorize_layer, notes_vocab = create_dataset(notes)
durations_seq_ds, durations_vectorize_layer, durations_vocab = create_dataset(
    durations
)
seq_ds = tf.data.Dataset.zip((notes_seq_ds, durations_seq_ds))
```

The full parsing and tokenization process is shown in Figure 11-4.

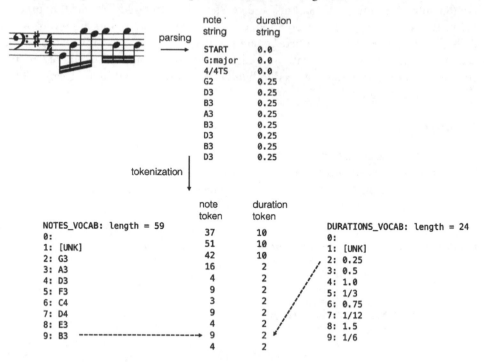

Figure 11-4. Parsing the MIDI files and tokenizing the notes and durations

Creating the Training Set

The final step of preprocessing is to create the training set that we will feed to our Transformer.

We do this by splitting both the note and duration strings into chunks of 50 elements, using a sliding window technique. The output is simply the input window shifted by one note, so that the Transformer is trained to predict the note and duration of the element one timestep into the future, given previous elements in the window. An example of this (using a sliding window of only four elements for demonstration purposes) is shown in Figure 11-5.

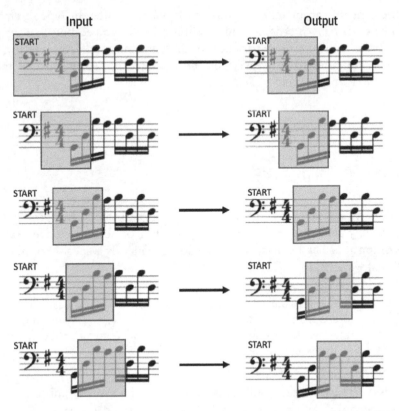

Figure 11-5. The inputs and outputs for the musical Transformer model—in this example, a sliding window of width 4 is used to create input chunks, which are then shifted by one element to create the target output

The architecture we will be using for our Transformer is the same as we used for text generation in Chapter 9, with a few key differences.

Sine Position Encoding

Firstly, we will be introducing a different type of encoding for the token positions. In Chapter 9 we used a simple Embedding layer to encode the position of each token, effectively mapping each integer position to a distinct vector that was learned by the model. We therefore needed to define a maximum length (N) that the sequence could be and train on this length of sequence. The downside to this approach is that it is then impossible to extrapolate to sequences that are longer than this maximum length. You would have to clip the input to the last N tokens, which isn't ideal if you are trying to generate long-form content.

To circumvent this problem, we can switch to using a different type of embedding called a *sine position embedding*. This is similar to the embedding that we used in Chapter 8 to encode the noise variances of the diffusion model. Specifically, the following function is used to convert the position of the word (*pos*) in the input sequence into a unique vector of length *d*:

$$PE_{pos, 2i} = \sin\left(\frac{pos}{10,000^{2i/d}}\right)$$

$$PE_{pos, 2i+1} = \cos\left(\frac{pos}{10,000^{(2i+1)/d}}\right)$$

For small *i*, the wavelength of this function is short and therefore the function value changes rapidly along the position axis. Larger values of *i* create a longer wavelength. Each position thus has its own unique encoding, which is a specific combination of the different wavelengths.

 Notice that this embedding is defined for all possible position values. It is a deterministic function (i.e., it isn't learned by the model) that uses trigonometric functions to define a unique encoding for each possible position.

The *Keras NLP* module has a built-in layer that implements this embedding for us—we can therefore define our `TokenAndPositionEmbedding` layer as shown in Example 11-4.

Example 11-4. Tokenizing the notes and durations

```
class TokenAndPositionEmbedding(layers.Layer):
    def __init__(self, vocab_size, embed_dim):
        super(TokenAndPositionEmbedding, self).__init__()
        self.vocab_size = vocab_size
        self.embed_dim = embed_dim
        self.token_emb = layers.Embedding(input_dim=vocab_size, output_dim=embed_dim)
        self.pos_emb = keras_nlp.layers.SinePositionEncoding()

    def call(self, x):
        embedding = self.token_emb(x)
        positions = self.pos_emb(embedding)
        return embedding + positions
```

Figure 11-6 shows how the two embeddings (token and position) are added to produce the overall embedding for the sequence.

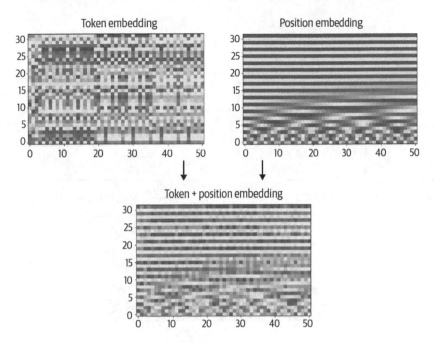

Figure 11-6. The `TokenAndPositionEmbedding` layer adds the token embeddings to the sinusoidal position embeddings to produce the overall embedding for the sequence

Multiple Inputs and Outputs

We now have two input streams (notes and durations) and two output streams (predicted notes and durations). We therefore need to adapt the architecture of our Transformer to cater for this.

There are many ways of handling the dual stream of inputs. We could create tokens that represent each note–duration pair and then treat the sequence as a single stream of tokens. However, this has the downside of not being able to represent note–duration pairs that have not been seen in the training set (for example, we may have seen a G#2 note and a 1/3 duration independently, but never together, so there would be no token for G#2:1/3.

Instead, we choose to embed the note and duration tokens separately and then use a concatenation layer to create a single representation of the input that can be used by the downstream Transformer block. Similarly, the output from the Transformer block is passed to two separate dense layers, which represent the predicted note and duration probabilities. The overall architecture is shown in Figure 11-7. Layer output shapes are shown with batch size b and sequence length l.

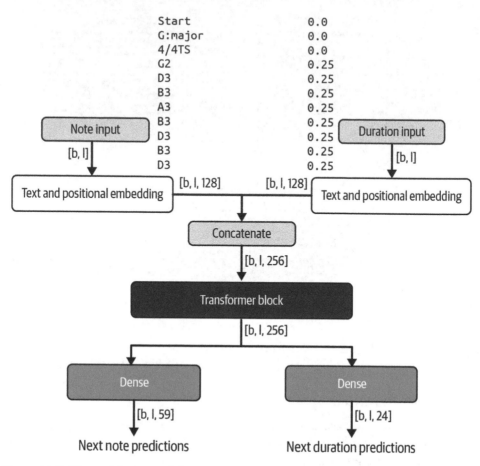

Figure 11-7. *The architecture of the music-generating Transformer*

An alternative approach would be to interleave the note and duration tokens into a single stream of input and let the model learn that the output should be a single stream where the note and duration tokens alternate. This comes with the added complexity of ensuring that the output can still be parsed when the model has not yet learned how to interleave the tokens correctly.

> There is no *right* or *wrong* way to design your model—part of the fun is experimenting with different setups and seeing which works best for you!

Analysis of the Music-Generating Transformer

We'll start by generating some music from scratch, by seeding the network with a START note token and 0.0 duration token (i.e., we are telling the model to assume it is starting from the beginning of the piece). Then we can generate a musical passage using the same iterative technique we used in Chapter 9 for generating text sequences, as follows:

1. Given the current sequence (of notes and durations), the model predicts two distributions, one for the next note and one for the next duration.

2. We sample from both of these distributions, using a temperature parameter to control how much variation we would like in the sampling process.

3. The chosen note and duration are appended to the respective input sequences.

4. The process repeats with the new input sequences for as many elements as we wish to generate.

Figure 11-8 shows examples of music generated from scratch by the model at various epochs of the training process. We use a temperature of 0.5 for the notes and durations.

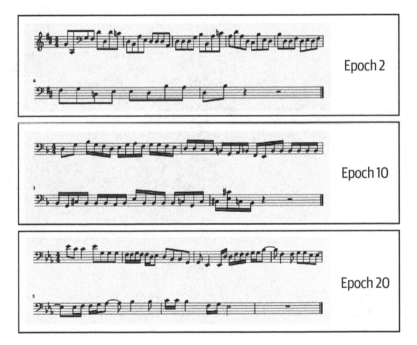

Figure 11-8. Some examples of passages generated by the model when seeded only with a START note token and 0.0 duration token

Most of our analysis in this section will focus on the note predictions, rather than durations, as for Bach's Cello Suites the harmonic intricacies are more difficult to capture and therefore more worthy of investigation. However, you can also apply the same analysis to the rhythmic predictions of the model, which may be particularly relevant for other styles of music that you could use to train this model (such as a drum track).

There are several points to note about the generated passages in Figure 11-8. First, see how the music is becoming more sophisticated as training progresses. To begin with, the model plays it safe by sticking to the same group of notes and rhythms. By epoch 10, the model has begun to generate small runs of notes, and by epoch 20 it is producing interesting rhythms and is firmly established in a set key (E ♭ major).

Second, we can analyze the distribution of notes over time by plotting the predicted distribution at each timestep as a heatmap. Figure 11-9 shows this heatmap for the example from epoch 20 in Figure 11-8.

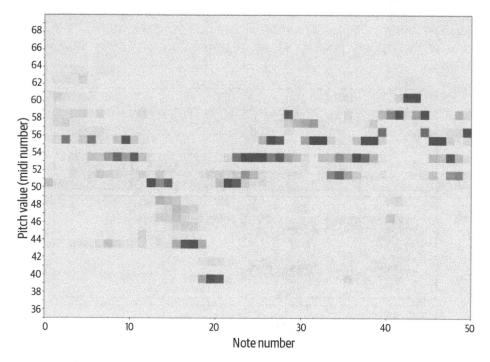

Figure 11-9. The distribution of possible next notes over time (at epoch 20): the darker the square, the more certain the model is that the next note is at this pitch

An interesting point to note here is that the model has clearly learned which notes belong to particular *keys*, as there are gaps in the distribution at notes that do not belong to the key. For example, there is a gray gap along the row for note 54 (corresponding to G♭/F♯). This note is highly unlikely to appear in a piece of music in the key of E♭ major. The model establishes the key early on in the generation process, and as the piece progresses, the model chooses notes that are more likely to feature in that key by attending to the token that represents it.

It is also worth pointing out that the model has learned Bach's characteristic style of dropping to a low note on the cello to end a phrase and bouncing back up again to start the next. See how around note 20, the phrase ends on a low E♭—it is common in the Bach Cello Suites to then return to a higher, more sonorous range of the instrument for the start of next phrase, which is exactly what the model predicts. There is a large gray gap between the low E♭ (pitch number 39) and the next note, which is predicted to be around pitch number 50, rather than continuing to rumble around the depths of the instrument.

Lastly, we should check to see if our attention mechanism is working as expected. The horizontal axis in Figure 11-10 shows the generated sequence of notes; the vertical axis shows where the attention of the network was aimed when predicting each note along the horizontal axis. The color of each square shows the maximum attention weight across all heads at each point in the generated sequence. The darker the square, the more attention is being applied to this position in the sequence. For simplicity, we only show the notes in this diagram, but the durations of each note are also being attended to by the network.

We can see that for the initial key signature, time signature, and rest, the network chose to place almost all of its attention on the START token. This makes sense, as these artifacts always appear at the start of a piece of music—once the notes start flowing the START token essentially stops being attended to.

As we move beyond the initial few notes, we can see that the network places most attention on approximately the last two to four notes and rarely places significant weight on notes more than four notes ago. Again, this makes sense; there is probably enough information contained in the previous four notes to understand how the phrase might continue. Additionally, some notes attend more strongly back to the key signature of D minor—for example, the E3 (7th note of the piece) and B-2 (B♭–14th note of the piece). This is fascinating, because these are the exact notes that rely on the key of D minor to relieve any ambiguity. The network must *look back* at the key signature in order to tell that there is a B♭ in the key signature (rather than a B natural) but there isn't an E♭ in the key signature (E natural must be used instead).

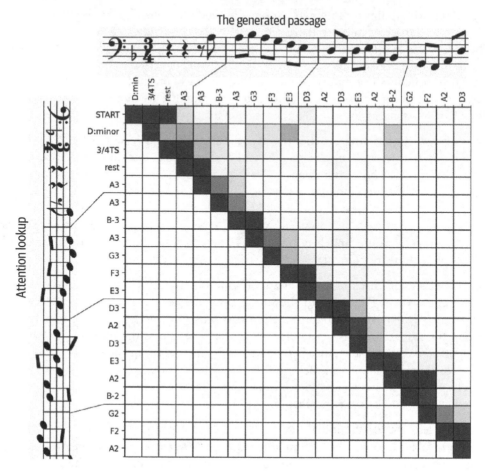

Figure 11-10. The color of each square in the matrix indicates the amount of attention given to each position on the vertical axis, at the point of predicting the note on the horizontal axis

There are also examples of where the network has chosen to ignore a certain note or rest nearby, as it doesn't add any additional information to its understanding of the phrase. For example, the penultimate note (A2) is not particularly attentive to the B-2 three notes back, but is slightly more attentive to the A2 four notes back. It is more interesting for the model to look at the A2 that falls on the beat, rather than the B-2 off the beat, which is just a passing note.

Remember we haven't told the model anything about which notes are related or which notes belong to which key signatures—it has worked this out for itself just by studying the music of J.S. Bach.

Tokenization of Polyphonic Music

The Transformer we've been exploring in this section works well for single-line (monophonic) music, but could it be adapted to multiline (polyphonic) music?

The challenge lies in how to represent the different lines of music as a single sequence of tokens. In the previous section we decided to split the notes and durations of the notes into two distinct inputs and outputs of the network, but we also saw that we could have interleaved these tokens into a single stream. We can use the same idea to handle polyphonic music. Two different approaches will be introduced here: *grid tokenization* and *event-based tokenization*, as discussed in the 2018 paper "Music Transformer: Generating Music with Long-Term Structure."[1]

Grid tokenization

Consider the two bars of music from a J.S. Bach chorale in Figure 11-11. There are four distinct parts (soprano [S], alto [A], tenor [T], bass [B]), written on different staffs.

Figure 11-11. The first two bars of a J.S. Bach chorale

We can imagine drawing this music on a grid, where the y-axis represents the pitch of the note and the x-axis represents the number of 16th-notes (semiquavers) that have passed since the start of the piece. If the grid square is filled, then there is a note playing at that point in time. All four parts are drawn on the same grid. This grid is known as a *piano roll* because it resembles a physical roll of paper with holes punched into it, which was used as a recording mechanism before digital systems were invented.

We can serialize the grid into a stream of tokens by moving first through the four voices, then along the timesteps in sequence. This produces a sequence of tokens $S_1, A_1, T_1, B_1, S_2, A_2, T_2, B_2, ...$, where the subscript denotes the timestep, as shown in Figure 11-12.

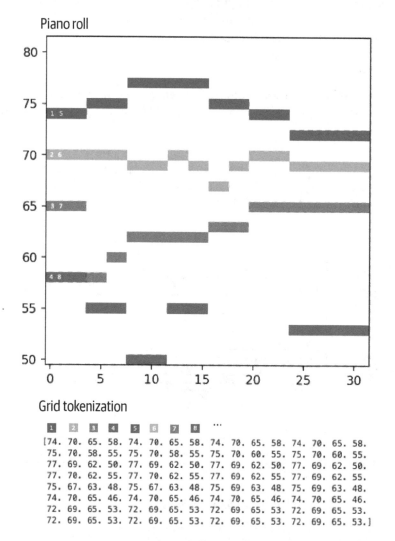

Figure 11-12. Creating the grid tokenization for the first two bars of the Bach chorale

We would then train our Transformer on this sequence of tokens, to predict the next token given the previous tokens. We can decode the generated sequence back into a grid structure by rolling the sequence back out over time in groups of four notes (one for each voice). This technique works surprisingly well, despite the same note often being split across multiple tokens with tokens from other voices in between.

However, there are some disadvantages. Firstly, notice that there is no way for the model to tell the difference between one long note and two shorter adjacent notes of the same pitch. This is because the tokenization does not explicitly encode the duration of notes, only whether a note is present at each timestep.

Secondly, this method requires the music to have a regular beat that is divisible into reasonably sized chunks. For example, using the current system, we cannot encode triplets (a group of three notes played across a single beat). We could divide the music into 12 steps per quarter-note (crotchet) instead of 4, that would triple the number of tokens required to represent the same passage of music, adding overhead on the training process and affecting the lookback capacity of the model.

Lastly, it is not obvious how we might add other components to the tokenization, such as dynamics (how loud or quiet the music is in each part) or tempo changes. We are locked into the two-dimensional grid structure of the piano roll, which provides a convenient way to represent pitch and timing, but not necessarily an easy way to incorporate other components that make music interesting to listen to.

Event-based tokenization

A more flexible approach is to use event-based tokenization. This can be thought of as a vocabulary that literally describes how the music is created as a sequence of events, using a rich set of tokens.

For example in Figure 11-13, we use three types of tokens:

- `NOTE_ON<pitch>` (start playing a note of a given pitch)
- `NOTE_OFF<pitch>` (stop playing a note of a given pitch)
- `TIME_SHIFT<step>` (shift forward in time by a given step)

This vocabulary can be used to create a sequence that describes the construction of the music as a set of instructions.

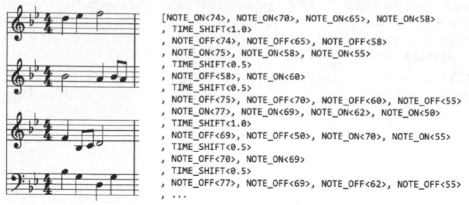

Event tokenization

```
[NOTE_ON<74>, NOTE_ON<70>, NOTE_ON<65>, NOTE_ON<58>
, TIME_SHIFT<1.0>
, NOTE_OFF<74>, NOTE_OFF<65>, NOTE_OFF<58>
, NOTE_ON<75>, NOTE_ON<58>, NOTE_ON<55>
, TIME_SHIFT<0.5>
, NOTE_OFF<58>, NOTE_ON<60>
, TIME_SHIFT<0.5>
, NOTE_OFF<75>, NOTE_OFF<70>, NOTE_OFF<60>, NOTE_OFF<55>
, NOTE_ON<77>, NOTE_ON<69>, NOTE_ON<62>, NOTE_ON<50>
, TIME_SHIFT<1.0>
, NOTE_OFF<69>, NOTE_OFF<50>, NOTE_ON<70>, NOTE_ON<55>
, TIME_SHIFT<0.5>
, NOTE_OFF<70>, NOTE_ON<69>
, TIME_SHIFT<0.5>
, NOTE_OFF<77>, NOTE_OFF<69>, NOTE_OFF<62>, NOTE_OFF<55>
, ...
```

Figure 11-13. An event tokenization for the first bar of the Bach chorale

We could easily incorporate other types of tokens into this vocabulary, to represent dynamic and tempo changes for subsequent notes. This method also provides a way to generate triplets against a backdrop of quarter-notes, by separating the notes of the triplets with TIME_SHIFT<0.33> tokens. Overall, it is a more expressive framework for tokenization, though it is also potentially more complex for the Transformer to learn inherent patterns in the training set music, as it is by definition less structured than the grid method.

 I encourage you to try implementing these polyphonic techniques and train a Transformer on the new tokenized dataset using all the knowledge you have built up so far in this book. I would also recommend checking our Dr. Tristan Behrens's guide to music generation research, available on GitHub (*https://oreil.ly/YfaiJ*), which provides a comprehensive overview of different papers on the topic of music generation using deep learning.

In the next section we will take a completely different approach to music generation, using GANs.

MuseGAN

You may have thought that the piano roll shown in Figure 11-12 looks a bit like a piece of modern art. This begs the question—could we in fact treat this piano roll as a *picture* and utilize image generation methods instead of sequence generation techniques?

As we shall see, the answer to this question is yes, we can treat music generation directly as an image generation problem. This means that instead of using Transformers, we can apply the same convolutional-based techniques that work so well for image generation problems—in particular, GANs.

MuseGAN was introduced in the 2017 paper "MuseGAN: Multi-Track Sequential Generative Adversarial Networks for Symbolic Music Generation and Accompaniment."[2] The authors show how it is possible to train a model to generate polyphonic, multitrack, multibar music through a novel GAN framework. Moreover, they show how, by dividing up the responsibilities of the noise vectors that feed the generator, they are able to maintain fine-grained control over the high-level temporal and track-based features of the music.

Let's start by introducing the the J.S. Bach chorale dataset.

Running the Code for This Example

The code for this example can be found in the Jupyter notebook located at *notebooks/11_music/02_musegan/musegan.ipynb* in the book repository.

The Bach Chorale Dataset

To begin this project, you'll first need to download the MIDI files that we'll be using to train the MuseGAN. We'll use a dataset of 229 J.S. Bach chorales for four voices.

You can download the dataset by running the Bach chorale dataset downloader script in the book repository, as shown in Example 11-5. This will save the MIDI files locally to the */data* folder.

Example 11-5. Downloading the Bach chorale dataset

```bash
bash scripts/download_bach_chorale_data.sh
```

The dataset consists of an array of four numbers for each timestep: the MIDI note pitches of each of the four voices. A timestep in this dataset is equal to a 16th note (a semiquaver). So, for example, in a single bar of 4 quarter (crotchet) beats, there are 16 timesteps. The dataset is automatically split into *train*, *validation*, and *test* sets. We will be using the *train* dataset to train the MuseGAN.

To start, we need to get the data into the correct shape to feed the GAN. In this example we'll generate two bars of music, so we'll extract only the first two bars of each chorale. Each bar consists of 16 timesteps and there are a potential 84 pitches across the 4 voices.

 Voices will be referred to as *tracks* from here on, to keep the terminology in line with the original paper.

Therefore, the transformed data will have the following shape:

```
[BATCH_SIZE, N_BARS, N_STEPS_PER_BAR, N_PITCHES, N_TRACKS]
```

where:

```
BATCH_SIZE = 64
N_BARS = 2
N_STEPS_PER_BAR = 16
N_PITCHES = 84
N_TRACKS = 4
```

To get the data into this shape, we one-hot encode the pitch numbers into a vector of length 84 and split each sequence of notes into two bars of 16 timesteps each. We are making the assumption here that each chorale in the dataset has four beats in each bar, which is reasonable, and even if this were not the case it would not adversely affect the training of the model.

Figure 11-14 shows how two bars of raw data are converted into the transformed piano roll dataset that we will use to train the GAN.

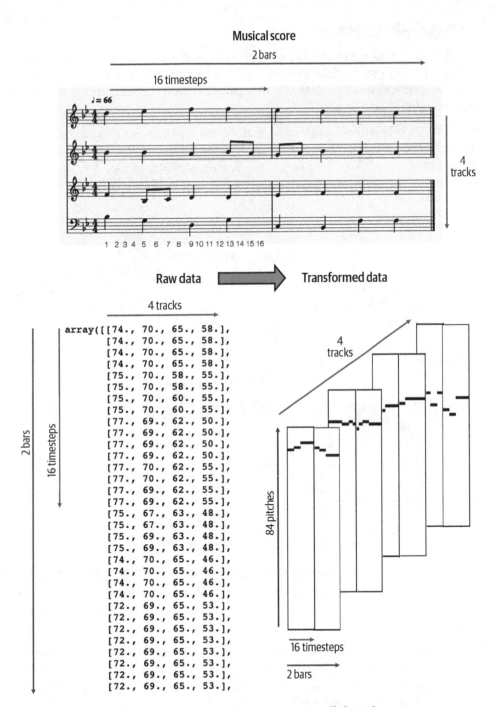

Figure 11-14. Processing two bars of raw data into piano roll data that we can use to train the GAN

The MuseGAN Generator

Like all GANs, MuseGAN consists of a generator and a critic. The generator tries to fool the critic with its musical creations, and the critic tries to prevent this from happening by ensuring it is able to tell the difference between the generator's forged Bach chorales and the real thing.

Where MuseGAN differs is in the fact that the generator doesn't just accept a single noise vector as input, but instead has four separate inputs, which correspond to four different characteristics of the music: chords, style, melody, and groove. By manipulating each of these inputs independently we can change high-level properties of the generated music.

A high-level view of the generator is shown in Figure 11-15.

THE MUSEGAN GENERATOR

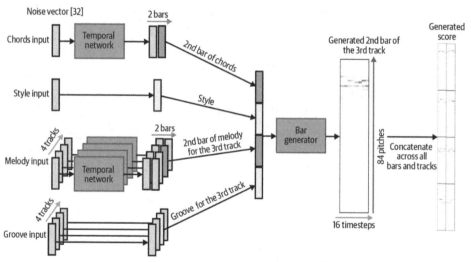

Figure 11-15. High-level diagram of the MuseGAN generator

The diagram shows how the chords and melody inputs are first passed through a *temporal network* that outputs a tensor with one of the dimensions equal to the number of bars to be generated. The style and groove inputs are not stretched temporally in this way, as they remain constant through the piece.

Then, to generate a particular bar for a particular track, the relevant outputs from the chords, style, melody, and groove parts of the network are concatenated to form a longer vector. This is then passed to a bar generator, which ultimately outputs the specified bar for the specified track.

By concatenating the generated bars for all tracks, we create a score that can be compared with real scores by the critic.

Let's first take a look at how to build a temporal network.

The temporal network

The job of a temporal network—a neural network consisting of convolutional transpose layers—is to transform a single input noise vector of length Z_DIM = 32 into a different noise vector for every bar (also of length 32). The Keras code to build this is shown in Example 11-6.

Example 11-6. Building the temporal network

```python
def conv_t(x, f, k, s, a, p, bn):
    x = layers.Conv2DTranspose(
                filters = f
                , kernel_size = k
                , padding = p
                , strides = s
                , kernel_initializer = initializer
                )(x)
    if bn:
        x = layers.BatchNormalization(momentum = 0.9)(x)

    x = layers.Activation(a)(x)
    return x

def TemporalNetwork():
    input_layer = layers.Input(shape=(Z_DIM,), name='temporal_input')  ❶
    x = layers.Reshape([1,1,Z_DIM])(input_layer)  ❷
    x = conv_t(
        x, f=1024, k=(2,1), s=(1,1), a = 'relu', p = 'valid', bn = True
    )  ❸
    x = conv_t(
        x, f=Z_DIM, k=(N_BARS - 1,1), s=(1,1), a = 'relu', p = 'valid', bn = True
    )
    output_layer = layers.Reshape([N_BARS, Z_DIM])(x)  ❹
    return models.Model(input_layer, output_layer)
```

❶ The input to the temporal network is a vector of length 32 (Z_DIM).

❷ We reshape this vector to a 1 × 1 tensor with 32 channels, so that we can apply convolutional 2D transpose operations to it.

❸ We apply Conv2DTranspose layers to expand the size of the tensor along one axis, so that it is the same length as N_BARS.

❹ We remove the unnecessary extra dimension with a `Reshape` layer.

The reason we use convolutional operations rather than requiring two independent vectors into the network is because we would like the network to learn how one bar should follow on from another in a consistent way. Using a neural network to expand the input vector along the time axis means the model has a chance to learn how music flows across bars, rather than treating each bar as completely independent of the last.

Chords, style, melody, and groove

Let's now take a closer look at the four different inputs that feed the generator:

Chords

The chords input is a single noise vector of length `Z_DIM`. This vector's job is to control the general progression of the music over time, shared across tracks, so we use a `TemporalNetwork` to transform this single vector into a different latent vector for every bar. Note that while we call this input chords, it really could control anything about the music that changes per bar, such as general rhythmic style, without being specific to any particular track.

Style

The style input is also a vector of length `Z_DIM`. This is carried forward without transformation, so it is the same across all bars and tracks. It can be thought of as the vector that controls the overall style of the piece (i.e., it affects all bars and tracks consistently).

Melody

The melody input is an array of shape `[N_TRACKS, Z_DIM]`—that is, we provide the model with a random noise vector of length `Z_DIM` for each track.

Each of these vectors is passed through a track-specific `TemporalNetwork`, where the weights are not shared between tracks. The output is a vector of length `Z_DIM` for every bar of every track. The model can therefore use these input vectors to fine-tune the content of every single bar and track independently.

Groove

The groove input is also an array of shape `[N_TRACKS, Z_DIM]`—a random noise vector of length `Z_DIM` for each track. Unlike the melody input, these vectors are not passed through the temporal network but instead are fed straight through, just like the style vector. Therefore, each groove vector will affect the overall properties of a track, across all bars.

We can summarize the responsibilities of each component of the MuseGAN generator as shown in Table 11-1.

Table 11-1. Components of the MuseGAN generator

	Output differs across bars?	Output differs across parts?
Style	X	X
Groove	X	✓
Chords	✓	X
Melody	✓	✓

The final piece of the MuseGAN generator is the *bar generator*—let's see how we can use this to glue together the outputs from the chord, style, melody, and groove components.

The bar generator

The bar generator receives four latent vectors—one from each of the chord, style, melody, and groove components. These are concatenated to produce a vector of length 4 * Z_DIM as input. The output is a piano roll representation of a single bar for a single track—i.e., a tensor of shape [1, n_steps_per_bar, n_pitches, 1].

The bar generator is just a neural network that uses convolutional transpose layers to expand the time and pitch dimensions of the input vector. We create one bar generator for every track, and weights are not shared between tracks. The Keras code to build a BarGenerator is given in Example 11-7.

Example 11-7. Building the BarGenerator

```python
def BarGenerator():

    input_layer = layers.Input(shape=(Z_DIM * 4,), name='bar_generator_input')  ❶

    x = layers.Dense(1024)(input_layer)  ❷
    x = layers.BatchNormalization(momentum = 0.9)(x)
    x = layers.Activation('relu')(x)
    x = layers.Reshape([2,1,512])(x)

    x = conv_t(x, f=512, k=(2,1), s=(2,1), a= 'relu',  p = 'same', bn = True)  ❸
    x = conv_t(x, f=256, k=(2,1), s=(2,1), a= 'relu', p = 'same', bn = True)
    x = conv_t(x, f=256, k=(2,1), s=(2,1), a= 'relu', p = 'same', bn = True)
    x = conv_t(x, f=256, k=(1,7), s=(1,7), a= 'relu', p = 'same', bn = True)  ❹
    x = conv_t(x, f=1, k=(1,12), s=(1,12), a= 'tanh', p = 'same', bn = False)  ❺

    output_layer = layers.Reshape([1, N_STEPS_PER_BAR , N_PITCHES ,1])(x)  ❻

    return models.Model(input_layer, output_layer)
```

❶ The input to the bar generator is a vector of length 4 * Z_DIM.

❷ After passing it through a Dense layer, we reshape the tensor to prepare it for the convolutional transpose operations.

❸ First we expand the tensor along the timestep axis…

❹ …then along the pitch axis.

❺ The final layer has a tanh activation applied, as we will be using a WGAN-GP (which requires tanh output activation) to train the network.

❻ The tensor is reshaped to add two extra dimensions of size 1, to prepare it for concatenation with other bars and tracks.

Putting it all together

Ultimately, the MuseGAN generator takes the four input noise tensors (chords, style, melody, and groove) and converts them into a multitrack, multibar score. The Keras code to build the MuseGAN generator is provided in Example 11-8.

Example 11-8. Building the MuseGAN generator

```python
def Generator():
    chords_input = layers.Input(shape=(Z_DIM,), name='chords_input')  ❶
    style_input = layers.Input(shape=(Z_DIM,), name='style_input')
    melody_input = layers.Input(shape=(N_TRACKS, Z_DIM), name='melody_input')
    groove_input = layers.Input(shape=(N_TRACKS, Z_DIM), name='groove_input')

    chords_tempNetwork = TemporalNetwork()  ❷
    chords_over_time = chords_tempNetwork(chords_input)

    melody_over_time = [None] * N_TRACKS
    melody_tempNetwork = [None] * N_TRACKS
    for track in range(N_TRACKS):
        melody_tempNetwork[track] = TemporalNetwork()  ❸
        melody_track = layers.Lambda(lambda x, track = track: x[:,track,:])(
            melody_input
        )
        melody_over_time[track] = melody_tempNetwork[track](melody_track)

    barGen = [None] * N_TRACKS
    for track in range(N_TRACKS):
        barGen[track] = BarGenerator()  ❹

    bars_output = [None] * N_BARS
    c = [None] * N_BARS
    for bar in range(N_BARS):  ❺
```

```
        track_output = [None] * N_TRACKS

        c[bar] = layers.Lambda(lambda x, bar = bar: x[:,bar,:])(chords_over_time)
        s = style_input

        for track in range(N_TRACKS):

            m = layers.Lambda(lambda x, bar = bar: x[:,bar,:])(
                melody_over_time[track]
            )
            g = layers.Lambda(lambda x, track = track: x[:,track,:])(
                groove_input
            )

            z_input = layers.Concatenate(
                axis = 1, name = 'total_input_bar_{}_track_{}'.format(bar, track)
            )([c[bar],s,m,g])

            track_output[track] = barGen[track](z_input)

        bars_output[bar] = layers.Concatenate(axis = -1)(track_output)

    generator_output = layers.Concatenate(axis = 1, name = 'concat_bars')(
        bars_output
    ) ❻

    return models.Model(
        [chords_input, style_input, melody_input, groove_input], generator_output
    ) ❼

generator = Generator()
```

❶ Define the inputs to the generator.

❷ Pass the chords input through the temporal network.

❸ Pass the melody input through the temporal network.

❹ Create an independent bar generator network for every track.

❺ Loop over the tracks and bars, creating a generated bar for each combination.

❻ Concatenate everything together to form a single output tensor.

❼ The MuseGAN model takes four distinct noise tensors as input and outputs a generated multitrack, multibar score.

The MuseGAN Critic

In comparison to the generator, the critic architecture is much more straightforward (as is often the case with GANs).

The critic tries to distinguish full multitrack, multibar scores created by the generator from real excerpts from the Bach chorales. It is a convolutional neural network, consisting mostly of Conv3D layers that collapse the score into a single output prediction.

Conv3D Layers

So far in this book, we have only worked with Conv2D layers, applicable to three-dimensional input images (width, height, channels). Here we have to use Conv3D layers, which are analogous to Conv2D layers but accept four-dimensional input tensors (n_bars, n_steps_per_bar, n_pitches, n_tracks).

We do not use batch normalization layers in the critic as we will be using the WGAN-GP framework for training the GAN, which forbids this.

The Keras code to build the critic is given in Example 11-9.

Example 11-9. Building the MuseGAN critic

```
def conv(x, f, k, s, p):
    x = layers.Conv3D(filters = f
                    , kernel_size = k
                    , padding = p
                    , strides = s
                    , kernel_initializer = initializer
                    )(x)
    x = layers.LeakyReLU()(x)
    return x

def Critic():
    critic_input = layers.Input(
        shape=(N_BARS, N_STEPS_PER_BAR, N_PITCHES, N_TRACKS),
        name='critic_input'
    ) ❶

    x = critic_input
    x = conv(x, f=128, k = (2,1,1), s = (1,1,1), p = 'valid') ❷
    x = conv(x, f=128, k = (N_BARS - 1,1,1), s = (1,1,1), p = 'valid')

    x = conv(x, f=128, k = (1,1,12), s = (1,1,12), p = 'same') ❸
    x = conv(x, f=128, k = (1,1,7), s = (1,1,7), p = 'same')

    x = conv(x, f=128, k = (1,2,1), s = (1,2,1), p = 'same') ❹
    x = conv(x, f=128, k = (1,2,1), s = (1,2,1), p = 'same')
```

```
x = conv(x, f=256, k = (1,4,1), s = (1,2,1), p = 'same')
x = conv(x, f=512, k = (1,3,1), s = (1,2,1), p = 'same')

x = layers.Flatten()(x)

x = layers.Dense(1024, kernel_initializer = initializer)(x)
x = layers.LeakyReLU()(x)

critic_output = layers.Dense(
    1, activation=None, kernel_initializer = initializer
)(x) ❺

return models.Model(critic_input, critic_output)

critic = Critic()
```

❶ The input to the critic is an array of multitrack, multibar scores, each of shape `[N_BARS, N_STEPS_PER_BAR, N_PITCHES, N_TRACKS]`.

❷ First, we collapse the tensor along the bar axis. We apply `Conv3D` layers throughout the critic as we are working with 4D tensors.

❸ Next, we collapse the tensor along the pitch axis.

❹ Finally, we collapse the tensor along the timesteps axis.

❺ The output is a `Dense` layer with a single unit and no activation function, as required by the WGAN-GP framework.

Analysis of the MuseGAN

We can perform some experiments with our MuseGAN by generating a score, then tweaking some of the input noise parameters to see the effect on the output.

The output from the generator is an array of values in the range [−1, 1] (due to the tanh activation function of the final layer). To convert this to a single note for each track, we choose the note with the maximum value over all 84 pitches for each timestep. In the original MuseGAN paper the authors use a threshold of 0, as each track can contain multiple notes; however, in this setting we can simply take the maximum to guarantee exactly one note per timestep per track, as is the case for the Bach chorales.

Figure 11-16 shows a score that has been generated by the model from random normally distributed noise vectors (top left). We can find the closest score in the dataset (by Euclidean distance) and check that our generated score isn't a copy of a piece of music that already exists in the dataset—the closest score is shown just below it, and we can see that it does not resemble our generated score.

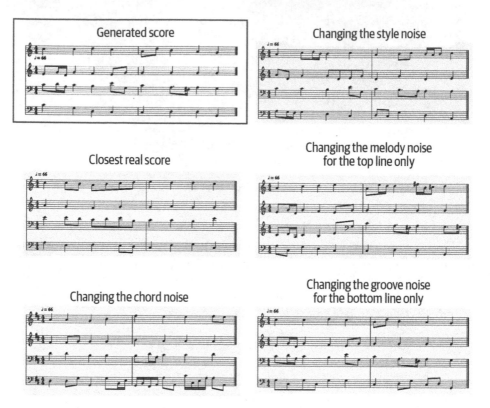

Figure 11-16. Example of a MuseGAN predicted score, showing the closest real score in the training data and how the generated score is affected by changing the input noise

Let's now play around with the input noise to tweak our generated score. First, we can try changing the chord noise vector—the bottom-left score in Figure 11-16 shows the result. We can see that every track has changed, as expected, and also that the two bars exhibit different properties. In the second bar, the baseline is more dynamic and the top line is higher in pitch than in the first bar. This is because the latent vectors that affect the two bars are different, as the input chord vector was passed through a temporal network.

When we change the style vector (top right), both bars change in a similar way. The whole passage has changed style from the original generated score, in a consistent way (i.e., the same latent vector is being used to adjust all tracks and bars).

We can also alter tracks individually, through the melody and groove inputs. In the center-right score in Figure 11-16 we can see the effect of changing just the melody noise input for the top line of music. All other parts remain unaffected, but the top-line notes change significantly. Also, we can see a rhythmic change between the two bars in the top line: the second bar is more dynamic, containing faster notes than the first bar.

Lastly, the bottom-right score in the diagram shows the predicted score when we alter the groove input parameter for only the baseline. Again, all other parts remain unaffected, but the baseline is different. Moreover, the overall pattern of the baseline remains similar between bars, as we would expect.

This shows how each of the input parameters can be used to directly influence high-level features of the generated musical sequence, in much the same way as we were able to adjust the latent vectors of VAEs and GANs in previous chapters to alter the appearance of a generated image. One drawback to the model is that the number of bars to generate must be specified up front. To tackle this, the authors show an extension to the model that allows previous bars to be fed in as input, allowing the model to generate long-form scores by continually feeding the most recent predicted bars back in as additional input.

Summary

In this chapter we have explored two different kinds of models for music generation: a Transformer and a MuseGAN.

The Transformer is similar in design to the networks we saw in Chapter 9 for text generation. Music and text generation share a lot of features in common, and often similar techniques can be used for both. We extended the Transformer architecture by incorporating two input and output streams, for note and duration. We saw how the model was able to learn about concepts such as keys and scales, simply by learning to accurately generate the music of Bach.

We also explored how we can adapt the tokenization process to handle polyphonic (multitrack) music generation. Grid tokenization serializes a piano roll representation of the score, allowing us to train a Transformer on a single stream of tokens that describe which note is present in each voice, at discrete, equally spaced timestep intervals. Event-based tokenization produces a *recipe* that describes how to create the multiple lines of music in a sequential fashion, through a single stream of instructions. Both methods have advantages and disadvantages—the success or failure of a Transformer-based approach to music generation is often heavily dependent on the choice of tokenization method.

We also saw that generating music does not always require a sequential approach—MuseGAN uses convolutions to generate polyphonic musical scores with multiple tracks, by treating the score as an image where the tracks are individual channels of the image. The novelty of MuseGAN lies in the way the four input noise vectors (chords, style, melody, and groove) are organized so that it is possible to maintain full control over high-level features of the music. While the underlying harmonization is still not as perfect or varied as Bach's, it is a good attempt at what is an extremely diffi-cult problem to master and highlights the power of GANs to tackle a wide variety of problems.

References

1. Cheng-Zhi Anna Huang et al., "Music Transformer: Generating Music with Long-Term Structure," September 12, 2018, *https://arxiv.org/abs/1809.04281*.

2. Hao-Wen Dong et al., "MuseGAN: Multi-Track Sequential Generative Adversarial Networks for Symbolic Music Generation and Accompaniment," September 19, 2017, *https://arxiv.org/abs/1709.06298*.

CHAPTER 12

World Models

Chapter Goals

In this chapter you will:

- Walk through the basics of reinforcement learning (RL).

- Understand how generative modeling can be used within a *world model* approach to RL.

- See how to train a variational autoencoder (VAE) to capture environment observations in a low-dimensional latent space.

- Walk through the training process of a mixture density network–recurrent neural network (MDN-RNN) that predicts the latent variable.

- Use the covariance matrix adaptation evolution strategy (CMA-ES) to train a controller that can take intelligent actions in the environment.

- Understand how the trained MDN-RNN can itself be used as an environment, allowing the agent to train the controller within its own hallucinated dreams, rather than the real environment.

This chapter introduces one of the most interesting applications of generative models in recent years, namely their use within so-called world models.

Introduction

In March 2018, David Ha and Jürgen Schmidhuber published their "World Models" paper.[1] The paper showed how it is possible to train a model that can learn how to perform a particular task through experimentation within its own generated dream environment, rather than inside the real environment. It is an excellent example of how generative modeling can be used to solve practical problems, when applied alongside other machine learning techniques such as reinforcement learning.

A key component of the architecture is a generative model that can construct a probability distribution for the next possible state, given the current state and action. Having built up an understanding of the underlying physics of the environment through random movements, the model is then able to train itself from scratch on a new task, entirely within its own internal representation of the environment. This approach led to world-best scores for both of the tasks on which it was tested.

In this chapter we will explore the model from the paper in detail, with particular focus on a task that requires the agent to learn how to drive a car around a virtual racetrack as fast as possible. While we will be using a 2D computer simulation as our environment, the same technique could also be applied to real-world scenarios where testing strategies in the live environment is expensive or infeasible.

In this chapter we will reference the excellent TensorFlow implementation of the "World Models" paper available publicly on GitHub (*https://oreil.ly/_OlJX*), which I encourage you to clone and run yourself!

Before we start exploring the model, we need to take a closer look at the concept of reinforcement learning.

Reinforcement Learning

Reinforcement learning can be defined as follows:

> Reinforcement learning (RL) is a field of machine learning that aims to train an agent to perform optimally within a given environment, with respect to a particular goal.

While both discriminative modeling and generative modeling aim to minimize a loss function over a dataset of observations, reinforcement learning aims to maximize the long-term reward of an agent in a given environment. It is often described as one of the three major branches of machine learning, alongside *supervised learning* (predicting using labeled data) and *unsupervised learning* (learning structure from unlabeled data).

Let's first introduce some key terminology related to reinforcement learning:

Environment
    The world in which the agent operates. It defines the set of rules that govern the game state update process and reward allocation, given the agent's previous action and current game state. For example, if we were teaching a reinforcement learning algorithm to play chess, the environment would consist of the rules that

govern how a given action (e.g., the pawn move e2e4) affects the next game state (the new positions of the pieces on the board) and would also specify how to assess if a given position is checkmate and allocate the winning player a reward of 1 after the winning move.

Agent
: The entity that takes actions in the environment.

Game state
: The data that represents a particular situation that the agent may encounter (also just called a *state*). For example, a particular chessboard configuration with accompanying game information such as which player will make the next move.

Action
: A feasible move that an agent can make.

Reward
: The value given back to the agent by the environment after an action has been taken. The agent aims to maximize the long-term sum of its rewards. For example, in a game of chess, checkmating the opponent's king has a reward of 1 and every other move has a reward of 0. Other games have rewards constantly awarded throughout the episode (e.g., points in a game of *Space Invaders*).

Episode
: One run of an agent in the environment; this is also called a *rollout*.

Timestep
: For a discrete event environment, all states, actions, and rewards are subscripted to show their value at timestep t.

The relationship between these concepts is shown in Figure 12-1.

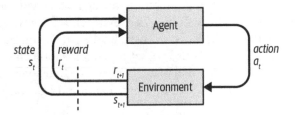

Figure 12-1. Reinforcement learning diagram

The environment is first initialized with a current game state, s_0. At timestep t, the agent receives the current game state s_t and uses this to decide on its next best action a_t, which it then performs. Given this action, the environment then calculates the next state s_{t+1} and reward r_{t+1} and passes these back to the agent, for the cycle to begin again. The cycle continues until the end criterion of the episode is met (e.g., a given number of timesteps elapse or the agent wins/loses).

How can we design an agent to maximize the sum of rewards in a given environment? We could build an agent that contains a set of rules for how to respond to any given game state. However, this quickly becomes infeasible as the environment becomes more complex and doesn't ever allow us to build an agent that has superhuman ability in a particular task, as we are hardcoding the rules. Reinforcement learning involves creating an agent that can learn optimal strategies by itself in complex environments through repeated play.

Let's now take a look at the `CarRacing` environment that simulates a car driving around a track.

The CarRacing Environment

`CarRacing` is an environment that is available through the Gymnasium (*https://gymnasium.farama.org*) package. Gymnasium is a Python library for developing reinforcement learning algorithms that contains several classic reinforcement learning environments, such as `CartPole` and `Pong`, as well as environments that present more complex challenges, such as training an agent to walk on uneven terrain or win an Atari game.

Gymnasium

Gymnasium is a maintained fork of OpenAI's Gym library—since 2021, further development of Gym has shifted to Gymnasium. In this book, we therefore refer to Gymnasium environments as Gym environments.

All of the environments provide a *step* method through which you can submit a given action; the environment will return the next state and the reward. By repeatedly calling the step method with the actions chosen by the agent, you can play out an episode in the environment. There is also a *reset* method for returning the environment to its initial state and a *render* method that allows you to watch your agent perform in a given environment. This is useful for debugging and finding areas where your agent could improve.

Let's see how the game state, action, reward, and episode are defined for the CarRacing environment:

Game state

A 64 × 64–pixel RGB image depicting an overhead view of the track and car.

Action

A set of three values: the steering direction (–1 to 1), acceleration (0 to 1), and braking (0 to 1). The agent must set all three values at each timestep.

Reward

A negative penalty of –0.1 for each timestep taken and a positive reward of 1,000/ N if a new track tile is visited, where N is the total number of tiles that make up the track.

Episode

The episode ends when the car completes the track or drives off the edge of the environment, or when 3,000 timesteps have elapsed.

These concepts are shown on a graphical representation of a game state in Figure 12-2.

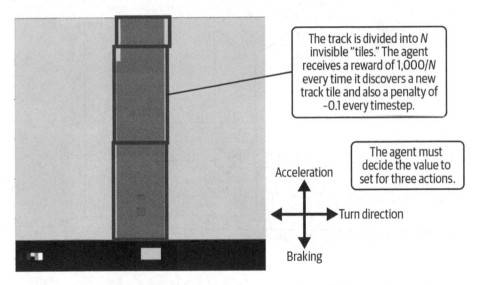

The track is divided into *N* invisible "tiles." The agent receives a reward of 1,000/*N* every time it discovers a new track tile and also a penalty of –0.1 every timestep.

The agent must decide the value to set for three actions.

Acceleration

Turn direction

Braking

Figure 12-2. A graphical representation of one game state in the CarRacing environment

Perspective

We should imagine the agent floating above the track and controlling the car from a bird's-eye view, rather than viewing the track from the driver's perspective.

World Model Overview

We'll now cover a high-level overview of the entire world model architecture and training process, before diving into each component in more detail.

Architecture

The solution consists of three distinct parts, as shown in Figure 12-3, that are trained separately:

V

A variational autoencoder (VAE)

M

A recurrent neural network with a mixture density network (MDN-RNN)

C

A controller

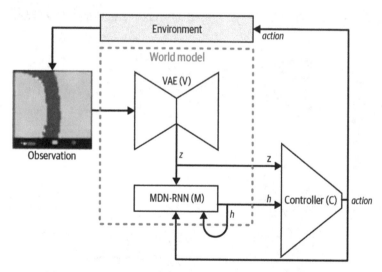

Figure 12-3. World model architecture diagram

The VAE

When you make decisions while driving, you don't actively analyze every single pixel in your view—instead, you condense the visual information into a smaller number of latent entities, such as the straightness of the road, upcoming bends, and your position relative to the road, to inform your next action.

We saw in Chapter 3 how a VAE can take a high-dimensional input image and condense it into a latent random variable that approximately follows a standard Gaussian distribution, through minimization of the reconstruction error and KL divergence. This ensures that the latent space is continuous and that we are able to easily sample from it to generate meaningful new observations.

In the car racing example, the VAE condenses the 64 × 64 × 3 (RGB) input image into a 32-dimensional normally distributed random variable, parameterized by two variables, mu and logvar. Here, logvar is the logarithm of the variance of the distribution. We can sample from this distribution to produce a latent vector z that represents the current state. This is passed on to the next part of the network, the MDN-RNN.

The MDN-RNN

As you drive, each subsequent observation isn't a complete surprise to you. If the current observation suggests a left turn in the road ahead and you turn the wheel to the left, you expect the next observation to show that you are still in line with the road.

If you didn't have this ability, your car would probably snake all over the road as you wouldn't be able to see that a slight deviation from the center is going to be worse in the next timestep unless you do something about it now.

This forward thinking is the job of the MDN-RNN, a network that tries to predict the distribution of the next latent state based on the previous latent state and the previous action.

Specifically, the MDN-RNN is an LSTM layer with 256 hidden units followed by a mixture density network (MDN) output layer that allows for the fact that the next latent state could actually be drawn from any one of several normal distributions.

The same technique was applied by one of the authors of the "World Models" paper, David Ha, to a handwriting generation (*https://oreil.ly/WmPGp*) task, as shown in Figure 12-4, to describe the fact that the next pen point could land in any one of the distinct red areas.

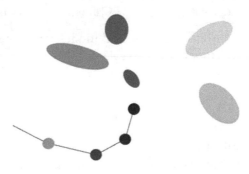

Figure 12-4. MDN for handwriting generation

In the car racing example, we allow for each element of the next observed latent state to be drawn from any one of five normal distributions.

The controller

Until this point, we haven't mentioned anything about choosing an action. That responsibility lies with the controller. The controller is a densely connected neural network, where the input is a concatenation of z (the current latent state sampled from the distribution encoded by the VAE) and the hidden state of the RNN. The three output neurons correspond to the three actions (turn, accelerate, brake) and are scaled to fall in the appropriate ranges.

The controller is trained using reinforcement learning as there is no training dataset that will tell us that a certain action is *good* and another is *bad*. Instead, the agent discovers this for itself through repeated experimentation.

As we shall see later in the chapter, the crux of the "World Models" paper is that it demonstrates how this reinforcement learning can take place within the agent's own generative model of the environment, rather than the Gym environment. In other words, it takes place in the agent's *hallucinated* version of how the environment behaves, rather than the real thing.

To understand the different roles of the three components and how they work together, we can imagine a dialogue between them:

> *VAE* (looking at latest 64 × 64 × 3 observation): This looks like a straight road, with a slight left bend approaching, with the car facing in the direction of the road (z).

> *RNN*: Based on that description (z) and the fact that the controller chose to accelerate hard at the last timestep (action), I will update my hidden state (h) so that the next observation is predicted to still be a straight road, but with slightly more left turn in view.

> *Controller*: Based on the description from the VAE (z) and the current hidden state from the RNN (h), my neural network outputs [0.34, 0.8, 0] as the next action.

The action from the controller is then passed to the environment, which returns an updated observation, and the cycle begins again.

Training

The training process consists of five steps, run in sequence, which are outlined here:

1. Collect random rollout data. Here, the agent does not care about the given task, but instead simply explores the environment using random actions. Multiple episodes are simulated and the observed states, actions, and rewards at each timestep are stored. The idea is to build up a dataset of how the physics of the environment works, which the VAE can then learn from to capture the states

efficiently as latent vectors. The MDN-RNN can then subsequently learn how the latent vectors evolve over time.

2. Train the VAE. Using the randomly collected data, we train a VAE on the observation images.

3. Collect data to train the MDN-RNN. Once we have a trained VAE, we use it to encode each of the collected observations into `mu` and `logvar` vectors, which are saved alongside the current action and reward.

4. Train the MDN-RNN. We take batches of episodes and load the corresponding `mu`, `logvar`, `action`, and `reward` variables at each timestep that were generated in step 3. We then sample a `z` vector from the `mu` and `logvar` vectors. Given the current `z` vector, `action`, and `reward`, the MDN-RNN is then trained to predict the subsequent `z` vector and `reward`.

5. Train the controller. With a trained VAE and RNN, we can now train the controller to output an action given the current `z` and hidden state, `h`, of the RNN. The controller uses an evolutionary algorithm, CMA-ES, as its optimizer. The algorithm rewards matrix weightings that generate actions that lead to overall high scores on the task, so that future generations are also likely to inherit this desired behavior.

Let's now take look at each of these steps in more detail.

Collecting Random Rollout Data

The first step is to collect rollout data from the environment, using an agent taking random actions. This may seem strange, given we ultimately want our agent to learn how to take intelligent actions, but this step will provide the data that the agent will use to learn how the world operates and how its actions (albeit random at first) influence subsequent observations.

We can capture multiple episodes in parallel by spinning up multiple Python processes, each running a separate instance of the environment. Each process will run on a separate core, so if your machine has lots of cores you can collect data much faster than if you only have a few cores.

The hyperparameters used by this step are as follows:

`parallel_processes`
    The number of parallel processes to run (e.g., 8 if your machine has ≥8 cores)

`max_trials`
    How many episodes each process should run in total (e.g., 125, so 8 processes would create 1,000 episodes overall)

`max_frames`
> The maximum number of timesteps per episode (e.g., 300)

Figure 12-5 shows an excerpt from frames 40 to 59 of one episode, as the car approaches a corner, alongside the randomly chosen action and reward. Note how the reward changes to 3.22 as the car rolls over new track tiles but is otherwise –0.1.

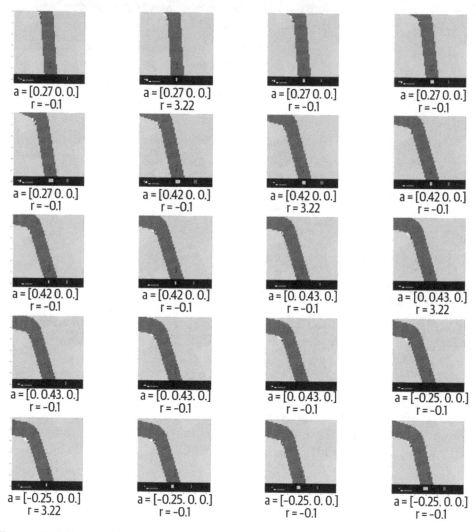

Figure 12-5. Frames 40 to 59 of one episode

Training the VAE

We now build a generative model (a VAE) on this collected data. Remember, the aim of the VAE is to allow us to collapse one $64 \times 64 \times 3$ image into a normally distributed random variable z, whose distribution is parameterized by two vectors, mu and logvar. Each of these vectors is of length 32. The hyperparameters of this step are as follows:

vae_batch_size
: The batch size to use when training the VAE (how many observations per batch) (e.g., 100)

z_size
: The length of latent z vector (and therefore mu and logvar variables) (e.g., 32)

vae_num_epoch
: The number of training epochs (e.g., 10)

The VAE Architecture

As we have seen previously, Keras allows us to not only define the VAE model that will be trained end-to-end, but also additional submodels that define the encoder and decoder of the trained network separately. These will be useful when we want to encode a specific image or decode a given z vector, for example. We'll define the VAE model and three submodels, as follows:

vae
: This is the end-to-end VAE that is trained. It accepts a $64 \times 64 \times 3$ image as input and outputs a reconstructed $64 \times 64 \times 3$ image.

encode_mu_logvar
: This accepts a $64 \times 64 \times 3$ image as input and outputs the mu and logvar vectors corresponding to this input. Running the same input image through this model multiple times will produce the same mu and logvar vectors each time.

encode
: This accepts a $64 \times 64 \times 3$ image as input and outputs a sampled z vector. Running the same input image through this model multiple times will produce a different z vector each time, using the calculated mu and logvar values to define the sampling distribution.

decode
: This accepts a z vector as input and returns the reconstructed $64 \times 64 \times 3$ image.

A diagram of the model and submodels is shown in Figure 12-6.

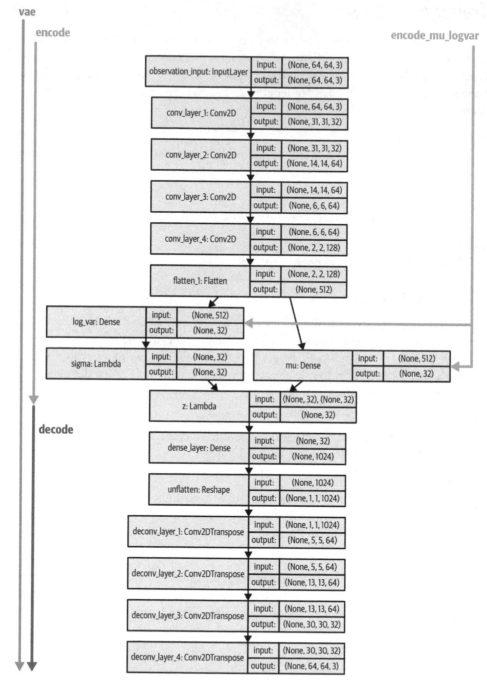

Figure 12-6. The VAE architecture from the "World Models" paper

Exploring the VAE

We'll now take a look at the output from the VAE and each submodel and then see how the VAE can be used to generate completely new track observations.

The VAE model

If we feed the VAE with an observation, it is able to accurately reconstruct the original image, as shown in Figure 12-7. This is useful to visually check that the VAE is working correctly.

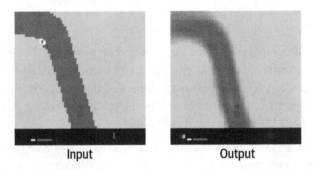

Input   Output

Figure 12-7. The input and output from the VAE model

The encoder models

If we feed the `encode_mu_logvar` model with an observation, the output is the generated `mu` and `logvar` vectors describing a multivariate normal distribution. The `encode` model goes one step further by sampling a particular `z` vector from this distribution. The diagram showing the output from the two encoder models is shown in Figure 12-8.

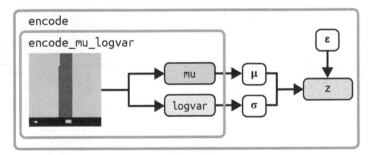

Figure 12-8. The output from the encoder models

The latent variable z is sampled from the Gaussian defined by mu and logvar by sampling from a standard Gaussian and then scaling and shifting the sampled vector (Example 12-1).

Example 12-1. Sampling z from the multivariate normal distribution defined by mu and logvar

```
eps = tf.random_normal(shape=tf.shape(mu))
sigma = tf.exp(logvar * 0.5)
z = mu + eps * sigma
```

The decoder model

The decode model accepts a z vector as input and reconstructs the original image. In Figure 12-9 we linearly interpolate two of the dimensions of z to show how each dimension appears to encode a particular aspect of the track—in this example z[4] controls the immediate left/right direction of the track nearest the car and z[7] controls the sharpness of the approaching left turn.

This shows that the latent space that the VAE has learned is continuous and can be used to generate new track segments that have never before been observed by the agent.

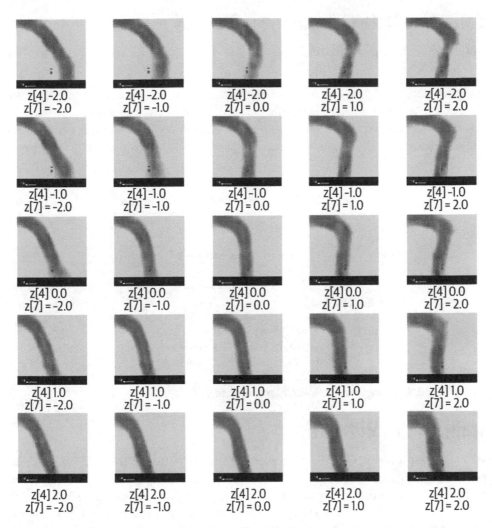

Figure 12-9. A linear interpolation of two dimensions of z

Collecting Data to Train the MDN-RNN

Now that we have a trained VAE, we can use this to generate training data for our MDN-RNN.

In this step, we pass all of the random rollout observations through the encode_mu_logvar model and store the mu and logvar vectors corresponding to each observation. This encoded data, along with the already collected action, reward, and done variables, will be used to train the MDN-RNN. This process is shown in Figure 12-10.

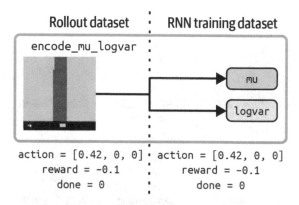

Figure 12-10. Creating the MDN-RNN training dataset

Training the MDN-RNN

We can now train the MDN-RNN to predict the distribution of the next z vector and reward one timestep ahead into the future, given the current z vector, current action, and previous reward. We can then use the internal hidden state of the RNN (which can be thought of as the model's current understanding of the environment dynamics) as part of the input into the controller, which will ultimately decide on the best next action to take.

The hyperparameters of this step of the process are as follows:

rnn_batch_size
> The batch size to use when training the MDN-RNN (how many sequences per batch) (e.g., 100)

rnn_num_steps
> The total number of training iterations (e.g., 4000)

The MDN-RNN Architecture

The architecture of the MDN-RNN is shown in Figure 12-11.

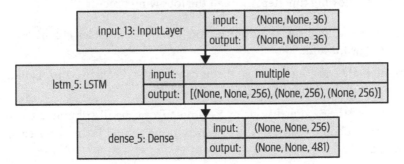

Figure 12-11. The MDN-RNN architecture

The MDN-RNN consists of an LSTM layer (the RNN), followed by a densely connected layer (the MDN) that transforms the hidden state of the LSTM into the parameters of a mixture distribution. Let's walk through the network step by step.

The input to the LSTM layer is a vector of length 36—a concatenation of the encoded z vector (length 32) from the VAE, the current action (length 3), and the previous reward (length 1).

The output from the LSTM layer is a vector of length 256—one value for each LSTM cell in the layer. This is passed to the MDN, which is just a densely connected layer that transforms the vector of length 256 into a vector of length 481.

Why 481? Figure 12-12 explains the composition of the output from the MDN-RNN. The aim of a mixture density network is to model the fact that our next z could be drawn from one of several possible distributions with a certain probability. In the car racing example, we choose five normal distributions. How many parameters do we need to define these distributions? For each of the 5 mixtures, we need a mu and a logvar (to define the distribution) and a log-probability of this mixture being chosen (logpi), for each of the 32 dimensions of z. This makes $5 \times 3 \times 32 = 480$ parameters. The one extra parameter is for the reward prediction.

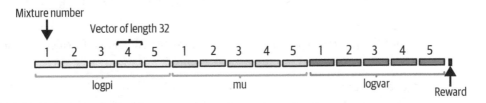

Figure 12-12. The output from the mixture density network

Sampling from the MDN-RNN

We can sample from the MDN output to generate a prediction for the next z and reward at the following timestep, through the following process:

1. Split the 481-dimensional output vector into the 3 variables (logpi, mu, logvar) and the reward value.

2. Exponentiate and scale logpi so that it can be interpreted as 32 probability distributions over the 5 mixture indices.

3. For each of the 32 dimensions of z, sample from the distributions created from logpi (i.e., choose which of the 5 distributions should be used for each dimension of z).

4. Fetch the corresponding values of mu and logvar for this distribution.

5. Sample a value for each dimension of z from the normal distribution parameterized by the chosen parameters of mu and logvar for this dimension.

The loss function for the MDN-RNN is the sum of the z vector reconstruction loss and the reward loss. The z vector reconstruction loss is the negative log-likelihood of the distribution predicted by the MDN-RNN, given the true value of z, and the reward loss is the mean squared error between the predicted reward and the true reward.

Training the Controller

The final step is to train the controller (the network that outputs the chosen action) using an evolutionary algorithm called the covariance matrix adaptation evolution strategy (CMA-ES).

The hyperparameters of this step of the process are as follows:

controller_num_worker
> The number of workers that will test solutions in parallel

controller_num_worker_trial
> The number of solutions that each worker will be given to test at each generation

controller_num_episode
> The number of episodes that each solution will be tested against to calculate the average reward

controller_eval_steps
> The number of generations between evaluations of the current best parameter set

The Controller Architecture

The architecture of the controller is very simple. It is a densely connected neural network with no hidden layers. It connects the input vector directly to the action vector.

The input vector is a concatenation of the current z vector (length 32) and the current hidden state of the LSTM (length 256), giving a vector of length 288. Since we are connecting each input unit directly to the 3 output action units, the total number of weights to tune is $288 \times 3 = 864$, plus 3 bias weights, giving 867 in total.

How should we train this network? Notice that this is not a supervised learning problem—we are not trying to *predict* the correct action. There is no training set of correct actions, as we do not know what the optimal action is for a given state of the environment. This is what distinguishes this as a reinforcement learning problem. We need the agent to discover the optimal values for the weights itself by experimenting within the environment and updating its weights based on received feedback.

Evolutionary strategies are a popular choice for solving reinforcement learning problems, due to their simplicity, efficiency, and scalability. We shall use one particular strategy, known as CMA-ES.

CMA-ES

Evolutionary strategies generally adhere to the following process:

1. Create a *population* of agents and randomly initialize the parameters to be optimized for each agent.
2. Loop over the following:
   a. Evaluate each agent in the environment, returning the average reward over multiple episodes.
   b. Breed the agents with the best scores to create new members of the population.
   c. Add randomness to the parameters of the new members.
   d. Update the population pool by adding the newly created agents and removing poorly performing agents.

This is similar to the process through which animals evolve in nature—hence the name *evolutionary* strategies. "Breeding" in this context simply means combining the existing best-scoring agents such that the next generation are more likely to produce high-quality results, similar to their parents. As with all reinforcement learning solutions, there is a balance to be found between greedily searching for locally optimal solutions and exploring unknown areas of the parameter space for potentially better solutions. This is why it is important to add randomness to the population, to ensure we are not too narrow in our search field.

CMA-ES is just one form of evolutionary strategy. In short, it works by maintaining a normal distribution from which it can sample the parameters of new agents. At each generation, it updates the mean of the distribution to maximize the likelihood of sampling the high-scoring agents from the previous timestep. At the same time, it updates the covariance matrix of the distribution to maximize the likelihood of sampling the high-scoring agents, given the previous mean. It can be thought of as a form of naturally arising gradient descent, but with the added benefit that it is derivative-free, meaning that we do not need to calculate or estimate costly gradients.

One generation of the algorithm demonstrated on a toy example is shown in Figure 12-13. Here we are trying to find the minimum point of a highly nonlinear function in two dimensions—the value of the function in the red/black areas of the image is greater than the value of the function in the white/yellow parts of the image.

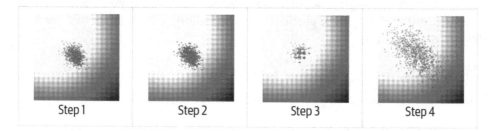

Figure 12-13. One update step from the CMA-ES algorithm (source: Ha, 2017)[2]

The steps are as follows:

1. We start with a randomly generated 2D normal distribution and sample a population of candidates, shown in blue in Figure 12-13.

2. We then calculate the value of the function for each candidate and isolate the best 25%, shown in purple in Figure 12-13—we'll call this set of points P.

3. We set the mean of the new normal distribution to be the mean of the points in P. This can be thought of as the breeding stage, wherein we only use the best candidates to generate a new mean for the distribution. We also set the covariance matrix of the new normal distribution to be the covariance matrix of the points in P, but use the existing mean in the covariance calculation rather than the current mean of the points in P. The larger the difference between the existing mean and the mean of the points in P, the wider the variance of the next normal distribution. This has the effect of naturally creating *momentum* in the search for the optimal parameters.

4. We can then sample a new population of candidates from our new normal distribution with an updated mean and covariance matrix.

Figure 12-14 shows several generations of the process. See how the covariance widens as the mean moves in large steps toward the minimum, but narrows as the mean settles into the true minimum.

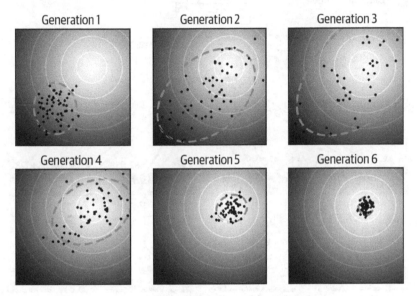

Figure 12-14. CMA-ES (source: Wikipedia (https://oreil.ly/FObGZ))

For the car racing task, we do not have a well-defined function to maximize, but instead an environment where the 867 parameters to be optimized determine how well the agent scores. Initially, some sets of parameters will, by random chance, generate scores that are higher than others and the algorithm will gradually move the normal distribution in the direction of those parameters that score highest in the environment.

Parallelizing CMA-ES

One of the great benefits of CMA-ES is that it can be easily parallelized. The most time-consuming part of the algorithm is calculating the score for a given set of parameters, since it needs to simulate an agent with these parameters in the environment. However, this process can be parallelized, since there are no dependencies between individual simulations. There is a orchestrator process that sends out parameter sets to be tested to many node processes in parallel. The nodes return the results to the orchestrator, which accumulates the results and then passes the overall result of the generation to the CMA-ES object. This object updates the mean and covariance matrix of the normal distribution as per Figure 12-13 and provides the orchestrator with a new population to test. The loop then starts again. Figure 12-15 explains this in a diagram.

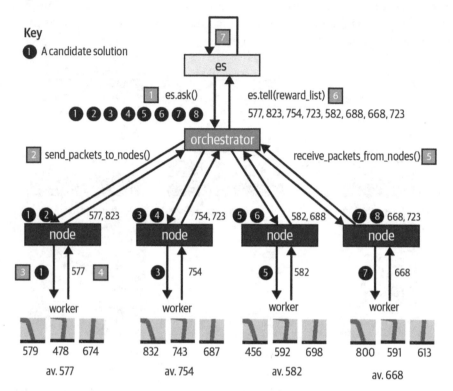

Figure 12-15. Parallelizing CMA-ES—here there is a population size of eight and four nodes (so t = 2, the number of trials that each node is responsible for)

❶ The orchestrator asks the CMA-ES object (**es**) for a set of parameters to trial.

❷ The orchestrator divides the parameters into the number of nodes available. Here, each of the four node processes gets two parameter sets to trial.

❸ The nodes run a worker process that loops over each set of parameters and runs several episodes for each. Here we run three episodes for each set of parameters.

❹ The rewards from each episode are averaged to give a single score for each set of parameters.

❺ Each node returns its list of scores to the orchestrator.

❻ The orchestrator groups all the scores together and sends this list to the es object.

❼ The es object uses this list of rewards to calculate the new normal distribution as per Figure 12-13.

After around 200 generations, the training process achieves an average reward score of around 840 for the car racing task, as shown in Figure 12-16.

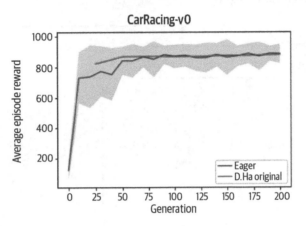

Figure 12-16. Average episode reward of the controller training process, by generation (source: Zac Wellmer, "World Models")

In-Dream Training

So far, the controller training has been conducted using the Gym CarRacing environment to implement the step method that moves the simulation from one state to the next. This function calculates the next state and reward, given the current state of the environment and chosen action.

Notice how the step method performs a very similar function to the MDN-RNN in our model. Sampling from the MDN-RNN outputs a prediction for the next z and reward, given the current z and chosen action.

In fact, the MDN-RNN can be thought of as an environment in its own right, but operating in z-space rather than in the original image space. Incredibly, this means that we can actually substitute the real environment with a copy of the MDN-RNN and train the controller entirely within an MDN-RNN-inspired *dream* of how the environment should behave.

In other words, the MDN-RNN has learned enough about the general physics of the real environment from the original random movement dataset that it can be used as a proxy for the real environment when training the controller. This is quite remarkable—it means that the agent can train itself to learn a new task by *thinking* about how it can maximize reward in its dream environment, without ever having to test out strategies in the real world. It can then perform well at the task the first time, having never attempted the task in reality.

A comparison of the architectures for training in the real environment and the dream environment follows: the real-world architecture is shown in Figure 12-17 and the in-dream training setup is illustrated in Figure 12-18.

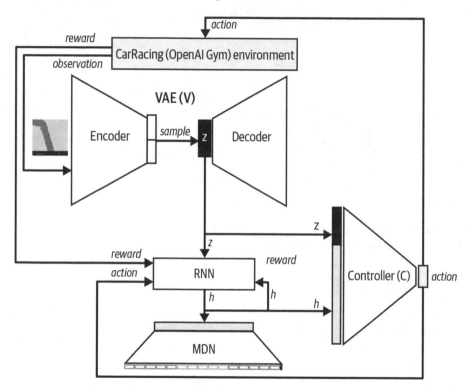

Figure 12-17. Training the controller in the Gym environment

Notice how in the dream architecture, the training of the controller is performed entirely in z-space without the need to ever decode the z vectors back into recognizable track images. We can of course do so, in order to visually inspect the performance of the agent, but it is not required for training.

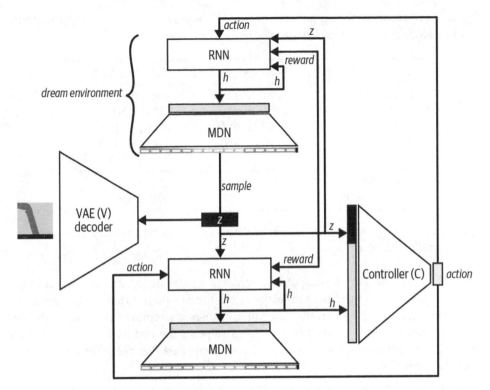

Figure 12-18. Training the controller in the MDN-RNN dream environment

One of the challenges of training agents entirely within the MDN-RNN dream environment is overfitting. This occurs when the agent finds a strategy that is rewarding in the dream environment but does not generalize well to the real environment, due to the MDN-RNN not fully capturing how the true environment behaves under certain conditions.

The authors of the original paper highlight this challenge and show how including a `temperature` parameter to control model uncertainty can help alleviate the problem. Increasing this parameter magnifies the variance when sampling z through the MDN-RNN, leading to more volatile rollouts when training in the dream environment. The controller receives higher rewards for safer strategies that encounter well-understood states and therefore tend to generalize better to the real environment. Increased temperature, however, needs to be balanced against not making the environment so volatile that the controller cannot learn any strategy, as there is not enough consistency in how the dream environment evolves over time.

In the original paper, the authors show this technique successfully applied to a different environment: `DoomTakeCover`, based around the computer game *Doom*.

Figure 12-19 shows how changing the `temperature` parameter affects both the virtual (dream) score and the actual score in the real environment.

TEMPERATURE τ	VIRTUAL SCORE	ACTUAL SCORE
0.10	2086 ± 140	193 ± 58
0.50	2060 ± 277	196 ± 50
1.00	1145 ± 690	868 ± 511
1.15	918 ± 546	1092 ± 556
1.30	732 ± 269	753 ± 139
RANDOM POLICY	N/A	210 ± 108
GYM LEADER	N/A	820 ± 58

Figure 12-19. Using temperature to control dream environment volatility (source: Ha and Schmidhuber, 2018)

The optimal temperature setting of 1.15 achieves a score of 1,092 in the real environment, surpassing the current Gym leader at the time of publication. This is an amazing achievement—remember, the controller has *never* attempted the task in the real environment. It has only ever taken random steps in the real environment (to train the VAE and MDN-RNN *dream* model) and then used the dream environment to train the controller.

A key benefit of using generative world models as an approach to reinforcement learning is that each generation of training in the dream environment is much faster than training in the real environment. This is because the z and reward prediction by the MDN-RNN is faster than the z and reward calculation by the Gym environment.

Summary

In this chapter we have seen how a generative model (a VAE) can be utilized within a reinforcement learning setting to enable an agent to learn an effective strategy by testing policies within its own generated dreams, rather than within the real environment.

The VAE is trained to learn a latent representation of the environment, which is then used as input to a recurrent neural network that forecasts future trajectories within the latent space. Amazingly, the agent can then use this generative model as a pseudo-environment to iteratively test policies, using an evolutionary methodology, that generalize well to the real environment.

For further information on the model, there is an excellent interactive explanation available online (*https://worldmodels.github.io*), written by the authors of the original paper.

References

1. David Ha and Jürgen Schmidhuber, "World Models," March 27, 2018, *https://arxiv.org/abs/1803.10122.*

2. David Ha, "A Visual Guide to Evolution Strategies," October 29, 2017, *https://blog.otoro.net/2017/10/29/visual-evolution-strategies.*

CHAPTER 13

Multimodal Models

Chapter Goals

In this chapter you will:

- Learn what is meant by a multimodal model.

- Explore the inner workings of DALL.E 2, a large-scale text-to-image model from OpenAI.

- Understand how CLIP and diffusion models such as GLIDE play an integral role in the overall DALL.E 2 architecture.

- Analyze the limitations of DALL.E 2, as highlighted by the authors of the paper.

- Explore the architecture of Imagen, a large-scale text-to-image model from Google Brain.

- Learn about the latent diffusion process used by Stable Diffusion, an open source text-to-image model.

- Understand the similarities and differences between DALL.E 2, Imagen, and Stable Diffusion.

- Investigate DrawBench, a benchmarking suite for evaluating text-to-image models.

- Learn the architectural design of Flamingo, a novel visual language model from DeepMind.

- Unpick the different components of Flamingo and learn how they each contribute to the model as a whole.

- Explore some of the capabilities of Flamingo, including conversational prompting.

So far, we have analyzed generative learning problems that focus solely on one modality of data: either text, images, or music. We have seen how GANs and diffusion models can generate state-of-the-art images and how Transformers are pioneering the way for both text and image generation. However, as humans, we have no difficulties crossing modalities—for example, writing a description of what is happening in a given photograph, creating digital art to depict a fictional fantasy world in a book, or matching a film score to the emotions of a given scene. Can we train machines to do the same?

Introduction

Multimodal learning involves training generative models to convert between two or more different kinds of data. Some of the most impressive generative models introduced in the last two years have been multimodal in nature. In this chapter we will explore how they work in detail and consider how the future of generative modeling will be shaped by large multimodal models.

We'll explore four different vision-language models: DALL.E 2 from OpenAI; Imagen from Google Brain; Stable Diffusion from Stability AI, CompVis, and Runway; and Flamingo from DeepMind.

The aim of this chapter is to concisely explain how each model works, without going into the fine detail of every design decision. For more information, refer to the individual papers for each model, which explain all of the design choices and architecture decisions in detail.

Text-to-image generation focuses on producing state-of-the-art images from a given text prompt. For example, given the input "A head of broccoli made out of modeling clay, smiling in the sun," we would like the model to be able to output a image that accurately matches the text prompt, as shown in Figure 13-1.

This is clearly a highly challenging problem. Text understanding and image generation are difficult to solve in their own right, as we have seen in previous chapters of this book. Multimodal modeling such as this presents an additional challenge, because the model must also learn how to cross the bridge between the two domains and learn a shared representation that allows it to accurately convert from a block of text to a high-fidelity image without loss of information.

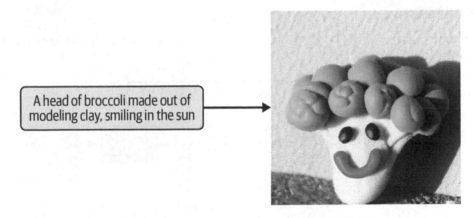

Figure 13-1. An example of text-to-image generation by DALL.E 2

Moreover, in order to be successful the model must be able to combine concepts and styles that it may never have seen before. For example, there are no Michelangelo frescos containing people wearing virtual reality headsets, but we would like our model to be able to create such an image if we ask it to. Equally, it would be desirable for the model to accurately infer how objects in the generated image relate to each other, based on the text prompt. For example, a picture of "an astronaut riding a doughnut through space" should look very different from one of "an astronaut eating a doughnut in a crowded space." The model must learn how words are given meaning through context and how to convert explicit textual relationships between entities to images that imply the same meaning.

DALL.E 2

The first model we shall explore is *DALL.E 2*, a model designed by OpenAI for text-to-image generation. The first version of this model, DALL.E,[1] was released in February 2021 and sparked a new wave of interest in generative multimodal models. In this section, we shall investigate the workings of the second iteration of the model, DALL.E 2,[2] released just over a year later in April 2022.

DALL.E 2 is an extremely impressive model that has furthered our understanding of AI's ability to solve these types of multimodal problems. It not only has ramifications academically, but also forces us to ask big questions relating to the role of AI in creative processes that previously were thought to be unique to humans. We will start by exploring how DALL.E 2 works, building on key foundational ideas that we have already explored earlier in this book.

Architecture

To understand how DALL.E 2 works, we must first survey its overall architecture, as shown in Figure 13-2.

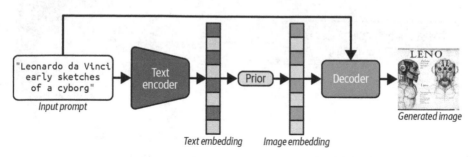

Figure 13-2. The DALL.E 2 architecture

There are three distinct parts to consider: the *text encoder*, the *prior*, and the *decoder*. Text is first passed through the text encoder to produce a text embedding vector. This vector is then transformed by the prior to produce an image embedding vector. Finally, this is passed through the decoder, along with the original text, to produce the generated image. We will step through each component in turn, to get a complete picture of how DALL.E 2 works in practice.

The Text Encoder

The aim of the text encoder is to convert the text prompt into an embedding vector that represents the conceptual meaning of the text prompt within a latent space. As we have seen in previous chapters, converting discrete text to a continuous latent space vector is essential for all downstream tasks, because we can continue to manipulate the vector further depending on our particular goal.

In DALL.E 2, the authors do not train the text encoder from scratch, but instead make use of an existing model called *Contrastive Language–Image Pre-training* (CLIP), also produced by OpenAI. Therefore, to understand the text encoder, we must first understand how CLIP works.

CLIP

CLIP (*https://openai.com/blog/clip*)[3] was unveiled in a paper published by OpenAI in February 2021 (just a few days after the first DALL.E paper) that described it as "a neural network that efficiently learns visual concepts from natural language supervision."

It uses a technique called *contrastive learning* to match images with text descriptions. The model is trained on a dataset of 400 million text–image pairs scraped from the internet—some example pairs are shown in Figure 13-3. For comparison, there are 14 million hand-annotated images in ImageNet. Given an image and a list of possible text descriptions, its task is to find the one that actually matches the image.

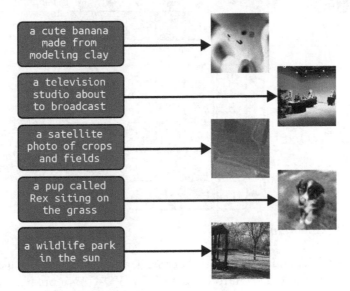

Figure 13-3. Examples of text–image pairs

The key idea behind contrastive learning is simple. We train two neural networks: a *text encoder* that converts text to a text embedding and an *image encoder* that converts an image to an image embedding. Then, given a batch of text–image pairs, we compare all text and image embedding combinations using *cosine similarity* and train the networks to maximize the score between matching text–image pairs and minimize the score between incorrect text–image pairs. This process is shown in Figure 13-4.

CLIP Is Not Generative

Note that CLIP is not itself a generative model—it cannot produce images or text. Is it closer to a discriminative model, because the final output is a prediction about which text description from a given set most closely matches a given image (or the other way around, which image most closely matches a given text description).

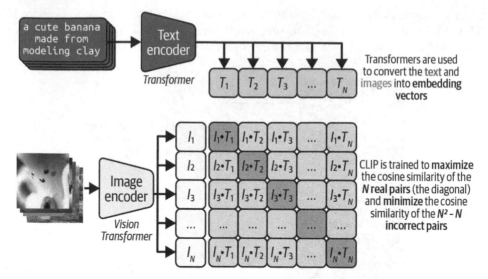

Figure 13-4. The CLIP training process

Both the text encoder and the image encoder are Transformers—the image encoder is a Vision Transformer (ViT), introduced in "ViT VQ-GAN" on page 292, which applies the same concept of attention to images. The authors tested other model architectures, but found this combination to produce the best results.

What makes CLIP especially interesting is the way it can be used for *zero-shot prediction* on tasks that it has never been exposed to. For example, suppose we want to use CLIP to predict the label of a given image in the ImageNet dataset. We can first convert the ImageNet labels into sentences by using a template (e.g., "a photo of a <label>"), as shown in Figure 13-5.

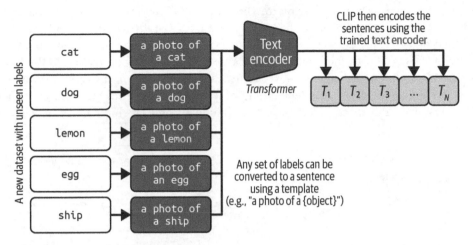

Figure 13-5. Converting labels in a new dataset to captions, in order to produce CLIP text embeddings

To predict the label of a given image, we can pass it through the CLIP image encoder and calculate the cosine similarity between the image embedding and all possible text embeddings in order to find the label with the maximum score, as shown in Figure 13-6.

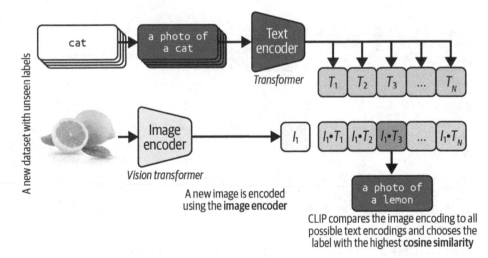

Figure 13-6. Using CLIP to predict the content of an image

Notice that we do not need to retrain either of the CLIP neural networks for it to be readily applicable to new tasks. It uses language as the common domain through which any set of labels can be expressed.

Using this approach, it is possible to show that CLIP performs well across a wide range of image dataset labeling challenges (Figure 13-7). Other models that have been trained on a specific dataset to predict a given set of labels often fail when applied to different datasets with the same labels because they are highly optimized to the individual datasets on which they were trained. CLIP is much more robust, as it has learned a deep conceptual understanding of full text descriptions and images, rather than just excelling at the narrow task of assigning a single label to a given image in a dataset.

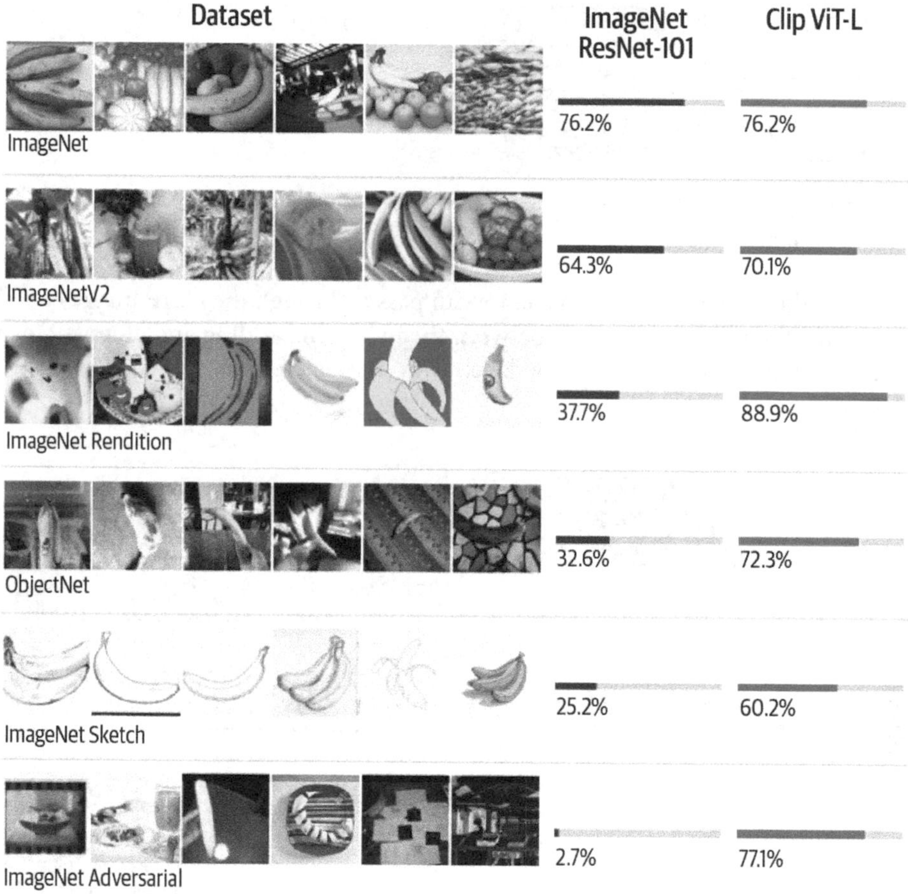

Dataset	ImageNet ResNet-101	Clip ViT-L
ImageNet	76.2%	76.2%
ImageNetV2	64.3%	70.1%
ImageNet Rendition	37.7%	88.9%
ObjectNet	32.6%	72.3%
ImageNet Sketch	25.2%	60.2%
ImageNet Adversarial	2.7%	77.1%

Figure 13-7. CLIP performs well on a wide range of image labeling datasets (source: Radford et al., 2021)

As mentioned, CLIP is measured on its discriminative ability, so how does it help us to build generative models such as DALL.E 2?

The answer is that we can take the trained text encoder and use it as one part of a larger model such as DALL.E 2, with frozen weights. The trained encoder is simply a generalized model for converting text to a text embedding, which should be useful for downstream tasks such as generating images. The text encoder is able to capture a rich conceptual understanding of the text, as it has been trained to be as similar as possible to its matching image embedding counterpart, which is produced only from the paired image. It is therefore the first part of the bridge that we need to be able to cross over from the text domain to the image domain.

The Prior

The next stage of the process involves converting the text embedding into a CLIP image embedding. The DALL.E 2 authors tried two different methods for training the prior model:

- An autoregressive model
- A diffusion model

They found that the diffusion approach outperformed the autoregressive model and was more computationally efficient. In this section, we'll look at both and see how they differ.

Autoregressive prior

An autoregressive model generates output sequentially, by placing an ordering on the output tokens (e.g., words, pixels) and conditioning the next token on previous tokens. We have seen in previous chapters how this is used in recurrent neural networks (e.g., LSTMs), Transformers, and PixelCNN.

The autoregressive prior of DALL.E 2 is an encoder-decoder Transformer. It is trained to reproduce the CLIP image embedding given a CLIP text embedding, as shown in Figure 13-8. Note that there are some additional components to the autoregressive model mentioned in the original paper that we omit here for conciseness.

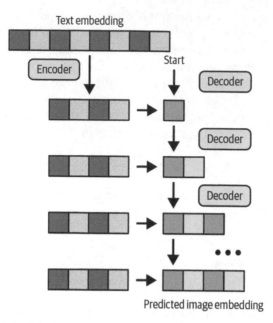

Figure 13-8. A simplified diagram of the autoregressive prior of DALL.E 2

The model is trained on the CLIP text–image pair dataset. You can think of it as the second part of the bridge that we need in order to jump from the text domain to the image domain: we are converting a vector from the text embedding latent space to the image embedding latent space.

The input text embedding is processed by the encoder of the Transformer to produce another representation that is fed to the decoder, alongside the current generated output image embedding. The output is generated one element at a time, using teacher forcing to compare the predicted next element to the actual CLIP image embedding.

The sequential nature of the generation means that the autoregressive model is less computationally efficient than the other method tried by the authors, which we'll look at next.

Diffusion prior

As we saw in Chapter 8, diffusion models are fast becoming the go-to choice for generative modeling practitioners, alongside Transformers. In DALL.E 2 a decoder-only Transformer is used as the prior, trained using a diffusion process.

The training and generation process is shown in Figure 13-9. Again, this is a simplified version; the original paper contains full details of how the diffusion model is structured.

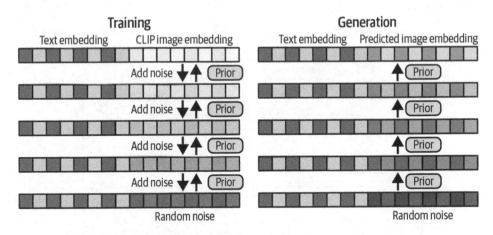

Figure 13-9. A simplified diagram of the diffusion prior training and generation process of DALL.E 2

During training, each CLIP text and image embedding pair are first concatenated into a single vector. Then, the image embedding is noised over 1,000 timesteps until it is indistinguishable from random noise. The diffusion prior is then trained to predict the denoised image embedding at the previous timestep. The prior has access to the text embedding throughout, so it is able to condition its predictions on this information, gradually transforming the random noise into a predicted CLIP image embedding. The loss function is the average mean-squared error across denoising steps.

To generate new image embeddings, we sample a random vector, prepend the relevant text embedding, and pass it through the trained diffusion prior multiple times.

The Decoder

The final part of DALL.E 2 is the decoder. This is the part of the model that generates the final image conditioned on the text prompt and the predicted image embedding output by the prior.

The architecture and training process of the decoder borrows from an earlier OpenAI paper, published in December 2021, which presented a generative model called Guided Language to Image Diffusion for Generation and Editing (GLIDE).[4]

GLIDE is able to generate realistic images from text prompts, in much the same way that DALL.E 2 can. The difference is that GLIDE does not make use of CLIP embeddings, but instead works directly with the raw text prompt, training the entire model from scratch, as shown in Figure 13-10.

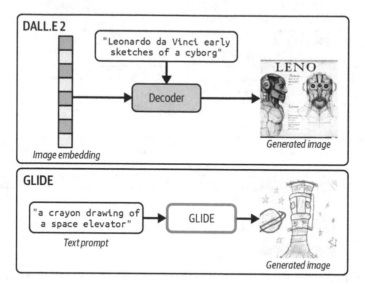

Figure 13-10. A comparison between DALL.E 2 and GLIDE—GLIDE trains the entire generative model from scratch, whereas DALL.E 2 makes use of CLIP embeddings to carry information forward from the initial text prompt

Let's see how GLIDE works first.

GLIDE

GLIDE is trained as a diffusion model, with U-Net architecture for the denoiser and Transformer architecture for the text encoder. It learns to undo the noise added to an image, guided by the text prompt. Finally, an *Upsampler* is trained to scale the generated image to 1,024 × 1,024 pixels.

GLIDE trains the 3.5 billion (B) parameter model from scratch—2.3B parameters for the visual part of the model (U-Net and Upsampler) and 1.2B for the Transformer. It is trained on 250 million text–image pairs.

The diffusion process is shown in Figure 13-11. A Transformer is used to create an embedding of the input text prompt, which is then used to guide the U-Net throughout the denoising process. We explored the U-Net architecture in Chapter 8; it's a perfect model choice when the overall size of the image should stay the same (e.g., for style transfer, denoising, etc.).

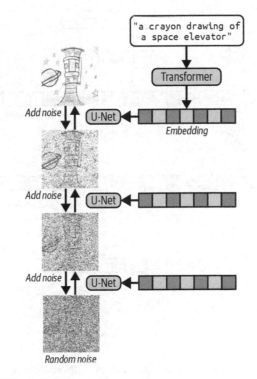

Figure 13-11. The GLIDE diffusion process

The DALL.E 2 decoder still uses the U-Net denoiser and Transformer text encoder architectures, but additionally has the predicted CLIP image embeddings to condition on. This is the key difference between GLIDE and DALL.E 2, as shown in Figure 13-12.

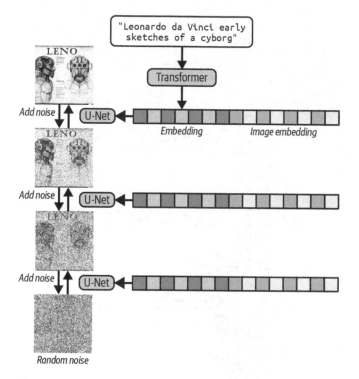

Figure 13-12. The DALL.E 2 decoder additionally conditions on the image embedding produced by the prior

As with all diffusion models, to generate a new image, we simply sample some random noise and run this through the U-Net denoiser multiple times, conditioned on the Transformer text encoding and image embedding. The output is a 64 × 64–pixel image.

Upsampler

The final part of the decoder is the Upsampler (two separate diffusion models). The first diffusion model transforms the image from 64 × 64 to 256 × 256 pixels. The second transforms it again, from 256 × 256 to 1,024 × 1,024 pixels, as shown in Figure 13-13.

Upsampling is useful because it means we do not have to build large upstream models to handle high-dimensional images. We can work with small images until the final stages of the process, when we apply the Upsamplers. This saves on model parameters and ensures a more efficient upstream training process.

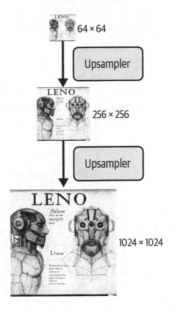

Figure 13-13. The first Upsampler diffusion model converts the image from 64 × 64 pixels to 256 × 256 pixels while the second converts from 256 × 256 pixels to 1,024 × 1,024 pixels

This concludes the DALL.E 2 model explanation! In summary, DALL.E 2 makes use of the pre-trained CLIP model to immediately produce a text embedding of the input prompt. Then it converts this into an image embedding using a diffusion model called the prior. Lastly, it implements a GLIDE-style diffusion model to generate the output image, conditioned on the predicted image embedding and Transformer-encoded input prompt.

Examples from DALL.E 2

Examples of more images generated by DALL.E 2 can be found on the official website (*https://openai.com/dall-e-2*). The way that the model is able to combine complex, disparate concepts in a realistic, believable way is astonishing and represents a significant leap forward for AI and generative modeling.

In the paper, the authors show how the model can be used for additional purposes other than text-to-image generation. One of these applications is creating variations of a given image, which we explore in the following section.

Image variations

As discussed previously, to generate images using the DALL.E 2 decoder we sample an image consisting of pure random noise and then gradually reduce the amount of noise using the denoising diffusion model, conditioned on the provided image embedding. Selecting different initial random noise samples will result in different images.

In order to generate variations of a given image, we therefore just need to establish its image embedding to feed to the decoder. We can obtain this using the original CLIP image encoder, which is explicitly designed to convert an image into its CLIP image embedding. This process is shown in Figure 13-14.

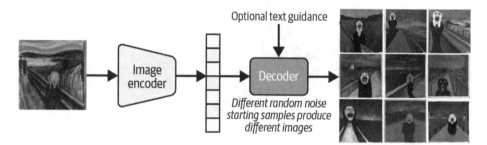

Figure 13-14. DALL.E 2 can be used for generating variations of a given image

Importance of the prior

Another avenue explored by the authors is establishing the importance of the prior. The purpose of the prior is to provide the decoder with a useful representation of the image to be generated, making use of the pre-trained CLIP model. However, it is feasible that this step isn't necessary—perhaps we could just pass the text embedding directly to the decoder instead of the image embedding, or ignore the CLIP embeddings completely and condition only on the text prompt. Would this impact the quality of the generations?

To test this, the authors tried three different approaches:

1. Feed the decoder only with the text prompt (and a zero vector for the image embedding).

2. Feed the decoder with the text prompt and the text embedding (as if it were an image embedding).

3. Feed the decoder with the text prompt and the image embedding (i.e., the full model).

Example results are shown in Figure 13-15. We can see that when the decoder is starved of image embedding information, it can only produce a rough approximation of the text prompt, missing key information such as the calculator. Using the text embedding as if it were an image embedding performs slightly better, though it is not able to capture the relationship between the hedgehog and the calculator. Only the full model with the prior produces an image that accurately reflects all of the information contained within the prompt.

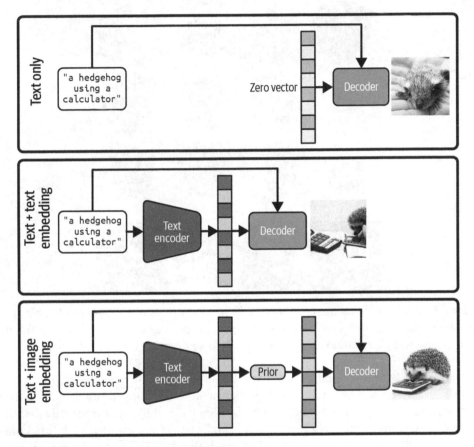

Figure 13-15. The prior provides the model with additional context and helps the decoder to produce more accurate generations (source: Ramesh et al., 2022)

Limitations

In the DALL.E 2 paper, the authors also highlight several known limitations of the model. Two of these (attribute binding and text generation) are shown in Figure 13-16.

Figure 13-16. Two limitations of DALL.E 2 lie in its ability to bind attributes to objects and reproduce textual information—top prompt: "A red cube on top of a blue cube"; bottom prompt: "A sign that says deep learning" (source: Ramesh et al., 2022)

Attribute binding is the ability of a model to understand the relationship between words in a given text prompt, and in particular how attributes relate to objects. For example, the prompt "A red cube on top of a blue cube" must appear visually distinct from "A blue cube on top of a red cube." DALL.E struggles somewhat with this, compared to earlier models such as GLIDE, though the overall quality of generations is better and more diverse.

Also, DALL.E 2 is not able to accurately reproduce text—this is probably due to the fact that the CLIP embeddings do not capture spellings, but instead only contain a higher-level representation of the text. These representations can be decoded into text with partial success (e.g., individual letters are mostly correct), but not with enough compositional understanding to form full words.

Imagen

Just over a month after OpenAI released DALL.E 2, the Google Brain team released their own text-to-image model called Imagen.[5] Many of the core themes that we have already explored in this chapter are also relevant to Imagen: for example, it uses a text encoder and a diffusion model decoder.

In the next section, we'll explore the overall architecture of Imagen and compare it with DALL.E 2.

Architecture

An overview of the Imagen architecture is shown in Figure 13-17.

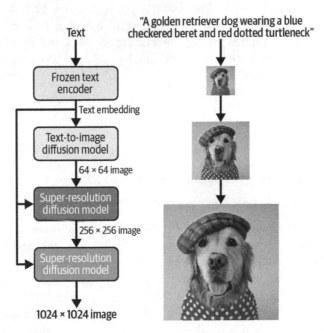

Figure 13-17. The Imagen architecture (source: Saharia et al., 2022)

The frozen text encoder is the pre-trained T5-XXL model, a large encoder-decoder Transformer. Unlike CLIP, this was trained only on text and not images, so it is not a multimodal model. However, the authors found that it still functions extremely well as a text encoder for Imagen and that scaling this model has more impact on overall performance than scaling the diffusion model decoder.

Like DALL.E 2's, Imagen's the decoding diffusion model is based on a U-Net architecture, conditioned on text embeddings. There are several architectural improvements made to the standard U-Net architecture, to produce what the authors call the *Efficient U-Net*. This model uses less memory, converges faster, and has better sample quality than previous U-Net models.

The Upsampler super-resolution models that take the generated image from 64×64 to $1,024 \times 1,024$ pixels are also diffusion models that continue to use the text embeddings to guide the upsampling process.

DrawBench

An additional contribution of the Imagen paper is *DrawBench*—a suite of 200 text prompts for text-to-image evaluation. The text prompts cover 11 categories, such as *Counting* (ability to generate a specified number of objects), *Description* (ability to generate complex and long text prompts describing objects), and *Text* (ability to generate quoted text). To compare two models, the DrawBench text prompts are passed through each model and the outputs given to a panel of human raters for evaluation across two metrics:

Alignment
    Which image more accurately describes the caption?

Fidelity
    Which image is more photorealistic (looks more real)?

The results from the DrawBench human evaluation are shown in Figure 13-18.

Both DALL.E 2 and Imagen are remarkable models that have made significant contributions to the field of text-to-image generation. Whilst Imagen outperforms DALL.E 2 on many of the DrawBench benchmarks, DALL.E 2 provides additional functionalities that are not present in Imagen. For example, because DALL.E 2 utilizes CLIP (a multimodal text–image model), it is able to accept images as input to generate image embeddings. This means DALL.E 2 is able to provide image editing and image variation capabilities. This is not possible with Imagen; the text encoder is a pure text model, so there is no way to input an image.

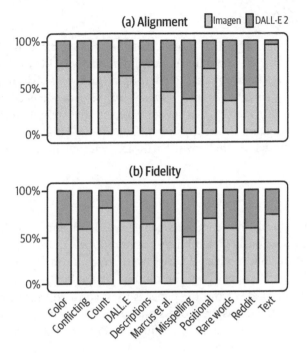

Figure 13-18. Comparison of Imagen and DALL.E 2 on DrawBench across alignment and image fidelity (source: Saharia et al., 2022)

Examples from Imagen

Example Imagen generations are shown in Figure 13-19.

| Three spheres made of glass falling into the ocean. Water is splashing. Sun is setting. | Vines in the shape of text "Imagen" with flowers and butterflies bursting out of an old TV. | A strawberry splashing in the coffee in a mug under the starry sky. |

Figure 13-19. Example Imagen generations (source: Saharia et al., 2022)

Stable Diffusion

The last text-to-image diffusion model that we shall explore is *Stable Diffusion*, released in August 2022 by Stability AI (*https://stability.ai*), in collaboration with the Computer Vision and Learning research group at Ludwig Maximilian University of Munich (*https://ommer-lab.com*) and Runway (*https://runwayml.com*). It is different from DALL.E 2 and Imagen in that its code and model weights have been released publicly, through Hugging Face (*https://oreil.ly/BTrWI*). This means that anyone can interact with the model on their own hardware, without having to use proprietary APIs.

Architecture

The main architectural difference between Stable Diffusion and the text-to-image models discussed previously is that it uses *latent diffusion* as its underlying generative model. Latent diffusion models (LDMs) were introduced by Rombach et al. in December 2021, in the paper "High-Resolution Image Synthesis with Latent Diffusion Models."[6] The key idea from the paper is to wrap the diffusion model within an autoencoder, so that the diffusion process operates on a latent space representation of the image rather than the image itself, as shown in Figure 13-20.

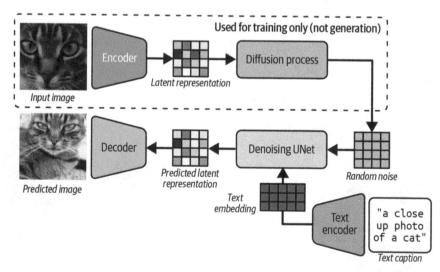

Figure 13-20. The Stable Diffusion architecture

This breakthrough means that the denoising U-Net model can be kept relatively lightweight, in comparison to U-Net models that operate on full images. The autoencoder handles the heavy lifting of encoding the image detail into latent space and decoding the latent space back to a high-resolution image, leaving the diffusion model to work purely in a latent, conceptual space. This gives a significant speed and performance boost to the training process.

The denoising process can also optionally be guided by a text prompt that has been passed through a text encoder. The first version of Stable Diffusion utilized the pre-trained CLIP model from OpenAI (the same as in DALL.E 2), but Stable Diffusion 2 has a custom trained CLIP model called OpenCLIP (*https://oreil.ly/RaCbu*), which has been trained from scratch.

Examples from Stable Diffusion

Figure 13-21 shows some example outputs from Stable Diffusion 2.1—you can try your own prompts through the model hosted on Hugging Face (*https://oreil.ly/LpGW4*).

"an insect robot preparing a delicious meal"   "a high tech solarpunk utopia in the the Amazon rainforest"   "a small cabin on top of a snowy mountain in the style of Disney, artstation"

Figure 13-21. Example outputs from Stable Diffusion 2.1

Exploring the Latent Space

If you'd like to explore the latent space of the Stable Diffusion model, I highly recommended the walkthrough (*https://oreil.ly/4sNe5*) on the Keras website.

Flamingo

So far we have looked at three different kinds of text-to-image models. In this section, we'll explore a multimodal model that generates text given a stream of text and visual data. Flamingo, introduced in a paper by DeepMind in April 2022,[7] is a family of visual language models (VLMs) that act as a bridge between pre-trained vision-only and language-only models.

In this section, we'll run through the architecture of Flamingo models and compare them to the text-to-image models we have seen so far.

Architecture

The overall architecture of Flamingo is shown in Figure 13-22. For conciseness, we shall explore the core components of this model—the Vision Encoder, the Perceiver Resampler, and the Language Mode—in just enough detail to highlight the key ideas that make Flamingo unique. I highly recommend reading the original research paper for a thorough review of each part of the model.

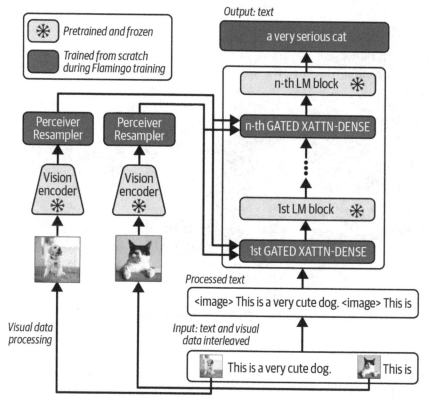

Figure 13-22. The Flamingo architecture (source: Alayrac et al., 2022)

The Vision Encoder

The first difference between a Flamingo model and pure text-to-image models such as DALL.E 2 and Imagen is that Flamingo can accept a combination of text and visual data interleaved. Here, *visual data* includes videos as well as images.

The job of the Vision Encoder is to convert the vision data within the input into embedding vectors (similar to the image encoder in CLIP). The Vision Encoder in Flamingo is a pre-trained Normalizer-Free ResNet (NFNet), as introduced by Brock et al. in 2021[8]—in particular, an NFNet-F6 (the NFNet models range from F0 to F6, increasing in size and power). This is one key difference between the CLIP image encoder and the Flamingo Vision Encoder: the former uses a ViT architecture, whereas the latter uses a ResNet architecture.

The Vision Encoder is trained on image-text pairs using the same contrastive objective as introduced in the CLIP paper. After training, the weights are frozen so that any further training of the Flamingo model does not affect the weights of the Vision Encoder.

The output from the Vision Encoder is a 2D grid of features that then gets flattened to a 1D vector before being passed to the Perceiver Resampler. Video is handled by sampling at 1 frame per second and passing each snapshot through the Vision Encoder independently to produce several feature grids; learned temporal encodings are then added in before flattening the features and concatenating the results into a single vector.

The Perceiver Resampler

Memory requirements in a traditional encoder Transformer (e.g., BERT) scale quadratically with input sequence length, which is why input sequences are normally capped at a set number of tokens (e.g., 512 in BERT). However, the output from the Vision Encoder is a vector of variable length (due to the variable input image resolution and the variable number of video frames) and is therefore potentially very long.

The Perceiver architecture is specifically designed to efficiently handle long input sequences. Instead of performing self-attention on the full input sequence, it works with a fixed-length latent vector and only uses the input sequence for cross-attention. Specifically, in the Flamingo Perceiver Resampler, the *key* and *value* are a concatenation of the input sequence and latent vector and the *query* is the latent vector alone. A diagram of the Vision Encoder and Perceiver Resampler process for video data is shown in Figure 13-23.

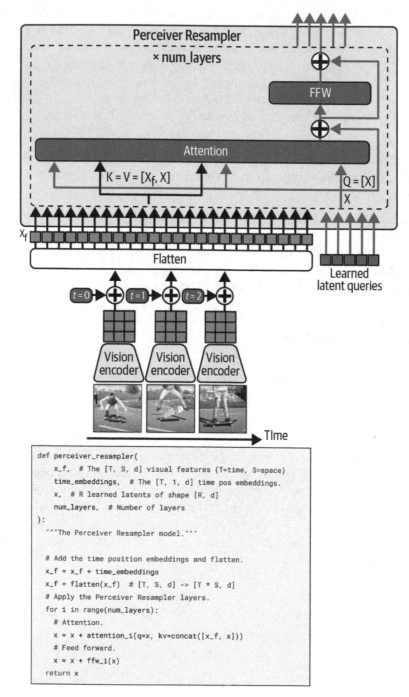

Figure 13-23. The Perceiver Resampler applied to video input (source: Alayrac et al., 2022)

The output of the Perceiver Resampler is a fixed-length latent vector that gets passed to the Language Model.

The Language Model

The Language Model consists of several stacked blocks, in the style of a decoder Transformer, that output a predicted text continuation. In fact, the majority of the Language Model is from a pre-trained DeepMind model called *Chinchilla*. The Chinchilla paper, published in March 2022,[9] showcases a language model that is designed to be considerably smaller than its peers (e.g., 70B parameters for Chinchilla compared to 170B for GPT-3), while using significantly more tokens for training. The authors show that the model outperforms larger models on a range of tasks, highlighting the importance of optimizing the trade-off between training a larger model and using a larger number of tokens during training.

A key contribution of the Flamingo paper is to show how Chinchilla can be adapted to work with additional vision data (X) that is interspersed with the language data (Y). Let's first explore how the language and vision input are combined to produce the input to the Language Model (Figure 13-24).

First the text is processed by replacing vision data (e.g., images) with an `<image>` tag and the text is divided into *chunks* using the `<EOC>` (end of chunk) tag. Each chunk contains at most one image, which is always at the start of the chunk—i.e., the subsequent text is assumed to relate only to that image. The beginning of the sequence is also marked with the `<BOS>` (beginning of sentence) tag.

Next, the sequence is tokenized and each token is given an index (`phi`) corresponding to the preceding image index (or `0` if there is no preceding image in the chunk). This way, the text tokens (Y) can be forced to only cross-attend to the image tokens (X) that correspond to their particular chunk, through masking. For example, in Figure 13-24 the first chunk contains no images, so all image tokens from the Perceiver Resampler are masked. The second chunk contains image 1, so these tokens are allowed to interact with the image tokens from image 1. Likewise, the final chunk contains image 2, so these tokens are allowed to interact with the image tokens from image 2.

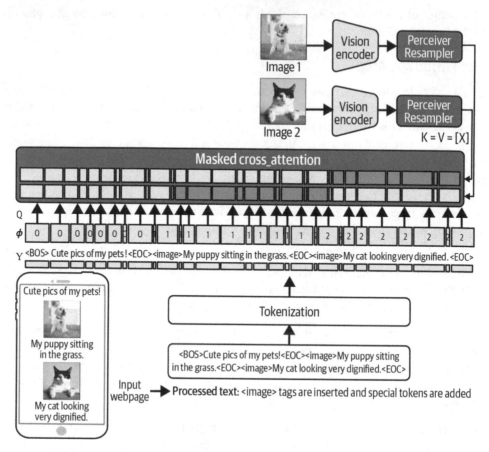

Figure 13-24. Masked cross-attention (XATTN), combining vision and text data—light blue entries are masked and dark blue entries are nonmasked (source: Alayrac et al., 2022)

We can now see how this masked cross-attention component fits into the overall architecture of the Language Model (Figure 13-25).

The blue LM layer components are frozen layers from Chinchilla—these are not updated during the training process. The purple GATED XATTN-DENSE layers are trained as part of Flamingo and include the masked cross-attention components that blend the language and vision information, as well as subsequent feed-forward (dense) layers.

The layer is *gated* because it passes the output from the cross-attention and feed-forward components through two distinct tanh gates, which are both initialized to zero. Therefore, when the network is initialized, there is no contribution from the GATED XATTN-DENSE layers—the language information is just passed straight through.

The `alpha` gating parameters are learned by the network, to gradually blend in information from the vision data as training progresses.

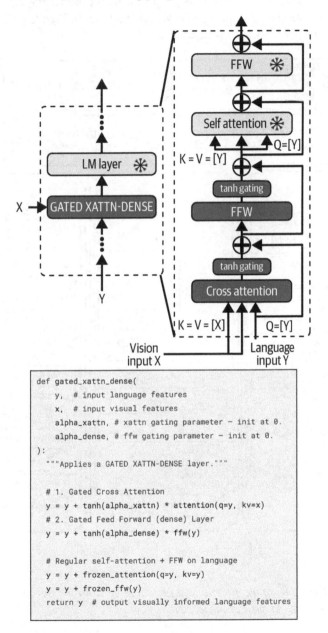

```
def gated_xattn_dense(
    y,  # input language features
    x,  # input visual features
    alpha_xattn, # xattn gating parameter — init at 0.
    alpha_dense, # ffw gating parameter — init at 0.
):
    """Applies a GATED XATTN-DENSE layer."""

    # 1. Gated Cross Attention
    y = y + tanh(alpha_xattn) * attention(q=y, kv=x)
    # 2. Gated Feed Forward (dense) Layer
    y = y + tanh(alpha_dense) * ffw(y)

    # Regular self-attention + FFW on language
    y = y + frozen_attention(q=y, kv=y)
    y = y + frozen_ffw(y)
    return y  # output visually informed language features
```

Figure 13-25. A Flamingo Language Model block, comprising a frozen language model layer from Chinchilla and a GATED XATTN-DENSE layer (source: Alayrac et al., 2022)

Examples from Flamingo

Flamingo can be used for a variety of purposes, including image and video understanding, conversational prompting, and visual dialogue. In Figure 13-26 we can see a few examples of what Flamingo is capable of.

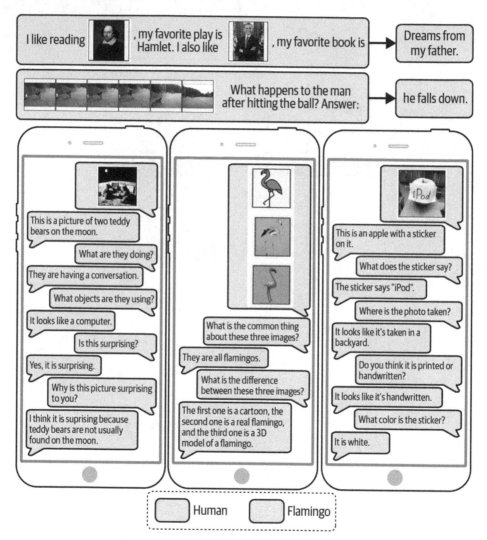

Figure 13-26. Examples of inputs and outputs obtained from the 80B parameter Flamingo model (source: Alayrac et al., 2022)

Notice how in each example, Flamingo is blending information from the text and the images in true multimodal style. The first example uses images in place of words and is able to suggest an appropriate book to continue the prompt. The second example shows frames from a video, and Flamingo correctly identifies the consequence of the action. The last three examples all demonstrate how Flamingo can be used interactively, to provide additional information through dialogue or probe with further questioning.

It is astonishing to see a machine being able to answer complex questions across such a wide range of modalities and input tasks. In the paper, the authors quantify Flamingo's ability across a set of benchmark tasks and find that across many benchmarks, Flamingo is able to surpass the performance of models that have been tailored to specifically tackle the one task in question. This highlights how large multimodal models can be rapidly adapted to a wide range of tasks and paves the way for the development of AI agents that aren't just tied to a single task, but instead are truly general agents that can be guided by the user at inference time.

Summary

In this chapter we have explored four different state-of-the-art multimodal models: DALL.E 2, Imagen, Stable Diffusion, and Flamingo.

DALL.E 2 is a large-scale text-to-image model from OpenAI that can generate realistic images across a range of styles given a text prompt. It works by combining pre-trained models (e.g., CLIP) with diffusion model architectures from previous works (GLIDE). It also has additional capabilities, such as being able to edit images through text prompting and provide variations of a given image. While it does have some limitations, such as inconsistent text rendering and attribute binding, DALL.E 2 is an incredibly powerful AI model that has helped to propel the field of generative modeling into a new era.

Another model that has surpassed previous benchmarks is Imagen from Google Brain. This model shares many similarities with DALL.E 2, such as a text encoder and a diffusion model decoder. One of the key differences between the two models is that the Imagen text encoder is trained on pure text data, whereas the training process for the DALL.E 2 text encoder involves image data (through the contrastive CLIP learning objective). The authors show that this approach leads to state-of-the-art performance across a range of tasks, through their DrawBench evaluation suite.

Stable Diffusion is an open source offering from Stability AI, CompVis, and Runway. It is a text-to-image model whose model weights and code are freely available, so you can run it on your own hardware. Stable Diffusion is particularly fast and lightweight due to the use of a latent diffusion model that operates on the latent space of an autoencoder, rather than the images themselves.

Finally, DeepMind's Flamingo is a visual language model—that is, it accepts a stream of interleaved text and visual data (images and video) and is able to continue the prompt with additional text, in the style of a decoder Transformer. The key contribution is showing how the visual information can be fed to the Transformer via a Visual Encoder and Perceiver Resampler that encode the visual input features into a small number of visual tokens. The Language Model itself is an extension of Deep-Mind's earlier Chinchilla model, adapted to blend in visual information.

All four are remarkable examples of the power of multimodal models. In the future, it is highly likely that generative modeling will become more multimodal and AI models will be able to easily cross modalities and tasks through interactive language prompting.

References

1. Aditya Ramesh et al., "Zero-Shot Text-to-Image Generation," February 24, 2021, *https://arxiv.org/abs/2102.12092.*

2. Aditya Ramesh et al., "Hierarchical Text-Conditional Image Generation with CLIP Latents," April 13, 2022, *https://arxiv.org/abs/2204.06125.*

3. Alec Radford et al., "Learning Transferable Visual Models From Natural Language Supervision," February 26, 2021, *https://arxiv.org/abs/2103.00020.*

4. Alex Nichol et al., "GLIDE: Towards Photorealistic Image Generation and Editing with Text-Guided Diffusion Models," December 20, 2021, *https://arxiv.org/abs/2112.10741.*

5. Chitwan Saharia et al., "Photorealistic Text-to-Image Diffusion Models with Deep Language Understanding," May 23, 2022, *https://arxiv.org/abs/2205.11487.*

6. Robin Rombach et al., "High Resolution Image Synthesis with Latent Diffusion Models," December 20, 2021, *https://arxiv.org/abs/2112.10752.*

7. Jean-Baptiste Alayrac et al., "Flamingo: A Visual Language Model for Few-Shot Learning," April 29, 2022, *https://arxiv.org/abs/2204.14198.*

8. Andrew Brock et al., "High-Performance Large-Scale Image Recognition Without Normalization," February 11, 2021, *https://arxiv.org/abs/2102.06171.*

9. Jordan Hoffmann et al., "Training Compute-Optimal Large Language Models," March 29, 2022, *https://arxiv.org/abs/2203.15556v1.*

CHAPTER 14

Conclusion

Chapter Goals

In this chapter you will:

- Review the history of generative AI from 2014 to the present day, including a timeline of key models and developments.

- Understand the current state of generative AI, including the broad themes that are dominating the landscape.

- See my predictions for the future of generative AI and how it will impact everyday life, the workplace, and education.

- Learn about the important ethical and practical challenges faced by generative AI going forward.

- Read my final thoughts on the deeper meaning of generative AI and how it has the potential to revolutionize our quest for artificial general intelligence.

In May 2018, I began work on the first edition of this book. Five years later, I am more excited than ever about the endless possibilities and potential impact of generative AI.

In this time we have seen incredible progress in this field, with seemingly limitless potential for real-world applications. I am filled with a sense of awe and wonder at what we have been able to achieve so far and eagerly anticipate witnessing the effect that generative AI will have on the world in the coming years. Generative deep learning has the power to shape the future in ways we can't even begin to imagine.

What's more, as I have been researching content for this book, it has become ever clearer to me that this field isn't just about creating images, text, or music. I believe that at the core of generative deep learning lies the secret of intelligence itself.

The first section of this chapter summarizes how we have reached this point in our generative AI journey. We will walk through a timeline of generative AI developments since 2014 in chronological order, so that you can see where each technique fits into the history of generative AI to date. The second section explains where we currently stand in terms of state-of-the-art generative AI. We will discuss current trends in the approach to generative deep learning and the current off-the-shelf models available to the general public. Next, we will explore the future of generative AI and the opportunities and challenges that lie ahead. We will consider what generative AI might look like five years in the future and its potential impact on society and business, and address some of the main ethical and practical concerns.

Timeline of Generative AI

Figure 14-1 is a timeline of the key developments in generative modeling that we have explored together in this book. The colors represent different model types.

To field of generative AI stands on the shoulders of earlier developments in deep learning, such as backpropagation and convolutional neural networks, which unlocked the possibility for models to learn complex relationships across large datasets at scale. In this section, we will study the modern history of generative AI, from 2014 onwards, that has moved at such breathtaking speed.

To help us understand how everything fits together, we can loosely break down this history into three main eras:

1. 2014–2017: The VAE and GAN era
2. 2018–2019: The Transformer era
3. 2020–2022: The Big Model era

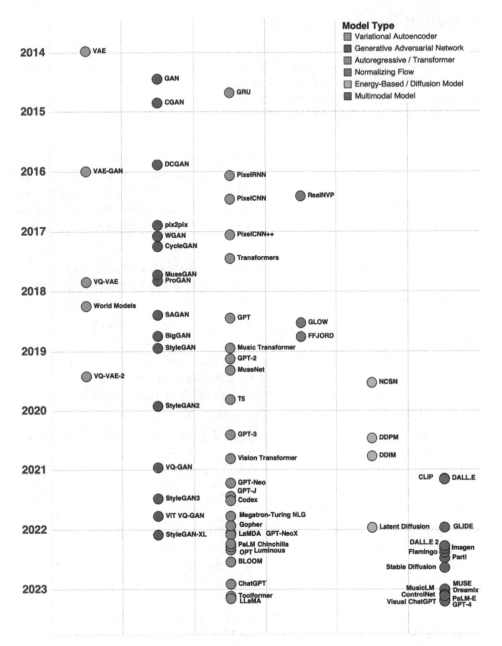

Figure 14-1. A brief history of generative AI from 2014 to 2023 (note: some important developments such as LSTMs and early energy-based models [e.g., Boltzmann machines] precede this timeline)

2014–2017: The VAE and GAN Era

The invention of the VAE in December 2013 can perhaps be thought of as the spark that lit the generative AI touchpaper. This paper showed how it was possible to generate not only simple images such as MNIST digits but also more complex images such as faces in a latent space that could be smoothly traversed. It was followed in 2014 by the introduction of the GAN, an entirely new adversarial framework for tackling generative modeling problems.

The following three years were dominated by progressively more impressive extensions of the GAN portfolio. In addition to fundamental changes to the GAN model architecture (DCGAN, 2015), loss function (Wasserstein GAN, 2017), and training process (ProGAN, 2017), new domains were tackled using GANs, such as image-to-image translation (pix2pix, 2016, and CycleGAN, 2017) and music generation (MuseGAN, 2017).

During this era, important VAE improvements were also introduced, such as VAE-GAN (2015) and later VQ-VAE (2017), and applications to reinforcement learning were seen in the "World Models" paper (2018).

Established autoregressive models such as LSTMs and GRUs remained the dominant force in text generation over this time. The same autoregressive ideas were also being used to generate images, with PixelRNN (2016) and PixelCNN (2016) introduced as new ways to think about image generation. Other approaches to image generation were also being tested, such as the RealNVP model (2016) that paved the way for later types of normalizing flow models.

In June 2017, a groundbreaking paper entitled "Attention Is All You Need" was published that would usher in the next era of generative AI, focused around Transformers.

2018–2019: The Transformer Era

At the heart of a Transformer is the attention mechanism that negates the need for the recurrent layers present in older autoregressive models such as LSTMs. The Transformer quickly rose to prominence with the introduction of GPT (a decoder-only Transformer) and BERT (an encoder-only Transformer) in 2018. The following year saw progressively larger language models being built that excelled at a wide range of tasks by treating them as pure text-to-text generation problems, with GPT-2 (2018, 1.5B parameters) and T5 (2019, 11B parameters) being standout examples.

Transformers were also starting to be successfully applied to music generation, with the introduction of, for example, the Music Transformer (2018) and MuseNet (2019) models.

Over these two years, several impressive GANs were also released that cemented the technique's place as the state-of-the-art approach for image generation. In particular, SAGAN (2018) and the larger BigGAN (2018) incorporated the attention mechanism into the GAN framework with incredible results, and StyleGAN (2018) and later StyleGAN2 (2019) showed how images could be generated with amazing fine-grained control over the style and content of a particular image.

Another field of generative AI that was gathering momentum was score-based models (NCSN, 2019), which would eventually pave the way for the next seismic shift in the generative AI landscape—diffusion models.

2020–2022: The Big Model Era

This era saw the introduction of several models that merged ideas across different generative modeling families and turbo-charged existing architectures. For example, the VQ-GAN (2020) brought the GAN discriminator into the VQ-VAE architecture and the Vision Transformer (2020) showed how it was possible to train a Transformer to operate over images. 2022 saw the release of StyleGAN-XL, a further update to the StyleGAN architecture that enables 1,024 × 1,024–pixel images to be generated.

Two models were introduced in 2020 that would lay the foundations for all future large image generation models: DDPM and DDIM. Suddenly, diffusion models were a rival for GANs in terms of image generation quality, as explicitly stated in the title of the 2021 paper "Diffusion Models Beat GANs on Image Synthesis." The image quality of diffusion models is unbelievably good and they only require a single U-Net network to be trained, rather than the dual-network setup of a GAN, making the training process much more stable.

Around the same time, GPT-3 (2020) was released—an enormous 175B parameter Transformer that can generate text on just about any topic in a way that seems almost impossible to comprehend. The model was released through a web application and API, allowing companies to build products and services on top of it. ChatGPT (2022) is a web application and API wrapper around the latest version of GPT from OpenAI that allows users to have natural conversations with the AI about any topic.

Over 2021 and 2022, a flurry of other large language models were released to rival GPT-3, including Megatron-Turing NLG (2021) by Microsoft and NVIDIA, Gopher (2021) and Chinchilla by DeepMind (2022), LaMDA (2022) and PaLM (2022) by Google, and Luminous (2022) by Aleph Alpha. Some open source models were also released, such as GPT-Neo (2021), GPT-J (2021), and GPT-NeoX (2022) by EleutherAI; the 66B parameter OPT model (2022) by Meta; the fine-tuned Flan-T5 model (2022) by Google, BLOOM (2022) by Hugging Face; and others. Each of these models is a variation of a Transformer, trained on a huge corpus of data.

The rapid rise of powerful Transformers for text generation and state-of-the-art diffusion models for image generation has meant that much of the focus of the last two years of generative AI development has been on multimodal models—that is, models that operate over more than one domain (for example, text-to-image models).

This trend was established in 2021 when OpenAI released DALL.E, a text-to-image model based upon a discrete VAE (similar to VQ-VAE) and CLIP (a Transformer model that predicts image/text pairs). This was followed by GLIDE (2021) and DALL.E 2 (2022), which updated the generative part of the model to use a diffusion model rather than a discrete VAE, with truly impressive results. This era also saw the release of three text-to-image models from Google: Imagen (2022, using Transformer and diffusion models), Parti (2022, using Transformers and a ViT-VQGAN model), and later MUSE (2023, using Transformers and VQ-GANs). DeepMind also released Flamingo (2022), a visual language model that builds upon their large language model Chinchilla by allowing images to be used as part of the prompt data.

Another important diffusion advancement introduced in 2021 was latent diffusion, where a diffusion model is trained within the latent space of an autoencoder. This technique powers the Stable Diffusion model, released as a joint collaboration between Stability AI, CompVis, and Runway in 2022. Unlike with DALL.E 2, Imagen, and Flamingo, the code and model weights of Stable Diffusion are open source, meaning anyone can run the model on their own hardware.

The Current State of Generative AI

As we come to end of our journey through the history of generative AI, it is important to now reflect on where we stand in terms of current state-of-the-art applications and models. Let's take a moment to assess our progress and key accomplishments in the field to date.

Large Language Models

Generative AI for text is now almost entirely focused on building large language models (LLMs), whose sole purpose is to directly model language from a huge corpus of text—that is, they are trained to predict the next word, in the style of a decoder Transformer.

The large language model approach has been adopted so widely because of its flexibility and ability to excel at a wide range of tasks. The same model can be used for question answering, text summarization, content creation, and many other examples because ultimately each use case can be framed as a text-to-text problem, where the specific task instructions (the *prompt*) are given as part of the input to the model.

Let's take GPT-3 (*https://oreil.ly/Pga1w*) as an example. Figure 14-2 shows how the same model can be used for text summarization and content creation.

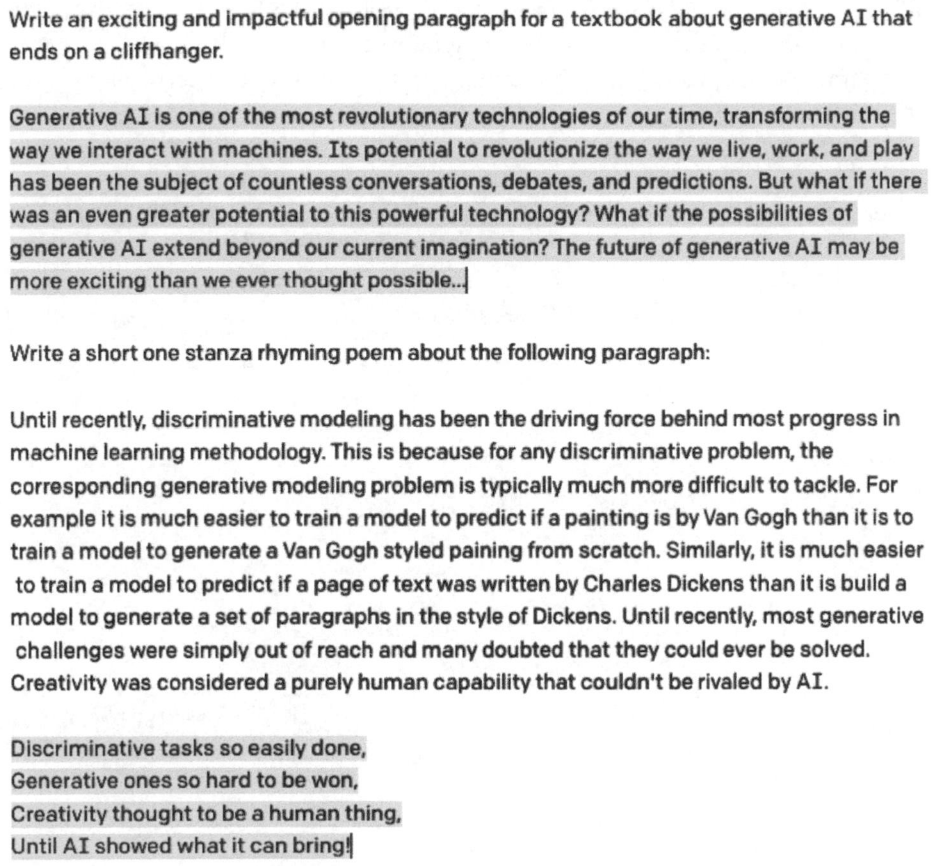

Write an exciting and impactful opening paragraph for a textbook about generative AI that ends on a cliffhanger.

Generative AI is one of the most revolutionary technologies of our time, transforming the way we interact with machines. Its potential to revolutionize the way we live, work, and play has been the subject of countless conversations, debates, and predictions. But what if there was an even greater potential to this powerful technology? What if the possibilities of generative AI extend beyond our current imagination? The future of generative AI may be more exciting than we ever thought possible...

Write a short one stanza rhyming poem about the following paragraph:

Until recently, discriminative modeling has been the driving force behind most progress in machine learning methodology. This is because for any discriminative problem, the corresponding generative modeling problem is typically much more difficult to tackle. For example it is much easier to train a model to predict if a painting is by Van Gogh than it is to train a model to generate a Van Gogh styled paining from scratch. Similarly, it is much easier to train a model to predict if a page of text was written by Charles Dickens than it is build a model to generate a set of paragraphs in the style of Dickens. Until recently, most generative challenges were simply out of reach and many doubted that they could ever be solved. Creativity was considered a purely human capability that couldn't be rivaled by AI.

Discriminative tasks so easily done,
Generative ones so hard to be won,
Creativity thought to be a human thing,
Until AI showed what it can bring!

Figure 14-2. Output from GPT-3—the non-highlighted text is the prompt and the green highlighted text is the output from GPT-3

Notice how in both cases, the prompt contains the relevant instructions. The job of GPT-3 is just to continue the prompt, one token at a time. It doesn't have a database of facts from which it can look up information, or snippets of text that it can copy into its answers. It is only asked to predict what token is most likely to follow the existing tokens and then append this prediction to the prompt to generate the next token, and so on.

Incredibly, this simple design is enough for the language model to excel at a range of tasks, as shown in Figure 14-2. Moreover, it gives the language model incredible flexibility to generate realistic text as a response to any prompt—imagination is often the limiting factor!

Figure 14-3 shows how large language models have grown in size since the original GPT model was published in 2018. The number of parameters grew exponentially until late 2021, with Megatron-Turing NLG reaching 530B parameters. Recently, more emphasis has been placed on building more efficient language models that use fewer parameters, as larger models are more costly and slower to serve in a production environment.

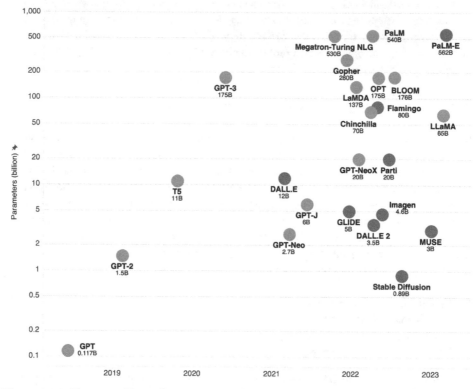

Figure 14-3. The size of large language models (orange) and multimodal models (pink) in number of parameters over time

OpenAI's GPT collection (GPT-3, GPT-3.5, GPT-4, etc.) is still considered by many to be the most powerful state-of-the-art suite of language models available for personal and commercial use. They are each available through a web application (*https://platform.openai.com/playground*) and API (*https://openai.com/api*).

Another recent addition to the large language model family is *Large Language Model Meta AI* (LLaMA) from Meta,[1] a suite of models ranging from 7B to 65B parameters in size that are trained purely on publicly available datasets.

A summary of some of the most powerful LLMs in existence today is shown in Table 14-1. Some, like LLaMA, are families of models of different sizes—in this case, the size of the largest model is shown here. Pre-trained weights are fully open source for some of the models, meaning that they are free for anyone to use and build upon.

Table 14-1. Large language models

Model	Date	Developer	# parameters	Open source
GPT-3	May 2020	OpenAI	175,000,000,000	No
GPT-Neo	Mar 2021	EleutherAI	2,700,000,000	Yes
GPT-J	Jun 2021	EleutherAI	6,000,000,000	Yes
Megatron-Turing NLG	Oct 2021	Microsoft & NVIDIA	530,000,000,000	No
Gopher	Dec 2021	DeepMind	280,000,000,000	No
LaMDA	Jan 2022	Google	137,000,000,000	No
GPT-NeoX	Feb 2022	EleutherAI	20,000,000,000	Yes
Chinchilla	Mar 2022	DeepMind	70,000,000,000	No
PaLM	Apr 2022	Google	540,000,000,000	No
Luminous	Apr 2022	Aleph Alpha	70,000,000,000	No
OPT	May 2022	Meta	175,000,000,000	Yes (66B)
BLOOM	Jul 2022	Hugging Face collaboration	175,000,000,000	Yes
Flan-T5	Oct 2022	Google	11,000,000,000	Yes
GPT-3.5	Nov 2022	OpenAI	Unknown	No
LLaMA	Feb 2023	Meta	65,000,000,000	No
GPT-4	Mar 2023	OpenAI	Unknown	No

Despite the impressive applications of large language models, there remain significant challenges to overcome. Most notably, they are prone to inventing facts and cannot reliably apply logical thought processes, as shown in Figure 14-4.

What is the fastest time to cross the Atlantic Ocean by foot?

The fastest time to cross the Atlantic Ocean by foot is 42 days, 5 hours, and 12 minutes, set by Andrew Towne in 2020.

If I was double my sister's age when I was 8, how old am I now my sister is 70?

You are now 70 x 2 = 140 years old.

Figure 14-4. While large language models excel at some tasks, they are also prone to mistakes related to factual or logical reasoning (GPT-3 output shown)

It is important to remember that LLMs are trained only to predict the next word. They have no other connection to reality that would allow them to reliably identify factual or logical fallacies. Therefore, we must be extremely cautious about how we use these powerful text prediction models in production—they cannot yet be reliably utilized for anything that requires precise reasoning.

Text-to-Code Models

Another application of large language models is code generation. In July 2021, OpenAI introduced a model called *Codex*, a GPT language model that had been fine-tuned on code from GitHub.[2] The model was able to successfully write novel coded solutions to a range of problems, prompted only with a comment on the problem to be solved, or a function name. The technology today powers GitHub Copilot (*https:// oreil.ly/P5WXo*), an AI pair programmer that can be used to suggest code in real time as you type. Copilot is a paid subscription-based service, with a free trial period.

Figure 14-5 shows two examples of autogenerated completions. The first example is a function that fetches tweets from a given user, using the Twitter API. Given the function name and parameter, Copilot is able to autocomplete the rest of the function definition. The second example asks Copilot to parse a list of expenses, by additionally including a free text description in the docstring that explains the format of the input parameter and specific instructions related to the task. Copilot is able to autocomplete the entire function from the description alone.

This remarkable technology is already beginning to change how programmers approach a given task. A significant proportion of a programmer's time is usually spent searching for examples of existing solutions, reading community Q&A forums such as Stack Overflow, and looking up syntax in package documentation. This means leaving the interactive development environment (IDE) through which you are coding, switching to a web browser, and copying and pasting code snippets from the web to see if they solve your specific problem. Copilot removes the need to do this in many cases, because you can simply tab through potential solutions generated by the AI from within the IDE, after writing a brief description of what you are looking to achieve.

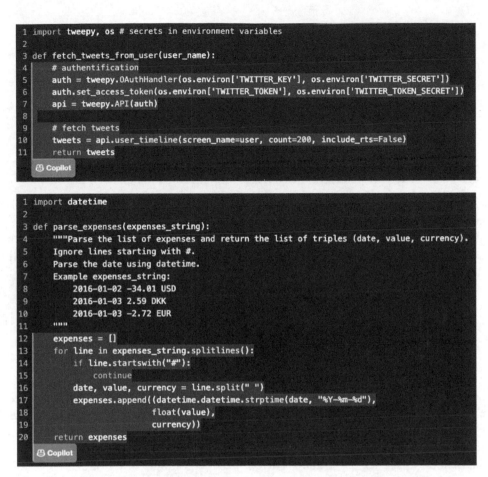

```
1  import tweepy, os # secrets in environment variables
2
3  def fetch_tweets_from_user(user_name):
4      # authentification
5      auth = tweepy.OAuthHandler(os.environ['TWITTER_KEY'], os.environ['TWITTER_SECRET'])
6      auth.set_access_token(os.environ['TWITTER_TOKEN'], os.environ['TWITTER_TOKEN_SECRET'])
7      api = tweepy.API(auth)
8
9      # fetch tweets
10     tweets = api.user_timeline(screen_name=user, count=200, include_rts=False)
11     return tweets
```
Copilot

```
1  import datetime
2
3  def parse_expenses(expenses_string):
4      """Parse the list of expenses and return the list of triples (date, value, currency).
5      Ignore lines starting with #.
6      Parse the date using datetime.
7      Example expenses_string:
8          2016-01-02 -34.01 USD
9          2016-01-03 2.59 DKK
10         2016-01-03 -2.72 EUR
11     """
12     expenses = []
13     for line in expenses_string.splitlines():
14         if line.startswith("#"):
15             continue
16         date, value, currency = line.split(" ")
17         expenses.append((datetime.datetime.strptime(date, "%Y-%m-%d"),
18                         float(value),
19                         currency))
20     return expenses
```
Copilot

Figure 14-5. Two examples of GitHub Copilot capabilities (source: GitHub Copilot)

Text-to-Image Models

State-of-the-art image generation is currently dominated by large multimodal models that convert a given text prompt into an image. Text-to-image models are highly useful as they allow users to easily manipulate generated images via natural language. This is in contrast to models such as StyleGAN, which, while extremely impressive, does not have a text interface through which you can describe the image that you want to be generated.

Three important text-to-image generation models that are currently available for commercial and personal use are DALL.E 2, Midjourney, and Stable Diffusion.

DALL.E 2 by OpenAI is a pay-as-you-go service that is available through a web application and API (*https://labs.openai.com*). Midjourney (*https://midjourney.com*) provides a subscription-based text-to-image service through its Discord channel. Both DALL.E 2 and Midjourney offer free credits to those joining the platform for early experimentation.

Midjourney

Midjourney is the service used to create the illustrations for the stories in Part II of this book!

Stable Diffusion is different because it is fully open source. The model weights and code to train the model are available on GitHub (*https://oreil.ly/C47vN*), so anyone can run the model on their own hardware. The dataset used to train Stable Diffusion is also open source. This dataset, called LAION-5B (*https://oreil.ly/2O758*), contains 5.85 billion image-text pairs and is currently the largest openly accessible image-text dataset in the world.

An important corollary of this approach is that the baseline Stable Diffusion model can be built upon and adapted to different use cases. An excellent demonstration of this is ControlNet, a neural network structure that allows fine-grained control of the output from Stable Diffusion by adding extra conditions.[3] For example, output images can be conditioned on a Canny edge map (*https://oreil.ly/8v9Ym*) of a given input image, as shown in Figure 14-6.

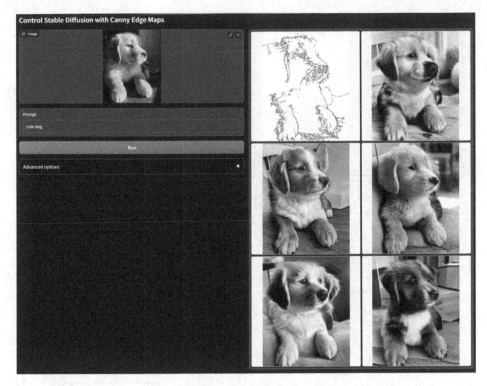

Figure 14-6. Conditioning the output of Stable Diffusion using a Canny edge map and ControlNet (source: Lvmin Zhang, ControlNet)

ControlNet contains a trainable copy of the Stable Diffusion encoder, alongside a locked copy of the full Stable Diffusion model. The job of this trainable encoder is to learn how to handle the input condition (e.g., the Canny edge map), whilst the locked copy retains the power of the original model. This way, Stable Diffusion can be fine-tuned using only a small number of image pairs. Zero convolutions are simply 1×1 convolutions where all weights and biases are zero, so that before training, Control-Net does not have any effect.

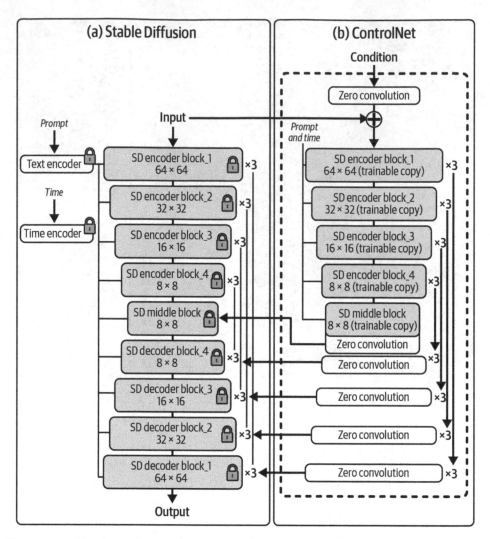

Figure 14-7. The ControlNet architecture, with the trainable copies of the Stable Diffusion encoder blocks highlighted in blue (source: Lvmin Zhang, ControlNet)

Another advantage of Stable Diffusion is that it is able to run on a single modestly sized GPU with only 8 GB of VRAM, making it possible to run on edge devices, rather than through calls to a cloud service. As text-to-image services are included in downstream products, the speed of generation is becoming increasingly more important. This is one reason why the size of multimodal models is generally trending downward (see Figure 14-3).

Example outputs for all three models can be seen in Figure 14-8. All of these models are exceptional and are able to capture the content and style of the given description.

A unicorn leaping over a magnificent river, beautiful oil painting, stunning natural scenery, award-winning art, golden lighting, intricate detail

Stable Diffusion v2.1   Midjourney   DALL.E 2

Figure 14-8. Outputs from Stable Diffusion v2.1, Midjourney, and DALL.E 2 for the same prompt

A summary of some of the most powerful text-to-image models in existence today is shown in Table 14-2.

Table 14-2. Text-to-image models

Model	Date	Developer	# parameters	Open source
DALL.E 2	Apr 2022	OpenAI	3,500,000,000	No
Imagen	May 2022	Google	4,600,000,000	No
Parti	Jun 2022	Google	20,000,000,000	No
Stable Diffusion	Aug 2022	Stability AI, CompVis, and Runway	890,000,000	Yes
MUSE	Jan 2023	Google	3,000,000,000	No

Part of the skill of working with text-to-image models is creating a prompt that both describes the content of the image you want to generate and uses keywords that encourage the model to produce a particular style or type of image. For example, adjectives such as *stunning* or *award-winning* can often be used to improve the quality of the generation. However, it is not always the case that the same prompt will work well across different models—it depends on the contents of the specific text-image dataset used to train the model. The art of uncovering prompts that work well for a particular model is known as *prompt engineering*.

Other Applications

Generative AI is rapidly finding applications across a variety of novel domains, from reinforcement learning to other kinds of *text-to-X* multimodal models.

For example, in November 2022 Meta published a paper on *CICERO* (*https://oreil.ly/kBQvY*), an AI agent trained to play the board game *Diplomacy*. In this game, players represent different countries in Europe before World War I and must negotiate with and deceive each other in order to gain control of the continent. It is a highly complex game for an AI agent to master, not least because there is a communicative element where players must discuss their plans with other players in order to gain allies, coordinate maneuvers, and suggest strategic goals. To achieve this, CICERO contains a language model that is able to initiate dialogue and respond to messages from other players. Crucially, the dialogue is consistent with the agent's strategic plans, which are generated by another part of the model to adapt to the constantly evolving scenario. This includes the ability for the agent to bluff when conversing with other players—that is, convince another player to co-operate with the agent's plans, only to then enact an aggressive maneuver against the player in a later turn. Remarkably, in an anonymous online *Diplomacy* league featuring 40 games, CICERO's score was more than double the average of the human players and it ranked in the top 10% of participants who played multiple games. This is an excellent example of how generative AI can be successfully blended with reinforcement learning.

The development of embodied large language models is an exciting area of research, further exemplified by Google's *PaLM-E* (*https://palm-e.github.io*). This model combines the powerful language model PaLM with a Vision Transformer to convert visual and sensor data into tokens that can be interleaved with text instructions, allowing robots to execute tasks based on text prompts and continuous feedback from other sensory modalities. The PaLM-E website showcases the model's abilities, including controlling a robot to arrange blocks and fetch objects based on text descriptions.

Text-to-video models involve the creation of videos from text input. This field, which builds on the concept of text-to-image modeling, has the additional challenge of incorporating a time dimension. For example, in September 2022 Meta published *Make-A-Video* (*https://makeavideo.studio*), a generative model that is able to create a short video given only a text prompt as input. The model is also able to add motion between two static images and produce variations of a given input video. Interestingly, it is trained only on paired text–image data and unsupervised video footage, rather than text–video pairs directly. The unsupervised video data is enough for the model to learn how the world moves; it then uses the text–image pairs to learn how to map between text image modalities, which are then animated. The *Dreamix* model (*https://oreil.ly/F9wdw*) is able to perform video editing, where an input video is transformed based on a given text prompt while retaining other stylistic attributes. For example, a video of a glass of milk being poured could be converted to a cup of coffee being poured, while retaining the camera angle, background, and lighting elements of the original video.

Similarly, *text-to-3D* models extend traditional text-to-image approaches into a third dimension. In September 2022 Google published *DreamFusion* (*https://dreamfu sion3d.github.io*), a diffusion model that generates 3D assets given an input text prompt. Crucially, the model does not require labeled 3D assets to train on. Instead, the authors use a pre-trained 2D text-to-image model (Imagen) as a prior and then train a 3D Neural Radiance Field (NeRF), such that it is able to produce good images when rendered from random angles. Another example is OpenAI's *Point-E* (*https:// openai.com/research/point-e*), published in December 2022. Point-E is a pure diffusion-based system that is able to generate a 3D point cloud from a given text prompt. While the output produced is not as high quality as DreamFusion's, the advantage of this approach is that is much faster than NeRF-based methods—it can produce output in just one to two minutes on a single GPU, rather than requiring multiple GPU-hours.

Given the similarities between text and music, it is not surprising that there have also been attempts to create *text-to-music* models. *MusicLM* (*https://oreil.ly/qb7II*), released by Google in January 2023, is a language model that is able to convert a text description of a piece of music (e.g., "a calming violin melody backed by a distorted guitar riff") into audio spanning several minutes that accurately reflects the description. It builds upon the earlier work *AudioLM* (*https://oreil.ly/0EDRY*) by adding the ability for the model to be guided by a text prompt; examples that you can listen to are available on the Google Research website.

The Future of Generative AI

In this final section, we will explore the potential impact that powerful generative AI systems may have on the world we live in—across our everyday lives, in the workplace, and within the field of education. We will also lay down the key practical and ethical challenges generative AI will face if it is to become a ubiquitous tool that makes a significant net positive contribution to society.

Generative AI in Everyday Life

There is no doubt that in the future generative AI will play an increasingly important role in people's everyday lives—particularly large language models. With OpenAI's ChatGPT (*https://chat.openai.com/chat*), it is already possible to generate a perfect cover letter for a job application, a professional email response to a colleague, or a funny social media post on a given topic using generative AI. This technology is truly interactive: it is able to include specific details that you request, respond to feedback, and ask its own questions back if something isn't clear. This style of *personal assistant* AI should be the stuff of science fiction, but it isn't—it's here right now, for anyone who chooses to use it.

What are the repercussions of this kind of application becoming mainstream? It is likely that the most immediate effect will be an increase in the quality of written communication. Access to large language models with a user-friendly interface will enable people to translate a sketch of an idea into coherent, high-quality paragraphs in seconds. Email writing, social media posts, and even short-form instant messaging will be transformed by this technology. It goes beyond removing the common barriers associated with spelling, grammar, and readability—it directly links our thought processes to usable output, often removing the need to engage with the process of constructing sentences at all.

Production of well-formed text is only one use of large language models. People will start using these models for idea generation, advice, and information retrieval. I believe we can see this as the fourth stage of our ability as a species to acquire, share, retrieve, and synthesize information. We started by acquiring information from those around us, or physically traveling to new locations to transfer knowledge. The invention of the printing press allowed the book to become the primary vessel through which ideas were shared. Finally, the birth of the internet allowed us to instantaneously search for and retrieve information at the touch of a button. Generative AI unlocks a new era of information synthesis that I believe will replace many of the current uses of today's search engines.

For example, OpenAI's GPT suite of models can provide bespoke holiday destination recommendations, as shown in Figure 14-9, or advice on how to respond to a difficult situation, or a detailed explanation of an obscure concept. Using this technology feels more like asking a friend than typing a query into a search engine, and for that reason, people are flocking to it extremely quickly. ChatGPT is the fastest-growing tech platform ever; it acquired 1 million users within 5 days of its launch. For context, it took Instagram 2.5 months to reach the same number of users and Facebook 10 months.

Provide me with three holiday destination suggestions in Europe that are off-the-beaten track and have both adventurous and relaxing activities nearby, for a family with teenage children. Give examples of why each is a perfect destination.

1. Riga, Latvia: Riga is a great holiday destination for a family with teenage children. It's off-the-beaten track and has something for everyone. It offers a wide range of activities, from adventure sports like kite surfing, kayaking, and rock climbing, to more relaxed activities like sightseeing and touring the city's historic sites. It's also a great base for exploring the Latvian countryside, with plenty of outdoor activities like hiking and camping.

2. Plitvice Lakes National Park, Croatia: Plitvice Lakes National Park is an ideal off-the-beaten-track destination for a family with teenage children. It offers a unique combination of activities, from relaxing boat rides and lake cruises to thrilling zip-lining and hiking. The park is also home to some of the most stunning waterfalls and cascades in Europe, making it a great place to explore and take in the incredible views.

3. Lofoten Islands, Norway: The Lofoten Islands in Norway are a great off-the-beaten-track destination for a family with teenage children. With its beautiful fjords, stunning coastal views, and abundant wildlife, there's plenty to explore in this remote archipelago. There are also plenty of activities to do, from fishing and kayaking to hiking and beachcombing. It's a great combination of adventure and relaxation.

Figure 14-9. Output from GPT-3, giving bespoke holiday recommendations

Generative AI in the Workplace

As well as general use, generative AI will find applications in specific jobs where creativity is required. A nonexhaustive list of occupations that may benefit follows:

Advertising
> Generative AI can be used to create personalized ad campaigns that target specific demographics based on their browsing and purchase history.

Music production
> Generative AI can be used to compose and produce original music tracks, allowing for a limitless range of possibilities.

Architecture
> Generative AI can be used to design buildings and structures, taking into account factors such as style and constraints around layout.

Fashion design
> Generative AI can be used to create unique and diverse clothing designs, taking into account trends and wearer preferences.

Automotive design
> Generative AI can be used to design and develop new vehicle models and automatically find interesting variations on a particular design.

Film and video production
> Generative AI can be used to create special effects and animations, as well as to generate dialogue for entire scenes or storylines.

Pharmaceutical research
> Generative AI can be used to generate new drug compounds, which can aid in the development of new treatments.

Creative writing
> Generative AI can be used to generate written content, such as fiction stories, poetry, news articles, and more.

Game design
> Generative AI can be used to design and develop new game levels and content, creating an infinite variety of gameplay experiences.

Digital design
> Generative AI can be used to create original digital art and animations, as well as to design and develop new user interfaces and web designs.

AI is often said to pose an existential threat to jobs in fields such as these, but I do not believe that this is actually the case. For me, AI is just another tool in the toolbox of these creative roles (albeit a very powerful one), rather than a replacement for the role itself. Those who choose to embrace this new technology will find that they are able to explore new ideas much faster and iterate over concepts in a way that previously was not possible.

Generative AI in Education

One final area of everyday life that I believe will be significantly impacted is education. Generative AI challenges the fundamental axioms of education in a way that we haven't seen since the dawn of the internet. The internet gave students the ability to retrieve information instantaneously and unambiguously, making exams that purely tested memorization and recall seem old-fashioned and irrelevant. This prompted a shift in approach, focused on testing students' ability to synthesize ideas in a novel way instead of only testing factual knowledge.

I believe that generative AI will cause another transformative shift in the field of education, necessitating a reevaluation and adjustment of current teaching methods and assessment criteria. If every student now has access to an essay-writing machine in their pocket that can generate novel responses to questions, what is the purpose of essay-based coursework?

Many would call for the use of such AI tools to be banned, in the same way that plagiarism is banned. However, it's not that simple, as detecting AI-generated text is much harder than detecting plagiarism and even harder to prove beyond doubt. Moreover, students could use AI tools to generate a skeleton draft for the essay and then add extra detail or update factually incorrect information as required. In this case, is it the student's original work, or the AI's?

Clearly, these are huge questions that need to be addressed in order for education and certifications to maintain their integrity. In my opinion, there is no sense in resisting the proliferation of AI tools within education—any such approach is doomed to fail, as they will become so widespread in everyday life that trying to restrict their use will be futile. Instead, we need to find ways to embrace the technology and ask how we can design *open-AI* coursework, in the same way that we allow *open-book* coursework, and encourage students to openly research material using the internet and AI tools.

The potential for generative AI to assist with the learning process itself is also immense and deeply profound. An AI-powered tutor could help a student learn a new topic (as shown in Figure 14-10), overcome a misunderstanding, or generate an entirely personalized study plan. The challenge of filtering truth from generated fiction is no different from what we currently have with information available on the internet and is a life skill that needs further attention across the curriculum.

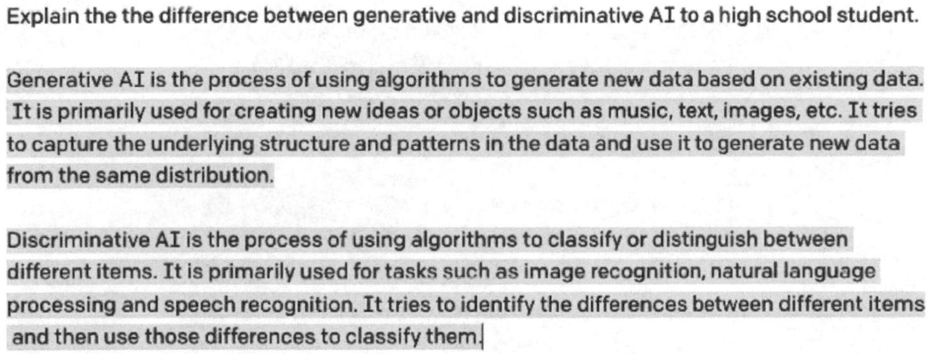

Explain the the difference between generative and discriminative AI to a high school student.

Generative AI is the process of using algorithms to generate new data based on existing data. It is primarily used for creating new ideas or objects such as music, text, images, etc. It tries to capture the underlying structure and patterns in the data and use it to generate new data from the same distribution.

Discriminative AI is the process of using algorithms to classify or distinguish between different items. It is primarily used for tasks such as image recognition, natural language processing and speech recognition. It tries to identify the differences between different items and then use those differences to classify them.

Figure 14-10. Output from GPT-3—an example of how large language models can be used for learning

Generative AI can be an incredibly powerful tool to level the playing field between those who have access to excellent teachers and the best learning materials and those who do not. I am excited to see the progress in this space, as I believe it could unlock massive amounts of potential across the globe.

Generative AI Ethics and Challenges

Despite the incredible progress that has been made in the field of generative AI, there remain many challenges to overcome. Some of these challenges are practical and others ethical.

For example, a major criticism of large language models is that they are prone to generate misinformation when asked about a topic that is unfamiliar or contradictory, as shown in Figure 14-4. The danger with this is that it is difficult to know if the information that is contained within a generated response is truly accurate. Even if you ask the LLM to explain its reasoning or cite sources, it might make up references or spout a series of statements that do not logically follow on from one another. This is not an easy problem to solve, as the LLM is nothing more than a set of weights that accurately capture the most likely next word given a set of input tokens—it does not have a bank of *true* information that it can use as a reference.

A potential solution to this problem is to provide large language models with the ability to call upon structured tools such as calculators, code compilers, and online information sources for tasks that require precise execution or facts. For example, Figure 14-11 shows output from a model called *Toolformer*, published by Meta in February 2023.[4]

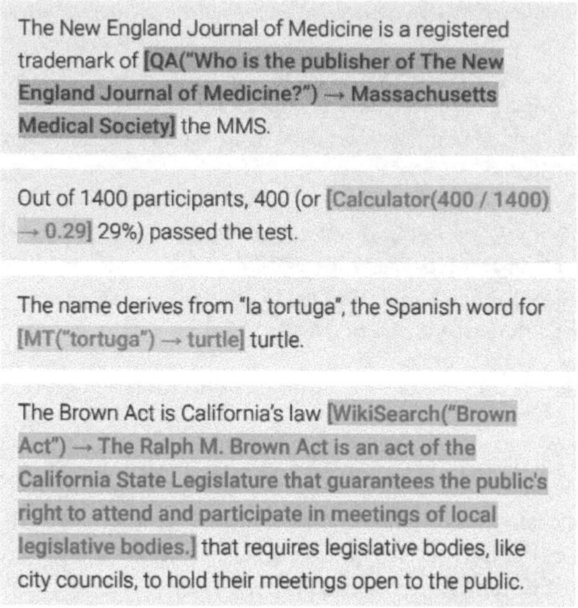

The New England Journal of Medicine is a registered trademark of [QA("Who is the publisher of The New England Journal of Medicine?") → Massachusetts Medical Society] the MMS.

Out of 1400 participants, 400 (or [Calculator(400 / 1400) → 0.29] 29%) passed the test.

The name derives from "la tortuga", the Spanish word for [MT("tortuga") → turtle] turtle.

The Brown Act is California's law [WikiSearch("Brown Act") → The Ralph M. Brown Act is an act of the California State Legislature that guarantees the public's right to attend and participate in meetings of local legislative bodies.] that requires legislative bodies, like city councils, to hold their meetings open to the public.

Figure 14-11. An example of how Toolformer is able to autonomously call different APIs in order to obtain precise information where necessary (source: Schick et al., 2023)

Toolformer is able to explicitly call APIs for information, as part of its generative response. For example, it might use the Wikipedia API to retrieve information about a particular person, rather than relying on this information being embedded in its model weights. This approach is particularly useful for precise mathematical operations, where Toolformer can state which operations it would like to enter into the calculator API instead of trying to generate the answer autoregressively in the useful fashion.

Another prominent ethical concern with generative AI centers on the fact that large companies have used huge amounts of data scraped from the web to train their models, when consent was not explicitly given by the original creators to do so. Often this data is not even publicly released, so it is impossible to know if your data is being used to train large language models or multimodal text-to-image models. Clearly this is a valid concern, particularly for artists, who may argue that it is usage of their artwork for which they are not being paid any royalties or commission. Moreover, an artist's name may be used as a prompt in order to generate more artwork that is similar in style to the originals, thereby degrading the uniqueness of the content and commoditizing the style.

A solution to this problem is being pioneered by Stability AI, whose multimodal model Stable Diffusion is trained on a subset of the open source LAION-5B dataset.

They have also launched the website *Have I Been Trained?* (*https://haveibeen trained.com*) where anyone can search for a particular image or text passage within the training dataset and opt out of future inclusion in the model training process. This puts control back in the hands of the original creators and ensures that there is transparency in the data that is being used to create powerful tools like this one. However, this practice is not commonplace, and many commercially available generative AI models do not make their datasets or model weights open source or provide any option to opt out of the training process.

In conclusion, while generative AI is a powerful tool for communication, productivity, and learning across everyday life, in the workplace, and in the field of education, there are both advantages and disadvantages to its widespread use. It is important to be aware of the potential risks of using the output from a generative AI model and to always be sure to use it responsibly. Nevertheless, I remain optimistic about the future of generative AI and am eager to see how businesses and people adapt to this new and exciting technology.

Final Thoughts

In this book we have taken a journey through the last decade of generative modeling research, starting out with the basic ideas behind VAEs, GANs, autoregressive models, normalizing flow models, energy-based models, and diffusion models and building upon these foundations to understand how state-of-the-art techniques such as VQ-GAN, Transformers, world models, and multimodal models are now pushing the boundaries of what generative models are capable of achieving, across a variety of tasks.

I believe that in the future, generative modeling may be the key to a deeper form of artificial intelligence that transcends any one particular task and allows machines to organically formulate their own rewards, strategies, and perhaps awareness within their environment. My beliefs are closely aligned to the principle of *active inference*, originally pioneered by Karl Friston. The theory behind active inference could easily fill another entire book—and does, in Thomas Parr et al.'s excellent *Active Inference: The Free Energy Principle in Mind, Brain, and Behavior* (MIT Press), which I highly recommend—so I will only attempt a short explanation here.

As babies, we are constantly exploring our surroundings, building up a mental model of possible futures with no apparent aim other than to develop a deeper understanding of the world. There are no labels on the data that we receive—a seemingly random stream of light and sound waves that bombard our senses from the moment we are born. Even when our someone points to an apple and says *apple*, there is no reason for our young brains to associate the two inputs and learn that the way in which light entered our eye at that particular moment is in some way related to the way the sound waves entered our ear. There is no training set of sounds and images, no training set of smells and tastes, and no training set of actions and rewards; there's just an endless stream of extremely noisy data.

And yet here you are now, reading this sentence, perhaps enjoying the taste of a cup of coffee in a noisy cafe. You pay no attention to the background noise as you concentrate on converting the absence of light on a tiny portion of your retina into a sequence of abstract concepts that convey almost no meaning individually but, when combined, trigger a wave of parallel representations in your mind's eye—images, emotions, ideas, beliefs, and potential actions all flood your consciousness, awaiting your recognition. The same noisy stream of data that was essentially meaningless to your infant brain is not so noisy anymore. Everything makes sense to you. You see structure everywhere. You are never surprised by the physics of everyday life. The world is the way that it is because your brain decided it should be that way. In this sense, your brain is an extremely sophisticated generative model, equipped with the ability to attend to particular parts of the input data, form representations of concepts within a latent space of neural pathways, and process sequential data over time.

Active inference is a framework that builds upon this idea to explain how the brain processes and integrates sensory information to make decisions and actions. It states that an organism has a generative model of the world it inhabits, and uses this model to make predictions about future events. In order to reduce the surprise caused by discrepancies between the model and reality, the organism adjusts its actions and beliefs accordingly. Friston's key idea is that action and perception optimization can be framed as two sides of the same coin, with both seeking to minimize a single quantity known as *free energy*.

At the heart of this framework is a generative model of the environment (captured within the brain) that is constantly being compared to reality. Crucially, the brain is not a passive observer of events. In humans, it is attached to a neck and a set of legs that can put its core input sensors in a myriad of positions relative to the source of the input data. Therefore, the generated sequence of possible futures is not only dependent on its understanding of the physics of the environment, but also on its understanding of *itself* and how it acts. This feedback loop of action and perception is extremely interesting to me, and I believe we have only scratched the surface of what is possible with embodied generative models that are able to take actions within a given environment according to the principles of active inference.

This is the core idea that I believe will continue to propel generative modeling into the spotlight in the next decade, as one of the keys to unlocking artificial general intelligence.

With that in mind, I encourage you to continue learning more about generative models from all the great material that is available online and in other books. Thank you for taking the time to read to the end of this book—I hope you have enjoyed reading it as much as I have enjoyed generating it!

References

1. Hugo Touvron et al., "LLaMA: Open and Efficient Foundation Language Models," February 27, 2023, *https://arxiv.org/abs/2302.13971*.

2. Mark Chen et al., "Evaluating Large Language Models Trained on Code," July 7, 2021, *https://arxiv.org/abs/2107.03374*.

3. Lvmin Zhang and Maneesh Agrawala, "Adding Conditional Control to Text-to-Image Diffusion Models," February 10, 2023, *https://arxiv.org/abs/2302.05543*.

4. Timo Schick et al., "Toolformer: Language Models Can Teach Themselves to Use Tools," February 9, 2023, *https://arxiv.org/abs/2302.04761*.

Index

About the Author

David Foster is a data scientist, entrepreneur, and educator specializing in AI applications within creative domains. As cofounder of Applied Data Science Partners (ADSP), he inspires and empowers organizations to harness the transformative power of data and AI. He holds an MA in Mathematics from Trinity College, Cambridge, an MSc in Operational Research from the University of Warwick, and is a faculty member of the Machine Learning Institute, with a focus on the practical applications of AI and real-world problem solving. His research interests include enhancing the transparency and interpretability of AI algorithms, and he has published literature on explainable machine learning within healthcare.

Colophon

The animal on the cover of *Generative Deep Learning* is a painted parakeet (*Pyrrhura picta*). The *Pyrrhura* genus falls under the family *Psittacidae*, one of three families of parrots. Within its subfamily *Arinae* are several macaw and parakeet species of the Western Hemisphere. The painted parakeet inhabits the coastal forests and mountains of northeastern South America.

Bright green feathers cover most of a painted parakeet, but they are blue above the beak, brown in the face, and reddish in the breast and tail. Most strikingly, the feathers on the painted parakeet's neck look like scales; the brown center is outlined in off-white. This combination of colors camouflages the birds in the rainforest.

Painted parakeets tend to feed in the forest canopy, where their green plumage masks them best. They forage in flocks of 5 to 12 birds for a wide variety of fruits, seeds, and flowers. Occasionally, when feeding below the canopy, painted parakeets will eat algae from forest pools. They grow to about 9 inches in length and live for 13 to 15 years. A clutch of painted parakeet chicks—each of which are less than an inch wide at hatching—is usually around five eggs.

Many of the animals on O'Reilly's covers are endangered; all of them are important to the world.

The cover illustration is by Karen Montgomery, based on a black and white engraving from *Shaw's Zoology*. The cover fonts are Gilroy Semibold and Guardian Sans. The text font is Adobe Minion Pro; the heading font is Adobe Myriad Condensed; and the code font is Dalton Maag's Ubuntu Mono.

Printed in the USA
CPSIA information can be obtained
at www.ICGtesting.com
JSHW061302110324
58992JS00013B/376

9 781098 134181